DORIS ALEXANDER

EUGENE O'NEILL'S CREATIVE STRUGGLE

THE DECISIVE DECADE, 1924–1933

D1450566

THE PENNSYLVANIA STATE UNIVERSITY PRESS
UNIVERSITY PARK, PENNSYLVANIA

..otations from the following plays are reprinted from *The Plays of Eugene O'Neill,* by permission of Random House, Inc., New York, and Jonathan Cape Limited, London:

Marco Millions, Copyright 1927 and renewed 1955 by Carlotta Monterey O'Neill; *The Great God Brown,* Copyright 1926 and renewed 1954 by Carlotta Monterey O'Neill; *Lazarus Laughed,* Copyright 1926, 1927 and renewed 1954, 1955 by Eugene O'Neill and Carlotta Monterey O'Neill; *Strange Interlude,* Copyright 1928 and renewed 1956 by Carlotta Monterey O'Neill; *Ah, Wilderness!,* Copyright 1933 by Eugene O'Neill and renewed 1961 by Carlotta Monterey O'Neill; *Desire Under the Elms,* Copyright 1924 and renewed 1952 by Eugene O'Neill; *Mourning Becomes Electra,* Copyright 1931 and renewed 1959 by Carlotta Monterey O'Neill; *Dynamo,* Copyright 1929 and renewed 1957 by Carlotta Monterey O'Neill; *Days Without End,* Copyright 1934 by Eugene O'Neill and renewed 1962 by Carlotta Monterey O'Neill.

Library of Congress Cataloging-in-Publication Data

Alexander, Doris.
   Eugene O'Neill's creative struggle : the decisive decade,
   1924–1933 / Doris Alexander.

        p.   cm.
   Includes index.
   ISBN 0-271-00813-X
   1. O'Neill, Eugene, 1888–1953.   2. Dramatists, American—20th
century—Biography.   I. Title.
PS3529.N5Z555   1992
812'.52—dc20
   [B]   91-29976
                                                          CIP

It is the policy of The Pennsylvania State University Press to use acid-free paper for the first printing of all clothbound books. Publications on uncoated stock satisfy the minimum requirements of American National Standard for Information Sciences—Permanence of Paper for Printed Library Materials, ANSI Z39.48–1984.

EUGENE O'NEILL'S
CREATIVE STRUGGLE

Also by Doris Alexander

Creating Characters with Charles Dickens
The Tempering of Eugene O'Neill

Contents

Acknowledgments

My work on Eugene O'Neill goes back so many years that I have a great many people to thank. I have already expressed my gratitude to the many friends and theater colleagues of Eugene O'Neill who gave me their recollections, and also to Carlotta Monterey O'Neill, and to the many librarians and curators who assisted my research in my earlier biographical study, *The Tempering of Eugene O'Neill*, which appeared in 1962. I am indebted since then to Max Wylie (who worked in close conjunction with Agnes Boulton when she was writing *Part of a Long Story* and he was working on his novel *Trouble in the Flesh*) for sharing documents with me, to Kenneth Macgowan for his recollections, and to John H. G. Pell for recollections of O'Neill and information on the fate of Eugene O'Neill's private library at Yale and at the C. W. Post College of Long Island University. I also thank Donald Ungarelli and the other librarians of C. W. Post College who assisted me there. I am also thankful for a fellowship from the Institute for the Arts and Humanistic Studies at The Pennsylvania State University, in the fall of 1968, which allowed me to do the solid reading in all of O'Neill's intellectual sources discovered from the books at Yale and those in the C. W. Post Collection.

I have friends to thank for support and assistance during the years when I was working on this book outside the United States, particularly for supplying me with suddenly needed books. I am especially grateful to Professor George Wellwarth of the State University of New York at Binghamton (who always does *more* than is asked of him), and grateful for the extraordinary time and trouble generously given by Professor Edward Margolies of the City University of New York; Professor Joann Ryan Morse of Barnard College, Columbia University; Professor Edith Link of the City University of New York; Professor John Shaw-cross of the University of Kentucky; and Professor Charles Mann, Chief of Rare Books and Special Collections at The Pennsylvania State University Libraries.

I had much encouragement from Professor Robert Proctor of Connecticut College, who was especially interested in the theory of creativity and its implications for teaching, and from Professor William Fisher of Rutgers University, who read the manuscript here in Italy and gave me an invaluable suggestion for revising the introduction. I also owe more than I can say to the great spirit of Professor Robert Worth Frank, Jr., Pennsylvania State University, to the large vision of my editor at Penn State Press, Philip Winsor, and to the nurturing over many years of my agent, Gunther Stuhlmann.

My debt to many libraries for assistance and for permission to quote from manuscripts in their collections is enormous. Yale University assisted over many years with its great wealth of manuscripts and letters of Eugene O'Neill and the Theatre Guild in the Collection of American Literature, Beinecke Rare Book and Manuscript Library, particularly the present curator of American Literature, Patricia C. Willis; the curator during the many years I did my research there, Donald Gallup; and the librarian of the American Literature Collection in those years, Anne Whelpley. Yale University also gave literary permission to quote extensively from manuscripts of Eugene O'Neill in their collection at Beinecke Library and from the collections of many other libraries. The cover photograph of Eugene O'Neill at Sea Island Beach by Carl Van Vechten was provided courtesy of the American Literature Collection, Beinecke Library, Yale University, and by permission of the Estate of Carl Van Vechten and its executor, Joseph Solomon.

Dorothy Commins provided personal help and recollections and allowed me to copy O'Neill's inscriptions to Saxe Commins in a number of his books. Her daughter, Frances Bennett gave permission to quote from one of these inscriptions and from letters of Eugene O'Neill to her father, Saxe Commins, and from several letters by her father. My thanks go also to Jean F. Preston, Curator of Manuscripts at Princeton University Library, where the letters to Saxe Commins are deposited. My quotations from those letters are by permission of Princeton University Library, as are quotations from several manuscripts and a number of other letters by Eugene O'Neill in Princeton's collection.

The Houghton Library, Harvard University, and its Curator of Manuscripts, Rodney G. Dennis, provided permission to quote from the correspondence between Eugene O'Neill and Agnes Boulton O'Neill, as well as from other letters of Eugene O'Neill and from his early poem "The Louse."

The New York Public Library, Astor, Lenox, and Tilden Foundations, allowed me to quote from materials in the Philip Moeller Collection and from the William J.M.A. Maloney Papers in the Rare Books and Manuscripts Division, and also gave me permission to quote from the materials on Susan Glaspell and Eugene O'Neill in the Henry W. and Albert A. Berg Collection.

My sincere thanks go also to Clifton Waller Barrett for his kindness to me when I worked at the University of Virginia Library and to Michael Plunkett, Curator of Manuscripts. Permission to quote from several letters in the Eugene O'Neill Collection (#6448) was given by the Clifton Waller Barrett Library, Manuscript Division, Special Collections Department, University of Virginia Library. The Dartmouth College Library and its Curator of Manuscripts, Philip N. Cronenwett, gave permission to quote from a number of letters in the Bella Landauer Collection. Kenneth Lohf, Librarian for Rare Books and Manuscripts, and the Columbia University Libraries gave permission to quote from letters in the Manuel Komroff Papers, Rare Book and Manuscript Library, Columbia University. New York University, Fales Library, and its librarian, Frank Walker, granted permission to quote from several letters of Eugene O'Neill. The Department of Rare Books, Cornell University Library, and James Tyler, Assistant Rare Book Librarian, gave permission to quote from letters in their collection. I owe thanks also for permissions to quote to the Manuscript Department, Lilly Library, Indiana University; to the Harry Ransom Humanities Research Center at the University of Texas at Austin; to the division of Rare Books and Special Collections and their Curator, James M. Mahoney, Dinand Library, College of the Holy Cross; and to the Theatre Collection of the Museum of the City of New York and its librarian, Kathryn Mets. Finally, many thanks to the Internationaal Instituut voor Sociale Geschiedenis (International Institute of Social History), Amsterdam for permission to quote from their Alexander Berkman and Emma Goldman collections and for their helpfulness to me during the weeks I worked there, some thirty years ago. Credit to all these sources is given in the notes as they occur.

Introduction:
The Mystery—and the Solving of It

"Source" studies have been done by the hundreds, many of them very convincing, but even in the best of them an immensity of unknowns, an abyss, cuts between the source and the work of literature supposedly derived from it. Somewhere, between the two, lies the mystery of the creative process, and that word "imagination," so often used to explain the mystery, evades rather than fills the emptiness.

This book sets out to fill in the blank, at least in the case of one author, Eugene O'Neill, by tracking him through nine consecutive plays to discover the whys and wherefores of what happens in them. If a "source" means a person or event the author knew, or his recollection of some other work of literature, or his use of a directive idea from his intellectual ambient, one can then ask, "Why did exactly this configuration of sources come together at the borderline of consciousness to shape characters, plot, conflict, events? How did they work toward and reach the dramatic resolution of the life experience in each play?"

In searching into these nine O'Neill plays—*Desire Under the Elms, Marco Millions, The Great God Brown, Lazarus Laughed, Strange Interlude, Dynamo, Mourning Becomes Electra, Ah, Wilderness!* and *Days Without End*—the "why" begins to show itself in the first two. O'Neill finished *Marco Millions* after he had written *Desire Under the Elms*, but he had begun it before, had done the scenario and written one act. Strangely enough, the act so insistent on being written first was the last act, the funeral and great mourning scene for his heroine, the Princess Kukachin. After that, the play went cold, and O'Neill put aside the writing of all the other acts, which are all concerned with a satirical comedy on American business values by way of Marco Polo and his father and uncle. O'Neill began with the end, with the funeral and mourning over the Princess, because at the time he was absorbed in grief and mourning over the death of his mother. And it was the same grief for his mother that caused him to drop *Marco Millions* after that one act and turn to other work, so that he became caught up in a play that had been born out of his mourning, *Desire Under the Elms,* the first idea for which had come to him shortly after his mother's death in 1922. What brought it instantly to life two years later was a dream about his mother fraught with her meaning for him, so that he could confront his grief and all the pulls it created in him directly by writing *Desire Under the Elms.* At that point he *had* to write it.

For Eugene O'Neill—as this book shows—a play was an opportunity to confront and solve a pressing life problem, and the order in which he tackled his plays, and the arousal in his mind of a particular configuration of memories and ideas to shape them, came from the urgency of the life problem that he was facing in each one. The great lure against which O'Neill was battling in *Desire Under the Elms* was the irresistible pull to join his mother in the grave. His need to struggle against that powerful undertow awakened the particular configuration of memories and ideas that would shape his drama. Before he had made a playwright of himself, O'Neill had fought just such a battle within his mind and lost. He had tried to kill himself, and only luck had saved him from succeeding. If he never attempted suicide again, he was preserved from it by the ability to fight out his battle against suicidal impulses with greater insight and wisdom in his plays.

He could fight that battle through his characters and their story with perspective and unflinching honesty because he himself remained unaware of the real battle he was fighting. He could declare, when asked about the theme of *Desire Under the Elms,* that he was writing a play about possessiveness—in money, in property, in love—and that theme certainly worked for him both in harmony and in counterpoint with his larger theme of the life-and-death battle. Both together created the play's ultimate shape, but all the richness, intensity, and significance of his characters and their fate in the play derive from the larger theme that impelled him to write. So, although O'Neill was perfectly clear that there was more to his play than the theme of possessiveness so easily definable, he was also clear that, whatever that "something more" was, he could write it into his play—but he could not capture it in an explicit statement.

All this will be seen in the chapter on *Desire Under the Elms*. What the play would have been had it been impelled only by the theme of possessiveness is revealed in one of the many notes that place this chapter in perspective. It shows that when O'Neill wrote a film scenario and deliberately cut all the dream-unconscious elements of his play as the most likely to be censored, he changed it into a simple sermon on avarice devoid of all the tragic power and poetry of his play.

One interesting question that arises from this study of O'Neill is whether the old categories of "conscious" and "unconscious" do not muddle the picture of his state of mind. He could be entirely unconscious of the fact that he was undertaking a great battle of the forces for life in him against the forces for death while he wrote *Desire Under the Elms*—yet only a year later, when he began work on *The Great God Brown*, be perfectly clear that his purpose was to create a real mystery drama, like the first plays that arose out of the worship of the god of life, Dionysus, in which, as in the mystery rites, the forces of life and eternal renewal triumph over death. So he was unconscious in one context of what was soon to become his explicitly reasoned purpose in another. And even though he followed *The Great God Brown* up with another mystery drama in *Lazarus Laughed*, he never gained conscious awareness that he had begun his mystery dramas with *Desire Under the Elms*. In other words, he had been creating his own future awareness, his own future conscious, but it never became retroactive. His own mind had engineered the entire battle of forces in *Desire Under the Elms*, yet he never saw that he had done so in that context, even though that victory had created in his mind a new purpose and new consciousness for his coming plays.

Indeed, the way in which O'Neill confronted in these nine plays his intense problems in love and marriage shows the same curious combination of knowing and not knowing at the same instant, and the same constant evolution in his thinking brought about by his actual knowledge of what refused to report itself in explicit reasoning. Thus we can watch the trouble in his marriage to Agnes Boulton already tangentially revealing itself in *Desire Under the Elms*, and powerfully charging the tragedy of *The Great God Brown*, until finally, unbeknownst to him, he sought and found in *Strange Interlude* (in which he combined the novel with the play form) the answer to his marriage problem. He was still fighting in real life to preserve his marriage after he had already seen in the form of his play that it could end only in divorce. The decision as to what to do with two such lovers as he and Agnes came a full year later in his life than in his play. Yet within the world of his plays, O'Neill fully understood—knew without knowing—that he had determined the future of his marriage in his novel-play. In fact, as soon as he finished it, he got an idea for a play about a man who works out the fate of his marriage by way of writing a novel. Yet O'Neill never saw that this play—which would be *Days Without End*—had originated with a decision to divorce Agnes. Nor did he discover the connection in the writing of it. Yet the two women between whom he had been torn, his wife Agnes and Carlotta Monterey, came together in both the wife of the play and the woman threatening her, not only as the real two women were when he first thought of the play, with Agnes the wife and Carlotta the threat, but also as they were when he came to write it, with Carlotta the wife and Agnes the threat to her. There is the strangest fusion of parts of the life story and character of these two women in both the women of his play. Nevertheless, even while he worked with these ambiguities, perfectly clear that he was seeking in this play a renewed faith in love to live by, he never saw the genesis of this play in the decision that he had made through writing his novel-play *Strange Interlude*.

The creation of his own consciousness, his own awareness, steadily taking place as he created his plays, is rendered particularly piquant by the surprises in his results, brought about by the conflicting forces within him. If O'Neill was a playwright, and exclusively a playwright, he was so because the life of a play is conflict and conflict was built into his personality. Not only was he swept by contradictory forces of life and death, of love and hate, but all his tendencies toward faith and positive affirmation were invariably accompanied by powerful forces of doubt and critical disbelief. His individual plays were charged with these conflicting forces, and he even conceived two of his plays at the same time, planning and writing the scenarios of both together, one of which, *Strange Interlude,* is ideologically antithetical to the other, *Lazarus Laughed.* We find him, in *Strange Interlude,* picking up the poetic images in celebration of faith of *Lazarus Laughed* and reversing them into images of despair. Even more surprising, after writing *The Great God Brown* and *Lazarus Laughed,* in which the god Dionysus and the goddess Cybele-Demeter are visible within his characters, he suddenly turned upon himself and attacked god-making with his play *Dynamo*. In *Dynamo* he investigated the twisted psychology behind the creation of gods—mother gods and father gods—in an astonishing breaking-down of the whole basis of his affirmations of faith before it.

And in *Dynamo* he also attacked his own compulsive doubt and skepticism, which had come from his never having really gotten past his rebellion against his father and his childhood faith. So O'Neill could then go on to create the last two plays of this study, *Ah, Wilderness!* and *Days Without End,* the first of which was born directly out of the frustration of trying to write the second, and those two plays, which critics saw as representing a complete return to his boyhood beliefs, actually represented (had his judges been able to see the struggle that produced them) O'Neill's victory in liberating himself both from the need to create gods and from his old compulsive reaction against faith and belief. Exactly at the point when almost everyone thought he had committed himself to a return to Catholicism, he had succeeded in liberating himself entirely from past compulsions and old rebellions that had bound him inextricably, if negatively, to those beliefs. In the excruciating struggle to create a renewed faith in life through *Days Without End,* O'Neill gave birth to the voice and larger perspective of the last plays he would write. Even though, in the end, he had to suppress that voice from *Days Without End* to reach a resolution of his old compulsive rebellion, it would sound out strong and clear in the plays he was still to write, particularly in the last three: *The Iceman Cometh, Long Day's Journey into Night,* and *A Moon for the Misbegotten.*

This story of the writing of nine of O'Neill's plays starts with the dream play *Desire Under the Elms* because it allows for a very intimate penetration into the life problem impelling him and the configuration of memories guiding him, and ends with another dream play, *Ah, Wilderness!* along with the play that gave birth to it, *Days Without End,* and its great struggle to achieve new balance. Although the focus is entirely on the plays, a moving story of one man's struggle for life understanding emerges. O'Neill's most intimate biography starts, not stops, at the door to his writing room, for it was there that all the great battles of his life were fought out to a steadily expanding understanding. If his plays have awakened an abiding worldwide interest, both in productions and as books to be read, it is so, certainly, because he has conveyed through them much of that expanding understanding and compassion for the human condition to others.

What stands, then, between the source and the finished work in O'Neill's case is the impelling power of a particular life problem and the configuration of interlocking memories that came to him as the raw materials for solving it. Of all his plays, *Marco Millions* depends most heavily on what is usually taken for a "source"—that is, on his readings about Marco Polo in the scholarly editions by Yule and Marsden, his own political orientation aimed at notorious scandals of his time, and his readings in Chinese philosophy and poetry. Yet even in this play, the magic that turns prosaic readings into the enchantment and poetry of the play is the configuration of memories that gave immediacy and life to the facts. The entire tragic story of the beautiful Princess Kukachin could never have taken shape from the few bare facts about her in the sources had she not become infused, through O'Neill's first vision of her as a dancing girl, with the poetry and beauty of his wife Agnes in her dancing photograph, and had she not become an outlet for his grief over his mother.

Take, for example, the Prologue to the play that resolves her whole tragedy. That tragedy had not been resolved by the last scene of the play—the one that O'Neill had written first—which had been full of O'Neill's doubt, for nothing in Chinese religion could deny death. Instead, he found his answer by writing a Prologue based on a long scholarly footnote in Yule about the legends of prophetic sacred trees, one of which Marco Polo had spoken of seeing. What transformed this lengthy footnote into drama was its infusion by specific memories of the funeral of O'Neill's mother. In fact, the entirely unhistorical funeral journey of the play's Princess from Persia, where she died, back to China for her funeral, had been born directly out of the actual journey of O'Neill's mother in her coffin from California, where she died, back to New York for the funeral and burial in New London. The dead Princess's taking on the power to speak when her coffin comes under the prophetic tree, so that she can deliver a message of eternal life and love, came partly from O'Neill's profound longing for a message of faith from his mother like the one he had taken from his dying father, and partly from the linkage of his mother to a tree that had been riveted in his mind through his writing of *Desire Under the Elms* with its maternal trees, for he had achieved through them his first victory over the pull of death, just before returning to the writing of *Marco Millions.*

The entire nine plays of this study show how plot, character, and imagery have been shaped by a specific nexus of personal memories brought into activity by a pressing life problem. Even something as seemingly external as the time sequence in a play may be determined by the particular memory impelling O'Neill's writing. For instance, *Lazarus Laughed,* a play that treats the fear of death, is charged with memories from the death of O'Neill's father. This play begins with the setting of the sun, and although there are gaps of months between the acts, all the scenes that follow are placed consecutively later and later, as if they were taking place all on one night, and the last four scenes actually do take place on the same night beginning at two o'clock in the morning and ending with the dawn of the next day. The same sequence had occurred to O'Neill for his much earlier play *The Emperor Jones,* in which he was also treating the psychology of fear and to which he had turned immediately after his father's death. In this play all the action takes place in the course of one night, starting with late afternoon and then moving later and later into the night until the final scene ends with dawn, just as in *Lazarus Laughed.* The odd thing about the time is that it follows that of the events when James O'Neill died.

O'Neill, with his mother and brother, had stayed with his father at the hospital until late that afternoon. They had been awakened by a telephone call close to midnight summoning them with the news that his father was dying. Back they rushed to the hospital, and they stayed there at the deathbed until James O'Neill breathed his last at 4:15 in the morning of August 10, 1920. Dawn was breaking when they left the hospital, as it breaks at the end of the two plays that emerged out of that traumatic night. Not only immediate time, but also the historical setting of a play, may emerge from the configuration of memories impelling it—such as the California gold rush setting of *Desire Under the Elms*.

That the nexus of memories behind a play works powerfully to shape it appears most dramatically in the instances (a number of which are noted in this study) where the memories assert themselves so intensely that they begin to break out of the play logic and actually contradict the facts of the play. For instance, memories of O'Neill's brother Jamie assert themselves so authentically in the character of Dion Anthony at some points in *The Great God Brown* that, just as Jamie had always insisted that he had created Eugene's success, so Dion insists that he had created Brown's, even though in the play Brown has already been a success before he began feeding on Dion's creative power.

Indeed, errors and inconsistencies sometimes arise in a play simply because a particular configuration of memories dominates the author's mind as he writes. In *The Great God Brown* O'Neill had at first stayed very close to his brother's last days in New London, as the early drafts show. Later he changed such scenes as the one in Jamie's old haunt, the local brothel, probably to avoid censorship, and he set this scene instead in the prostitute's own cottage. Yet he has Brown look for Dion there as if it were a well-known haunt of his, although as the play facts stand, Dion has turned up there by chance for the first time that night. O'Neill himself never caught this error from changing one major fact in the memory system that he was taking for granted as he wrote.

Of course, the human mind—even in processes that take place before ideas report themselves to consciousness—does not work literally and mechanistically, but always has the capacity of itself to create out of the facts symbolic images that get at an emotional or intellectual essence. One cannot penetrate the creative process merely by making a point-by-point comparison of the facts in the memory system and the facts in the play. One must go beyond to an understanding of habitual ways of seeing life on the author's part. For instance, O'Neill could transmute his mother's fatal journey to California to realize the money on some property James O'Neill had purchased there into an idea for a play about the California gold rush with death at its finale because he had been in the habit of seeing his father's financial investments as the gold buried on the island of Monte Cristo in the play that had made him rich. To reach any understanding of the transformation of memory facts into the living imagery of the play, one needs to know not only the facts of the particular memory feeding it, but also the habitual structure of thought and ways of interpreting life that have operated in the author from boyhood. In O'Neill many of these can be discovered from his images in letters, and also from some of the cruder imagery in his earliest apprentice plays. Also, as we shall see in the analysis that follows, O'Neill had a tendency to repeat certain crucial wishes or symbolic ideas, so that they recur in several plays. The Princess in the Prologue of *Marco Millions* is not the only woman who rises momentarily out of death to deliver a message of life and love; two others do so in the course of these nine plays. Also, Dion Anthony in *The Great God Brown* is one out of quite a procession of men in O'Neill's plays who get down on their knees before a beloved woman.

In comparing memory with play, neither can one arrive at truth by assuming a one-to-one relationship between character and original. A number of O'Neill's critics have thought that a father in an O'Neill play must ipso facto be his own father, a mother his own mother, and a son himself. Thus most critics have taken the old father Ephraim in *Desire Under the Elms* for O'Neill's father, and the son Eben who cuckolds him for O'Neill. But this character comes not as a reproduction of James O'Neill, but as an embodiment of O'Neill's identification with his father, so that as the play progresses, Ephraim expresses O'Neill's own philosophy of life and creativity and embodies the distrust and loneliness that O'Neill himself felt at the core of his marriage. O'Neill certainly recognized Ephraim as a self-portrait—he actually said he was—but his critics have been so imbued with the preconception that father in literature is father in life that they have managed to misconstrue his words. No more does O'Neill's mother make her appearance in O'Neill's plays necessarily as a mother. She is as likely to appear as a child.

Another misinterpretation of what is going on in an O'Neill play comes from the assumption, slipped into by some of his psychoanalytic critics, that O'Neill was unconscious of the Freudian implications of his characters, as if psychoanalytic theory was a secret to which outsiders had no access. They have thought that O'Neill had no idea of the psychological significance of Eben's sexual attraction to his stepmother in *Desire Under the Elms*. They assume that O'Neill had been releasing by way of Eben his own unconscious incestuous wishes. Actually, O'Neill was perfectly aware of these psychoanalytic implications, for he had examined critically not only the theories of Freud but also those of Stekel and Jung. It is impossible to assess correctly what forces had been acting to shape an O'Neill play without knowing well the whole range of his intellectual equipment.

Another assumption that obscures the dynamics of O'Neill's creativity sees him as mechanically subject to influences, so that ideas from others fell dead into his head. Actually, as these nine plays reveal, O'Neill no sooner grasped an idea than he was transforming it creatively. In his very fruitful association with Kenneth Macgowan and Robert Edmond Jones, O'Neill had no sooner taken up an idea of theirs than he was in turn influencing them by all the original applications and combinations of it to which he had leapt ahead. His active intellectual life was a potent force in shaping his plays, working hand in hand with the memory systems leading him to resolve urgent life problems. Always he used ideas flexibly, critically transforming them, and the history of these nine plays shows his critics limping along after him, trying to catch, in their limited ideological nets, conceptions built on fields of knowledge that are totally unfamiliar to them. We shall also see that his most artistically successful works show a reinforcing harmony between the memory system nourishing them and the intellectual conceptions operating through them.

These shaping forces are put forth here as if they had all been set up a priori. Actually they came out of an analysis, play by play, of the configuration of memories within each, carried out with awareness of all the pitfalls lying in wait in such an approach. A major danger in trying to reconstruct the memory system operating in a play by comparing play facts with life facts is that there are many specious, farfetched resemblances that can be read into the process. How can one be sure that a particular set of memories actually was operating in a play and that they really had been activated by the need to solve a particular life problem? The best confirmation lies in the extent of the configuration. Two or three resemblances of minor details may come through sheer chance or through intellectual straining on the part of the analyst. But if a whole scheme of details, most of them major, fit one another, the identification is probably correct. In such a configuration one or two details may indeed be erroneous, but the mass of them, in all probability, will be trustworthy.

In the making of this analysis, a number of trails had to be abandoned because they never achieved a sufficiently convincing solidity. No hint of the trial and error is apparent in the final chapters, but traces appear in the Notes at the end of this book. Indeed, the Notes do more than identify the sources of quotations and information. Many of them reinforce the evidence in the chapters and explain why one interpretation is more likely than another. A few comparisons have been allowed to stand, even though more needs to be known about them, because they are suggestive in the light of other evidence. For all the major points, however, the weight of evidence is substantial enough to carry conviction.

If one is certain of the memory system, how can one be sure that it had been set in motion, not only because the author wanted to create a play with a plot, characters, scenes, and confrontations, but also because all these elements allowed him to tackle major problems in his life? Analysis reveals the problems, as it reveals the memories they have summoned up. One can deduce the problem from the memory system itself, from the genesis and awakening in O'Neill's mind of a play, from the way he aligned the forces in his life among the characters and conflicts of the play, and from the way that the balance achieved in a play influenced O'Neill. The most efficient check is this last one of seeing what changes took place in O'Neill's life after completion of a particular play. If the memory system in the play was impelling him to certain basic decisions, once he made them for his play he would inevitably take a fresh perspective on his living and act upon it.

The chapters present all the evidence, as far as possible, so that even one who is unfamiliar with O'Neill can follow and evaluate the analysis. Of course, what is true for O'Neill may not necessarily be true for other writers. Only further studies of individual authors will make for a genuine science of creativity. Nevertheless, this picture of how O'Neill faced life problems in his plays, and how the memory systems awakened by them shaped plot, character, and imagery, suggests the likelihood that other writers—probably many other writers—create their works in a similar way.

If this is so, a whole range of aesthetic values may be traced to the creative process behind the work. The unity and richness of tone and imagery, even much that is thought of as "style," may come from the intensity of the memory system directing a writer. Probably the validity of a work of art depends on how honestly and penetratingly the author has perceived and stored his life experience, as well as how fully memories of those experiences nourish his writing. If he is striving, even though unconsciously, to solve his life problems honestly through them, then the motive power behind literature is essentially healthy, rather than diseased as some critics have believed. The value of the work lies in how profoundly reality has been faced and resolved in it. If it is based on valid memories, it should give a reader a wider life experience than the living of his one life can, and should enlarge his understanding of what it means. Thus the value of reading great literature would be similar to the value of writing great literature—that of reaching a greater wisdom in living.

One may answer all kinds of critical questions by way of this idea of the creative process. Why, for instance, does a literary collaboration—even one between, say, a writer of the grandeur of Joseph Conrad and the potential excellence of Ford Madox Ford—produce a work bereft of the emotional intensity and scope of meaning that each could create alone? Apparently the collaboration allows neither to work profoundly with his life through the writing, and thus excludes its nourishment by a transforming personal memory system. Indeed, the reason why one potboiler remains merely a potboiler and another achieves literary value probably depends on whether the chosen subject allows for the infusion of a profound memory system impelled by the urgency to come to terms with some aspect of living.

In O'Neill's case the memory system that shapes his play remains largely unconscious. Most of the time O'Neill is not consciously recalling old experiences, yet they steadily direct and inform him. Here and there an aspect of the memory may be registered consciously, but never the intricate nexus that brings the work to life. This is probably a characteristic of the way memory of personal experience operates as a force in any confrontation of life, not only of the way an artist creates. Certainly a man in a stressful situation—say, with a tiger in his path—cannot spare any part of his consciousness from watching the tiger and perceiving his options for safety. When a pounce on the part of the tiger sets him to act, he will do so out of a combination of a push from activated memories of similar dangers and the necessities of his immediate situation. He could not cope at all with the peril were he to turn his conscious attention to mulling through old experience, for he would lose his awareness of what the tiger is about to do. The mind of the creative artist apparently works the same way that the human mind works to determine very different lines of action. The brain can work intricately and purposefully without reporting itself to consciousness. And for the writer, the unconsciousness serves to insulate him from the lethal charge of his materials until he has put them, by way of the writing, into a managable form.

Reports from creative people suggest that the arousal of memory, even though unconscious, is not simply a passive procedure, with the materials inert but available, like a file taken out of a cabinet. It seems that the memories awaken to violent activity, with some reinforcing others and some canceling one another out, so that by themselves they are moving toward a solution. A number of persons in the thick of creativity have noticed the strange combination, at certain stages, of a physical sense of tension, excitement, and a perfectly blank mind. Charles Dickens—that most acute observer—in the act of generating a new novel reported long periods of a blank mind and an almost unbearable feeling of restlessness, so that he was driven to walk for miles and miles, or had the feeling that he must set out instantly for some distant part of the world. He would find himself walking around and around his study carpet, stepping compulsively on the same parts of the pattern, with no idea why he was doing so. Clearly immense tension from inner mental activity was impelling him, and an active attempt to "think" at that particular point would only have impeded the process.

Writers are always being surprised, sometimes astounded, by what comes out in the writing. The author of *Light on the Path,* for example, a woman fatally bitten by the spiritualist bug, felt herself to be merely taking dictation from a holy man who had died centuries before choosing her as a channel for his wisdom. Her explanation may be absurd, but she came up with it to account for an authentic sensation that a number of less obsessed authors have observed and reported. Of course, the entire creative process does not take place unconsciously. That is why, in the chapters to follow, much care has been taken to register all of O'Neill's conscious critical perceptions of what he was doing, as well as all his conscious planning and theorizing. To weigh accurately all the forces interacting in the writing, these must be known. But certainly for O'Neill, with all his intellectual directives, the most intense part of the creative process—the push of the memory system directing him—reported itself only through the writing. His experience with *Ah, Wilderness!* where he woke up with the whole play shaped and ready to write differs only in degree from the generation of his other works. It demonstrates visibly how—with a life problem impelling him—he came quite unconsciously to plot, events, and characters. When a draft of *Ah, Wilderness!* was all written, he could then attack it critically and add a final scene to give its resolution greater appropriateness for his mature life. From these nine plays by O'Neill, a fascinating picture emerges of the way a body of closely related memories, of which the author was largely unconscious, worked to shape his plot, setting, characters, and imagery and to determine the ultimate resolution of the play's conflicts.

Chronology of Important Events Leading Up to This Story

July 14, 1877	James O'Neill, the popular young actor, marries Mary Ellen Quinlan ("Ella"), daughter of his old friend Thomas J. Quinlan, former city circulator of the *Cleveland Plain Dealer* and partner in Quinlan & Spirnaugle Liquor and Cigars. The ceremony is performed quietly in the rectory of St. Ann's Church on 12th Street in New York City.
September 28, 1878	James O'Neill, Jr., is born in San Francisco.
February 12, 1883	James O'Neill opens in New York in the Fechter version of *Monte Cristo* under the management of John Stetson.
Summer 1883	James O'Neill builds a summer home on the water at 325 Pequot Avenue, New London, Connecticut, where his wife's aunt and her family live.
ca. September 19, 1883	Edmund Burke O'Neill is born.

ca. January 1885

James O'Neill buys the Fechter version of *Monte Cristo* from Stetson and, as actor-manager, becomes caught by the popular role, so that he goes on playing it alone or in repertory until 1912.

March 4, 1885

The O'Neills receive a telegram in Denver, Colorado, that their baby Edmund, left in New York with Mary's mother, is mortally ill with measles. He dies the same day, shortly after his mother boards the train to go to him.

October 16, 1888

Eugene Gladstone O'Neill is born in New York City.

ca. October 1889

English nurse Sarah Sandy enters the family and becomes a second mother to Eugene O'Neill.

1889–1895

With his mother and nurse, Eugene O'Neill follows his father's tours, often watching performances from a box. Summers he finds "home" in the house at 325 Pequot Avenue, New London.

Fall 1895

Just before his seventh birthday, Eugene O'Neill is sent to boarding school at Mount St. Vincent-on-the-Hudson, where he stays until his First Communion (May 24, 1900), spending winter vacations with his nurse and summers in New London with his family.

Fall 1900

Just before his twelfth birthday, Eugene O'Neill enters De La Salle Institute in New York City, where he remains for two years.

September 1902

Just before his fourteenth birthday, Eugene O'Neill enters Betts Academy at Stamford, Connecticut, where he remains until graduation in 1906, with summers in New London. During these years he reads Shaw, Ibsen, and Carlyle voraciously and is led to a passion for

	poetry—especially Wilde, Swinburne, Rossetti, Dowson, Kipling, and Omar Khayyám—by his brother Jamie.
Summer 1903	Almost fifteen, Eugene O'Neill learns from his brother Jamie that his mother has been addicted to morphine ever since her illness following his birth.
1903–1904	Sometime in his fifteenth year, Eugene O'Neill begins drinking with his older brother Jamie.
1904–1905	Sometime in his sixteenth year, O'Neill is taken to his first prostitute by Jamie.
Fall 1906	Just before his eighteenth birthday, Eugene O'Neill enters Princeton, where he is bored by what he later calls "professorial dry rot." Outside classes he discovers Nietzsche's *Thus Spake Zarathustra* at Benjamin Tucker's anarchist bookstore in New York, and it becomes the bible of his youth.
March 1907	Eugene O'Neill sees Alla Nazimova in Ibsen's *Hedda Gabler* at the Bijou Theatre in New York and returns to see it again for ten successive nights, enraptured by his first vision of "a modern theatre where truth might live."
April 1907	Eugene O'Neill is suspended from Princeton for throwing stones at and breaking the glass insulators on the trolley line from Princeton Junction after a spree with classmates in Trenton. He decides to drop out of the university.
September 1907	O'Neill watches his father rehearse a new repertory of *Virginius, Julius Caesar,* and *Monte Cristo* in New York and enters Henry Brittain's New York–Chicago Supply Company, which goes bankrupt soon after in the depression of 1908.

1908–1909   Eugene O'Neill writes poetry on an allowance
                                 from his father, sharing a studio in the Lincoln
                                 Arcade in New York with his old New London
                                 friend Ed Keefe, now an artist, and another
                                 young artist, George Bellows, and an advertis-
                                 ing illustrator, Edward Ireland. He becomes
                                 involved with an attractive young woman,
                                 Kathleen Jenkins.

October 2, 1909   Two weeks before his twenty-first birthday,
                                 Eugene O'Neill marries Kathleen Jenkins se-
                                 cretly at Trinity Protestant Episcopal Church
                                 in Hoboken, New Jersey, and then, helped by
                                 his father, sets out at once alone for a new life
                                 by joining a gold prospector bound for Hon-
                                 duras.

October 1909–1910   Eugene O'Neill finds in Honduras a hell of
                                 insects, and no gold and comes down with
                                 malaria. He joins his father, opening in *The
                                 White Sister* in St. Louis on March 14, 1910.

May 7, 1910   Mrs. Jenkins reveals the marriage of her
                                 daughter to Eugene O'Neill and the birth of
                                 his son Eugene O'Neill, Jr., to a reporter for
                                 the *New York World*.

June 6, 1910   Eugene O'Neill sails from Boston for Buenos
                                 Aires and a job at Westinghouse Electric with
                                 the secret hope of reaching China.

July 17, 1911   Back in New York, Eugene O'Neill signs on
                                 for his last voyage as seaman: New York to
                                 Southampton and return.

December 29, 1911   Eugene O'Neill arranges to be seen in bed
                                 with a prostitute as evidence for a divorce
                                 from Kathleen.

January 1912   At twenty-three, Eugene O'Neill attempts sui-
                                 cide by an overdose of sleeping tablets in a

hall bedroom at "Jimmy the Priest's" roominghouse, but doesn't die.

January 1912	Eugene O'Neill returns to his family in time to join his father's opening at the Orpheum in New Orleans in a final vaudeville version of *Monte Cristo*.
July 5, 1912	The divorce from Kathleen is granted.
August 1912	Eugene O'Neill begins work as a night reporter on the *New London Telegraph* (published by his father's friend Judge Latimer) and he contributes light verse to its Laconics column.
December 24, 1912	Eugene O'Neill is admitted to Gaylord Farm after an attack of pleurisy reveals tubercular signs at the right apex of his lung.
First half of 1913	At the sanatorium, twenty-four-year-old Eugene O'Neill begins writing plays.
June 3, 1913	Eugene O'Neill is discharged from the sanatorium and rejoins his family in New London.
1913–1914	Eugene O'Neill writes plays in New London.
Spring 1914	Eugene O'Neill falls in love with Beatrice Ashe. By early summer they are engaged.
1914–1915	Eugene O'Neill goes to Harvard as a special student of play-writing in Professor Baker's class.
January 1, 1916	Eugene O'Neill helps put out the anarchist weekly *Revolt*, edited by Hippolyte Havel, until federal agents suppress it after the February 19 issue.
Spring 1916	As Beatrice continues to hold off marriage, Eugene O'Neill relapses badly into drinking.
Tuesday, July 25, 1916	Eugene O'Neill writes Beatrice Ashe that he is helping to direct his play *Bound East for*

Cardiff, to be put on by the Provincetown Players at Cape Cod on the next Friday and Saturday nights (July 28 and 29), giving him his first production at twenty-seven.

August 1916	Eugene O'Neill rushes back to New London to urge Beatrice to marry him. She breaks their engagement.
August & September 1916	Eugene O'Neill drinks. He is rescued from it by Louise Bryant.
November & December 1916	Eugene O'Neill has first New York productions by the Provincetown Players in New York's Greenwich Village.
January & February 1917	Eugene O'Neill drinks. He is again rescued by Louise Bryant.
Fall 1917	Eugene O'Neill meets beautiful Agnes Boulton in Greenwich Village and takes her to Provincetown after the November productions of his plays.
April 12, 1918	At twenty-nine, Eugene O'Neill is married to Agnes Boulton by a "delightful, feeble-minded, Godhelpus, mincing Methodist minister."
October 30, 1919	Agnes gives birth to O'Neill's son Shane Rudraighe O'Neill in Provincetown.
February 2, 1920	Eugene O'Neill's first Broadway opening comes with his full-length play *Beyond the Horizon* in a series of special matinees, watched from a box by his proud parents, and it wins O'Neill the first of his Pulitzer prizes.
March 1, 1920	James O'Neill suffers a stroke and is revealed to have cancer.
August 10, 1920	Eugene O'Neill, his mother, and his brother watch James O'Neill die at the Lawrence Memorial Hospital, New London.

November 1, 1920

The Emperor Jones, O'Neill's most original and successful work to date, opens at the Provincetown Playhouse in Greenwich Village and by January 29, 1921, moves uptown to Broadway.

Fall 1921

O'Neill meets his son Eugene Jr. for the first time since his birth and undertakes his support.

February 28, 1922

Eugene O'Neill's mother dies of a brain tumor in Los Angeles.

March 9, 1922

The Hairy Ape—always a favorite for O'Neill as his greatest advance to date over surface realism—opens to brilliant success, while O'Neill himself is devastated by grief over his mother's body arriving that day in New York.

November 8, 1923

James O'Neill Jr. dies of cerebral apoplexy at Riverlawn Sanatorium in Paterson, New Jersey.

January 1, 1924

In the early hours after midnight, Eugene O'Neill dreams of his dead baby brother Edmund.

1

Desire Under the Elms

It was grief—grief for his mother—that set off *Desire Under the Elms* in Eugene O'Neill's mind. After her death, he made a note of it with the title "Under the Elms" and the date "1922": "Play of New England—laid on farm in 1850, time of California gold rush—make N.E. farmhouse and elm trees almost characters." It had a "hard" father who has "killed off wives (2) with work," along with "3 sons—all hate him." The old man's "possessive pride" is in the farm because "it is so hard." In his "old age in moment of sensual weakness" he marries a young woman and brings her back to the farm. The "youngest son falls for her" and brings on the tragedy.

The clue to O'Neill's grief lies in the California gold rush setting. Of course, the lust for possession is a central theme, and the gold rush expresses it, but O'Neill might have chosen another symbol for it, and later he did hesitate about whether to make it the Silver City silver rush. California and the gold rush won out because they came straight out of memories of his mother's death journey. At the beginning of January 1922 his mother and his brother Jamie had set out for California. No sooner had they arrived than his mother was felled by a brain tumor. She was dead by February 28.

They had gone to realize the money on a piece of property—suddenly booming in value—his father had bought out there years ago. The pursuit of his father's money had powerful associations for O'Neill. He had always seen it as the gold buried on the island of Monte Cristo in the play that had made his father rich from years of starring in it. After his father died, he had written the family friend George C. Tyler that his mother was putting the estate in order: "The treasures of Monte Cristo are buried deep again in prairie dog gold mines, in unlubricated oil wells," he said, but he hoped that with his mother's capable direction "some dividends may finally accrue from the junk buried on the island of Monte Cristo." The modest allowance from his father during his wild years had always appeared to him a withholding of love, and he had always resented the odd investments in which his father had buried the money. Two of his early plays, *Where the Cross Is Made* (1918) and *Gold* (1920), had dealt with a son madly determined to go after his father's treasure of gold buried on a desert island—gold that ironically is actually "junk." Out of these old associations his mother's fatal pursuit of his father's gold buried in California earth naturally transmuted itself for him into a tragedy of the California gold rush with death at the end.

The plot had come to him with three sons, the number his mother had had, and dominated by the image of a house brooded over by two elm trees and pervaded by memories of two dead mothers. The description of the trees in the play shows that they were meant to express the pull out of the past of those two dead women:

> Two enormous elms are on each side of the house. They bend their trailing branches down over the roof. They appear to protect and at the same time subdue. There is a sinister maternity in their aspect, a crushing, jealous absorption. They have developed from their intimate contact with the life of man in the house an appalling humanness. They brood oppressively over the house. They are like exhausted women resting their sagging breasts and hands and hair on its roof, and when it rains their tears trickle down monotonously and rot on the shingles.

The house is of a "sickly grayish" color with faded green shutters under its shingled roof, recalling the house in New London where O'Neill spent his boyhood summers, which also had gray paint and shutters and shingles. The extraordinary thing about the two maternal trees that brood over it and their association with two dead women is that O'Neill had actually had *two* mothers. He himself would draw up a "Diagram" of his early emotional life with three love lines in it: one for his father, and two more close together, one labeled "mother love" and the second labeled "nurse love," connected to the other with a line and the word "meaning." So he had mother love from his actual mother and "nurse love meaning mother love" from his nurse Sarah Sandy. When he broke off both lines in adolescence, he terminated Sarah's with the words "breaking away from nurse as mother value." His two mothers often mingled in his mind. He had called the ship that would get the father's gold in *Where the Cross Is Made* the "Mary Allen," a name just one letter off his mother's name, "Mary Ellen." In *Gold* the name combined both mothers to become the "Sarah Allen." The dead spinster Sarah would be floating in the back of his mind when he wrote the square dance scene for *Desire Under the Elms,* for he had the fiddler call out to one of the guests, "Ye're walkin' like a bride down the aisle, Sarah! Waal, while they's life they's allus hope, I've heerd tell." So the two maternal trees and the two dead mothers of his 1922 plot emerged directly out of the double mother of his infancy, called up by his grief for his actual one.

O'Neill did not spell out the "tragedy" of this first plot, but he must have had in mind the killing of the old man, and the subsequent immolation of the young lovers. It was so much the obvious ending for the love conflict that afterward, when O'Neill discarded it, he had to explain it away by having the woman realize confusedly, "That's what I ought t' done, hain't it?" But the murder of the old man did not interest O'Neill. He tried to prod his thinking on the murderous rivalry of father and son by reading pertinent case histories in one of Wilhelm Stekel's psychoanalytic books. It was early November 1923, and Malcolm Cowley happened to be visiting him in his home at Ridgefield, Connecticut. As Cowley recalled, he talked of plans for a "New England" play and showed him Stekel's book, which, he said, had plots enough for "all the playwrights who ever lived." He pointed out particularly—so Cowley recalled—the case record of a mother who seduced her son and drove him mad. (Actually the case—from *Twelve Essays on Sex and Psychoanalysis*—was closer to O'Neill's plot than Cowley remembered, for the seducing mother was really a stepmother, and the son in it was torn by conflicting thoughts of his good mother and his "whore" stepmother in a manner similar to O'Neill's character.) But Stekel did not bring his idea to life. He needed something more meaningful than the murder of the old man to plunge him into participation.

The plunge came when he woke up on New Year's morning in 1924 with his mind still pervaded by a dream. It gave him, he realized, just the right tragic ending for his play. It added *Desire* to the title, making it "Desire Under the Elms." It added a baby to the characters and changed the tragedy to that of a mother who kills her baby to prove her greater love for its father. Like the first plot, this idea came out of his grief, for it recalls the major tragedy of his mother's life back in 1885, more than three years before he himself was born. His father, James O'Neill, had been on tour in *Monte Cristo* out west and had become desperately lonely for his wife, whom he had left in New York with the two children: Jamie, who was seven, and the baby Edmund. For love of her husband, Mary Ellen O'Neill left the two children with her mother and went out to join him. They had just reached Denver when they received a telegram telling them that the baby Edmund was mortally ill. She took the first train back on March 4, but he died that very day. The older boy had caught the measles, and her mother had carelessly allowed him to infect the baby. She felt that if she had been there she could have kept them apart. She felt she had killed the baby by abandoning him, and she was haunted by guilt for the rest of her life.

Eugene O'Neill had been born into the dead baby's place. All his mother's bereavement had focused—so he wrote in a sketched "family history"—into a "fierce concentration of affection" for him. From that time on, he was her baby. She was still calling him "my baby" after he had a baby son of his own, Shane. She ended a letter to him with love for his wife, his baby, "and the biggest baby of the three, *You*." So he was linked eternally to the dead baby whose place he had taken. When he came to write his autobiographical play *Long Day's Journey into Night*, he actually exchanged names with the dead baby, making the live son "Edmund" and the dead baby himself, "Eugene." His brother Jamie had longed only to follow their mother into the grave, and he had had his wish—had succeeded in drinking himself to death—only a little less than two months before Eugene O'Neill dreamed his New Year's dream. The same wish was in the dream of the dead baby which brought the play to such urgent life for O'Neill that he started in on it at once.

The dream had been fraught with his current feelings for his wife Agnes, who was—so he told her—"mother of the best of me" and whose baby he also was, as her letters to him show. "My own dear big baby," she would write, urging him to take care of himself, or, "You poor, poor dear baby," wanting to take care of him. Somewhere behind the dream of the beloved dead baby had lurked his growing unhappiness as the live baby of Agnes. He had founded his life on his love for her, but their marriage had been "unhappy." He had said so after only two years of it, and after six, abysses of silence had begun to open between them, and more and more frequently destructive quarrels broke out between them. He had always felt uncertain of his wife's love. She had come to him out of a precociously complicated love past that made him doubt her. She herself was chronically jealous, and so she had always instinctively reassured herself of his love by provoking his jealousy. Besides, he had a basic distrust of love because of his traumatic discovery at the age of fifteen that his mother was addicted to morphine. So great had been this shock to his faith in life and love that he had discontinued his mother's love line in his "Diagram" at this point. All that basic distrust had been accentuated in his marriage, blending his feeling for his mother with his feeling for Agnes inextricably.

Blended too were his feelings of guilt toward both his wife and his mother. He was convinced that his own birth had shattered his mother's health and made her vulnerable to addiction when her doctor prescribed morphine. He felt the same guilt in his marriage for all the pain that he caused his wife. So Agnes joined his mother to enter both into the dead mother of his play and into Abbie, the new "Maw." O'Neill drew Eben's overall guilt toward his mother from his own, but the concrete example of it recalls Agnes at the time shortly after their marriage when they lived in her house at Point Pleasant on the New Jersey shore. She knew the house, so he had let her take care of the coal stoves, which—Agnes said—needed "to be shaken down every day and the ashes taken out." Only after some time did he awake to the fact that the work was much too heavy for his fragile wife. Then, remorsefully, he took over. His remorse enters the play as Eben's haunted vision of his mother "come back all cramped up t' shake the fire, an' carry ashes, her eyes weepin' an' bloody with smoke an' cinders same's they used t' be." Agnes enters into the stepmother too. Although O'Neill called this character "Abbie" because it is a typically New England name, he could never have chosen a name so close to his pet name for Agnes, "Aggie," had not Abbie been imbued with his feeling for her. All his distrust of Agnes enters Eben's distrust of Abbie when she first enters his life, and after their union, when it sets off her proof of love by infanticide. The same distrust of Agnes invests Abbie as the betraying wife and pulls O'Neill into the betrayed old man.

O'Neill found that he could use for *Desire Under the Elms* some ideas that he had used for a one-act play back in 1918 called *The Rope*. It had also been a farm play, and he had apparently based it on the story of a real farmer he knew, probably from the Truro area near his Provincetown summer home. O'Neill changed him from the fragile old lunatic of *The Rope* into a powerful patriarch for *Desire Under the Elms* but kept his other features. In both plays he is tall, gaunt, stoop-shouldered, and has very weak eyesight. He quotes scripture, often wrathfully. By hard work he has made his farm extraordinarily valuable for the area, but he is a miser and has an ugly history of driving an earlier wife to death. In *The Rope* he has had a second, much younger wife, who has been flagrantly unfaithful. She became the third wife, Abbie, of *Desire Under the Elms*. In both plays he has a hidden treasure of twenty-dollar gold pieces.

The younger son of *Desire Under the Elms* digs it up from under the floor-boards to buy out his brother's share in the farm with the boatfare to California. In *The Rope* the coins are attached to a noose the old man has set up in the barn, supposedly for his son to hang himself but actually to shower him with the gold.

O'Neill's most intimate feelings toward his family had gone into *The Rope*, for it is an ironical version of the prodigal son story. During his wild years of wandering, O'Neill saw himself as a prodigal son, and he had longed for the prodigal's fated return to the love of his father. The idea of a return to love became permanently linked for him with his feeling of being the prodigal. When he was coming back to New London from Harvard to see his beloved Beatrice Ashe in the fall of 1914, he told her once to expect her "Prodigal Bridegroom" and another time to expect her "Prodigal Husband." A year be-fore he wrote *The Rope*, his own father had literally turned into the prodigal's father, for he had taken that role in *The Wanderer*, a play based on the parable in the Bible. O'Neill had watched him deliver the moving words "For this my son was dead, and is alive again" months before he put them into the mouth of the miser father in his play. Quite naturally all his ambivalent feelings for his own father had gone along with them: all the "resentment & hatred" (so labeled in his "Diagram") that he had felt when his father had exiled him to boarding school, all his longing for the love he had had before, all his later resentment at his father's miserly withholding of his "gold," and all the longing to take it. In the play, the father's gold is actually waiting for his son, if he can triumph over his fear of the invitation to hang himself with the rope.

Although the prodigal's mother has already died in *The Rope*, O'Neill found a way to bring his own mother into the play along with all his distrust of her. She enters in the form of a "soft-minded" child whose commonplace name is actually her own: "Mary." The play opens with the child enacting a little pan-tomime with her doll strangely expressive of O'Neill's mother with her "baby" Eugene. (In *The Great God Brown* O'Neill would have his protagonist see his mother as a child and himself as her "doll," and have him say, "She played mother and child with me for many years.") He gave the child Mary in *The Rope* his mother's "fierce concentration of affection" for her baby. Startled by a noise, she "quickly snatches up the doll, which she hugs fiercely to her breast," and then she runs to hide. She is very like his picture of his mother Mary in his later autobiographical play *Long Day's Journey into Night*, who "hugs him with a frightened, protective tenderness" and hides herself in the depths of her drug addiction. Indeed, the "soft-minded" child stands in the place of his mother, soft-minded from the drug, and she gives herself away by a curious parody of his mother's gestures. In *Long Day's Journey into Night* he describes them: "Her hands flutter up to pat her hair in their aimless, distracted way." Under the drug, she "settles back in relaxed dreaminess, staring fixedly at nothing. Her arms rest limply along the arms of the chair." The child Mary is first seen "staring fixedly" at her doll, and her "hands flutter about aimlessly in relaxed, flabby gestures"—a combination of his mother's tremor with her limpness under the drug. It is this "mother-child" (O'Neill actually once called Beatrice that) who brings down the father's gold by swinging on the rope that the prodigal son feared to touch. At the play's end she is foolishly tossing the goldpieces one by one into the sea. If there is an "unconscious" substratum in all this, it reads like this: the father's gold (love), ardently desired by the son, goes to the mother, but it is "thrown away" on her, soft-minded as she is from the drug.

Both O'Neill's mother and father, trailing the shapes that they had taken in *The Rope,* pushed their way into *Desire Under the Elms.* The miser father even takes on the same age at the end of the play as O'Neill's father when he died in 1920, seventy-six. He also takes on his actual vitality in his old age. Even as late as 1913, James O'Neill's interviewers were rapturous over "the robust power of his features and the strength—physical and mental—that has made him what he is." An echo of the soft-minded child of *The Rope* sounds in the lines of *Desire Under the Elms* on the dead mother of Eben. His father comments on him: "Soft-headed. Like his Maw." O'Neill's own father had thought that he was out of his head during his wild youth, and had always considered him "a bundle of nerves like his mother." O'Neill was so possessed by this oneness with her, and by thoughts of her death as he wrote, that he had the old man at one point threaten to take his shotgun to his son "an' blow his soft brains t' the top o' them elums!" That gives Eben—and O'Neill with him—a death like his mother's death of brain tumor. It merges his soft brains with hers (at the top of the maternal tree). If O'Neill's parents had haunted *The Rope,* written when they were both alive, they could only do so more intensely in *Desire Under the Elms,* written when they were both dead, his mother after his father, united with the dead baby Edmund in the New London earth.

No wonder, then, that as he wrote, the house with its brooding elms became a haunted house, drenched in past sorrow, pervaded by the memory of the dead mother. The set shows all four rooms of the house with its elms, the sky, and a piece of the road, and O'Neill deliberately contrasted its haunted interior with the freedom and promise of the sky and road. The indoor scenes are all set in the shadows of twilight, dawn, or candlelit night. The dead mother pervades these shifting shadows, first in her kitchen where her son Eben sees her come back "all cramped up" to stand by her stove, and then even more palpably in the tomblike parlor—O'Neill says that it is like a "tomb"—where she was laid out. Even the old man senses the chill of her presence, "droppin' off the elums, climbin' up the roof, sneakin' down the chimney, pokin' in the corners!" By contrast, almost all the outdoor scenes are flooded with golden light. A golden sunset begins the play, and the opening lines link it with the longing for love and the gold in California. It is golden sunrise when the two older brothers break free of the farm and go capering off down the road bound "fur the gold fields o' Californi-a." It is golden sunrise again when Eben and Abbie find love, and it is most intensely golden sunrise at the end of their tragedy when they stand for a moment, transfigured by love and sacrifice, "looking up raptly in attitudes strangely aloof and devout."

No one could have sensed more sharply than Eugene O'Neill the push of all these memories arising to direct his plot, his set, his dialogue. He was used to looking beyond the surface in himself and others. He had chosen the Swedish playwright Strindberg as his "master," because Strindberg had led the way that he wanted to go with dramas that pierced the banal exterior of life to reveal the immense realities—psychological, biological, sociological—that work behind them. O'Neill had selected one of the most difficult of Strindberg's "behind-life" dramas, *The Spook Sonata,* for the very first production of a new theater group he had formed with Kenneth Macgowan and Robert Edmond Jones, and, even though he hated essay-writing, he took the trouble to write an explanation of Strindberg's greatness for the program. It would serve to prepare audiences for coming productions of his own plays by educating them to his intention to cut through surface realism. (*The Spook Sonata* had opened on January 3, 1924, two days after his New Year's dream.) Of course, this was his intention in *Desire Under the Elms.*

After it went on he told his friend George Jean Nathan: "What I think everyone missed in 'Desire' is the quality in it I set most store by—the attempt to give an epic tinge to New England's inhibited life-lust, to make its inexpressiveness poetically expressive, to release it." He was not reproducing New England speech literally; he was "trying," he said, "to write a synthetic dialogue which should be, in a way, the distilled essence of New England." He had his characters speak in powerful fragments and piquant arrangements of New England clichés that convey their inexpressiveness yet become vivid poetry. The two older brothers sum up Eben and his belief that he is "Maw—every drop o' blood!" with an ironic refrain that comes up three times, each with variations:

SIMEON.   Like his Paw.
PETER.   Dead spit an' image!
SIMEON.   Dog'll eat dog!

O'Neill knew that a playwright works "as Beethoven did" (so he declared in an interview) "molding tones, giving them color, new meaning, thus creating music." In the dialogue of *Desire Under the Elms,* O'Neill creates a musical theme and variations on the New England stones beginning with Peter's chant "Here—it's stones atop o' the ground—stones atop o' stones," and going on to Eben's "stone atop o' stone—makin' walls till yer heart's a stone," to reach a climax in the old man's "God's in the stones! Build my church on a rock—out o' stones an' I'll be in them! That's what he meant t' Peter! Stones. I picked 'em up an' piled 'em into walls. Ye kin read the years o' my life in them walls, every day a hefted stone."

Both in action and in words his characters recall the animals they live with. The older brothers come in from work "like two friendly oxen" and move clumsily toward their food, "their bodies bumping and rubbing together." Simeon sees their escape from the farm as if they really were oxen: "The halter's broke—the harness is busted—the fence bars is down—the stone walls air crumblin' an' tumblin'! We'll be kickin' up an' tearin' away down the road!" Going off to visit Min, the village prostitute, young Eben is "all slicked up like a prize bull," and when he takes her for the first time he begins "t' beller like a calf." All the women—Min, Eben's Maw, and Abbie—are called cows. His characters see life as did the ancient agricultural civilizations that created all the mythical cow-mother goddesses and all the bull gods. O'Neill knew them from reading Sir James Frazer's *The Golden Bough* and Carl Jung's analysis of the myth-making unconscious in *The Psychology of the Unconscious,* the psychoanalytic book that had interested him most. He explained, "I never intended that the language of that play should be a record of what the characters actually said. I wanted to express what they felt subconsciously."

Subconsciously, all his characters make the age-old equation of the fertile woman with the fertile land. They see in the cultivation of the earth, just as all the ancient cults did, "the fertilization of the mother." They think of the farm as a woman. Eben says that Min, the prostitute, "smells like a wa'm plowed field," and when he takes her, a woman his father and his brothers have possessed before him, he is making his opening battle to possess his mother's farm. The new stepmother, Abbie, lusting for him, "squirms desirously" under the masculine sun, receiving it as if she were the fertile earth. "Hain't the sun strong an' hot?" she asks Eben pointedly. "Ye kin feel it burnin' into the earth— Nature—makin' thin's grow—bigger an' bigger—burnin' inside ye—makin' ye want t' grow—into somethin' else." The old man looks upon her directly as the fertile earth that he possesses. He tells her: "Sometimes ye air the farm an' sometimes the farm be yew!" He pounds his fist on his knee, crying, "Me an' the farm has got to beget a son!" Eben takes possession of the farm by possessing Abbie. Coming upon his father right afterward, he reverses their roles and orders the old man to get to work. "Ay-eh! I'm bossin' yew! Ha-ha-ha! See how ye like it! Ha-ha-ha! I'm the prize rooster o' this roost." The primeval life-lust creates mythical overtones in his characters so that their struggle takes on an "epic tinge." He told George Jean Nathan, "It's just that—the poetical (in the broadest and deepest sense) vision illuminating even the most sordid and mean blind alleys of life—which I'm convinced is, and is to be, *my* concern and justification as a dramatist. . . . It's where the poetic is buried deep beneath the dull and crude that one's deep-seeing vision is tested."

Later, asked point-blank what *Desire Under the Elms* was all about, O'Neill answered, " 'Desire,' briefly, is a tragedy of the possessive—the pitiful longing of man to build his own heaven here on earth by glutting his sense of power with ownership of land, people, money—but principally the land and other people's lives." He did shape his play with this idea in mind, and saw to it that his principal characters transcended their lust for possession through tragic suffering. But O'Neill himself realized instantly the inadequacy of his own explanation, and he added: "Of course, there's more to it than that, and the above is so crude as to misrepresent, but it's the best I can do."

Actually, the meaning of the play emerged from the directive push of the dead-baby dream working itself out within the channels of his theme of possessiveness. His memories formed no passive reservoir but a shaping force. Abbie is driven toward her tragic apotheosis by the same force that impelled O'Neill's mother toward hers. O'Neill derives her passion to possess the farm out of her bitterly homeless state. Homelessness had been his mother's agony. As a touring actor's wife, she had moved endlessly from one alien hotel room to another. In his "family history," O'Neill said that "her bitterest resentment" against her husband had been "that she never had [a] home." In *Long Day's Journey into Night* she attributes the baby's death to that, declaring, "Women need homes, if they are to be good mothers." Abbie enters the play with a passionate utterance of the word "Hum!" and repeats almost the same words with a New England accent: "A woman's got t' hev a hum!" Within the play logic, she seduces her stepson primarily to get a baby that will give her title to the farm (with lust and pique intermixed). The seduction brings her love, so that when Eben discovers that his baby gives her the farm and furiously rejects her, she proves her greater love for him by killing the baby she loves. Out of the magnitude of her sacrifice for love, she rises to tragic exaltation.

The scenes that deal with the baby's death were shaped by O'Neill's sense of oneness with the dead baby Edmund. He has the old man celebrate the birth of the baby with a square dance at which he flaunts his pride in begetting a son so late in life. The scene was called up in O'Neill by his own birth. In his "family history" he wrote of it: "Husband very proud of his birth (confirmed by stories to me)—44 years old at time." The transfer of that pride from his forty-four-year-old father to one seventy-six is enough to make it grotesque, but it is made far more so by the savage irony with which O'Neill designed these scenes. His picture of the old man dancing in triumph before his neighbors what is actually his disgrace emanated from a witches' brew of self-loathing and hatred in himself set off by this proxy vision of his birth (the birth that had caused—so he believed—his mother's addiction). The same witches' brew must have been boiling up in him twelve years before his dream of the dead baby, when he had tried to kill himself. That had been shortly after he supplied the evidence for his divorce from Kathleen Jenkins late in December 1911. It had been a New York divorce, with adultery the only legal grounds, and so he had had to arrange to be seen in bed with a prostitute by several witnesses. That degrading scene had demonstrated intolerably for him the mess he had made of life and love. After it, he had tried to kill himself with an overdose of sleeping tablets. Somewhere in that rush to die out of the loveless world in which he found himself must have been the desire to become what his brother Edmund had always been, his mother's eternally beloved baby. That desire had created his New Year's dream, and so he merged both the baby's birth and his death with his own. Abbie's words on it are redolent of his own suicide attempt: "I left the piller over his little face. Then he killed himself. He stopped breathin'."

The old suicidal pull drew O'Neill more powerfully now that becoming the dead baby meant joining his mother in the grave. That pull sweeps Eben to his tragic end. His is the greatest triumph over possessiveness and the greatest sacrifice for love. Abbie's sacrifice had aimed at possessing him, but his sacrifice of farm, liberty, and life is directed only at sharing her suffering in "prison 'r death 'r hell." Through Eben's tragic end, O'Neill shares with his mother the guilt for the dead baby that proved her love for his father and at the same time is united to her forever as the dead baby. So powerful was this drive toward a reunion in death that it almost broke into complete expression before the tragic climax of the play during the scene in which Abbie and Eben are joined in love. Within the play logic, he takes her in the parlor haunted by his dead mother because the act revenges his mother on his father. But the union vibrates with overtones of a consummation in death. It takes place in a room that looks like "a tomb in which the family has been interred alive." (O'Neill's whole family was in the grave as he wrote.) Its candles summon up the image of Eben's Maw laid out in death, and he takes his new Maw in her name. This initial union with her foreshadows the ultimate union at the end of the tragedy, when he joins her in death.

Those final moments reveal the ultimate aim of that drive toward death. Logically, the Sheriff (alerted by Eben in his first horror at the murder of the baby before his love triumphs) enters at the last as a mere dramatic device to carry the lovers off at the apotheosis of their sacrifice. Actually he comes out of the very heart of the dream wish. O'Neill gives him a quite unnecessary personal name, which rings out with peculiar insistence in the last few lines of the play. It turns out to be that commonplace name—so redolent of meaning for O'Neill—his father's name, "Jim." It is pronounced three times in the space of a few seconds and emerges yet again in the last words of the play, in which the story logic meets the dream logic: "It's a jim-dandy farm, no denyin'. Wished I owned it!" By joining the mother in death through his protagonist, O'Neill is taken up with her into the eternal custody of a father figure in authority (like James O'Neill, who was usually called "the Governor" among theater friends), and he actually bears O'Neill's father's name, "Jim." The image emerges wordlessly out of O'Neill's earliest image of felicity in love. As a real baby, he had been doubly encircled in love, first in the protective arms of his mother and then along with her, in the greater love of his father, that "indefinite hero" of his infancy (so O'Neill called him in his "Diagram"). The same image had inspired his plays of the son who strives to attain his father's gold by way of a mother ship. Eben is impelled by O'Neill's own longing to join his mother in love and death and so attain eternal custody by his father.

With such a powerful death-urge sweeping through his play, O'Neill might easily have been swept along with it. But he was writing drama, the essence of which is conflict, and so he could struggle against it within his play. He fought out his battle by way of his warring father and son. Their clash represents all the life forces in Eugene O'Neill struggling against the lure of death. O'Neill had been drawn into both characters—in part—because he had a powerful sense of being both father and son at this time. He was living among the stony Connecticut farms of Ridgefield, which called up his boyhood New London, Connecticut, summer home surrounded by fields a long walk over the railroad trestle away from the town. "I have a place at New London where I bury stones in the summer," his father had said of it. Eugene O'Neill had raised chickens as a boy, and now his son Shane repeated him, running about with his pet rooster. His other son from his first marriage, Eugene Jr., had been staying for the Christmas holidays with him just before he dreamed his New Year's dream, and he arranged a ticket for him to see *The Spook Sonata* when he returned to school in New York, just as his own father had arranged New York theater tickets for him when he was a boy at school in Stamford, Connecticut. He also had vivid recollections of his father in his roles as the father of the biblical prodigal son in *The Wanderer* and even more as the patriarch Jacob in the play *Joseph and His Brethren,* in which he had toured from 1913 to 1915. (Echoes of the Joseph story crept into *Desire Under the Elms,* such as in Abbie's advances toward Eben and her revenge when repulsed by accusing the boy, which recall Potiphar's wife with Joseph.) All that winter O'Neill had been reading the Old Testament to himself. He later told Lawrence Langner: "Ridgefield always drove me to hard cider, acidosis, and the Old Testament in the weepy, muddy, slush-and-snow days." He was also writing a "Book of Revelation" adaptation from the New Testament when he dreamed his New Year's dream. (Robert Edmond Jones wanted to use it as a medium for experiment with dance movements as theatrical expression.) Finishing it had kept him from starting in on *Desire Under the Elms* after the dream. When he did begin, on January 15, he fit smoothly into the scripture-quoting old man of his play.

This character had originally been conceived as the most possessive of all, one who could gladly set fire to the farm when he died so as to know that "it was all a-dying with me an' no one else'd ever own what was mine, what I'd made out o' nothin' with my own sweat an' blood!" But, as O'Neill wrote, old Ephraim came virtually to transcend the possessiveness that dominates him because he values the farm, not for itself but for its expression of his own creative power. "When ye kin make corn sprout out o' stones, God's livin' in yew!" he says. Ephraim takes on grandeur because O'Neill's most intimate life philosophy flowed into him. Whereas Eben had been impelled to his tragic destiny by O'Neill's sense of oneness with his mother, Ephraim became impelled by O'Neill's realization that he was also "spit an' image" of his strong-willed father. He had early absorbed the striving spirit that had transformed his father from a poor Irish immigrant file-cutter with a heavy brogue into a prominent actor-manager famous for the beauty of his diction. James O'Neill's anecdotes all stress his enthusiasm for overcoming limitations and triumphing over difficulties. One of his favorites had the dying Charlotte Cushman advising him—after their last tour together—to "work, *work*, WORK!"He made a creed of that "work, *work*, WORK!" He often told of his flat failure when he first stepped into the role of Monte Cristo with no time to rehearse, and of how he got at the part "hammer and tongs" to convert it into success. O'Neill had taken over the striving philosophy of his "Hero Father" (so called in his "Diagram"). At eighteen he had discovered Friedrich Nietzsche's *Thus Spake Zarathustra,* and he went on to reread it almost every year of his life thereafter. Its philosophy of striving to create and live by higher values, he found, blended easily into his heritage from his father. Nietzsche has a dialogue between a diamond and a piece of charcoal over the virtues of hardness and softness, with the diamond being hard as all "creators are hard" and suggesting the new commandment: "*Become hard!*" O'Neill had accepted that commandment, and the *hard*, the *difficult*, became his object. Outlining his ideal program for life, he described it as "years of undisturbed hard and difficult work." In his program explanation of *The Spook Sonata*, he said that they had chosen it because "the difficult is properly our special task." "Easy" was his favorite term of contempt. He insisted: "Truth, in the theatre as in life, is eternally difficult just as the easy is the everlasting lie." He never had forgotten his father's regrets in his old age at missing his opportunity to become a great Shakespearean actor. O'Neill thought that he had given in to the lure of "easy" popularity and money with *Monte Cristo,* and he swore on his deathbed to "remain true to the best that is in me though the heavens fall." He knew he could go on writing one successful *Anna Christie* after another, but he declared scathingly, "It would be too easy!" He meant to follow his dream unswervingly so that "my real significant bit of truth, and the ability to express it, will be conquered in time—not tomorrow nor the next day nor any near, easily-attained period, but after the struggle has been long enough and hard enough to merit victory."

He put this entire creative philosophy into the old man of his play, even to his own way of using the words "hard" and "easy." Ephraim says:

> When I come here fifty odd year ago—I was jest twenty an' the strongest an' hardest ye ever seen—ten times as strong an' fifty times as hard as Eben. Waal—this place was nothin' but fields o' stones. Folks laughed when I tuk it. They couldn't know what I knowed. When ye kin make corn sprout out o' stones, God's livin' in yew! They wa'n't strong enuf fur that! They reckoned God was easy. They laughed. They don't laugh no more. . . . They're all underground—fur follerin' arter an easy God. God hain't easy.

As O'Neill rejected easy wealth from repeating plays like *Anna Christie,* Ephraim has rejected the easy money he could have had from farming the fertile lands out west. "I could o' been a rich man—but somethin' in me fit me an' fit me—the voice o' God sayin': 'This hain't wuth nothin' to' Me!' " He sums up O'Neill's faith as a creator in four words: "God's hard, not easy!"

O'Neill gave the old man his own loneliness as a creator—his own loneliness as a man. Ephraim is "allus lonesome" because everyone covets the farm he has created "without knowin' what it meant." O'Neill had experienced that loneliness deeply in his marriage. Agnes had felt crushed by his triumph as a writer, which was so much greater than her own. Yet she never could grasp his advice to write only out of the best that was in her, and instead had been turning out easy items for money. The abyss between their viewpoints became ever wider; silence divided them. O'Neill put all the pathos of his own "inexpressiveness" into his lonely and betrayed old New Englander's one effort to break his silence and communicate his deepest thinking to his wife. She does not hear a word of it, absorbed as she is in her own designs. Bitterly, the old man tells her to pray "fur understandin'." He foreshadows O'Neill's words to Agnes when all was over between them: "But what do you understand of me or I of you?"

Into the old man too he put his own realization of his tragic possessiveness—particularly in love. The fiercely repeated "my" and "mine" of his characters came right out of his own self-knowledge. His letters to Agnes call her "My Own" or "Own Sweetheart" or "Own little wife." He had been struggling throughout their marriage to adapt to her need for superficial socializing and to accept the invasions of Ridgefield by her impecunious family or casual friends. He did not feel he had conquered it until they moved to their Bermuda home later, and then he told her: "I love Spithead—and not with my old jealous bitter possessiveness—my old man Cabotism!—but as ours, not mine except as mine is included in ours." He had given old Ephraim Cabot his own possessiveness in love, which echoed his father's. In the "family history" O'Neill describes his father as "morbidly jealous of her, even of her affection for children" when he took his wife from them and Edmund died. O'Neill knew he had within him the same "jealous bitter possessiveness." His sense of himself as "spit an' image" of his father shaped old Ephraim Cabot and determined his end.

So powerful was that sense of his father as a directive ideal working within him that he contradicts Ephraim's history in the play to make him fulfill it. His father had been for him the supreme example of romantic married love. He had held him up as a model to live by when he wrote Agnes from his deathbed of the enduring power of his love for his wife. He had been, O'Neill said, "a husband to marvel at." Despite Ephraim's history of working his former wives to death, O'Neill converts him into a standard and model for love. He says of the dead baby, "He'd ought t' been my son, Abbie. Ye'd ought t' loved me. I'm a man. If ye'd loved me, I'd never told no Sheriff on ye no matter what ye did, if they was t' brile me alive!" (At his father's funeral O'Neill had heard William F. Connor sum up James O'Neill as "a man in every sense and in the noblest interpretation of the word.") It is Ephraim who grudgingly praises Eben for his decision to share Abbie's guilt. "Purty good—fur yew!" he says. Although O'Neill devoted the last moment of his play to his exalted lovers walking "hand in hand" out of life, the most impressive final figure is that of the old man, bereft of love and money, relinquishing an impulse to follow his elder sons to California and going back to work with the words "Waal—what d'ye want? God's lonesome, hain't He? God's hard an' lonesome!" If, in the end, the old man took on the most pronounced epic tinge of all, it was because O'Neill put into him his own philosophy of work, taken up from his father, and it was that philosophy beyond everything else that bound him to life. Through Ephraim all the life forces in Eugene O'Neill triumph over the lure of death. O'Neill knew well how much of himself had gone into this character. He said, "I have always loved Ephraim so much! He's so autobiographical!"

If Eugene O'Neill found a theater ready for this play of adultery and infanticide in 1924 America, he did so only because he had taken care to create the theater for it. He had been the prime mover in resurrecting Jig Cook's Provincetown Playhouse and bringing to it the fresh creative talents of Kenneth Macgowan and Robert Edmond Jones. A flurry of productions in their new theater had actually split the writing of *Desire Under the Elms* into two distinct parts. O'Neill had just finished part one at the end of January when he was swept into rehearsals for no less than four of his plays: *Welded, All God's Chillun Got Wings, The Emperor Jones* (a revival with Paul Robeson, who would also take the lead in *All God's Chillun Got Wings*), and an adaptation of Coleridge's *Rime of the Ancient Mariner* (like his adaptation of the last book of the New Testament, which he called the "Book of Revelation," for Robert Edmond Jones to experiment with dance movement). Not until May 24 could O'Neill get back to *Desire Under the Elms.* He finished it on June 16, 1924, and a week later he was reading it to his partners Kenneth Macgowan and Bobby Jones in a hospital where Jones happened to be "laid up." They decided to open *Desire Under the Elms* that fall in their Greenwich Village theater and fill the smaller Provincetown Playhouse with a revival of four of O'Neill's one-act sea plays combined into a cycle to be called "S.S. Glencairn." Rehearsals got under way October 18. O'Neill found himself, as often before, rushing from play to play, with *Desire Under the Elms* rehearsing all morning and afternoon and "S.S. Glencairn" in the evening.

They were painfully handicapped by lack of time and money. Even a brilliant set designer like Bobby Jones could not, in such short time, create elms redolent of a "sinister maternity" which would participate in the play like characters. (In the opening scene, for instance, they were to glow green to make the house they oppress "pale and washed out by contrast.") Neither the elms nor "the house as character" with its "flow of life from room to room" came through as

O'Neill knew they could. He had divided each of the three parts of his play into four quick scenes punctuated by moments of darkness. Unfortunately, in performance, these were extended to intermissions with lights turned up in the theater. Later, he declared, "It ruined my idea in 'Desire Under the Elms,' that lights up business! What I want is black out, curtain down, change made in a few seconds, curtain up, then lights again." In compensation, O'Neill was delighted with Walter Huston's acting in the role of the old man. It was, he said, "exactly what I had in mind." He added: "Walter's work was as fine as any I've seen in a theatre. He was infinitely superior to Mary Morris [as Abbie], who was good in sections but had nothing to contribute but stock acting and pumped emotion when something deeply passionate was demanded. The part carried her a lot of the time. Yet it was Mary who made the biggest hit with the public, who received most publicity and critical praise." They opened on November 11, and the first-night critics did their best to kill the play. Most of them thought it a "gruesome morbid" thing. It was the subscription audiences who turned it into a success.

When they moved uptown to the Earl Carroll Theater in January, the District Attorney of New York, Joab Banton, provoked a sudden run on their box office by attacking the play as obscene and threatening to close it. Later that year, when O'Neill payed his dentist, Dr. Lief, he remarked humorously, "But don't thank me, thank that so-amiable District Attorney! Seriously though, his press-agent work is bad in the long run. It attracts the low-minded, looking for smut, and they are highly disappointed or else laugh wherever they imagine double-meanings." The threat to close was opposed so vigorously by those who saw the play's greatness that Banton finally agreed to submit the question to a play jury, which the Authors League had suggested as a way of getting censorship out of the hands of ignorant officials and into those of people competent to judge. When the jury cleared it, laughingly O'Neill said to Kenneth Macgowan: "All's well what ends in publicity only."

In the midst of the Banton uproar O'Neill had asked his agent, Richard Madden: "Do you have to send in script of 'Desire' to committee to make it eligible for Pulitzer Prize? If so, do so. Of course, I know there's no chance for it, but *I do,* for the sake of principle, want to *make* them pass it up." They did pass it up. The prize went to Sidney Howard's comedy *They Knew What They Wanted,* which had opened at about the same time. Howard's own judgment was better. He had rushed to O'Neill's defense during the Banton threat with a letter to the *New York Times* (December 14, 1924) in which he said, "I only ask to be shown anything produced in the English-speaking theatre of recent generations which is half so fine or true or brave as 'Desire Under the Elms.' " The play ran eleven months in New York and then set out for a road tour.

Macgowan thought that they might avoid trouble by softening the most objectionable words, and O'Neill agreed: "Yes, 'harlot' could substitute for 'whore' and 'femalin' ' or 'sluttin' ' or something of the kind for 'whorin'." Trouble came anyway. O'Neill told Upton Sinclair, "I hear they have 'pinched' my play 'Desire Under the Elms' in your Holy City, Los Angeles. Well, well, and so many of the pioneers are said to have come from New England! Boston has also barred it." In England, the Lord Chamberlain prohibited any production of it. (It had its first very successful opening in London sixteen years later in the midst of World War II, when O'Neill was astounded that "a war ravaged England should show such an interest in a play like 'Desire.' ") Long before that it had been produced all over Europe. O'Neill was fascinated by the "stir raised in Moscow" when the Kamerny Theater produced *Desire Under the Elms*. He told Alexander Berkman, the old anarchist: "It seems they held a public trial of the character 'Abby' in the play on the charge of having murdered a child. An audience of the intellegentsia were the jury." She had been declared innocent unanimously because of the pressure on her of "the curse of private property and inhibited New England morals." Berkman assured him that he was right in taking the trial as a sign of the play's popularity. By chance, O'Neill was able to see the Kamerny production of *Desire Under the Elms* when they brought it to Paris in June 1930. Despite the translation into Russian, O'Neill found that they had captured "the inner spirit" of his work. So brilliant was their production that he felt they had fulfilled his lifelong dream of a "theatre of creative imagination."

American critics had greeted the book *Desire Under the Elms* when it appeared in 1925 far more favorably than the first-night play reviewers had. The Freudian critics grasped the father-son rivalry and praised the play as an illustration of the Oedipus complex. O'Neill remarked, "The Freudian brethren and sisteren seem quite set up about it and, after reading astonishing complexes between the lines of my simplicities, claim it for their own. Well, so some of them did with 'Emperor Jones.' They are hard to shake!" To a student who asked him point-blank if he were dramatizing Freud, O'Neill explained the hypothetical nature of scientific theory: "To me, Freud only means uncertain conjectures and explanations about the truths of the emotional past of mankind that every dramatist has clearly sensed since real drama began. Which, I think, answers your question. I respect Freud's work tremendously—but I'm not an addict!"

By this time most critics found *Desire Under the Elms* worth fighting over and began disputes as to whether Abbie, Eben, or Ephraim was the central character, as to whether the theories of Freud or Jung, or a play by Strindberg or by Ibsen, or specifically *They Knew What They Wanted* by Sidney Howard, were the central source, and as to whether the play meant this or that. Even when the Banton conflict was raging, O'Neill himself was already two plays on. Far too busy to be deflected by what he called "the megaphone men," he carried on unswervingly his pursuit of the real realities.

2

Marco Millions

When Eugene O'Neill was bundled off on the *Charles Racine* to "make good" in Argentina, his own secret hope was to go on and reach China. "I've always longed to go to the East—it was the ultimate goal of my sailor days but I never made it," he confessed. So later, when he began to read up on Ponce de León for his play *The Fountain* in 1921, he discovered that Ponce thought he would repeat Marco Polo's voyage to the golden cities of Kublai Khan. O'Neill gave his Ponce a vision—fraught with his own China dreams—of Kublai Khan in all his worldly power, accompanied by Beauty in a Chinese dancing girl and Truth in a venerable old poet. They really did not belong in a play about Ponce de León, so he cut them, but he found himself haunted by his three characters in search of a play, and he longed even more urgently for China. Agnes wanted to go to Europe, but, as he told a friend, "Europe somehow means nothing to me. Either the South Seas or China, say I." He wanted to "wind up in China," and he saw that he could do so by setting out with Marco Polo by way of a play to reach the golden cities of Kublai Khan, the dancing girl, and the venerable poet.

He rushed out and bought the best scholarly editions of *The Book of Ser Marco Polo*—the one edited by Yule and the one edited by Marsden—and set to work taking copious notes from them. He was delighted with Yule's description of Marco Polo as "a practical man, brave, shrewd, prudent, keen in affairs, and never losing his interest in mercantile details, very fond of the chase, sparing of speech."

"The American Ideal!" O'Neill exclaimed. He saw that he could make his Marco an embodiment of the 1920s American businessman and take off on all the crude money values of his boyhood New London world, against which he had revolted so heartily in adolescence. In fact, he saw Marco Polo, his father, and his uncle as three typical American traveling salesmen. Marco Polo even had an American enthusiasm for millions and millionaires. When he returned to Venice he "would always make use of the term *millions*," his biographer Giovanni Battista Ramusio reported, so that the Venetians "gave him the nickname of Messer MARCO MILLIONI." O'Neill translated it as "Marco Millions," and so he took for his play the title that newspapermen would misreport incorrigibly as "Marco's Millions."

O'Neill had long been wondering what would happen if America should suddenly find its soul and see "the true valuation of all our triumphant brass band materialism; should see the cost—and the result in terms of eternal verities. What a colossal, ironic, one hundred per cent American tragedy that would be—what?" In *Marco Millions* he wanted to reveal that tragedy yet keep his satirical view of the Polos, and he realized that he could do so by making his play Chinese in form as well as in content. He had bought Kate Buss's *Studies in the Chinese Drama,* and from her meager pages had taken a great vision of how he could go ahead as the Chinese had, to mingle comedy and tragedy, realism and fantasy, and drama with music, dance, pantomime, poetry, and sheer spectacle. It would be exciting but difficult, and he told Kenneth Macgowan: "The child will be either a surpassing satiric Beauty or a most Gawdawful monster."

As a matter of fact, he would even follow the Chinese custom of making his play go on and on. He had dreamed for a long time of breaking out of conventional play time, and now he saw his opportunity to make *Marco Millions* a two-part play—really two plays in one, to be played on two consecutive evenings in the theater. In the first play he would take young Marco Polo—who had been fifteen when he set out for China with his father and uncle—from all the romance, poetry, and possibilities of youth into complete and devastated Polohood inspired by no dream but the acquisition of money. In the second he would offer him a splendid opportunity for redemption.

So he began his Marco Polo where he himself had begun his insight into the tragic voids in American life values, when he too had had everything to start with—innocent love, poetry, sentiment, hope. Marco Polo's thirteenth-century

Venice became strangely infused with recollections of his own watery New London, with the river flowing into Long Island Sound in front of his house. He set up a moon like the moons of his romantic youth and put young Marco in a gondola under the window of a twelve-year-old Donata, to pledge their troth while all the "sentimental singing voices and guitars" of Venice rise about them "in celebration of love." The last perfectly innocent love of O'Neill's boyhood had been a girl with "big naïve wondering dark eyes" whose image would haunt him again a decade after *Marco Millions* in another play about his loss of innocence, *Ah, Wilderness!* Marco tries to write a poem to his love, and in it he describes her eyes as "black pearls." O'Neill's own wayward path away from his dark-eyed child sweetheart gave him Marco's voyage away from love.

Superficially, of course, young Marco and his two mentors, his father and uncle, could not have been more unlike himself and his two heroes, his father and much older brother Jamie, but O'Neill could not help putting the spirit of his own initiation into that of Marco. His brother had pulled him out of the pure love of his youth to throw him into his own raffish world of lechery and bought lust. As a matter of fact, Jamie was curiously linked with the traveling salesmen Polos in his mind, for the one long role Jamie had played outside his father's company had been that of a salesman in a play called *The Traveling Salesman.* Besides, O'Neill had always felt that his father had himself given in to "the lure of easy popularity and easy money," and he never forgot his father's pressure on him to "make good" financially. A touch of his father went into the elder Polos, along with a touch of Jamie, and they became a composite of the middle-class values O'Neill had seen in his New London relatives and their friends, and so, impalpably, some of his affectionate glow toward them all in boyhood carried over to his satire. He told Kenneth Macgowan, "I actually grow to love my American pillars of society, Polo Brothers & Son."

First Marco is laughed out of his poetry by his elders. O'Neill's own family had encouraged his poetry; indeed, he had come out of a background of poetry. His father had burst into Shakespeare instead of singing in the bathtub, and his brother was always reciting Swinburne and Kipling. It had been the neighbors who had tried to laugh him out of his. He gave Marco a very different kind of heritage from his family—the salesman's art of the dirty joke—and had him observe his elders exchanging sly stories along the way of their travels until finally he too tries to tell one. In this O'Neill remembered laughingly his own first awkward attempt at recitation, and had Marco's audience fall asleep while his father stares at him "bitterly" and his uncle watches with "contemptuous pity." The scene is reminiscent of the time that O'Neill and his brother bet their father that they could learn Macbeth's role as quickly as he had as a young actor. Jamie had recited and taken his money. When Eugene's turn came his father fed him his cues and he recited without a hitch. "It was a terrible ordeal, I remember, hearing you murder the lines," he would have his father say of it in *Long Day's Journey into Night.* "I kept wishing I'd paid over the bet without making you prove it."

Second, Marco loses his innocence in love. In O'Neill's own case his brother had simply thrown him to a prostitute when he was sixteen, and that actuality— virtually a rape by the woman—had come as a major shock to his romantic dreams. Yet he had also been proud to become such a "wise guy" so very young and had gone back at once for more. Later he told a classmate at Harvard, Corwin Willson, about those times, and Willson commented: "Gene's abundance of early experience with women in ways that psychically were without beauty and were actually degrading colored his entire outlook." For O'Neill himself those experiences and the prostitutes had all seemed the same one, and he gave Marco a prostitute who reappears ubiquitously along his travels to initiate him into bought lust and grind the remains of his dream love for his dark-eyed child sweetheart into dust.

Despite her ubiquity, the prostitute bears a strong resemblance to the realistic picture of a first prostitute that O'Neill later depicted in *Ah, Wilderness!* Both seem to be recollections of the actual women who seduced him as a very handsome young boy. Both call the boy "Handsome," and both offer themselves as "a gift," except that the one in *Ah, Wilderness!* says she would "do it for nothing" for such a "handsome kid" only she owes her room rent. Both boys fight shy, with Marco saying, "You see I promised someone I'd never—," and the *Ah, Wilderness!* boy saying that he has taken "an oath I'd be faithful." Only, unlike the *Ah, Wilderness!* boy, Marco follows O'Neill's example to become an old customer of the prostitute, and she grinds his poem to Donata under foot, chanting, "Going! Going! Gone! Your soul! Dead and buried!"

O'Neill had realized that simple quotes of the banal remarks in the real Marco's journal would be funny in themselves, and he knew that Marco often included materials that his father and uncle had reported to him of their first trip to China, so he had the elder Polos read their notes to him in each place they arrive, setting their matter-of-fact comments on oil, flocks, goats, and horses against the mysterious and gorgeous panorama of life in Turkey, India, and Mongolia. No pointing up was needed to make laughable such actual comments as "The women wear cotton drawers. This they do to look large in the hips, for the men think that a great beauty." The Polos are particularly blind on religious questions, and the closer to their own beliefs the idea is, the more certain they are of its heathen madness. Hearing about the Buddha's virgin birth, his renunciation of riches, and his ultimate godhead, Marco says, "Died and became a God? So that's what they believe about that stone statue, is it?"

His comments and those of the elder Polos are set in sharp contrast to the spectacular vision of life they move through. Each scene shows a throned ruler flanked by the two supports of his power, the priest and the warrior, while beneath him spreads the whole cycle of life in a semicircle of figures going from birth through childhood, love, to old age and death. In the beginning Marco gapes at the figures and reacts, if embarrassedly, to birth, love, and death, but at the point where he has given his soul to the prostitute and has told his first dirty joke he is no longer capable of seeing anything but his own crude values. He has arrived at the epitome of Polohood when he reaches China, and what he has become forms the final "smashing" contrast to Chinese culture when he appears in the gorgeous throne room of Kublai Khan.

O'Neill's Pope had said that Marco could stand in place of the "hundred able teachers of science and religion" that the Khan had asked the Polos to bring back with them, so that they could discuss their ideas with his Confucians, Taoists, and Buddhists. Just as Marco loses his soul completely, he comes before the Khan as an epitome of Western manhood and its dream of a soul that lives after death. The urgent question for O'Neill's Chinese trio—Kublai Khan, his venerable adviser Chu Yin, and the beautiful dancing girl—is whether this typical American has, or can develop, even a mortal soul, let alone one that lives after death. The climax of the first part has Marco demonstrate the direction he will go. O'Neill had noted Yule's account of "a record in the Chinese Annals of the Mongol Dynasty, which states that in the year 1277, a certain POLO was nominated a second-class commissioner or agent attached to the Privy Council." In O'Neill's play Maffeo takes Marco aside and suggests that he ask for a second-class agency because a first-class one is all brass buttons and no opportunity. "A Second Class travels around, is allowed his expenses, gets friendly with all the dealers, scares them into letting him in on everything—and gets what's rightfully coming to him!" When Marco doubts that this is "square," his uncle replies crushingly, "You'd think I was advising you to steal—I, Maffeo Polo, whose conservatism is unquestioned!" O'Neill was laughingly alluding to the first horrid revelations of thievery in the "conservative" Harding administration, just then appearing in the newspapers, and particularly to Harding's Attorney General, Harry M. Daugherty, who had turned down an initial offer of the Secretaryship of State for the lesser office—and it was becoming only too clear why he had done so. This opening demonstration of what power will mean to Marco—O'Neill's typical American businessman—brings part one to a climax full of foreboding of the cost in all that makes life worth living of his brass band materialism.

The second part of *Marco Millions* offers Marco—America—a possibility of redemption, and O'Neill placed it in the most important of all values for life, love. Marco's actual wife Donata gave little hope for it. Her marriage had been arranged by the families, and in the two historical records of her she appears to be grasping of money. In one, she sells her husband Marco some property next to his, and in the other she is fined for filching money from bags sequestered on a debtor claim in her house. So O'Neill turned to his old vision— Ponce's vision—of Beauty in the shape of a Chinese dancing girl. When he came to study Yule's introduction he discovered a far more romantic historical figure, the Tartar Princess Kukachin. Even the real Marco had thought her "a very beautiful and charming person." She had given the real Polos their opportunity to leave China, for the Khan was sending her off to be married to the Emperor of Persia. War had broken out on the overland route, and her Tartar escorts were ignorant of ships, so the experienced Venetians offered to guide their ships to Hormuz. It was a long, dangerous journey, and most of the Princess's retinue died. She arrived safely only because the Polos had so carefully "watched over and guarded" her. When they reached Hormuz, she had "wept for sorrow at the parting." She had barely become Queen of Persia, when she died. O'Neill decided to interpret both her tears and her death as coming from unrequited love of Marco.

So O'Neill fused the dancing girl of Ponce's vision with the historical Princess, but he never lost her image as a dancing girl, for it had come out of his most profound image of Beauty, his wife Agnes. Agnes had been away when he was writing the vision for Ponce in *The Fountain,* and O'Neill had told her: "Your dancing snapshot is in a frame on my desk. It looks beautiful—you— luring and enchanting—my Love forever." So the dancing image became ineradicably part of his "Queen of Beauty," the Princess Kukachin. He had his Khan say, "Her little feet danced away the stamp of armies," and turn from the court dancers because "dancing makes me remember Kukachin whose little dancing feet—." O'Neill could not give up the dancing image, even though Kukachin never dances in the play, for his Tartar Princess had taken over all that he loved most in his beautiful, poetical wife Agnes.

He brought Kukachin into his play on a wave of poetry, for Agnes and he were one in that. The Princess appears chanting about her coming exile to Persia in spare images like those of Li Po, in the volume of his verses that O'Neill had, and in the form of the *Cantonese Love Songs* he had also bought for background. O'Neill filled the ship scene with the Princess's poetry and

even created for the Boatswain an odd hybrid of a sea chantey and the Confucian Odes in the *She-King*, which he also studied for *Marco Millions*. The Princess took on Agnes's sweetly whimsical way about her, her fierce readiness to
become jealous—about which he had teased Agnes often in the early days of
their marriage—and her need to try "pitifully to arouse his jealousy." Yet he felt
at one with Agnes, and so his own feelings of loss and pain at the frequent
conflicts in their marriage found an outlet in the Princess's longing too.

O'Neill wrote *Marco Millions* in two summers—beginning in the summer of
1923, a half-year before the dream that brought *Desire Under the Elms* to life—
while he was still grieving deeply over his mother's death. His old sense of unity
with his mother went into the Princess too. Her death—the death of love in the
play—became inextricably interlocked with his mother's death. Indeed, the one
extraordinary fiction he added to the historical Princess's death came as compulsive repetition of the facts of his mother's death in California, for he put in
a quite impossible duplicate of his mother's funeral journey from California to
New York. He had the Princess's body brought all the way from Persia overland
to China—despite the wars that had closed that route to the live Princess—
although historically Kukachin had been buried in Persia. O'Neill needed a
scene of Kublai Khan mourning over her coffin for release of his own mourning
over his mother's coffin when it reached New York. So important to him was
this mourning scene, the last scene of the play, that he wrote it first, after he
finished the scenario.

Pain of loss in love—exile from love—had been the first trauma of his childhood. In his "Diagram" he placed it at age seven, when he started as a boarding
student at Mount St. Vincent-on-the-Hudson, where he first felt, he said, "resentment and hatred of father as cause of school (break with mother)." His old
exile to school as a boy became joined to the great theme of exile in Chinese
poetry, and both entered into the Princess's exile to Persia. The lovelorn Kukachin became the viewpoint through which he could register the cost in eternal verities and the ironic tragedy of Marco's failure to develop a soul. Through
their love for her, Kublai Khan and his adviser Chu Yin would feel it also. So
he found a way to channel through his Chinese trio all the pain of his old
separation from love brought on by his father. His rebellion had begun in that
old resentment and had later moved into his conviction that his father had sold
out his great artistic possibilities for easy money. The same pain and love had
gone into his larger conviction that his country, America, had also sold out its
possibilities as the first republic of the modern world in a scramble for money.

In the second part of *Marco Millions*, Marco comes bursting in as the epitome of America's brass band materialism. He enters deafeningly with an actual

brass band. In his fantastic garb as "Cock of Paradise" in the order he has established of "Mystic Knights of Confucius," he is all "child-actor," and through this satire of America's fraternal orders O'Neill held remembrance of his actor father's lifelong membership in the Mystic Knights of Columbus. Even the memory of his father's burial in the baldric and sword of the Fourth Degree knights emerged to make him veritably "Cock of Paradise." Marco resembles an American "movie star at a masquerade ball, disguised so that no one can fail to recognize him," and his face is "arranged into the grave responsible expression of a Senator from the South of the United States of America about to propose an amendment to the Constitution restricting the migration of non-Nordic birds into Texas, or prohibiting the practice of the laws of biology within the twelve-mile limit."

The actual Marco Polo had become governor of the city of Yang-Chau. O'Neill calls him "Mayor" and has him come to the court to tell the Khan how he "sweated out" such a bonanza in taxes. He says, "I simply reversed the old system. For one thing I found they had a high tax on excess profits. Imagine a profit being excess! Why, it isn't humanly possible! I repealed it. And I repealed the tax on luxuries. I found out the great majority in Yang-Chau couldn't afford luxuries. The tax wasn't democratic enough to make it pay! I crossed it off and I wrote on the statute books a law that taxes every necessity in life, a law that hits every man's pocket equally, be he beggar or banker!" Marco's plan is simply that of America's multimillionaire Treasury Secretary Andrew Mellon during the Harding and Coolidge administrations as O'Neill wrote. Mellon had repealed the excess profits tax, cut income taxes drastically (particularly on incomes over $66,000 a year), and compensated for the loss of revenue by putting a sales tax on all consumer goods. Marco sums up expansively, "And I got results!"

"In beggars?" asks O'Neill's Chu Yin. Only a few years after O'Neill wrote these lines, Mellon's beggars would actually stretch in breadlines as far as the eye could see all over the United States.

O'Neill was working as closely with his world when he had Mayor Marco stamp out culture in the city of Yang-Chau. Even as O'Neill was writing this play, Mayor Hylan of New York had done his best to prevent the Provincetown Players' opening of O'Neill's *All God's Chillun Got Wings*—which dealt with America's tragic color prejudices—and a couple of years before that authorities had tried to close O'Neill's play *The Hairy Ape,* first by charging violation of the Sunday Law and then by declaring it "impure, obscene and indecent" in a city where burlesque and brothels ran wide open. (In the first draft of *Marco Millions,* later cut, O'Neill had Nicolo and Maffeo Polo intoning the benefits of

Marco's mayorship. They chant, "Houses of ill fame and theatres closed" and then add hastily, "But sacred concerts may be housed in barrel-houses, hooker shanties, dance halls, and peep-shows." They don't want, they say, to prohibit "legitimate entertainment.") As O'Neill wrote, a general exodus of poets from the United States to Paris was taking place, and he was thinking of it when he had Chu Yin hear of Marco's devastation of culture in Yang-Chau from "a poet who had fled from there in horror."

O'Neill wanted to cut deeper, and he found his opportunity in the historical Marco's fascination with Chinese paper money. Marco Polo had thought of it as a form of "alchemy" in which the Khan distilled gold out of paper. O'Neill decided in his notes that he would have Marco invent paper money, the means "through which man loses all contact with the worth—and exchange—of the goods he produces." O'Neill saw that he could also use the legend that Marco Polo had invented gunpowder out of Chinese firecrackers and combine it with his historical construction of "mangonels," slings that cast great stones, to aid the Khan in his siege of the city of Saianfu. The Polos had demonstrated the slings before the whole court and convinced the Khan dramatically that the city would "surrender incontinently." O'Neill had his Marco invent the cannon, and so create explosives that make war "heroically meaningless and constantly more horrible."

In front of the Khan, Marco sets up a toy cannon against a fortress of children's blocks and falls into the real Marco's "vein of bombastic commonplaces" in describing battle. He acts out the scene, challenging the fortress in his normal voice, answering himself in mock heroic falsetto, and then shooting off his cannon. The Khan asks whether he conquered the "immortal soul" of the city's hero who refused surrender, preferring death to defeat. Marco tells him, "Well, you can't consider souls when you're dealing with soldiers, can you?"

His inspiration for the cannon came, Marco explains, during Easter, when he suddenly thought "of Our Lord as the Prince of Peace." He realized that there was nothing in history about "heroes who waged peace." Then he suddenly saw that the only "workable way" to end wars was "to conquer everybody else in the world so they'll never dare fight you again." He tells the Khan it can be done easily with his two little inventions: "You conquer the world with this— (*He pats the cannon-model*) and you pay for it with this. (*He pats the paper money—rhetorically*) You become the bringer of peace on earth and good-will to men, and it doesn't cost you a yen hardly." O'Neill's Marco is really summing up the logic behind America's entry into World War I. Woodrow Wilson had presented it as a war to end wars waged to secure "the ultimate peace of the world."

World War I had been for O'Neill a painful shock to his search for a better life for mankind. Before America's entry he had written a poem urging his fellow men to cease this "Fratricide," and take up the cry,

> All workers on the earth
> Are brothers and WE WILL NOT FIGHT!

He had written about the sufferings of war in a play called *The Sniper* in Professor Baker's play-writing class at Harvard, and the following year he had helped Hippolyte Havel put out the anarchist weekly *Revolt,* strongly urging peace, until federal agents confiscated the magazine and threatened them with prison. Later O'Neill had been distressed by the Versailles Treaty, which concluded the war. He saw it as a game played by "professional swindlers" selling "the future of peoples down the river of power politics." More war would come of it. O'Neill put in a second scene, after his Marco leaves China, in which the Khan's General Bayan tries to get a war under way in the name of "Buddha, the Prince of Peace." He finally declares war on "unscrupulous Japanese trade-pirates," who, he says, "are breeding and maintaining silkworms for purposes of aggression!"

When World War II came, as O'Neill had feared it would, and yet another peace treaty was under way, he saw little hope for an end to wars. "As Marco tells the Khan in 'Marco Millions': 'I've never read much in any history about heroes who waged peace.' If there are any noble-minded statesmen or diplomats in the world to-day who can be relied on to make an unselfish peace and then keep on waging it, I don't see them. They all seem to believe any end justifies any means—and the end to that is total ruin for man's spirit." His laughter in *Marco Millions* had an undercurrent of tragic foresight.

Marco's last chance for a soul lies in the voyage with the Princess Kukachin. The Khan has given him up. Marco, he says, "has not even a mortal soul, he has only an acquisitive instinct." He tells Chu Yin, "He has looked at everything and seen nothing. He has lusted for everything and loved nothing. He is only a shrewd and crafty greed. I shall send him home to his native wallow." But the Princess believes in his soul and believes that he can learn to feel love and perceive beauty. In a last hope of either curing her or awakening him so that "his soul may be born," Chu Yin orders him to look into her eyes each day on the voyage. Marco sees it as fever prevention. He departs China in an uproar of brass band and mechanized labor, full of his own viewpoint, expressed in such declarations as "I hate idleness where there's nothing to occupy your mind but thinking" or "If you look before you leap, you'll decide to sit down. Keep

on going ahead and you can't help being right! You're bound to get somewhere!"

Marco's inability to develop a soul is a tragedy only for the Princess and for
the Khan and Chu Yin through her. In the voyage scene in which he remains
impervious to Beauty and Love embodied in her, he suffers nothing. But into
the Princess flowed all O'Neill's old pain at being shut out of love when he was
sent to boarding school. He knew—for he wrote it into his "Diagram"—that in
his infancy his father had been no rival but an "indefinite hero" to him, and
that even after he had begun to resent him for exiling him he lived in a world
of "Fantasy" with his "Father as Hero." In the play, the Princess has come to
love Marco because, in her childhood, she saw him rarely as "a strange, mysterious dream-knight" always "acting the hero"—as O'Neill had seen his father
acting the hero on stage. Marco also acts the hero on the voyage to Persia, as
the Princess acknowledges, for he has saved her life three times. Into each went
one of O'Neill's particularly vivid childhood images of his father as hero. In the
first, Marco has swum to her when she was drowning and pulled her to safety.
One of O'Neill's first efforts to imitate his father had been as a swimmer, and
swimming remained a lifelong passion with him. One of his father's favorite
stories—repeated many times—was of how he had swum to a friend who was
drowning and pulled him to safety. In the second, Marco defends the Princess
from pirates with his "brave sword" and strikes them dead at her feet. O'Neill's
father had acted the hero as swordsman in the duel scene of *Monte Cristo,* and
even more memorably as D'Artagnan in a spectacular New York opening of *The
Three Musketeers* in 1899, which Eugene saw many times and once brought a
party of schoolmates from Mount St. Vincent-on-the-Hudson to watch from a
box.

The *Dramatic Mirror* had held James O'Neill up as a model to young actors,
saying, "Mark the effectiveness of O'Neill's sword-play, the fire of his lovemaking, his buoyant and agile grace of movement, his mobile facial expression,
the ease with which he doffs his plumed hat, and the swagger with which he
wears his ever-ready rapier." Certainly Eugene and his schoolmates had
marked it all, for one of them recalled that, afterward, "Eugene, I and others
vigorously fenced with foils made from the mulberry and cherry trees."

The third way that Marco saves the Princess recalls O'Neill's most intimate
of all infant memories. The Princess tells Marco that during her illness he
watched "by my bedside like a gentle nurse, even brewing yourself the medi-
cines that brought me back to life." In his "Diagram," O'Neill recalled as crucial his awakenings from nightmares, when his parents would come to his bedside and his father would mix him a little "whiskey and water" to soothe him.

He thought he had taken to alcohol because it had been the "Drink of Hero Father." In *Long Day's Journey into Night* the whiskey would be attributed to James O'Neill's Irish peasant family, who honestly believed that "whiskey is the healthiest medicine for a child who is sick or frightened." Marco tells the Princess, "My mother's recipes. Simple home remedies—."

With the theme of longing for love, came, in these last scenes of the play, a powerful undertow pull toward death. The Princess chants:

> When love is not loved it loves Death.
> When I sank drowning, I loved Death.
> When the pirate's knife gleamed, I loved Death.
> When fever burned me I loved Death.
> But the man I love saved me.

All O'Neill's suicidal yearnings went into her, along with memories of his own suicide attempt back when he had despaired of love after supplying the evidence for the divorce from Kathleen. He had taken an overdose of sleeping tablets, and the Princess's longing to be "asleep in green water" had been his own. Marco—who thinks her love is fever—tells her to "go to sleep." She pulls out a dagger and cries, "I obey! I shall sleep forever!" Marco again rescues her, stammering bewilderedly, "I never believed people—sane people—ever seriously tried—." O'Neill had his own father say of his suicide attempt in *Long Day's Journey into Night:* "You weren't in your right mind. No son of mine would—."

For one precarious moment, Marco, looking into the Princess's eyes for the last time, almost conceives a soul, but at that moment his uncle, counting their profits, slaps a stack of coins down and calls out, "One million!" Marco is instantly diverted back to acquisition, and Beauty, Love, and Truth are lost forever. It had happened that during the historical Princess's two-year voyage, the Emperor Arghun Khan died, and so the new Emperor, his son Ghazan Khan, came to claim her for his bride. O'Neill used Ghazan as a sharp contrast to Marco. Ghazan instantly sees that Kukachin will be "Queen of Love," as well as of Persia, and he tells her, "Persia shall be your conquest and everywhere where songs are sung they shall be in praise of your beauty!" But the heartbroken Princess can see only the failure of her dream. She calls hectically for a chest of gold coins, and her final contempt explodes in a gesture that was very much O'Neill's own for an acquisitive world. He had once told a New London friend—at the peak of his youthful rebellion—that he would like to hire a carriage and ride down Main Street scattering coins for the populace to scramble after. The Princess throws a shower of coins over the kneeling Polos crying, "Here! Guzzle! Grunt! Wallow for our amusement!"

But the rage is momentary. The Princess is Love—Eternal Love—and so she can only go on loving or die. And it is the knowledge that she will die, brought by message to Kublai Khan, which brings home the tragic cost of Marco's acquisitiveness to him. In a first rage at the senseless destruction of Love and Beauty, Kublai wants further destruction—a war to wipe out the West. Of Marco, the epitome of its values, he cries, "There shall not be a fragment of bone nor an atom of flesh which will not have shrieked through ten days' torture before it died!" Even this outburst had come out of remembered resentment at loss of love. O'Neill's father had actually suffered "incredible tortures" before he died, and the ten days of those tortures probably came from the day of his death, August 10. His oldest memories of destroyed love entered into and became part of this vision of a greedy world where Love, Beauty, and Truth could not live.

His clown Marco Polo remains a clown to the end, and O'Neill had the Khan and Chu Yin watch through a crystal his triumphant return to Venice—America. In this case the historical legend of Marco Polo's return needed little exaggeration to turn it into a clown act. The real Polos had held a great banquet for the Venetians, who had not recognized them in their shabby Tartar clothes. Before their assembled guests they entered "clothed in crimson satin, fashioned in long robes." They had thrown these splendid garments to retainers to be "cut up and divided among the servants," and donned even more magnificent robes of "crimson damask." These too they threw to the servants and put on even more costly crimson velvet. Then they had their shabby Tartar traveling clothes brought in and slit the seams to pour out streams of "rubies, sapphires, carbuncles, diamonds, and emeralds." O'Neill had only to shape the comedy by having his Polos wear all the robes at once, to peel off one layer after another to be thrown to the servants along with handfuls of gold coins until they reach their shabby clothes. Then, to a great blare of music, they slit the sleeves and pour out their "glittering multicolored" final display of wealth. At the last the guests have disappeared behind a perfect mountain of food on the table, and Marco is delivering a chamber of commerce speech on China, of which, in the uproar of guzzling and clattering, only his favorite word can be heard, "Millions! . . . millions! . . . millions!" The Khan says, "The Word became their flesh, they say. Now all is flesh! And can their flesh become the Word again?"

This question echoes through the final tragic funeral scene, where the Khan mourns over the Princess after her long funeral journey back to China. All O'Neill's grief over his mother's body when it reached New York went into it.

For all the gorgeous Chinese trappings, his scene is filled with images out of his mother's Catholic funeral—with bells and swinging censors of incense. Into the Princess herself came his old association of his beautiful mother Mary with the Virgin Mother Mary. Kukachin appears "wrapped in a winding sheet of deep blue" like the Virgin's blue mantle, and her face, "white and clear as a statue's," recalls both O'Neill's last glimpse of his mother's face and the statues of the Virgin he had knelt to in his devout Catholic boyhood. Kukachin wears a jeweled crown like the one worn by the Queen of Heaven after her ascension. She actually appears to be ascending, for she is surrounded by "incense ascending in clouds . . . as if it were bearing her soul with it."

His mourning Khan loses all grip on worldly power in the humility of his grief, just as O'Neill had lost all the glory of the triumphant opening of his play *The Hairy Ape* the evening of the day his mother's body arrived in New York. Years afterward, when once again his life was bitter with lost love, he would tell Agnes, "Do you remember 'The Hairy Ape' opening night with my mother's body in the undertaking parlor? 'So ist das Leben,' I guess. Or at least my 'Leben.' 'The power and the glory' always pass over—or under—my head." The Khan feels the irony of being called "Greatest of the Great" in the desolation of grief. Not satisfied with the pathos of an old man weeping over a young woman, O'Neill put into this scene all the pathos in his old image of his mother as a child. Alone with Kukachin, the Khan says, "You are a little girl again. You are playing hide and seek. You are pretending." Then he turns to what was O'Neill's own yearning for the protective love of his mother and his sense of himself as her beloved dead baby. He tells her, through the Khan, "I—I am dead and you are living! Weep for me, Kukachin! Weep for the dead!"

At this point, O'Neill himself was in the position of his Khan, who says that Marco's "example has done much to convert me to wisdom—if I could find the true one!" O'Neill saw in the Khan and his request to the Pope for one hundred wise men from the West an open, inquiring intellect like his own. Through the Khan he could ask his own fundamental questions in this play that was to be a reexamination of all values, preliminary to the search for faith. He had his Khan follow the example for rulers set by the good King of T'ang in Confucius's *Shu-King*. Like him, Kublai does "not ignore advice," does "not look for perfection" in others, and is "conscious of his defects." He accepts a steady criticism of his philosophy of power from Chu Yin, the Taoist mystic. When he bursts into rage at Marco, Chu Yin tells him: "The noble man ignores self. The wise man ignores action. His truth acts without deeds. His knowledge venerates the unknowable. To him birth is not the beginning, nor is death the end." Afterward

O'Neill said that the two great philosophers of Tao, "Lâo-zse and Chuang Tzŭ probably interested me more than any other oriental writing."

O'Neill wrote his final funeral scene first of all, in an urgent search for the answer to death—to the death of his mother that had followed so hard upon the death of his father. All his doubts entered into this last scene written first. The Khan's advisers—Buddhist, Taoist, and Confucian—can give no answer but acceptance of the fact: "Death is." O'Neill himself saw no answer—only questions—after his first summer of work on *Marco Millions,* and so he decided to lay it aside. He was "reaching toward the artistic wisdom," he told Kenneth Macgowan, of treating "each play with more and more concentration of mind and effort over a longer period of time." Only after writing *All God's Chillun Got Wings* and *Desire Under the Elms* did he return to *Marco Millions* in the summer of 1924, and only at the end of his work in the fall did he find his statement of faith. He had written his last scene first, and now he wrote a first scene, a Prologue, last to shed its glow over all that was to follow.

Curiously, he found his faith in the very heart of his skepticism, and it took shape from the least likely source imaginable—from a long learned footnote in Yule. In it Yule had gone into a perfect prodigy of citation, starting at the end of one page and taking over the entire ten full pages following it with small print to explain Marco Polo's references to a Holy Tree near the Persian frontier. The extraordinary thing about all the legends of sacred trees was their power of prophetic speech. This power answered O'Neill's deepest need in coming to grips with the death of his mother. He had taken from his dying father a message of hope and a faith to live by. From his father's deathbed he had written Agnes of his father's certainty that he was going to a "better sort of life— somewhere." His father had died hugging to his heart "my mother's love and his for her" and believing "that it will go with him wherever he is going—the principal reason he is not afraid to go, I believe!" No such message had come from his dying mother. She had reached New York wrapped in the impenetrable silence of death. In his yearning for her old protective love, his feeling that she should be weeping for him, O'Neill must have had a powerful wish for reassurance of his father's faith in eternal life and love. He had just finished *Desire Under the Elms,* with its strange association of his dead mother with a tree, when he took up *Marco Millions* again in the summer of 1924. While he wrote, the idea of the mother-tree and that yearning for a message struck fire out of the footnote in Yule, and from it sprang the poetry and beauty of O'Neill's Prologue to *Marco Millions.*

His scene opens on an enormous sacred tree standing in a great plain that recalls Yule's description of the one that he had seen in the midst of the Suez

Desert. It also recalls two other sacred trees that Yule described in a suburb of
Ispahan and in a garden at Shiraz. Like them, O'Neill's tree is hung with "votive
offerings, pieces of cloth torn from clothing, bangles, amulets, ornaments, tapers." In Yule, O'Neill had read all the strange beliefs of Christians, Buddhists,
Magians, and Mohammedans about the origins of these trees. Under the shade
of his tree O'Neill brought together three traveling salesmen—a Christian, a
Magian, and a Buddhist—and by simply condensing the statement of their beliefs in Yule he was able to show what he had originally meant his Khan to
perceive: the amazingly "contradictory manner" in which the religious truths
of Christ, Buddha, and Zoroaster become "distorted in human life, the dogma
of religion." In the Prologue, the Buddhist explains—quite literally out of
Yule—that the tree sprang from "a twig" Buddha had plucked "to cleanse his
teeth." The Christian thinks that is ridiculous, and declares the real origin of it
to be Adam's staff, which "was handed down to Moses who used it to tap water
out of stones" and then became the cross on which Christ was crucified. The
Magian tells the other two that they have been "duped by childish lies": it is
really a shoot of the "Tree of Life" which Zoroaster brought from Paradise and
planted. They are about to come to blows over the question when a great train
of men drawing a wagon is whipped in from across the plain. The Moham-
medan captain—who has requisitioned the men in place of the animals they
hid—comes to inform them that they are all wrong. The tree really took root
from the "staff of Mahomet," he says.

Had the real Princess taken the strange funeral journey O'Neill created for
her, she would have passed close to the sacred tree near the Persian frontier
described by Marco Polo, which had set off Sir Henry Yule's spate of scholar-
ship. The Captain reveals the Princess in a glass coffin on the wagon, aglow
with living beauty, and under the influence of the prophetic sacred tree above
her she rises out of death for an instant and joins its music to deliver the message that O'Neill had yearned for. She says, "Say this, I loved and died. Now I
am love, and live." Her voice and the music of the tree melt into laughter "of
an intoxicating, supernatural gaiety."

O'Neill meant that faith to shed its glow over the entire story of Marco Polo
to follow. Clearly, if O'Neill had no hope for his particular American Marco
Polo, he had hope for his America. He gave his play an Epilogue in which,
when the curtain goes down on the last scene, Marco Polo is found rising with
the audience in the theater. Although he himself remains blind to the significance of his own story, its lesson is there for the audience to perceive. In his
heart O'Neill believed that his United States was "in the throes of a spiritual

awakening," and he hoped that *Marco Millions* would help deliver that soul of his people which slowly, in travail, was "being born."

O'Neill thought David Belasco was the only producer likely to give his play a really spectacular production, with "forestage, music, many scenes, large crowds." He sent it to him on November 22, 1924, and hoped he would not be put off by the fact that "*it seems to last two nights*—to be *two* plays, in fact!" By January 14, 1925, O'Neill had decided that the two-play, two-night form would not stand up, and he set to work in the next few weeks condensing it into one. He cut out opening and closing scenes in the prison at Genoa, where the real Marco Polo, taken in battle, had dictated his travels. He cut also a final scene in part one in which Marco's Chinese tutors had given him up as hopeless. On March 13 he learned jubilantly that "Belasco has bought the play and promises to spend the small fortune required to do it right." The fortune was $200,000, and Belasco talked about sending Robert Edmond Jones to China at once to work out the sets. As luck had it, shortly afterward, Belasco suffered heavy losses and drew back from any immediate risk. He was still hesitating over *Marco Millions* a full year later when his contract ran out. O'Neill knew Belasco's "reputation of holding plays for a long, long time," and to push him he demanded that Belasco forfeit his advance if he did not produce at once, refusing to accept another advance to be subtracted from royalties. Frightened, Belasco backed out altogether. Later he telegraphed O'Neill, when the play finally opened: "One of the regrets of my life will be that there were misunderstandings between us, and that I lost 'Marco.' "

The play went to Gilbert Miller, but he gave up when the actor he found for Marco thought the role that of a "romantic, handsome hero" and saw no irony in it. Arthur Hopkins gave up on staging it too. By the spring of 1927 it had come to the Theatre Guild. The Guild's Lawrence Langner happened to be visiting Bermuda at the time, and O'Neill let him read part of the play he was working on, *Strange Interlude*. Electrified, Langner rushed back to New York to tell the Guild that the "psychological moment" had come for them to link up with O'Neill. He urged them to start by accepting *Marco Millions*. The committee members were full of doubts. They were afraid to risk the money for a "heavy spectacular" production, which Lee Simonson estimated at $30,000, and they feared that the mass scenes weighed down the comedy; they thought the play should be scaled down drastically.

O'Neill replied that they could do it either on "a super-grand scale with great masked crowds" or "very simply" and "symbolically and suggestively." Any halfway, he thought, "would be ultra-fatal," and he considered Lee Simonson's

$30,000 distinctly halfway. He thought the travel scenes could be done with painted drop curtains that could lift after a brief blackout to give a "feeling of movement, of a journey." (Simonson later found that the semicircle of living people could not be substituted by painted ones lest the "ironic climax" of Marco's developing incapacity to see life be lost, along with the sense "of the patient pattern of Eastern civilization.") O'Neill wanted to keep the spectacular scene at Cambulac as a "smashing brilliant contrast' to the sordid Polos, but he was ready to cut "down to nothing," if necessary, by shifting the scene to the simple summer palace at Xanadu with a handful of courtiers. Also, he was ready to cut all the pageantry from the funeral scene. In this form *Marco Millions* finally opened on January 9, 1928—shorn of all its gorgeous Chinese innovations of dance, pantomime, and pageantry.

O'Neill had hoped that the evanescently lovely Lillian Gish would play Kukachin, but the Guild told him the choice would "wreck their company with jealousy and dissention." So he accepted Margalo Gillmore and cheered himself with the thought that Alfred Lunt "should make a remarkable 'Marco.' He is a fine actor." He took the loss of spectacle philosophically. "One can't have everything in our American theatre," he said. "The Guild is our best and they are certainly doing their best by me."

Critics and audiences found the play joyful and enchanting. It was "still bringing home the bacon"—so O'Neill learned gratefully in April—and it went on doing so through a long road tour in repertory. Much of its warning and prediction became stark reality with the coming of the Great Depression before it closed. Much happened to O'Neill too. Between the time he finished writing it and the time of its opening, he had passed far beyond its vision. He had written three extraordinary plays that cut to the heart of his life experience, altering its course forever and transforming him.

3

The Great God Brown

"Where do I belong?" O'Neill was still asking himself that question long after he had put it to "Yank," his proletarian hero of *The Hairy Ape,* back in 1921. That play had no sooner opened than he was thinking of a sequel to it that would put the same question to "the intellectual, the occupant of the Ivory Tower." His first note in 1922 makes the intellectual an architect, a failure who drinks. His "friend and rival," a successful businessman, loves the same "good, unimaginative girl." O'Neill planned to put the Earth into this play in the shape of the old fertility goddess Cybele, who has been "corrupted into prostitute symbol."

A clue to the source of this plot appears in the architect who is a failure. He came out of memories of O'Neill's first failure in life, which had precipitated during the depression of 1908–9. He had lost the job his father had found him at the New York–Chicago Supply Company when the firm went bankrupt. His father had kept urging him to find another "bread and butter" job, and he had fled the family pressure by moving in with two young artists, Ed Keefe and George Bellows, who shared a large studio in the Lincoln Arcade Building at 65th Street and Broadway in New York City and were glad to divide the rent. Keefe's father had agreed to pay for his study of painting in New York, on the condition that he get practical experience each summer as a draftsman in an architect's office back in New London. That summer of 1909 Keefe had given up his struggle to live for art and had gone back to the architect's office for good. At the same time, O'Neill had lost his hope of becoming a poet through his entanglement with Kathleen Jenkins, that "good, unimaginative girl." The destruction of his own "highest hopes" had become inextricably linked in his mind with Keefe's, and so later he blended Keefe and himself in the failed artist of one of his earliest plays, "Bread and Butter," written in 1914. Its hero, a young painter like Keefe, struggles against his family's pressure to drive him into a "bread and butter" job. They are a set of "muddy spirits" named "Brown" from a small town in Connecticut like New London. The painter looks just like Keefe, with large black eyes "deep-set and far apart," an "oval" face, and a mouth that is "full-lipped and small." He follows the advice of an older painter, just as Keefe had followed Robert Henri, the leader of the "Ash Can" school of painters in those days, whose studio was right down the hall in the Lincoln Arcade. O'Neill had this young artist lose his strength for creativity, as he himself had, by laboring on the docks for money. Like O'Neill too, he is destroyed altogether as an artist when he marries a conventional girl, for whom he must earn money. It is probably not chance that O'Neill's name for her, "Maude Steele," takes the initials of Maibelle Scott, a girl with whom he almost repeated the Kathleen Jenkins disaster, or that her first name is that of a prostitute he knew at about the same time, Maude Williams. Maude worked in a "house" not far from the one where O'Neill arranged to be caught in adultery for his divorce from Kathleen, and he had used her for additional evidence. According to the court testimony, she had "committed adultery" with him "divers times" in June, July, August, and September of 1911. Despair over his failure in love had made O'Neill try to kill himself, and so he had the hero of "Bread and Butter" kill himself at the end. *The Great God Brown* recalls that old play. O'Neill named his businessman "Brown" after those old "muddy spirits." He even took his title from them. He substituted the name of his successful clod Brown for that of the Great God Pan—the creative life principle—whose worship he has supplanted. He also recalled Ed Keefe's name in the name he first thought of for his hero "Stan Keith." He put in the disastrous marriage to a good girl, and the ghost of his old good girl–prostitute association haunted this play too.

By 1925, when O'Neill began to write *The Great God Brown,* Keefe had changed from a dreamy-eyed boy with a shock of black hair into a balding small-town architect with a penchant for drink. Only George Bellows had become a real painter. By luck he happened to see *Desire Under the Elms,* and, thrilled by it, he had written O'Neill asking to paint him. Before the letter

reached O'Neill in Bermuda on January 16, 1925, Bellows was dead of a ruptured appendix, so poignant memories of Bellows joined those of Keefe in the
two young friends condemned to architecture by their families in his play. Bellows's father had been as eager as Keefe's to make his boy an architect, for he
wanted him to bring prestige to his firm of builders and contractors. In O'Neill's
play Billy Brown's father talks similarly of how his son will make the firm one
of *"architects* and builders—instead of *contractors* and builders." Bellows had
killed that hope by leaving Ohio State University without taking his degree to
study painting in New York. In the play, Dion Anthony drops architecture for
painting, as had Bellows, while Billy Brown obediently finishes his course in
architecture and becomes a success designing buildings like those that were
transforming New London from a pleasant seaside village into another hideous
American small city as O'Neill wrote. The tragedy of Dion is that he must give
up his dream of creating beauty to work as a draftsman in Brown's office, just
as Keefe had done.

With memories of Keefe, O'Neill mingled those of other New London intellectuals, such as his close friend Hutch Collins, who had taken to drink. Ironically, exactly at the point where Hutch was trying to taper off, he had contracted
influenza in the pandemic of 1919 and died of resulting pneumonia. O'Neill
gave Hutch's splendid "athletic" frame to Billy Brown, and his own "lean and
wiry" physique to Dion. His two friends echo the curiously ambivalent mingling
of dependence, affection, envy, and resentment that characterized Hutch's attachment for him. Hutch had been planted right in the middle of O'Neill's great
love for Beatrice Ashe and had often passed between them. Once, in 1916,
Hutch had failed to keep a promise to bring Beatrice to Christine's restaurant
in Greenwich Village, where O'Neill could see her, at a time when he was afraid
to go to her because of a drinking bout. All his bitterness at Hutch for failing
him came out after Beatrice had forgiven him. He wrote her a "story" called
"The Passing of Hutch Collins," telling how he, O'Neill, a popular "fixture in
Bohemia," had taken Hutch around and introduced him everywhere, but after
a few months everyone had protested against Hutch as a "bore" and a
"sponger" who appreciated nothing that was done for him. O'Neill himself
would have been spared days of "hell" had Hutch kept his promise. The two
friends of his play have a similarly ambivalent relationship—Brown, like Hutch,
following after his more creative friend.

These memories flowed into and joined O'Neill's poignant recollection of the
most tragic failure of all New London's promising intellectuals. Jamie, his ten-
year-older brother, had been the "hero" of his boyhood and the leader of his
intellectual awakening. From Jamie he had caught the love of modern poetry

that he shared with Hutch Collins. No one had promised so brilliantly as Jamie, and no one had failed more dismally. Jamie was just a little more than one year dead when O'Neill began writing *The Great God Brown*, and he knew that Jamie "had never found his place. He had never belonged." He could only "hope like my 'Hairy Ape,' he does now." So Jamie entered the failed intellectual of his play, and with him the hope that, like the hero of *The Hairy Ape*, Jamie had found some kind of apotheosis in death.

O'Neill asked himself immediately how he could dramatize what was really an inner drama of souls. In his very first note he hit on his technique: "Play of masks—remarkable—the man who really is and the mask he wears before the world." His excitement about masks came from Kenneth Macgowan, who at this time was writing a book around a fascinating collection of photographs of masks, religious and theatrical, which he and Herman Rosse had collected. It came out as *Masks and Demons* in 1923, and in it Macgowan pointed out that masks convey a "curious and oppressive sense of the dead made living, the spirit given flesh, the god or demon brought into physical contact." O'Neill took off from there and began to invent ways to use masks in their experimental theater. Masks would be perfect, he decided, for acting out *The Spook Sonata* because Strindberg himself had talked of unmasking the people in that play. For his own dramatization of Coleridge's *Ancient Mariner*, O'Neill decided on greenish drowned masks for the chorus of living dead men and on gothic angel masks for the seraph band. Those masks had been startlingly effective, and right after O'Neill saw them at rehearsals he jotted down in his *Work Diary* on April 29, 1924, that he now saw how he would use masks in *The Great God Brown*. He had learned from Nietzsche that it is "not the worst things of which one is most ashamed." A man might be masking a delicate inner spirit with a coarse exterior, just as precious wine is enclosed in a clumsy barrel. Nietzsche had declared: "Every profound spirit needs a mask; nay, more, around every profound spirit there continually grows a mask, owing to the constantly false, that is to say, *superficial* interpretation of every word he utters, every step he takes, every sign of life he manifests." O'Neill saw that he could show that misunderstanding of his characters with masks. He saw that he could express a split personality by contrasting a character's mask with his face. He could even dramatize changes in psychology by changes in the masks. Indeed, he could express the central event of his play, the transfer of personality from one man to another, by simply transferring the mask.

At the same time, he saw how to reveal instantly the falsity of life's surface, so that an audience could plunge through it into the psychological reality made visible by the masks. He had caught from Robert Edmond Jones a vision of what could be done with painted backdrops for scenery. Jones had used them to satirize the overly "realistic" scenery of the Victorian era when they did a "spoofing" production of *Fashion,* a Victorian comedy. Jones had made those paintings of magnificent furniture laughable by having the actors pretend to drape themselves about it. O'Neill decided that deliberately overdetailed painted backdrops would make rooms and offices appear as obviously artificial as the "stereotyped paintings" found in certain American houses. He wanted his audience to realize at once that the "family kodak" conception of reality has "nothing to do with the truth." He even thought to illustrate the falsity of photographic reality in his first draft by having Dion, as mock photographer, suddenly freeze his family into woodenness by ordering them: "Smile! Think of nothing!" They vanish altogether in "the noise, flash and smoke of a flashlight" followed by darkness.

In the middle of *The Great God Brown,* Dion Anthony dies and leaves his creative power with his mask to William Brown. This was no mere dramatic trick. Just such a transfer of personality had taken place in O'Neill's life. At the time when Jamie had introduced him to poetry, rebellion, drink, and sex, O'Neill had taken his brother's personality into himself and had begun to live in imitation of him. The result was a split in his soul between the shy, idealistic child he had been, devoutly Catholic and strongly identified with his mother, and a new mocking, skeptical self clothed in Jamie's bold masculinity. O'Neill always insisted that the real genius of his family had been Jamie—the most brilliant, the most witty, the most inventive of them all. Jamie might have achieved anything, but all his gifts had been drowned in drink. There had been a brief resurrection after their father died, when Jamie had stopped drinking and had even started to win his bets on the horses. But after their mother died, Jamie had "lost all hold on life and simply wanted to die as soon as possible." That last year of alcoholic poisoning, delirium, blindness, and death had been so unendurably painful for O'Neill that he had kept—as far as possible—away from Jamie in sheer self-preservation. Only after Jamie's death from cerebral apoplexy in Riverlawn Sanatorium on November 8, 1923, could O'Neill allow himself to remember his old hero-worship and to think of the tragedy of that terrible waste. He staved off his grief at first by immersing himself in work, writing *Desire Under the Elms,* guiding his other plays through rehearsals, finishing *Marco Millions,* and then rehearsing *Desire Under the Elms.* The day after that play opened on November 11, 1924, O'Neill began to drink, and he could not stop. He found himself virtually reliving Jamie's last days. He had never been addicted to gambling, but on Boxing Day in Bermuda he found himself, like Jamie, at the horse races betting on the "bang tails" and so dead drunk—as he himself said—that he "didn't know one from another." In the first days of the New Year he tried desperately to cut down drinking but felt "too miserably disorganized to really make it." When he finally could start work on *The Great God Brown,* on January 28, 1925, he was painfully alive to his tragic heritage from Jamie. He had actually experienced in himself Jamie's tragic rush toward death and the pangs of his corroded genius.

So into this play about the fate of creativity in the modern world went all of his experience of it in Jamie, as well as all he had seen of it in Ed Keefe, Hutch Collins, and other frustrated New London intellectuals. He knew that their tragedy of failure was only the other side of the tragedy of success. The same sterile values that poisoned creativity made for the spiritual emptiness of American success. O'Neill knew the full danger and hollowness of success, for he had it. He was writing at this time some very personal poems, not meant for publication, in which he expressed his despair at a world where all dreams became "Soiled and true." His carefully nurtured "milk-white horse" in a "stall of ivory" had not sprouted wings and become Pegasus but had remained merely a "fat" white horse, and so he had given it to the "Circus," where it "was eaten by a flea-bitten lion." He felt honest only when he strove to wring the truth of life out of writing, but later, when he came to what he would describe as "that dreary ordeal of disillusionment and compromise called rehearsals," he began to despair. When his works were martyred in the Roman circus of production-publicity and his dream became "soiled and true," he was filled with horror. He had watched his play *Anna Christie*—in which he had meant to convey the threat of fate and chance hanging over human life—become transformed into a conventional happy-ending love story by the producer Arthur Hopkins and as such into a huge success. Afterward he had been overcome by "a great and self-blighting loathing for the world in general." Curiously, in a last explosion of drunken hatred, envy, and frustration, Jamie had burst into obscenities during a performance of that very play and had to be rushed out of the theater. A "most disgraceful scene" O'Neill called what he heard of it. Jamie had reacted with loathing like his own to the same success. Later, when the critic Benjamin De Casseres wrote up O'Neill as a Prometheus freed of his vultures, he got back an instant disclaimer. O'Neill told him: "I would feel a success and a total loss if they should ever desert me to gorge themselves fat and comforted on what the newspaper boys naively call fame." So it was that O'Neill was able to put himself into both the artist failure and the business success of his play, for he understood both as victims of the same forces.

His two friends in the play are truly brothers: brothers in that the failure of one and the empty success of the other emerge from the same deformed values of their world, and brothers in the way they are bound to one another, as he and Jamie had literally been. Cybel the Earth Mother says so: "You're brothers, I guess, somehow." Although O'Neill had entered largely into Brown, he made him "the Big Brother," for he had taken that role toward Jamie in those last years. (He would have his mother say to him in *Long Day's Journey into Night,* "You'd think you were the one ten years older.") In that last self-destructive year of Jamie's life, O'Neill had learned—so he said—"that the more I should urge him toward one course of action, the more obstinate and determined he will be to do the opposite." The same exasperated attempts at guidance on Brown's part and resistance on Dion's part went into the play.

When he began writing, O'Neill found that he was bound tightly by the actual facts of Jamie's last days in New London. He called the town of the play "New Caledonia, Connecticut," and he set the beginnings of Dion's plunge toward destruction in one of Jamie's own haunts, the parlor of the New London brothel, called in this version "Madame May's." Dion has been rescued and brought there by a prostitute named Estelle, who found him dead drunk, betting on the horses in "Nolan's dump," where he was about to be "rolled." "Nolan's dump" is clearly Jamie's other favorite New London refuge, Louis Montague's "gambling joint." Jamie had actually been rolled during those last days while drunk, but not at Louis's joint. Once O'Neill had written down these facts, he was able to pass beyond them. In a second draft, he erased the name of the town, made the horse-betting general gambling, and cut out the town brothel and the dump like Louis Montague's. The prostitute became more distinctly the Earth Mother Cybele. She is actually called "Cybel," and she has the dignity of her own cottage. In the first draft, Billy Brown had come looking for Dion at Madame May's because the brothel was a notorious hangout of his. After it was cut a strange improbability arose. Brown still looks for Dion in Cybel's cottage, but Dion has never been there before. (Cybel has found him sleeping off a drunk on her doorstep.) Neither O'Neill nor his audiences were disturbed by it, for in this play surface logic is treated consistently as a veil over the psychological truth that lies beyond it.

The two friends of his play are especially brothers as rivals in love. O'Neill designed the two women they share out of his deepest insight. They come from two views of his mother. One, the eternally innocent girl Margaret, reflects his old view of his mother as a child. He put it into Dion's thoughts on his mother's death: "And my mother? I remember a sweet, strange girl, with affectionate, bewildered eyes as if God had locked her in a dark closet without any explanation. I was the sole doll our ogre, her husband, allowed her and she played mother and child with me for many years in that house until at last through two years I watched her die with the shy pride of one who has lengthened her dress and put up her hair. And I felt like a forsaken toy and cried to be buried with her, because her hands alone had caressed without clawing. She lived long and aged greatly in the two days before they closed her coffin. The last time I looked, her purity had forgotten me, she was stainless and imperishable, and I knew my sobs were ugly and meaningless to her virginity; so I shrank away, back into life, with naked nerves jumping like fleas, and in due course of nature another girl called me her boy in the moon and married me and became three mothers in one person. . . ." O'Neill had Dion watch his mother die as Jamie had, but the rest of the recollection is his own of *The Hairy Ape's* opening day, when his mother's coffin arrived in New York. As he wrote it first, he had shrunk back "capering," as the hairy hero of his play might have, "in the nude nerves like a flayed ape." O'Neill repeats consciously the unconscious image in *The Rope* of his mother as a child playing with her doll. She is not merely the eternally innocent girl, she is the eternal virgin ("my sobs were ugly and meaningless to her virginity"), so that she merges, as she had in O'Neill's description of the dead Princess Kukachin, with the Virgin Mother Mary, whose name she bore. Indeed, O'Neill carries his Catholic imagery further when Dion sees himself married to a Holy Trinity of mothers, "three mothers in one person." They came from the two mothers of his childhood—his real mother and his nurse mother—who had entered into and become one with his mother-wife.

Jamie must have had a similar image of the innocent girl mother, and it must have made the revelation of her dope addiction all the more devastating for him. Jamie recalls that discovery in *Long Day's Journey into Night:* "Never forget the first time I got wise. Caught her in the act with a hypo. Christ, I'd never dreamed before that any women but whores took dope!" From that point on—it seems—Jamie carried an unconscious image of his mother as a prostitute because she took dope. She took her place beside his consciously "sainted" mother—or so he actually called her. Certainly Jamie had such a double image of his mother, and O'Neill came to know it. Perhaps he could not have put it into words when he was writing *The Great God Brown,* but he could and did write it into his late plays *Long Day's Journey into Night* and *Moon for the Misbegotten,* his last word on Jamie. In *Long Day's Journey into Night,* Jamie tells how he reacted to his mother's relapse into addiction. He went to Mamie Burns's brothel and chose a prostitute called "Fat Violet," whom Mamie was about to fire because she was fat and she got too "boiled" to play the piano, her particular job. All the early imagery of the play shows that this fat piano-playing prostitute is a grotesque proxy for his mother. Mary has been described over and over as "fat" from her cure, and she has bewailed her inability to play the piano because her hands have become crippled. With this proxy prostitute-mother, Jamie has enacted a strange ritual of compassion and hatred, weeping with her but exclaiming savagely afterward, "Pah! Imagine me sunk to the fat girl in a hick town hooker shop! Me! Who have made some of the best-lookers on Broadway sit up and beg!" O'Neill carried out the same idea in *Moon for the Misbegotten*. In it Jamie confesses appallingly that he has picked up "a blonde pig" with "a come-on smile as cold as a polar bear's feet" on the train carrying his mother's body to New York. The cold stranger with "parlor house written all over her" is another prostitute proxy for his mother who—in death—has become for him a "stranger": "cold and indifferent." With all his power to attract women, Jamie had preferred prostitutes, had selected prostitutes, and behind that choice had lain the trauma of his mother's addiction. O'Neill came to know that, and perhaps ultimately he even suspected that his brother's insistence on bringing him into rapport with prostitutes so early in his life came of a compulsion to extend their sharing of the mother symbolically to include the proxy prostitute. A foreshadowing of that knowledge created the two women his "brothers" share in *The Great God Brown:* the eternal girl and the prostitute Mother Earth, both of whom are revealed to be two aspects of one person at the end of the play.

Of course, O'Neill never lost sight of the fact that Cybel, the play prostitute, represents the ancient fertility goddess. Through her, Dion achieves friendship with the Earth and the profound life instincts, while Brown can find in her only what his shame allows him to see, her mask, "the rouged and eye-blackened countenance of the hardened prostitute." Everything around Cybel points out her meaning. In her cottage the painted backdrop expands the room into a vision of the earth's fertility. The wallpaper gives "a blurred impression of a fallow field in early spring," when Dion first sees it, and when he comes there just before his death the cycle of growth has been completed in a new wallpaper of "crimson and purple flowers and fruits" tumbling over one another in profusion. Her player piano comes out of O'Neill's unquenchable nostalgia for those "nickel-in-the-slot" automatons that had been ubiquitous in the dives of his youth, but it also celebrates the Earth Mother by banging out "a sentimental medley of 'Mother-Mammy' tunes." Cybel herself suggests the statues of fertility goddesses with her "full-breasted and wide-hipped" body. Her langorous animal movements recall the cow-mother goddesses. She actually "chews gum like a sacred cow forgetting time with an eternal cud." Dion calls her either "old Sacred Cow" or "Mother Earth." She delivers her words standing "like an idol." Yet, despite her godhead, she took up O'Neill's direct memories of his prostitute-mother—that is, his mother as she appeared under the influence of the drug. Then she too had taken on the remote unearthly calm of an idol, and she had spoken, as Cybel does, in a "far-off voice." She had even received the plea for love of her sons as Cybel receives Brown's, staring "ahead unmoved as if she hadn't heard." Indeed, O'Neill's conscious symbolism and his memories blended so perfectly that the Earth Mother Cybel merges altogether into his intimate longing for his mother become earth. Dion, like both Jamie and O'Neill, has wanted "to be buried" with his mother, and the culminating image of this play shows Brown snuggling gratefully against Cybel and murmuring "The earth is warm" as he dies. So in the two brothers and their Earth Mother, O'Neill was able to reach for a larger vision of man's destiny directly out of the living tissues of remembered love.

O'Neill entered into both Dion and Brown, even though much of Dion is straight Jamie. Dion's mask starts out with his own boyhood view of Jamie as a "reckless, defiant, gayly scoffing and sensual young Pan." The mask changes during the seven-year leap between the Prologue and act one just as Jamie's face had changed. By 1912, when *Long Day's Journey into Night* takes place, its "habitual expression of cynicism" had given it a distinctly "Mephistophelian cast." So Dion's mask becomes "more defiant and mocking, its sneer more forced and bitter, its Pan quality becoming Mephistophelean." The mask changes again before Dion's death to resemble Jamie's face before his death: "All its Pan quality has changed into a diabolical Mephistophelean cruelty and irony." So far Dion follows Jamie, but his inner self comes out of O'Neill's own "spiritual, poetic, passionately supersensitive" one, filled with a "childlike, religious faith in life." He felt himself so deeply Dion in the first part of the play, and Brown in the second part, that he wanted the same actor to play both. Both came of his feeling that he had stolen his brother's personality.

Of course, he modeled Dion's dying very faithfully on Jamie's. In the Earth Mother, Dion finds the same brief interlude of peace that Jamie found with his mother after his father died. With her and for her, Jamie had been able to stop drinking. Just before he and his mother set out on their fatal California journey, O'Neill had written of him to their friend Harold DePolo: "He hasn't had a drink in almost a year and a half now! Fact, I swear to you! My mother got him to go on the wagon and stick—and he *has* stuck." Similarly, in the play, Dion is free of his drinking in the interludes with Mother Earth, for the drinking belongs to his Mephistophelian mask and he needs no mask with her. Dion also has with Cybel the pure relationship of mother and son, while Brown carries on a sexual relationship with her empty proxy, the mask of the hardened prostitute.

Dion's last devastating attack upon Brown, in which he tears apart his vacuity, his sterility, and his complacency, came directly as recollection of Jamie's "tongue like an adder" during those last frenzied outbursts before his death. Indeed, Jamie enters into and speaks so passionately through the dying Dion that he almost—but not quite—breaks out of the surface logic of the play to become pure Jamie lashing his brother Eugene with hatred. He is also Eugene O'Neill at one with his brother in loathing of his own "success." Dion cries, "I've been the brains! I've been the design! I've designed even his success—drunk and laughing at him—laughing at his career! Not proud! Sick! Sick of myself and him!" Actually this is straight Jamie accusing O'Neill, for Brown has been a success before he started stealing Dion's designs. "I've designed even his success" almost breaks out of the play into pure anguished recollection. Later, in *Long Day's Journey into Night,* he would have Jamie say: "And because I once wanted to write, I planted it in your mind that someday you'd write! Hell, you're more than my brother. I made you! You're my Frankenstein!"

"When I die, he goes to hell!" So Dion says, and so Brown does after he steals Dion's mask at his death. Brown himself had no mask, for he had no self, only a mass of conventional beliefs. But the poisoned creativity of Dion, once his, brings him suffering, and out of his suffering, the beginnings of a soul. In *Masks and Demons* Kenneth Macgowan had pointed out that primitive people had a special ritual for taking off and putting on a mask. "If the savage ignores the ritual he knows that disaster will follow," he had said. "The god who came into him when he wore the fetish will remain in his flesh, tortured and torturing." O'Neill felt sure that the same instinct that directed primitive peoples would allow a modern audience to see the tormenting and tormented presence of Dion in Brown once he has stolen his mask. Of course, long before O'Neill had even met Kenneth Macgowan he had experienced in himself the torturing presence of his brother's Mephistophelian personality, and he had even written about it. Several months after he had attempted suicide he had told of it in a poem, "The Lay of the Singer's Fall," which appeared in the *New London Telegraph* on November 27, 1912. He himself was the singer, the poet, and at his birth a "Devil of Doubt" had whispered that he would enter into him and "abide for aye" at the moment he learned "the meaning of sin." Jamie had been his "Devil of Doubt," and Jamie had taught him the meaning of sin when he introduced him to sex. In the poem, his "Devil of Doubt" rapidly kills his faith in "Truth," "Love," and "God" and finally kills him with the lure of suicide. He had known all about having a "Devil of Doubt" inside him long before he gave Dion's mask to Brown. In fact, Dion leaves Brown his mask as a "gnawing of a doubt" and predicts that it will "thrive and breed and become multitudes and eat until Brown is consumed!" In Brown and his Dion mask, O'Neill could work out the whole of his heritage from his brother: all that he knew, all that he sensed, all that he dimly divined. His stage directions have Brown reach for Dion's mask "like a dope fiend after a drug." Then he puts "out one hand to touch the mask like a frightened child reaching out for its nurse's hand." The actions expose his sense of self without his brother's masculinity superimposed upon it. The "dope fiend" makes him one with his addicted mother. At the same time, he is the frightened child reaching for the hand of his second mother, the nurse Sarah Sandy. His pre-Jamie self had been child-woman, and that self still lived intact within his adult masculinity.

He had become part Jamie with that first sex experience, and it must have held for him a strange ambiguity. If—as it appears—he went into it a woman-identified child, he must have felt even more passively one as he submitted to what had virtually been a rape. Although he had been filled with pride at taking over in himself his hero brother's bold masculinity, he must in his depths have felt a twinge of uncertainty as to whether he was his brother proving himself upon the prostitute, or whether the prostitute was not in some mysterious way his brother working upon him. That dim confusion as to who was who and what was taking place must have clouded all his repetitions. The woman for him was always the object—the woman and only the woman—but somehow she carried with her that infantile memory of how his mother's encircling arms always brought the love of the hero father. So the prostitute was woman, and yet redolent of the two heroes of his boyhood, his brother and father, even at the moment when he was most closely identified with their masculinity. Whatever he felt, he always behaved very differently with prostitutes, amateur and pro-fessional, than he did with the "good" girls whom he loved romantically. During his year at Harvard (1914–15) he happened to tell a classmate of his, Corwin Willson, all about his many early experiences with prostitutes and easy women. Willson later explained: "He seemed somehow to meet numbers of the kind of young women who are sexually aggressive nymphomaniacs." O'Neill had told him in detail, he said, "how such a girl began embracing him in a normally fervent manner and then passionately ended by 'going down on him.'" Also, "O'Neill described to me *in detail* the way various prostitutes had gone after him professionally in a similar manner." What struck Willson later in all these stories was "his own passive role in them": "He never discussed homosexuality with me but he sure was hipped on what over-amorous women can do to a rather passive man. Always Gene's stories ended by the woman hungrily pounc-ing on him." From all evidence, O'Neill's behavior was absolutely different in romantic love. There he definitely took active lead. Certainly the youthful

O'Neill who seemed such a peril to New London parents of conventional girls, and the young O'Neill who found himself a father so early in life, had taken the lead with "nice" girls most emphatically. The striking difference of his behavior with them and with prostitutes reflects the ambiguity in his first experience.

This ambiguity appears in Brown's behavior with Dion's mask. As a matter of fact, it emerges strikingly because it joins O'Neill's intention to show Brown as sterile, uncreative, alienated from life. Brown was to illustrate Zarathustra's comment on conventional men—"Also ye love the earth, and the earthly: . . . but shame is in your love, and a bad conscience. . . ." It is the combined love and shame that makes Brown want to buy the Earth Mother Cybel but allows him to get only the prostitute mask. He envies Dion's creative power, and he tries to steal it, first in his architectural designs and then in his mask itself. He is really trying to steal Pan, the male life force, when he steals Dion's mask. In the end, when he is goaded into confessing his love for Margaret, Dion instantly turns upon him crying, "No! That is merely the appearance, not the truth! Brown loves me! He loves me because I have always possessed the power he needed for love, because I am love!" And he is proved right. Brown behaves toward Dion's mask with all the ambiguity that had clouded O'Neill's own graduation into his brother's masculine power. As he puts on Dion's clothes he says to the mask, "Hurry, Brother! It's time we were home. Our wife is waiting! Come with me and tell her again I love her! Come and hear her tell me how she loves you! (*He suddenly cannot help kissing the mask*) I love you because she loves you! My kisses on your lips are for her! (*He puts the mask over his face and stands for a moment, seeming to grow tall and proud—then with a laugh of bold self-assurance*) Out by the back way! I mustn't forget I'm a desperate criminal, pursued by God, and by myself!" O'Neill had laid bare this confusion of who was who and what was what only by tearing pitilessly into his own complexities.

All this digging into masculinity-creativity went to the heart emotional impulse of the play: romantic love. *The Great God Brown* begins and ends in the enchanted moonlit summer nights of O'Neill's first youthful loves. Love spreads its glow over the Prologue, when his characters are young, and over the Epilogue, a generation later. It is love that brings suffering to Dion and Brown, love for Margaret. O'Neill chose for her the name of Faust's Marguerite—Gretchen—who is caught up in Faust's search for meaning but remains spiritually innocent of it. Margaret is the "eternal girl-woman," O'Neill said, "properly oblivious to everything but the means to her end of maintaining the race." He put into her all the conventional girls he had ever known—the Kathleen Jenkinses and the Maibelle Scotts of his life. Indeed, the moonlit pier of the

Prologue seems, at one point, to have melted for him into "Scott's wharf," which stretched into the Thames River to one side of the O'Neill house at 325 Pequot Avenue, where O'Neill had often joined Maibelle Scott in the June evenings long ago. But the agony Margaret provokes comes from fresher wounds; it wells up out of O'Neill's suffering in his marriage. Of course, Agnes had been anything but a conventional girl. She was poetical, mystical, imaginative, and had taken up his religion of love with fervor. At first she had tried hard to keep faith with the best that was in him. He had written her a letter about their love on the way to New York, and she had answered that his letter from the train had given her a "deep" peace, a feeling of humble silent prayer before their "Holy of Holies." Their faith, their dream, *would* endure. She had too often judged him by commonplace standards, but inwardly, instinctively, she never misjudged his fineness, his truth. She ended by saying that she beat herself three times upon the breast, for their difficulties had been her fault, her fault, her most "grievous" fault. But as the years had gone on, she had slipped back into judging him more and more by common standards, into attributing mean motives to him as his silences became more and more impenetrable to her. The quarrels that shattered their unity became progressively more excruciating for him, and all that suffering in love went into the two men of his play.

He had Dion feel reborn at first, as he had felt, through his love. Sure of Margaret for the first time, he cries, "Now I am born—I—the I!—one and indivisible—I who love Margaret!" Just so, O'Neill had felt through Agnes that he became "a whole, a truth." Faith in love allows Dion to put aside his mask, and union with the woman-mother brings the wider circle of the father's love—just as it did in O'Neill's infancy—only in this case it is God the Father. Dion says, "O God, now I believe!" A moment later, Margaret herself shatters the double circle of love and faith. She shrieks in fear at his unmasked self: "Who are you! Why are you calling me? I don't know you!" Only hidden under his mask can Dion win her, and once his faith in the reality of her love is destroyed, his faith in God goes too. He tells her: "Watch the monkey in the moon! See him dance! His tail is a piece of string that was left when he broke loose from Jehovah and ran away to join Charley Darwin's circus!" For O'Neill, faith in love and faith in God were one.

In direct opposition to his more and more "Mephistophelean" mask, Dion's inner self becomes "more selfless and ascetic," ever "more spiritual, more saintlike." O'Neill did and yet did not describe himself. He was proud of his inquiring spirit, and he had been convinced by Nietzsche that the essence of Christian asceticism is "the sacrifice of all freedom, all pride, all self-confidence of spirit; it is at the same time subjection, self-derision, and self-mutilation."

O'Neill had opted, with Nietzsche, for proud participation in Life's struggle to achieve higher forms. Nevertheless, he kept the ideal of the selfless saint at the heart of his marriage. If he had followed his brother's attitude toward sex, he had followed even more decisively his father's attitude toward romantic love. He knew that his father had been "a husband to marvel at" and that he had set a pattern of gallant and selfless devotion to his wife in all her trouble. He had once declared, "Life is really worth living, after all," through "the fortunate circumstances which enable one to come to the assistance of a fellow-being." O'Neill took up his ideal of service, and in one of the very first long plays he ever wrote, *Servitude* (1914), he gave the secret of life as "Servitude in love, love in servitude." Always, his play heroes had reached exaltation through sacrifice for love, and they had always ended on their knees before the beloved woman. In *All God's Chillun Got Wings* O'Neill had even called his married lovers "Jim" and "Ella"—the nicknames of his father and mother—because Jim would demonstrate the same sublime self-sacrificing love for his mentally disturbed wife as his father had shown for his addicted mother. In that play Jim ends "on his knees," his eyes "shining," his face "transfigured" before his wife. In *Desire Under the Elms,* Eben throws "himself on his knees" for Abbie, and in *The Great God Brown* Dion Anthony repeats the gesture. Just before he dies, he tears off his mask crying, "Behold your man—the sniveling, cringing, life-denying Christian slave you have so nobly ignored in the father of your sons!" His inner self is revealed "radiant with a great pure love for her," and he cries out, "O woman—my love—that I have sinned against in my sick pride and cruelty—forgive my sins—forgive my solitude—forgive my sickness—forgive me!" Then he "kneels and kisses the hem of her dress." If O'Neill's play heroes end on their knees—in that gesture of reverence and humility out of his Catholic boyhood—it was forced upon them by the insistence on that posture within him for his religion of love.

The split and suffering Dion partook of all the pain in O'Neill's marriage to Agnes, and Brown intensified it after he took over Dion's mask. "Paradise by proxy! Love by mistaken identity!" he cries bitterly. He is not only unseen under Dion's mask, he has the peculiar torture of hearing Margaret speak of him with "devastating contempt" to the mask. In O'Neill's marriage, the moments of peace and love were often marred by the haunting echo of what she had said during their quarrels. When the rupture came, he told her, "There have been too many insults to pride and self-respect, too many torturing scenes that one may forgive but which something in one cannot forget and which no love, however strong, can continue to endure and live." So the pain of Dion and the greater pain of Dion-Brown caught up all of O'Neill's anguish in his marriage to cry out the loneliness of all the stifled souls in the world.

Through suffering Dion and Brown reach their apotheosis, for out of it they forge a soul. O'Neill thought that the very nature of life makes it a condemnation to suffering. In *The Hairy Ape* he had Yank reply to a policeman's question "What you been doin'?": "Enuf to gimme life for! I was born, see? Sure, dat's de charge." In his sequel *The Great God Brown,* O'Neill illustrates the idea. He arranges the benches on the pier in the Prologue to suggest a courtroom and has two trials take place there. First Brown stands before his mother as judge with his father as advocate and is condemned to architecture. Then Dion stands before his father as judge with his mother as advocate and receives the same sentence. O'Neill repeats the "same courtroom effect" in Dion's home, where he is condemned by Margaret to give up his creative struggle and go back to the architect's office. When Dion is destroyed, he sentences Brown, declaring "like a cruel malignant condemnation" that Brown "will devote his life into renovating the house of my Cybel into a home for my Margaret"—that is, he must carry on Dion's painful struggle to make the Earth a place where love can live. The "condemnation" is underlined in the last scene, where the same literal-minded policeman of *The Hairy Ape*—thoroughly bewildered as to who has done what—appears to threaten Cybel into identifying his culprit, the dying hero. Her answer is "Man!" Cybel's rapturous hymn to the eternal return of all things had at first spoken of "Spring bearing the intolerable Condemnation of life again!" Later O'Neill enlarged the meaning of the condemnation, making it "Spring bearing the intolerable chalice of life again!" to suggest the cup of the crucifixion, the cup of Communion, and the promise of resurrection.

Out of his "condemnation" man works out his own redemption, because suffering brings spiritual growth. Dion and Brown are Nietzsche's "down-going ones" who go "beyond." O'Neill accepted his own condemnation to life and suffering in that hope. When he assured Benjamin De Casseres that his vultures were still tearing him, he found in them a "test" and a "self-justification": "Each visit they wax stronger and more pitiless—which is, naturally, a matter of boast between them and me!—and I look forward to some last visit when their wings will blot out the sky and they'll wrench the last of my liver out; and then I predict they'll turn out to be angels of some God or other who have given me in exchange the germ of a soul." His brother's suffering, his own suffering, the suffering of all the frustrated creative spirits he had ever known had been a "test" from which they might emerge with higher life values. Their failure, like the failure of Dion and Brown, had been their triumph. In the words of Nietzsche's Zarathustra: "What wonder even that ye have failed and only half-succeeded, ye half-shattered ones! Doth not—man's *future* strive and struggle in you?"

The woman Margaret who brings his tragic heroes suffering and redemption became invaded by Agnes as he wrote. It happened that Agnes was pregnant, and she gave birth right after he had given birth to the play. In it he had blended images of pregnancy with his vision of the eternal renewal of life. At her very first appearance in the moonlit Prologue, Margaret is already redolent of renewal. Her instinct speaks through her, and she thinks, "Dion is the moon and I'm the sea. I want to feel the moon kissing the sea. I want Dion to leave the sky for me. I want the tides of my blood to leave my heart and follow him." The moon's power over female fertility joins the power of her lover, and both merge with the baby they will produce, so that she feels herself pregnant with all three. "And I'll be Mrs. Dion—Dion's wife—and he'll be my Dion—my own Dion—my little boy—my baby! The moon is drowned in the tides of my heart, and peace sinks deep through the sea!" The same vision of the eternal renewal of Man through Woman went into his image of Margaret in the Epilogue. She takes Dion's mask from under her cloak as if from her womb and speaks as the eternally pregnant mother of life: "You are sleeping under my heart! I feel you stirring in your sleep, forever under my heart."

It had all come together—his most intimate experience, his most searching psychological analysis, and his apocalyptic vision of the meaning of all the lives he had ever known. He saw that he could make Life the hero of his play. He had been reading and rereading *The Birth of Tragedy* and had become fascinated by Nietzsche's idea that "all the celebrated figures of Greek tragedy"—such as Oedipus and Prometheus—are in reality masks of the "original hero, Dionysus," the god of life and fertility out of whose ritual celebration Greek drama developed. They represented "the suffering Dionysus of the mysteries, the god experiencing in himself the agonies of individuation." As Nietzsche saw it, the "mystery doctrine of tragedy" asserted the "oneness of everything existent," placed "the prime cause of evil" in the separation of life into individuals, and presented the "joyous hope that the bonds of individuation may be broken in augury of restored oneness." O'Neill realized that he already had in his play the two principal figures of the Eleusinian mysteries and of all the mystery celebrations of life: the Earth Mother Cybele and the God Pan-Dionysus. His was a "tragic mystery drama of Life," and he decided to call his hero "Dion" to show that he is really Dionysus, Life. Like the God, Dion dies and is reborn; he goes down as Dion Anthony and is renewed as Dion Brown. So excited was O'Neill by this idea that he wanted the mask to show the reborn God in Brown. First "a trace of Pan" was to come "alive in it again." Then it was to lose its "dissipated, bitter, diabolical quality" and emerge as "a young, healthy, mockingly-laughing, ironically inquisitive Pan." At the very end it was to transcend individuality altogether and take on "the remote, objective quality of a God done in stone." No sooner had O'Neill formed this plan than he saw that it would be difficult to manage. If he obliterated the Mephistopheles in the mask entirely, the audience might never realize that Brown had stolen a poisoned product in Dion's mask. With time to experiment, O'Neill could have found a way to do both. As it was, in both the acted play and the published version, he simply gave up and left the mask in its ravaged Mephistophelian state from Dion's death to the end. Yet everything in his play called for the mask of the reborn god. Pan is shown, toward the end, escaping his confinement in Brown. He tears up the hideous plan for a state capitol building and throws away as "dead" the mask of his own success William Brown (which he has alternated with that of Dion). Then he leaps to freedom with the "quick prancing movement" of the goat god, "his head thrown back, shaking with silent laughter." The final escape of the God from "the bonds of individuation" comes when he lets the police shoot him in the mask of Dion as the murderer of William Brown.

The climax gave O'Neill fulfillment of his dearest personal wish and a celebration of life like that of the Greek tragedies. His hero returns to Cybel, Life renews itself through Mother Earth, and O'Neill and his brother James become one with their mother in the New London earth. The same assurance of eternal life and love O'Neill had the Princess deliver in *Marco Millions* is given to the dying hero. Cybel assures him, "There is only love." As Mother God she brings the Father God by declaring with certainty, "Our Father Who Art!" And she delivers the hero's epitaph in the form of a hymn to the eternal renewal of all things: "Always spring comes again bearing life! Always again! Always, always forever again! Spring again!—life again!—summer and fall and death and peace again!—but always, always, love and conception and birth and pain again—spring bearing the intolerable chalice of life again!—bearing the glorious, blazing crown of life again!" Right afterward the individual Margaret shows herself to be one with the eternal Mother of Life, and she gives her personal assurance of renewal to the mask of Dion (shed by the dying Brown), calling it, "My lover! My husband! My boy!" As the eternally pregnant girl-mother, she tells it: "You will live forever! You will sleep under my heart! I will feel you stirring in your sleep, forever under my heart!" The cycle is completed in the Epilogue. Margaret stands with her three grown sons on the same moonlit pier of her youth, as each goes off to begin the cycle of love and birth over again with another eternal girl. (O'Neill named them for his own romantic dream girls: "Mabel" for Maibelle Scott, "Bee" for Beatrice Ashe, and "Alice" for Alice Cuthbert, to whose joy and youth he had just written a poem.) O'Neill's two "brothers," who embody the God of the mysteries, resolve their suffering, as Nietzsche resolved the God's—by restoration to "the eternally creative primordial mother, eternally impelling to existence, eternally self-sufficient amid this flux of phenomena." Margaret presents the final image out of the mystery celebrations. She stands as the eternally pregnant mother with the mask of her son-lover who will be endlessly reborn through her. "It's only our lives that grow old," she says. "We *are* where centuries only count as seconds and after a thousand lives our eyes begin to open."

O'Neill was sure that the same perception of the cycle of seasons and renewal of life that had created the original mystery celebrations would allow his audiences to see the tragic mystery drama of life behind "the recognizable human beings" in his play: Dion, Brown, Margaret, and Cybel. As he explained, "I meant it always to be mystically within and behind them, giving them a significance beyond themselves, forcing itself through them to expression in mysterious words, symbols, actions they do not themselves comprehend. And that is as clearly as I wish an audience to comprehend it."

O'Neill was "hot at work on 'Brown'" and found it "coming good" when he almost lost his stride at finding himself once again attacked by the same noncreative, anti-life Browns of the United States who had tried to suppress *The Hairy Ape* and *All God's Chillun Got Wings.* This time they were trying to close his play *Desire Under the Elms* as obscene, seeing, as they always did in Life, only what their deformed values showed them: "the rouged and eye-blackened countenance of the hardened prostitute." O'Neill forced himself to turn his back on their machinations, so that frustration could not corrode his joy in celebrating life. Yet his anger found its way into his hero's final rejection of the Brown in himself along with his plan for a state capitol, which he knows will please the politicians with its "fat-bellied finality": "Only to me will that pompous facade reveal itself as the wearily ironic grin of Pan as, his ears drowsy with the crumbling hum of past and future civilizations, he half listens to the laws passed by his fleas to enslave him!" Exploding into a "few goatish capers," he chants ironically: "Long live Chief of Police Brown! District Attorney Brown! Alderman Brown! Assemblyman Brown! Mayor Brown! Congressman Brown! Governor Brown! Senator Brown! President Brown! Oh, how many persons in one God make up the good God Brown?" A good part of these American gods, including New York City's Chief of Police, District Attorney, and Mayor, were doing their best to destroy the Pan in him as he worked. For him there was nothing abstract about the great God Brown of his play. The entire work rushed out in two months of hard writing. He concluded it on March 25, 1925. The next day he wrote George Jean Nathan: "I've just finished a devastating, crucifying new one called 'The Great God Brown,' which I think marks my 'ceiling' so far, and I feel right cheerful!" That summer he saw how high that ceiling was when he had to take up and polish his play of three years earlier, *The Fountain,* which they were going to produce in their Greenwich Village theater. He hated going back to that "old thing." He told Kenneth Macgowan that "Brown" was "worth a dozen 'Fountains.'"

The Great God Brown was to go on after it, and O'Neill fretted because the cast was not lined up and thus they could not begin on the masks, which would have to look like the real actors. By the time they had found the actors there was no time left to perfect all that had to be communicated through the masks. Afterward O'Neill wrote Macgowan: "Do the masks in 'Brown' do what the script requires of them? They do not. They only get across personal resemblance of a blurry meaninglessness." Later he told Benjamin De Casseres, "I quite understand the masks confusing you when you saw it. They were never right and we had neither the time nor the money to experiment and get them right before we opened—the old story that prevents anything really fine from ever being done in the American theatre!" Far from expressing the psychological complexities or the struggle of life forces, O'Neill continued, "They suggested only the Brownidic, hypocritical and defensive double-personality of people in their personal relationships—a thing I never would have needed masks to convey." Indeed, the masks could barely be seen from the back of the theater. Perhaps, O'Neill thought, "I should have made them twice as large—and conventionalized them, so the audience could get the idea at once."

After seeing the play in rehearsal, Barrett Clark told O'Neill that it would not last more than two weeks. "You may be right," O'Neill said, "but I somehow feel there's enough in it to get over to unsophisticated audiences. In one sense *Brown* is a mystery play, only instead of dealing with crooks and police it's about the mystery of personality and life." When they showed the play to an audience of critics the night before its public opening on January 23, 1926, most of them agreed with Clark. They were as bewildered and hostile—in the main—as they had been at the opening of *Desire Under the Elms.* Later O'Neill said, "Everyone seems to think now that these two plays got a very good press but the facts are that the majority vote was against them, very much so." The audiences saved it. As O'Neill had predicted to Clark, it fascinated many who did not "bother too much over every shade of meaning" but followed it "as they follow any story. They needn't understand with their minds; they can just watch and feel." Four days after the regular opening, O'Neill noted, " 'Brown' looks like big hit." After five weeks, they were able to move it to a larger theater uptown. O'Neill became jubilant. Here was a masked drama with all its values "psychological, mystical, and abstract," yet it had run "in New York for eight months, nearly all of that time in Broadway theatres." That proved, he thought, both "the deeply responsive possibilities in our public" and the validity of masks as a theatrical device. Even years later he was sure that *The Great God Brown* was "one of the most interesting and moving" of his plays. It had "its faults," he knew, but it had truly been a "tragic mystery drama of Life." He always declared it a "favorite" of his. He even said: "It's very near—and dear—to me, that play—(I'm not sure it isn't the best beloved of them all)."

4

Lazarus Laughed

The "germ of idea" for his play about Lazarus came to O'Neill on August 20, 1924, while he was creating his lovelorn suicidal Princess in *Marco Millions*. She was emerging out of memories of his own failure in love and his own suicide attempt. He had risen from it, just as Lazarus had risen from the dead. With Lazarus as his hero, he could face death directly and fight his fear that only nothingness lay beyond it. "To feel one's life blown out like the flame of a cheap match!" he had exclaimed, by way of Dion, in *The Great God Brown*. When he discovered that he could make Life—Dionysus—his real hero, he was ready to begin. On September 1, 1925, he sat down to sketch a scenario about a Lazarus reborn as Dionysus to give a message of hope to the world very much as Nietzsche's Zarathustra—also an embodiment of Dionysus—had in the book that had been the Bible of his youth, *Thus Spake Zarathustra*. Nietzsche had used his Zarathustra to contrast the joyous pagan acceptance of living with the Christian rejection of life in this world. According to Zarathustra, Jesus himself would have overcome his death-directed philosophy had he lived long enough to conquer his Hebrew melancholy, his pity for man, and his loathing for the Pharisees—those conventionally "good and just" men. Nietzsche even predicted what Jesus might have become in the parable of a shepherd who triumphantly bites off and spits out a suffocating snake that has sunk fangs into his

mouth. Freed, the shepherd springs up "a transfigured being, a light-surrounded being, that *laughed*. Never on earth laughed a man as *he* laughed!"
This laughing hero merged for O'Neill with his memories of a light-refulgent
Christ rising from the tomb, and he decided that his Lazarus, free of the fear
of death, would rise radiant and full of laughter in joyous affirmation of unending life. So his title came to him as a rejection of the biblical words "Jesus
wept," and he called his play "Lazarus Laughed."

He had been stirred particularly by Nietzsche's idea of "dance" as a "parable
of the highest things," for it suggested both the dancing celebrants of Dionysus
in the mystery rites and the dancing choruses of Greek tragedy. He saw his
resurrected Lazarus surrounded by dancing crowds freed from the fear of
death by his joyous laughter. He saw him faced also with hostile crowds, for
man's fear herds him into warring sects and nations. The decadent Roman
Empire of Lazarus's day showed, he thought, how the drive for power comes
from fear and life-hatred. O'Neill's Emperor Tiberius—hoping that Lazarus is
a Jewish sorcerer with a charm against death—has a legion bring him from
Bethany (where the Bible drops him), across conquered Greece to Rome, and
to the core of its fear and cruelty in the notorious villa of Tiberius at Capri. On
the way, he converts mobs of cruel life-haters into laughing, dancing celebrants.

O'Neill had looked into the actual mystery religions of the ancient world and
had written out the cosmic views of Plotinus, Vatius Valens, and Pythagoras
(which he had found in a book by Samuel Angus, *The Mystery Religions and
Christianity*). He saw that the Pythagorean view extended the oneness of living
things to include all nature in a way that let him hold on to God the Father, for
Pythagoreans believed that all things come from Deity and return into Deity:
that Deity "pervades all, earth and expanse of sea, and the deep vault of
heaven." They believed that men do not die but "fly up alive into the ranks of
the stars." Here, O'Neill saw, was an authentic mystery religion of Lazarus's
own time that blended beautifully with modern astronomy's view of a universe
in perpetual creation. He gave it to Lazarus and became just a bit intoxicated
with it himself. Lazarus tells his followers that they die to become dancing dust
in space and so they can "love the stars as equals," for "new stars are born of
dust eternally." When he learns that Jesus has been crucified, he tells his followers, "See! a new star has appeared!" Free of the division into individuals that
bound them to death, his followers can join in Laughter—which is Deity—and
become one with the eternally renewed cosmos.

At this point, all O'Neill's dreams for the theater joined Pythagoras and the
mystery rites in one gorgeous vision of how to make this play live on stage. He,
Robert Edmond Jones, and Kenneth Macgowan had reciprocally set off each

other's creativity. Jones had first awakened his interest in rhythmical movements and sculpturesque pose as a theatrical language (ideas Jones had formed when working with the great dancer Nijinsky on "Tyl Eulenspiegel"). To give Jones an opportunity, O'Neill had arranged Coleridge's poem *The Rime of the Ancient Mariner* for a narrator and a masked chorus and had participated in Jones's unusual way of training his choruses: teaching them to feel the emotions of the lines and then to fall naturally into postures and gestures expressive of them. O'Neill decided to dramatize his crowds in Jones's way. The first view of Lazarus's followers presents a joyous prophecy of their future as dancing dust among the stars. They move diaphonously among myriads of candles that give "a throbbing star-like effect." Outside two hostile crowds, one of Orthodox Jews and the other of Nazarene Jews, express their hatred and fear by hopping, jerking, and twisting in a "bestial parody of the dance of the Followers." Later, they fuse in one indistinguishable whirling mass of hatred, above which "knives and swords flash" and hands are raised "in every tense attitude of striking, clutching, tearing." He used sculpturesque pose as dramatically. At one point Lazarus's followers are frozen in dance around him "like figures in a frieze." Bereft of Lazarus, they huddle into dark bunches, their arms stretched "out in every direction supplicatingly."

O'Neill saw his crowds as masked by their fear. The masks express the herds of Jews, Greeks, Romans they hide in, as well as the seven ages of man and seven defensive outer personalities. O'Neill had been caught by the Pythagorean enthusiasm for numbers and became rapt by the magic number seven. He saw his own life in seven-year stages. In his "Diagram" he marked "7 years old—complete break—school" and a second break at "Adolescence," when he learned of his mother's addiction. His disastrous first marriage had come at 21, and he had found Agnes at 28. For a future play he would see a procession of his "dead selves" as masked figures at "7, 14, 21, 28, 35, 42." This intimate number virtually obsessed him in *Lazarus Laughed*. He put into it seven guests, seven citizens of Athens, seven senators. He constructed all his crowds in multiples of seven, and he spearheaded each crowd with a chorus of seven made up of the age-group and personality type that expressed its mass emotion. A chorus of seven old men of the "Sorrowful, Resigned" type leads the melancholy neighbors of Lazarus, and a chorus of seven young men of the "Proud, Self-Reliant" type spearheads the Greeks. As O'Neill saw it, these masked masses would be the real scenery of the play.

Silhouetted against them, Lazarus would play out his brief second life on earth. Already at resurrection, he would look like "a statue of a divinity of Ancient Greece," and he would grow more like one, and also ever younger, as

O'Neill had wanted the reborn Dionysus to do in *The Great God Brown*. By the time he reaches Athens, he resembles the "positive masculine Dionysus, closest to the soil of the Grecian Gods, . . . soul of the recurring seasons, of living and dying as processes in eternal growth." He is unmistakable to the audience, for O'Neill took advantage of the tendency in the ancient world to blend all worship into that of Dionysus (he had read about it in Angus) to make the Greeks hail Lazarus as Dionysus. He is drawn in a chariot like old paintings of the god, and a group of bacchantes await him, stained with wine lees and clad in goat skins like "the old followers of Dionysus." They throw the Dionysian bull's hide over his shoulders and press into his hand "the mystic rod of Dionysus with a pine cone on top."

With Dionysus as his hero and a chorus of celebrants, O'Neill had the major elements of a mystery rite. All he needed to complete it was the mother goddess—Cybele or Demeter—always celebrated with Dionysus. She appears in the form of Lazarus's perfectly fictitious wife—the New Testament gives no hint of one—who resembles the Demeter "sunk in eternal sorrow," described by Nietzsche in *The Birth of Tragedy*. She symbolizes "a world torn asunder and shattered into individuals," in contrast to Dionysus, who represents eternal oneness. Because she represents individuation, and therefore death, O'Neill put her into mourning for her dead children and reversed Lazarus's growing younger to have her grow rapidly older, ever more clearly the "sad, resigned mother of the dead." She stands, a black figure expressing pity and supplication, next to the radiant Lazarus rapt in joyous contemplation. The two of them make for a timeless tableau of Dionysus and Demeter: Dionysus the triumphant symbol of eternal life and eternal oneness, Demeter the subordinate symbol of the change, pain, and individual dying within the endless renewal of life.

These two mythological figures leaped to life within him because they held his most intimate experience. Lazarus sprang forth out of his own resurrection. O'Neill had risen, if not instantly transfigured, certainly transformed, and for the first time in his life able to seek a way to earn his bread that would let him live true to the best that was in him. Within a year of his suicide attempt, he found full resurrection out of despair as a dedicated playwright—and he found it where his father's life-enjoyment had showed him the way: the theater. He had been reborn into the spirit of his father's striving, and so his Lazarus became saturated with his boyhood hero-worship of James O'Neill. Lazarus is primarily a father. He addresses the crowds of the play as if they were "a group of inquisitive children." The Greeks and Romans hear his voice and become frozen into "the sheepish shame of children caught in mischief." He sets the old Emperor Tiberius straight "smiling—as if he were correcting a child." He particularly reacts to Caligula as to a child, "gently patting his head" and answering his ferocity by smiling "affectionately as at a child in a tantrum."

The smile was typically James O'Neill's. One reporter said it was "a lamp to the path of the hopeless," a "torch" in "a place of darkness": "It is kindly, rarely intelligent, and plays odd pranks with the corners of his lips, that tell the story of a merriment he seeks to repress." His son, trying to create a biblical prophet transformed into a laughing Greek god, actually achieved a composite recollection of his smiling hero father on and off stage. Like Lazarus, James O'Neill had been thought to resemble a Greek god. He was considered "one of the handsomest men," and critics believed he would be "till he dies, for the outline of his face is cut boldly, and brow, nose and chin have almost a classic strength and beauty." Eugene O'Neill had powerful recollections of him, both biblical and Roman, particularly as the patrician hero of *Virginius* in the fall of 1907 in New York. His white-robed Lazarus took on the appearance of his father in that play. "I never knew how much of majesty might inhere in a human being until I saw James O'Neill play Virginius," the critic for the *Dramatic Mirror* had declared. "His walk is as stately as the movement of a newly launched ocean liner making its proud way out to sea. His voice is like a deep toned bell. His eyes, big and luminous like Novelli's, bespeak a boundless vitality." Just such a figure came to his son for Lazarus.

Even his idea of having Lazarus grow younger, so that he seems to have found a charm against age, fit into the myth surrounding his father. "James O'Neill's Marvelous Secret of Eternal Youth Laid Bare," one article on him had been called. When he was more than sixty years old he was thought to have "boyish eyes, the eyes of everlasting youth." Even trying to make fun of him in his perennial *Monte Cristo,* Alan Dale had accentuated the myth. He found James O'Neill "young to look at, and filled with an uncanny sprightliness." As the young Dantes, he said, "the actor frolics like an inspired calf. He positively bounds in and out. He frisks. He gambols. He is younger than youth. While the lines of the play are so melodramatically old that they are no longer funny even as burlesque, this actor, who has assimilated 5,000 well-shaken doses of the stuff, makes us all look like old codgers."

James O'Neill had been most famous for his voice, and his son conceived of Lazarus chiefly as a voice—the sheer sound of which could create faith in multitudes. He wanted the greatest "voice" of his own day to play Lazarus: the opera singer Chaliapin. Only Chaliapin could "give speech the quality of music—and that's exactly what Lazarus must do," he told Barrett Clark. Critics had always praised the "melodious splendor" of his father's voice. One of them had pointed out at length how "unaffectedly and unforcedly" James O'Neill could evoke "every note of melody that is inherent in the words he speaks." As a boy O'Neill had heard that voice thrill audiences. Indeed, writing, he became literally a boy again in a box beside his mother, looking into a theater full of spectators hypnotized by his father on stage, and he designed his scenes from that viewpoint. Lazarus first appears on "a raised platform" with his neighbors seated below him, and then he addresses crowds beneath him from the flat roof of his house. He enters Athens on a chariot to waiting crowds. The ranks of senators in Rome react to his appearance like a theater audience, leaning "forward in their seats, fascinated by his face. A low murmur of admiration comes from them." In the palace of Tiberius, Lazarus is placed on a raised dais with the courtiers grouped around it "in a big semicircle as of spectators in a theatre." The culminating scene actually shows an amphitheater crowded with spectators watching Lazarus. Through all these scenes, O'Neill wanted a spotlight trained on Lazarus—so he explained to Kenneth Macgowan—as "an arrowhead of concentration directed at the one man who is real and true and alive in the midst of false, dead people." He declared that with the right actor for Lazarus they could play *Lazarus Laughed* "with a spotlight, a couple of tables, two soap boxes, a black curtain and the Hudson Duster Gang." The spotlight seems to have come first as well as last. Long before he had read of Nietzsche's light-surrounded being, even before he had seen paintings of the refulgent Christ, he had watched his father brilliantly spotlighted on stage. That had been the "star" he worshiped as a boy, and the whole of his later Pythagorean preoccupation with the stars came perhaps from the insistence of one word echoing in his mind. When he saw the hope after death of joining the stars, he was perhaps merely projecting the dream of his lonely boyhood when his father had been indeed a distant star moving in theatrical constellations far from Mount St. Vincent-on-the-Hudson, a star he could hope to join for a summer of love at the end of the school year.

O'Neill's mother is just as evident in Lazarus's wife. This figure in "deep black" rushing into white-haired old age comes out of O'Neill's last memory of his mother in deep mourning for the death of his father. She also shows the mark of her death and burial soon after in the New London earth. She wears a mask of the "pure pallor of marble"—that is, of her face as seen in death—and beneath it her own skin is "sunburned and earth-colored" in token of her actual return into the earth and of her Earth Mother promise of renewal. She emerges clearly as the mother of the beloved dead baby into whom O'Neill's identity flowed. He gave her inward-looking eyes that "dream down on the child forever in memory at her breast." He might have called her by his mother's name had not the Bible already given Lazarus a sister Mary. As next best he called her by the Hebrew for Mary: "Miriam."

Miriam accompanies her husband as a lonely and even incongruous figure in his triumphal passage through Athens to Rome and Capri, and so she takes on a curious resemblance to Mary Ellen O'Neill in endless accompaniment of James O'Neill on his theatrical tours across the United States. And their farm in Bethany takes on a curious resemblance to the O'Neill summer home outside New London, where, like Lazarus, James O'Neill had been—so he said—"a farmer and nothing but a farmer." She even talks of dying before her husband, just as Mrs. O'Neill might have talked of going back to New London alone to open up the house. "Say what you like, it is much better I should go home first, Lazarus," she said. "We have been away so long, there will be so much to attend to about the house." At the same time, she talks of dying in Capri as if she were certain to be buried worlds away in Bethany, and as if the resurrected Lazarus beside her were still in his grave there. She longs to go to "our tomb near our home, Lazarus, in which you and my children wait for me." So she speaks as Mary Ellen O'Neill might have spoken, dying in California, of being buried across the continent in New London where her baby Edmund and her husband James O'Neill were actually waiting for her.

Above all, Miriam has in her marriage absolute love. Lazarus gives her the unaltering fidelity that James O'Neill gave his wife. Like him, Lazarus is "a husband to marvel at," and despite his growing young while his wife rapidly ages, he does not stray. Just as James O'Neill was never tempted by the women who idolized him, so Lazarus passes untouched although "herds of women" throw themselves upon him, begging for love. Indeed, the chief impetus to *Lazarus Laughed* came from his father's faith. O'Neill's letters to Agnes from the hospital reveal it. Agnes and he had fought the night before he left Provincetown to go to his father in New London. She wrote to him that their quarrel had left her with a "frightful" feeling of hopelessness. It had dragged out—they had made up—and then, in the midst of their embraces, they had broken out in hatred again. The horror of it had given her a dream in which she discovered that he had been steadily unfaithful to her ever since their marriage. She could not tell him with what a "drained" hopeless feeling she had awakened. Writing back, O'Neill pinned his hope for their love on his father's faith. He told Agnes that they must stop fighting and hurting each other. It was a sin against their love. He could see that the one vital thing for his father was "my mother's love and his for her. He has thrown everything else overboard, but that remains— the real thing of the seventy-six years—the only meaning of them—the justification of his life because he knows that, at least, is fine and that it will go with him wherever he is going—the principal reason he is not afraid to go, I believe! So let us protect our love against ourselves—that we may always have the inner courage, the faith to go on—with it to fall back on."

From that strange border between Life and Death his father had tried to communicate his faith. Pitifully, cruelly, ironically, he could no longer talk plainly. Only his cries of agony could be understood, O'Neill told Agnes. "And all through life his greatest pride has been in his splendid voice and clear articulation!" At one point he had called O'Neill over and made a frightful effort to speak clearly. He was glad to go—was going to a "better sort of life," somewhere—but the rest was mumbled. Hard as he tried, O'Neill could not understand. His father's somewhere did not seem to be a Catholic heaven. He had tried to tell him, and O'Neill never would get over his anguish at being unable to understand. With the faith and love in his marriage falling away from him, O'Neill needed his father's message urgently. *Lazarus Laughed* came as a desperate effort to call his father back from the dead so that he could deliver—this time in the magnificent voice of his prime and with "surpassing clearness"—his message of eternal life and love.

Outside of that hope, everything about his dying had been designed to convey horror and terror. He had suffered "incredible tortures" that no palliatives could allay. Suffering with him, Eugene O'Neill had felt his "last illusion" of the "soft beauty of death" torn rudely from him. He asked, "Then why should he suffer so—when murderers are granted the blessing of electric chairs? Mankind—and myself—seem to me meaningless gestures, to be mocked at with gales of dreary laughter." He had been gripped so forcibly by that horror right after his father's death that it took over a play he began about the mob-murdered President Sam of Haiti—who had boasted that he could be killed only with a silver bullet—and made it a study in the psychology of fear. In this play, *The Emperor Jones,* his own fear drove the fear-haunted Emperor through the night forest. The Emperor's courage had cracked with the rising in him of indistinct wormlike shapes of fear emitting "a tiny gale of low mocking laughter." So O'Neill had seen his own and mankind's courage in the face of his father's undeserved agony as "meaningless gestures to be mocked at with gales of dreary laughter." The same horror arose in him when he started to write *Lazarus Laughed,* and once again it made its assault at night. Of course, he had good reason to begin *Lazarus Laughed* in the late afternoon, and to set all the scenes at night with a finale at dawn, just as he had done in *The Emperor Jones.* He needed darkness to contrast his light-surrounded Lazarus and to dramatize masks with flashes from torches, lightning, or flames. But it was memory, not reason, that insisted on night for his study of the fear of death in *Lazarus*

Laughed as it had in *The Emperor Jones*. Night and fear became one when—
after their last afternoon in the hospital—he and his mother and brother were
jangled into wakefulness in the middle of the night with a call from the hospital
that his father was dying. He had never forgotten that drive through the dark
of New London. Death had taken his father at 4:15 in the morning of August
10, 1920, and they had left the hospital at dawn.

Like *The Emperor Jones, Lazarus Laughed* is a study of fear, and this time
O'Neill had an opportunity to work with mass fear. Masks, he realized, would
preserve his mobs from what he called "the illusion-shattering recognitions by
an audience of the supers on stage." He was full of memories of his father's
portrayal in repertory of both Virginius, and also of Mark Antony in Shakespeare's *Julius Caesar,* in the fall of 1907. He recalled vividly the faults of those
productions. "Have you ever seen a production of *Julius Caesar?*" he asked in
his notes on masks. "Did the Roman mob ever suggest to you anything more
Roman than a gum-chewing Coney Island Mardi Gras?" At the time, even the
New York Telegraph of September 17, 1907, had remarked: "And when we
behold a Roman maiden chewing gum, as one of the mob did last night, or see
a Roman citizen with a French beard, we are not particularly interested with
the versimilitude of the reproduction. For Mr. O'Neill all praise. . . . But the
company around him were neither Romans nor actors." Eugene O'Neill knew
that masks were the answer. With the right actor for Lazarus—an actor like his
father—and masked mobs, the supporting cast could be the Hudson Dusters,
those seedy gangsters of his Greenwich Village youth. Masks would transcend
their individuality.

More, he knew that he could express "mob psychology" with masks. Masked
crowds would appear not as a mere "random collection of individuals" but as
"an entity" with one mind and one emotion. He showed his crowds of Pharisees
and Nazarenes become possessed by a "queer excitement" to form "crowd
mind" by weaving in and out in accelerating "jerky steps to the music" and
raising "clenched fists" or "threatening talons." Beginning with shouts of
"Shameless! Wanton! Dirty!" they pass imperceptibly into crowd desire: "Madness! Blood! Adultery! Murder! We burn! We kill! We crucify!" It all gave him
an idea for a play about a lynch mob pursuing a murderer, showing its forma-
tion from "harmless human units" into an entity possessed by the same "lust
and fear that made him commit his crime," so that they kill him "in the same
spirit—of enjoyment, of gratified desire." He would show their degeneration
into "Brutes" through masks and have the murderer—like his Emperor Jones
"but *white*"—revert to a gibbering beast through fear. Meanwhile, in *Lazarus
Laughed* he worked out the way that fear, life-hatred, and boredom in the

perverts of Tiberius's palace transfer into a hectic appetite for cruelty and death. They urge on the murder of Lazarus's wife, Miriam, "squatting on their hams like savages" and projecting one "concentrated death wish."

In combat with the mass fear of the mobs stands the joyous confidence of Lazarus and his followers, echoing the way his father's faith had contrasted with his own fear and horror. He was haunted by the sounds he heard at the hospital. An automobile accident victim lay dying a floor above his father's room and kept "howling monotonously with every expulsion of breath," his "hollow cries" reverberating through the wide halls. Against that, he had listened to his father's groans and cries of pain. In the play the fear-ridden crowds echo these terrible sounds, primarily in howls, punctuated by screams, yells, groans and wails. O'Neill heard the play as a war of sounds with all the nuances of Lazarus's laughter affirming faith over the discordant "jeering howls" of fear from the mobs.

The chief contrast to Lazarus is Caligula, who enters the play at Athens to pit his fear against Lazarus's faith. O'Neill found his facts on Caligula in Edgar Saltus's *Imperial Purple* and in Suetonius's *Lives of the Twelve Caesars,* although he had read many other books on Rome. Suetonius had described Caligula as "ill-shaped" with "very slender" legs and a hairy body. O'Neill took off from there with an "almost malformed" Caligula who has "short, skinny, hairy legs like an ape's." His Caligula leaps crazily, breaks into grotesque dances, or crouches on his hams. Echoing in O'Neill's mind was Nietzsche's bitter comment that man who was once an ape is still "more of an ape than any of the apes." Zarathustra had asked, "What is the ape to man? A laughing-stock, a thing of shame. And just the same shall man be to the Superman." Those words had already reverberated in O'Neill's play *The Hairy Ape.* Much of himself had gone into his proletarian hero, who is shocked into realizing that he is merely an ape in a steel cage. Tragically unable to find his way to living by higher standards, he ends by deciding—in Nietzsche's words—that he would "rather go back to the beast than surpass man." O'Neill realized that an apelike Caligula, besotted with lust for worldly power to hide his fear, would make a perfect contrast to his higher man, Lazarus, liberated from fear and its palliative, power over others. At their first meeting in Athens, Caligula "cuts a hopping caper" to Lazarus's chariot, "where he squats on his hams and, stretching out his hand, fingers Lazarus' robe inquisitively and stares up into his face in the attitude of a chained monkey." He is a laughingstock, and toward the play's end, in a flash of liberation, he can follow Lazarus's advice to laugh at himself and confess that he is merely "a trained ape, a humped cripple."

According to Suetonius, Caligula kept shifting between "excessive confidence and the most abject timidity." O'Neill saw these as the result of his upbringing as a "Child of the Camp," alternately spoiled and terrified by the soldiers. O'Neill invested him with his own shock as an innocent boy when he was thrown into his brother's hard world. He had tried to become hard, and later had chosen the companionship of rough sailors. For a companion, he gave Caligula a rough Roman General, Cneius Crassus, who blends two of his own old seagoing pals, a barge captain named Chris Christopherson, whom he had described in *Anna Christie* (1921) as "squat, broad-shouldered," and "muscular," and a stoker named Driscoll, whose "battered features" appear in *Bound East for Cardiff* (1914). Like them, Crassus is "a squat, muscular man" with "a heavy battered face full of coarse humor." In contrast, Caligula, the portrait of fear, acts the frightened child O'Neill had been, who retreated into a fantasy world with his father as hero. He had imitated his father's heroic swordplay as D'Artagnan during his schooldays, only to cower in terror at night when the menacing branches of trees swept the windows of the boy's cottage. Similarly, he had Caligula flourish his sword at one moment only to throw it away the next, hide his face, and weep. "Men still need their swords to slash at ghosts in the dark," Lazarus says. The play ends with Caligula acting out a fantasy before an empty amphitheater, saluting himself with "crazy intensity," lunging "with his spear at imaginary foes, jumping, dodging from side to side, yelping." O'Neill had been struck by Caligula's attempts to look terrifying by shaping his face "before a mirror into the most horrible contortions," and by Domitian's lining of his room with mirrors so that no one could stab him in the back. Both combined in his mind to form one image of the isolated, posturing, self-deluded human soul: "Tragic is the plight of the tragedian whose only audience is himself! Life is for each man a solitary cell whose walls are mirrors. Terrified is Caligula by the faces he makes!"

Caligula embodied his most merciless self-loathing. Through Caligula's recorded drunkenness, O'Neill could flay his own periodic alcoholism—his way out of unbearable tension from the age of fifteen. He had gotten drunk (April 3) after he finished *The Great God Brown,* and he had been drinking when his daughter Oona was born on May 14. He stopped, only to begin again July 17, and he sobered up late in August only to relapse again in September, October, and November. Only on New Year's Eve, December 31, 1925, was he ready to initiate a new era of sobriety. Caligula became the image of his former drunkenness. He appears "half-drunk" in the senate scene when fear threatens to triumph over faith, flourishing a large goblet while a "slave with an amphora of wine crouches on the steps by his chair." Without his old drunkenness, O'Neill felt, he said, "the void left by those companionable or (even when most horrible) intensely dramatic phantoms and obsessions, which, with caressing claws in my heart and brain, used to lead me for weeks at a time, otherwise lonely, down the ever-changing vistas of that No-Man's-Land lying between the D.T.'s and reality as we suppose it." With his new sobriety, hallucinatory phantoms poured so tumultuously into *Lazarus Laughed* that they took over completely the last two acts. The heart of fear was Tiberius's palace, and ghosts swarmed through it, although it had sprung, initially, out of O'Neill's Roman readings. Edgar Saltus saw "Imperial Purple" as a symbol of the bloody regimes of the Caesars and had pictured the first Caesar with face and arms painted vermillion in a toga of Tyrian purple and gold. O'Neill adopted a similar color scheme for Tiberius, dressing him in "deep purple, fringed and ornamented with crimson and gold," and filling his palace with "crimson-purple" lights. He is surrounded by prostitutes in crimson, purple, and "blotched heliotrope." These male and female prostitutes were historical, and were there—so Suetonius said—for the practice of "abominable lewdness." O'Neill saw in this brothel-like palace the first brothel of his own life, where his ideals of romance had been shattered. Oddly enough, its "crimson-purple" decor found its way back into the parlor of the prostitute mother in *The Great God Brown,* which he had left in the manuscript with a backdrop of "rare-colored flowers and fruits." After sketching Tiberius's palace in scenario, he changed it to "crimson and purple flowers and fruits." The prostitute mother from it had already found her way into the brothel-palace of Tiberius. She fuses the two major shocks to O'Neill's faith in love: his realization of his mother's addiction and his rape by the first prostitute. So the scene leading to Lazarus's entrance into the brothel-palace became dominated by that obstreperous phantom, his brother Jamie, who had brought both shocks upon him.

Jamie had not found a place in any of the major characters, so he forced his way into as many minor ones as he could. Even before Lazarus came to the palace, Jamie had materialized at Rome in the person of the First Senator. (Jamie was the firstborn O'Neill.) His presence is proclaimed by the Senator's cynicism, self-loathing, and longing for death. He alone of the senators bandies words with Caligula—the image of O'Neill's self-loathing—who tells him, "I heard you wish for death, Lucius. When I am Caesar you shall scream and pray for it!" The threat is fraught with memories of their father's cries and prayers for death, and of Jamie's own screaming in the D.T.'s, when he had been taken, "nuts complete"—as O'Neill had said—to the sanatorium. The First Senator is the only one given a persistently repeated name, "Lucius." Jamie—in a Roman toga—had played the role of "Lucius" in his father's production of *Virginius.*

Jamie pervades the scene before the brothel-palace, and he comes redolent of his destructive leadership in O'Neill's life. Even dying, he had been the leader, for O'Neill had taken up his suicidal drinking to the very brink of delirium and death. In the play, Jamie takes the shape of a crucified lion set up in front of Tiberius's palace (so Caligula tells Lazarus) as a "lesson" and "example for other lions—not to roar—or laugh—at Caesar!" Jamie had died in agony, "crucified," and O'Neill had reason to see him as a lion. He told his son Shane that he loved lions for their strength and beauty and that his brother, "your Uncle Jim," who died could make a sound just like a lion's roar, and for a joke he would go up to the lion's cage in the zoo when the lion slept and roar into his ear. When the lion woke up and began to roar too, Jim would walk away, "laughing to himself." O'Neill's brother Jim was the lion who went ahead of him into death, his roaring and laughing silenced forever. Lazarus goes up to the cross and "gently pushes the lion's hair out of its eyes." Jamie had been *"almost blind* from bad booze" when he died, and the gesture compassionately clears his vision. In actuality, O'Neill had only been able to exclaim helplessly, "What the hell can be done about him is more than I can figure. He'll only get drunk again, I guess, after he gets out [of the sanatorium] and then he'll be all blind." Lazarus expresses O'Neill's pity and remorse. "Poor brother!" he exclaims. "Forgive me your suffering!"

The rest of the scene acts out Jamie's destructive role. A character called Marcellus emerges from the palace in "a stream of reddish light" and passes "under the crucified lion without a glance," and the phantom of Jamie moves into him. In the autobiographical play *Long Day's Journey into Night,* O'Neill has Jamie confess that he has been a "rotten bad influence" and warn him to look out: "I'll be waiting to welcome you . . . and give you the glad hand, and at the first good chance I get stab you in the back." Marcellus welcomes Lazarus flatteringly, only to try to stab him in the back a moment later. With the knife raised, he is stopped by Lazarus's affectionately understanding laughter. In *Long Day's Journey into Night* Jamie concludes his confession with the words "Know you absolve me, don't you, Kid? You understand." In *Lazarus Laughed* absolution is given to Marcellus with an affectionate farewell, and also to Jamie on the cross, before whom Lazarus pauses and "raises his hand as if blessing the dead lion." Caligula then pushes Marcellus to suicide, saying, "Judge yourself!" So O'Neill worked out his guilt toward Jamie as well as his understanding forgiveness. He also linked Jamie's death to their father's faith in everlasting life. Lazarus joins the dying Marcellus in laughter to the chant of the Roman guards, "Death is dead!"

Within the palace, O'Neill reenacts his fear—as his father lay dying—that love itself was dying out of his life. Caligula's feeling for Tiberius expresses all the resentment O'Neill had ever felt toward his father for loss of love. Tiberius embodies the negative image of his father that joined his heroic ideal father after his exile to boarding school, and so Tiberius came to resemble his dying father. In the scenario, O'Neill made him "79," but in the play he took the age of James O'Neill at death, "76." Caligula's impatience for Tiberius to die caricatures O'Neill's during the days he waited for death to take his father. His most hideous recollections of them came out in Caligula. "I kept listening to the beating of his heart," Caligula tells Lazarus. "It sounded slow, slower than when I last heard it. Did you detect that, Lazarus? Once or twice I thought it faltered—." O'Neill had found out at once, "it is only Papa's *marvelously strong heart* that is keeping him alive." The doctors kept telling him, "It's practically a miracle the way his heart holds out." O'Neill reported to Agnes, "All those 'in the know' at the hospital expect him to depart every night—morning, rather—between two and five, the hours of least resistance. Every morning they seem astonished to find him still alive." Like Caligula he had listened for the faltering of that heart. The terrible reality of his father's loss of speech—which the entire play is designed to negate—emerges through Caligula. He says of Tiberius: "His words are a thick babble I could not hear. They well from his lips like clots of blood from a reopened wound." The push of O'Neill's memory here almost broke up the play logic, for the comment comes after a long, clear account by Tiberius of his life story. Caligula also gives vent to the most horrible hospital memory of all. O'Neill told Agnes on the first day, "Internal decomposition has set in—while he is still living! There is a horrible, nauseating smell in the room, the sickening, overpowering odor of a dead thing." After Tiberius exits, Caligula gloats over what is really O'Neill's own liberation from it when his father died: "He is gone! I can breathe! His breath in the same air suffocates me."

The palace became impregnated with his father's last bitter words on the world: "This sort of life—froth!—rotten! All of it—no good!" That judgment joined with the ambiguity of his first brothel experience to create the people surrounding Tiberius. Suetonius had said that the palace was filled with "companies of girls and catamites." O'Neill accentuated their ambiguity by turning them into a "train of Lesbians and pederasts" like those Saltus had described following Nero. All the females wear wigs in "short boyish mode" and male robes and speak in "harsh, strident, mannish" voices. All the males wear curly wigs of frizzed female hair and "women's robes" adorned with "anklets and bracelets and necklaces," and speak in "affected, lisping, effeminate" voices. Everything female is male and everything male is female, and within these rotten precincts love is killed by lust. O'Neill had been haunted for years by Oscar Wilde's poem "The Harlot's House," in which "Love passed into the

house of lust" and died. Jamie quotes it apropos of his visit to the proxy prostitute in *Long Day's Journey into Night*. The central episode in the brothel-
palace is the murder of love (embodied in Lazarus's wife, Miriam) by lust (embodied in Tiberius's favorite mistress, Pompeia). The murder also reenacts the
killing of the pure mother with the drug by the prostitute mother. Although a
mask of "perverted passion" covers Pompeia's face, beneath it her "gentle,
girlish mouth" can be seen "set in an expression of agonized self-loathing." She
has the "tender" and youthful mouth of Miriam, which is really that of O'Neill's
convent girl mother, and it is set in "self-contempt" at her addiction as in *Long
Day's Journey into Night*.

Roman history offered O'Neill a perfect parallel for morphine. Tiberius had
been suspected of getting rid of his enemies by poisoned fruit. O'Neill had
Pompeia force one upon Miriam. "Poison" was his father's word for morphine.
He uses it repeatedly in *Long Day's Journey into Night:* ". . . that's the way the
poison acts on her always"; "Up to take more of that God-damned poison. . . ."
In the play, poison kills the pure mother, leaving only the prostitute mother.
O'Neill even put in his guilty feeling that he had caused his mother's addiction
by being born. Caligula—the image of his self-loathing—eggs on the poisoning
and ends by pounding his head against the steps to the dais on which the pure
mother died, "laughing with grief and remorse."

Miriam also became invested with O'Neill's obsessive recollection of his
mother laid out in the funeral parlor, the memory that had forced its way into
the image of the dead Princess in *Marco Millions*. Miriam, having rushed into
old age, and Lazarus, having rushed into youth, have reached the ages of
O'Neill and his mother when she died. She is laid out in semidarkness with a
single lamp shining on "the white mask of her face," while Lazarus sits beside
her "like a young son who keeps watch by the body of his mother." O'Neill
could not resist getting from her once again the reassurance that he had made
the dead Princess give in unearthly laughter and the words "Now I am love,
and live." Lazarus begs Miriam, "Call back to me! Laugh!" He repeats O'Neill's
desolation in the funeral parlor, weeping and confessing, "I am lonely!" Miriam
responds by rising from the dead to announce, with "unearthly sweetness,"
"There is only life!" Although Lazarus should know this from his own death, he
needs—as O'Neill so desperately needed—her message in order to break into
laughter of a "terrible, unbearable power and beauty" that can beat down Caligula's laughter of "grief and remorse," Pompeia's of "horror and self-loathing," and Tiberius's of "the agony and terror of death."

O'Neill needed his mother to confirm his father's faith in eternal love. His
own faith in love was crumbling with his marriage. Everything in this play or

omitted from it proclaims dissolution. The romantic girl is gone from it, even in *The Great God Brown* she had brought only pain, and she vanishes altogether from *Lazarus Laughed*. The eternal girl in Miriam can barely be discerned under her mask of sorrow, and she is quickly lost in white-haired age. Miriam becomes only a mother—even to her husband Lazarus. Her only sexual meaning lives in the prostitute who survives her, and O'Neill charged that image of his early disillusion with all his current distrust of Agnes. According to the play logic, Pompeia poisons Miriam out of lust for Lazarus and resentment because he loves only humankind. She pours out her frustration very much as Agnes did. Agnes left a fragment of a story with the characters "Almado" and "Eugenia" as thin disguises for "Agnes" and "Eugene," expressing her resentment. In it, she says that Almado expects of his wife the same loyalty now when he gives her little tenderness, less sex, and takes everything for granted, as when he expressed his love tenderly and frequently. Her resentment had sharpened after the birth of Oona, when O'Neill took a separate bedroom so he could start writing directly on awakening in the morning. Pompeia attacks Lazarus as a writer, a maker of phrases: "Did you think I would . . . give you love and passion and beauty in exchange for phrases about man and gods—you who are neither a man nor a god but a dead thing without desire!"

The final scenes—dominated by the prostitute—are full of yearning for a lost romantic ideal. Caligula confesses that he is sick, "sick of cruelty and lust and human flesh and all the imbecilities of pleasure." Tiberius confesses that he wants "youth again because I loathe lust and long for purity." O'Neill endows Tiberius with his own longing for a lost faith—lost first in his mother and last in his beautiful wife Agnes when she vanished into the cruel whore of their quarrels. His Tiberius has been forced to divorce his first pure love, Agrippina, by his heartless mother so that he can marry the "whore" Julia as a step to becoming Caesar. Tiberius's disillusion in love comes from his mother, even as O'Neill's own, so that he longs for youth to "play again about her feet with the love I felt for her before I learned to read her eyes." O'Neill had read his mother's addiction in her eyes. "Take a look at your eyes in the mirror!" he had Jamie exclaim to her in *Long Day's Journey into Night*.

With romantic love—the core of his marriage—lost, O'Neill felt a horror of lust. The last vital link between him and Agnes was desire, and it accentuated the agony of their quarrels. When he finally left her, he said, "You've tortured your last torture." Lazarus dies by torture brought upon him by the frustrated whore Pompeia. His torture combines O'Neill's suffering in his marriage with the "incredible tortures" of his dying father. Even as O'Neill struggled to affirm his father's faith in love, he sensed obscurely inside himself that his love for

Agnes was already doomed. The life-hatred, fear, and horror he had been combating throughout the play were his own. His own romantic love had died, and left him terribly vulnerable to all the ambiguities of sex and to the old lure of death.

They welled into the play's mysticism. The laughter itself—meant to be expressive of the creative push toward endless renewal—took on inevitable sexual overtones. As a result, whenever it broke out between "brothers" it became fraught with ambiguity, and crowds of evangelical brothers pervade this play about the oneness of all things. The language of sexual love pushed its way into and clouded the mystical references to brothers and fathers. Lazarus, looking back at "My Brother," who has just resurrected him, begins "to laugh softly like a man in love with God." Marcellus (pervaded by Jamie) gives up his backstabbing and "smiles back at Lazarus—the curious, sheepish, bashful smile of one who has fallen in love and been discovered." The mass death of the followers reported by the laughing male legions to Lazarus becomes fraught with the reversal of roles when the first prostitute assaulted him, and with orgiastic overtones. Crassus says, "They charged upon us, laughing! They tore our swords away from us, laughing, and we laughed with them! They stabbed themselves, dancing as though it were a festival! They died, laughing, in one another's arms!" The words are accentuated by "terrific flashes of lightning and crashes of thunder" like "a responsive accompaniment from the heavens."

Along with these ambiguities, suicidal yearnings wove their way into the entire play logic. He felt that love was in the grave with his father, and showed it by making all the living people in his play "dead," so that the only one truly alive is the corpse Lazarus. The only way that the followers, or Marcellus, or Miriam, or ultimately Tiberius, can affirm life is by dying. The pull of the play takes up Lazarus and rushes him back through the years of growing up, so that in the final moments he passes through boyhood, infancy, and a return through the womb to rejoin the love out of which he had been created.

Yet O'Neill managed to channel both the ambiguity and the pull out of life into his mystical affirmation. He was able to resolve both affirmatively in his play—and indeed, in his life. Had the life-hatred, ambiguity, and disillusionment with women in the play been all-powerful, he would have been left with no alternative but suicide when his marriage finally went to pieces. Everything he did in the months after finishing this play shows that he had found through it the answer to the death of love in his marriage. Although his brain was still powerfully set on a faithful love for Agnes, the rest of him instinctively took the logical way out of his impasse. In the summer he became powerfully attracted—for the first time in his faithful marriage—to another woman, Carlotta

Monterey, and that fall when Agnes left him alone in New York he felt shot into the sky by the realization that it was love. When he went back to Bermuda he talked it over with Agnes, and then tried desperately hard to fight down his new love and preserve his marriage. He went on struggling for a full year, until the accentuated distrust of Agnes and their fierce bickering finally convinced all of him of what part of him had already known, and he asked Agnes to divorce him so that he could carry out his father's faith in a new romantic love.

The way he would choose had already been forecast in the resolution he found for his play. The final scene shows Lazarus being burned at the stake after his torture before an immense amphitheater of spectators all asking the question that O'Neill had been asking himself throughout the writing of the play:

> Is there hope of love
> For us on earth?

O'Neill found the answer for himself and for his play where all the images of infantile felicity had always led him. He refused to rest content with the prostitute mother—the image of his disillusionment with women. So he transformed Pompeia. First he changed her lust into love, and then he purified her love of selfishness, so that by the time Lazarus burns she has become the pure woman-mother—and not the old one who died in Miriam. Lazarus's voice has already taken on the "fresh, clear quality of boyhood," and in her ears, it goes further back to infancy. "I hear him crying to me!" she says, and then, "I must go to him." So she throws herself into the fire to unite with him in laughter and "flaming toward the stars." Reunion with the mother leads to the love of God the Father. The pure mother came into Pompeia several months before O'Neill found Carlotta Monterey that summer in Maine. Once he had, she became one with that ideal. He talked of having her act the role of Pompeia well before he thought of asking her to become his wife. Carlotta resolved all ambiguities in renewed romantic love. To her he inscribed a typescript of *Lazarus Laughed* with the very words that Lazarus had addressed to God the Father: "I am your laughter—and you are mine!"

The pull of death was also dissolved in the final mystical solution of his play. Lazarus joins God the Father to become one with eternal life and love. O'Neill had already tried to join his father by creating Lazarus, who takes up his message of faith and delivers it with "surpassing clearness." Yet he felt shaky in that union and that faith. (All the uncertainties in the characterization of Lazarus show it.) O'Neill wanted to become entirely one with his father's faith. A canceled passage put that purpose explicitly. Miriam says in it, "Lazarus—my husband—died—and is gone from me. Thou art—my son reborn from earth!" Lazarus whispers, "Sssshh!" and adds, "I shall always need you, Woman!" Through the woman, the father is reborn in the son. O'Neill would say it all again in his next play (*Strange Interlude*), where his "Woman" declares, "Sons are always their fathers. They pass through the mother to become their father again."

The final moments of *Lazarus Laughed* underline that idea. The image of fear—Caligula—resolves the play in a double murder of faith. He falls upon and strangles Tiberius—the negative father image—at the very moment that Tiberius is ready to join Lazarus in laughter and dying. The he spears Lazarus so that both images of the father die together. The last moments of the play show Caligula—the crazed epitome of fear—prancing about as Caesar, only to fall abjectly groveling and imploring Lazarus to save him from fear. The responsive laughter of Lazarus then "rises and is lost in the sky like the flight of his soul back into the womb of infinity." Caligula acts out his yearning for a union with faith—laughter—the father. He reaches up to the laughter like a child wanting to be picked up, "on tip-toes, his arms straining upward to the sky, a tender, childish laughter of love on his lips." So O'Neill achieved oneness with his father's faith in love and life and triumphed over the groveling image of his fear.

O'Neill had done a hasty first draft of *Lazarus Laughed* in October and November of 1925, but his real writing began on March 6, 1926. He finished by May 11, except for separating Lazarus's speeches from the play to make sure of a "progression of his ideas from scene to scene." On June 10 he wrote in his *Work Diary*, "done." It was "fine stuff," he thought, but "no one will ever produce it." That summer at Belgrade Lake in Maine he broke a long silence between himself and David Karsner to say, "There can be no such thing as an Ivory Tower for a playwright. He either lives in the theater of his time or he never lives at all." He was determined to give *Lazarus* life. He thought first of his own theater with Kenneth Macgowan. (Jones, disillusioned, had opted out.) To strengthen their finances, Macgowan had amalgamated with the "Actors' Theater." O'Neill thought that they had simply allowed themselves to be "swallowed up by a vastly inferior, quite brainless organization." He hoped that—for *Lazarus Laughed*—they might ditch the "Actors combine" and do the play creatively with the old crowd and Jimmy Light directing—if they could ever find the money. Richard Skinner, the *Commonweal* critic, suggested Catholic support for it. Macgowan tried to get it, failed, and began thinking of the Protestants. "The decision of the Catholics, I knew all along, having once been one myself," O'Neill told him. He thought Skinner was either a "dull boy" or not much of a Catholic if he did not realize that the play denied Catholicism's basic dogmas. The same would be true of the Protestants. The mysticism of *Lazarus Laughed,* he knew, was strictly nonsectarian. "And to the members of a sect that's more anathema than even the doctrine of a rival creed."

In rapid order, he tried Arthur Hopkins—who said that he was "impressed—but didn't 'get' it"; the Theatre Guild, which dropped it like a hot potato; the Jewish Art Theatre, which was afraid "it would offend their Orthodox audiences"; and Horace Liveright, the publisher, who (O'Neill correctly suspected) was "only talking big." For a while Max Reinhardt spoke of joining O'Neill and Macgowan for a New York production if they could work out an arrangement with Morris Gest, to whom he was under contract. He also thought he might do it later independently in Germany. Nothing came of it. Then the great Russian director Dantchenko, touring the United States with the Moscow Art Theatre, became enthusiastic about it even before he had a copy in Russian to read, and talked of doing it as soon as he finished his Hollywood film contract. He might, he said, even do a film of it. So Eleanor Fitzgerald sent off a copy to be translated into Russian by her old friend the anarchist leader Alexander Berkman, who had been living in St. Cloud, France, after his political deportation from the United States. O'Neill had met Berkman years ago at Romany Marie's restaurant, and Berkman wrote that he was sure he remembered O'Neill better than O'Neill remembered him. "You have become famous since, and I more infamous than ever before." O'Neill answered from the heart: "As for my fame (God help us!), and your infame, I would be willing to exchange a good deal of mine for a bit of yours. It is not so hard to write what one feels as truth. It is damned hard to live it." When Dantchenko left the United States for the Soviet Union he had Berkman's Russian translation with him, but he never produced it there. Years later he confessed that it had been found "too mystical." In the end only one brief twenty-eight-day production came to *Lazarus Laughed* by a subsidized amateur group in Pasadena at the California Community Playhouse in April 1928, with Irving Pichel as Lazarus. Reviewers found it "effective, tense, terrible," but no commercial producer dared to risk the money it took.

On November 11, 1927, O'Neill allowed the book of *Lazarus Laughed* to appear to fine reviews and an enthusiastic reading public. He had given it the subtitle "A Play for an Imaginative Theatre." He meant by that, he said, the old, true theater, the theater "of the Greeks and Elizabethans" which "could dare to boast—without committing a farcical sacrilege"—of being a legitimate descendant of the first theater that sprang out of the worship of Dionysus. It would be "a theatre returned to its highest and sole significant function as a Temple" for the celebration of Life. O'Neill had copied Samuel Angus's definition of a mystery religion as "a *divine drama*" showing "the travail of nature in which life ultimately triumphs over death, and joy is born out of pain." In *Lazarus Laughed* he had created just such a divine drama. As for his "Imaginative Theatre," O'Neill was clear that it did not exist in his times. It would have to be a genuinely creative theater in which imaginative directors, scene designers, lighting specialists, and actors would work together to make his play "live as Life." O'Neill knew that this play represented the "best writing I've done for the theater." It was really a score for production, "a producer's play." The laughter needed to be directed as music. Shelley's "Ode to a Skylark" had been echoing in his mind as he wrote. He saw the Laughter of Lazarus as "a great bird song triumphing in depths of sky," rising "like a lark from a field." It ran through every modulation of human happiness. Only a great voice could perform it. When O'Neill lost hope of Chaliapin, he began to think of Paul Robeson. He told Agnes, "It's a good hunch." Robeson could make up as a white, just as whites made up to play blacks. O'Neill thought Robeson was the only actor who could "do the laughter," and that was of first importance. But the money was never raised in Robeson's time.

With the years, O'Neill lost hope of finding a great enough voice or voices, and he decided that the laughter would have to be aided by an instrumental composition that would seem as if it "sprang from their laughter, went along with it, dominated it, and finally became pure music." With the years, he also lost hope of a Great Imaginative Theatre. He was ready to sacrifice all his pageantry in *Lazarus Laughed* and do a "condensed version with masks omitted," with lighting down to a spotlight, and with "crowds done by off-stage choral effect." But even that was never done. In the desperate search for untouched O'Neill after his death, Broadway was ready to do anything, even a shapeless first draft (*More Stately Mansions*) that O'Neill had ordered destroyed. But no one thought of *Lazarus Laughed*.

5

Strange Interlude

The idea for a "woman play" came to O'Neill in April 1923 just after he finished *Welded,* in which he treated the religion of love that had inspired his marriage to Agnes. Woman was the central mystery of that religion, and he hoped to reveal her significance by taking one who had lost her ideals and needed to find her place in life. His plot came that summer in Provincetown when "an aviator, formerly of the Lafayette Escadrille" told him the story of a girl "whose aviator fiancé had been shot down just before the armistice." She had become "neurotic and desperate," had "started drinking and having promiscuous sex affairs," and finally had married without love, hoping that motherhood would bring her "a measure of contentment in life." It was hardly a plot for a play, but O'Neill saw in it a chance to realize an old ambition. He could wed "the theme for a novel to the play form in a way that would still leave the play master of the house." So he planned a psychological "novel-play" dealing with "the outer and inner life of a woman from the age of young womanhood until forty-five."

It became ripe for writing at the same time as *Lazarus Laughed.* O'Neill wrote the scenarios for both in September 1925 and began *Strange Interlude* even before he had completed *Lazarus Laughed.* Both came out of the misery in his marriage. *Lazarus Laughed* overcame it by taking up his father's faith in an eternity of love. *Strange Interlude* released the doubt he had suffocated to achieve that triumph. It allowed him to enter into his mother and her disillusioning secret—which had set off his doubt in the first place—and try to reach truth from there.

His childhood faith had rested on a lie, on ignorance of the threatening secret within the seeming safety of his family. His family life with Agnes also hid a secret, that of their increasingly terrible quarrels. In his "woman play" he wanted to break through the surface lie, face the reality, and strive to reach a higher truth out of it. He decided, at first, to bring a novelist into his novel-play, to reveal realities by speaking his thoughts out loud in a new use of the old "soliloquy" and "aside." Then he realized that he could have all his characters think their thoughts out loud. Excitedly he noted, "Method: start with soliloquy—perhaps have the whole play nothing but a thinking aloud (or this extreme for other play)—anyway the thinking aloud being more important than the actual talking—speech breaking through thought as a random process of concealment, speech inconsequential or else imperfectly expressing the thought behind—." Thinking aloud could puncture the surface lies of life continually and express, as no other method could, a "special type of modern neurotic, disintegrated soul" prevalent among upper-middle-class Americans.

His woman would be surrounded by conventional men who live by lies. The novelist in his novel-play would write in the genteel manner of Henry James and, like James, would fly the realities of his America in the guise of an Anglicized gentleman. A steady ironic disparity would appear between the world of his novels, in which he is "a hush-hush whisperer of lies," and the realities he is forced to look upon in the play. Another "fugitive from reality" would appear in the woman's father, a professor who has withdrawn into the culture of the past and who hides his fear of life behind the "complacent, superior manner of the classroom." The woman would marry a man who has been nurtured—as O'Neill himself had been—on a long lie about his family, only he would never discover the lie. He would make his fortune by selling lies—in advertising—and die a typical 1920s "success," his whole life founded on lies. The woman's lover, after her loveless marriage, would be a different kind of fugitive from reality, a young scientist hiding from his own emotions and ignoring the unknowns by absolute belief in current scientific theories and surface facts. The woman herself would say of him, "Did you ever know a young scientist, Charlie? He believes if you pick a lie to pieces, the pieces are the truth!" Through these fugitives, O'Neill could release all his doubt in a steady puncturing of the lies people live by.

The woman herself, at her most despairing, was to be most conscious of the lie. She tells the novelist: "Say lie—(*She says it, drawing it out*) L-i-i-e! Now say life. L-i-i-f-e! You see! Life is just a long drawn out lie with a sniffling sigh at the end!" She is a fulcrum for doubt in the play, yet also an Everywoman experiencing all the fulfillment and loss that woman is heir to. In appearance, she fuses O'Neill's two great loves. (They had once before joined in the heroine of *Welded.*) Nina Leeds has the magnificent athletic body of O'Neill's lost love Beatrice Ashe joined to his wife Agnes's face, which is "striking, handsome rather than pretty, the bone structure prominent, the forehead high, the lips of her rather large mouth clearly modelled above the firm jaw. Her eyes are beautiful and bewildering, extraordinarily large and a deep greenish blue." So were Agnes's eyes and, like Agnes, Nina is blonde. Her last name, "Leeds," recalls the fact that Agnes was born in England, and her first name, "Nina," recalls Nina Jones—a beautiful and intellectual girl from a socially elite family (as Nina was to be) whose friendship for O'Neill spanned both his great loves, Beatrice and Agnes. (His memory of meeting Nina Jones on boat day of 1915 in New London and watching the races with her and her mother probably worked to place act eight of *Strange Interlude* at a boat race.) This much of his woman came from outside him. Her torn spirit, her searching, the whole of her struggle for meaning came from O'Neill himself. Through her he became one with his mother's tragic secret and with all the doubt and disillusionment created in him by it.

FIRST PART

Act one picks up Nina Leeds almost a year after her bereavement, at the point when she breaks away from her father, forcing him to confess that he has secretly put her fiancé, Gordon Shaw, on his honor not to marry her until after the war, in the hope that Gordon would be killed. She is hectically determined to make up for her failure to consummate her love. These details came from two of O'Neill's memories, both saturated with regret. First he recalled the frustration of his long, futile engagement to Beatrice Ashe. At the time (1914–15), he had been studying play-writing with Professor Baker at Harvard and had been thrilled one evening when the Professor invited him for a long talk in the study of his home on Brattle Street. It was an unheard-of honor, and—so O'Neill had told Beatrice—his hopes for the future had soared in that book-lined sanctuary before an open log fire. O'Neill set three acts of *Strange Interlude* in just such a study and gave his Nina memories of sitting with her professor-father before a similar fire, her "dreams like sparks soaring up to die in the cold dark" as his own hopes of Beatrice had ultimately died. Along with Professor Baker, O'Neill put into her father earlier memories of the provincial snobbery and prim conventionality of the Princeton professors he had fled after his freshman year (1906–7), because he had felt—so he said—"instinctively, that we were not in touch with life or on the trail of the real things."

At Harvard, O'Neill had been in the same position as Nina's fiancé, a promising student, but without the position and money to marry. O'Neill had to wait, and his frustration exploded just before Christmas of 1914 when his father failed to send him the money for his train fare to New London and Beatrice. He told her that he was so "peeved" he was ready to bite cement. He waited on "pins and needles," and even though it finally came he expected no good from his father from then on. As soon as he learned that the tour of *Joseph and His Brethren* was closing, he was sure that his father would come back in "abominable humor" and take it out on him. He knew that together they would have gotten along like a "cage full of wounded wild-cats." All the frustration of being kept on tenterhooks by Beatrice came to be attributed to his father— who had first exiled him from love by sending him to boarding school long ago. He resented his father because his love for Beatrice remained unconsummated, and so it was that act one of *Strange Interlude* took shape as a battle between Nina and her father in which she forces him to confess his guilt in her frustration.

O'Neill's frustration had been absolute, for he had given up all sex to remain pure for Beatrice. He had been the "honorable code-bound Gordon" who kept telling himself, as Nina recalls, "No, you mustn't, you must respect her." His desire for Beatrice had become agony the night before he had to leave her at the end of the Christmas recess to go back to Cambridge. Afterward he recalled how they had been upon "the rack" in each other's arms. He was proud of his "self-overcoming," but he felt "loneliness unutterable." Out of that memory came Nina's anguished recollection of the night before Gordon left for the front—"in his arms until my body ached—kisses until my lips were numb"— and her desolate loneliness afterward. Nina's despair at remaining "Gordon's silly virgin" was his own, and her regret was his, then and always, that his great love for Beatrice never was consummated.

To that poignant loss he joined another that gave him both Nina's grief and her father's remorse. The grief, he had seen in Susan Glaspell when her husband George Cram Cook—"Jig," who had started their Provincetown Playhouse—died suddenly in Greece in January 1924. Susan had become sick with sorrow. Even six months afterward—so O'Neill told Kenneth Macgowan—"Susan is in bad shape physically, from what I hear, and still plunged in grief."

Remembering her, he had Nina become "very ill," even "perilously so," from her grief at Gordon's death. As a writer Susan had tried to master her grief by creating a book about Jig, and at first had asked O'Neill to contribute to it. Then she decided to make it a biography and began to write *The Road to the Temple*. In act four, O'Neill had Nina follow Susan, even though she is no writer, with an adoring biography of Gordon Shaw, and had the novelist Marsden help her.

Jig's death had filled O'Neill with remorse. The night before Jig had sailed for Greece, both he and O'Neill had been drunk and had quarreled bitterly. Railing at the mess their theater was in, O'Neill must have said very much what he later told Eleanor Fitzgerald. It was, he said, "all Jig's fault." He had driven their most talented people away because they dared to disagree with him, and then "beat it to Greece leaving a hollow shell as a monument to his egotism." They needed "new blood," lots of it, for their theater, but Jig would see it as an attempt to ruin him "by taking *his* theatre out of *his* hands." Certainly O'Neill did not want Jig to come back and take control again. So it seemed his own wish had become hideously true when Jig died, and he was overcome with guilt. He wrote, "As for Jig—when I heard of his death, Susan, I felt suddenly that I had lost one of the best friends I had ever had or ever would have—unselfish, rare and truly noble!" And when he thought of never having said so to Jig, and of the other things "I said and wished unsaid, I felt like a swine, Susan. Whenever I think of him it is with the most self-condemning remorse. It made me afraid to face you in New York." He put these feelings into the Professor's more clear-cut guilt before his daughter's unspoken accusation, as well as into his remorseful thought, "And it's true, you contemptible . . . !"

All of O'Neill's affection for Jig came flooding back with his death. They had both loved ancient Greek tragedy. Jig had read Greek, and he had wanted to immerse himself in it when he fled to Delphi. Only two years after Jig's death O'Neill began to study ancient Greek. He told Manuel Komroff that he hoped in a few years to be able to enjoy the tragedies in their original Greek, and if he could, he would "have made a grand refuge for my soul to dive deeply and cooly into at moments when modern life—and drama—become too damn humid and shallow to be borne." So—for himself and Jig—when he began writing *Strange Interlude* he changed Nina's father from a professor of psychology into a classics professor, and gave him the same refuge he and Jig had sought in the culture of the past. Out of Jig and Susan and himself he created both the love-bereaved daughter and the guilty father in act one.

Nina's determination to break with home and learn to give herself came out of O'Neill's youthful idealism in loving Beatrice. One of his last letters begged

Beatrice to join him in a marriage of two struggling artists. To find her own soul, he told her, she must free herself from home and parents; she must throw overboard her "moral excess baggage"; she must surrender herself to life and not count the cost. Beatrice had not taken his advice, but a year later Agnes came into his life, and she had already surrendered herself to life most recklessly. Agnes's past was always a thorn in their marriage, an incitement to "mistrust." So O'Neill had come to see the dangers in that early idealism of his, and he used it to motivate Nina's disastrous fling into promiscuity. The wreck of his idealism went into the shattering of hers.

O'Neill began his novel-play with a soliloquy by the novelist Charlie Marsden. He designed this character's psychology as a reexamination of Dr. Gilbert Van Tassell Hamilton's diagnosis. Dr. Hamilton had briefly analyzed O'Neill to help him overcome his alcoholism, and he had told O'Neill that he suffered from an Oedipus complex. O'Neill tried out the Oedipus complex on Charlie Marsden. Marsden begins by recalling two of O'Neill's crucial memories: his introduction to sex and his father's death. O'Neill's changes to adapt them for Marsden show how different his history would have been had he really had an Oedipus complex. Marsden loses his father in adolescence, the period when O'Neill's own most traumatic experience had been his loss of faith in his mother. He had Marsden feel only alienation from his father rather than his own passionate identification with him. As for the brothel experience, Marsden is forced into it by two prep school companions rather than a heroic older brother, and so he reacts with shame, not pride. Instead of following it up with O'Neill's compulsive repetitions, Marsden is paralyzed from ever again engaging in sex. His love for Nina, therefore, has "its real maturity blocked." Under his surface fatherly friendship for her, he is perpetually torn between conflicting desire and terror.

As O'Neill began *Strange Interlude* he reacted violently against his affirmation of faith in *Lazarus Laughed*. Act one took shape as a deliberate negation of the triumph of Lazarus, as the reverse of Lazarus's arrival at eternal life and love by "flaming toward the stars." Nina's hero has been "brought down in flames" to become "ashes dissolving into mud! . . . mud and ashes!" Instead of exultant faith, there is only a cry of desperate loneliness from the bereaved Nina, which sounds ever louder in this act to climax in the cry of loneliness and fear of her father at the end: "I feel cold . . . alone! . . . this home is abandoned! . . . the house is empty and full of death!" The act ends with the Professor pulling a book at random from his shelves and reading "aloud sonorously like a child whistling to keep up his courage in the dark." The Latin he quotes comes from Manilius's *Astronomica*. It was one of the star-quotes O'Neill copied out of Samuel Angus's *The Mystery Religions and Christianity* to create his ecstatic vision of eternal life among the stars in *Lazarus Laughed.* Transferred to the frightened Professor, it becomes O'Neill's confession that he had also only been "whistling to keep up his courage in the dark."

O'Neill was so compelled by his statement of the finality of death in act one that he found he could not write act two unless he could carry it on. He had written two unsuccessful versions at the sanatorium where Nina has been promiscuous, and found his stride only when he brought her home at the death of her father, accompanied by Dr. Darrell and Sam Evans. She continues O'Neill's rejection of the star-visions of *Lazarus Laughed.* Instead of finding faith among the stars, Nina finds only doubt, as O'Neill himself was finding as he read astronomy in those days. She says, "I tried hard to pray to the modern science God. I thought of a million light years to a spiral nebula—one other universe among innumerable others. But how could that God care about our trifling misery of death-born-of-birth? I couldn't believe in Him, and I wouldn't if I could! I'd rather imitate His indifference and prove I had that one trait at least in common!" She denies Lazarus's God the Father who laughs, and she declares: "We should have imagined life as created in the birth-pain of God the Mother. Then we would understand why we, Her children, have inherited pain, for we would know that our life's rhythm beats from Her great heart, torn with the agony of love and birth. And we would feel that death meant a reunion with Her, a passing back into Her substance, blood of Her blood again, peace of Her peace!" Instead of God the Father and eternal life, there is God the Mother and the peace of death.

Act two deals with O'Neill's most lethal shock to love, his disillusioning brothel trauma and its repetitions. In the Oedipal Charlie Marsden it had blocked all sex. In Nina, O'Neill portrayed his own compulsive returns to it. She has "kept on, from one to one, like a stupid driven animal," even as had O'Neill, and she has reached a despair like his own. (His suicide attempt had been set off by his having to repeat the encounter with the brothel prostitute before witnesses in order to get a divorce from Kathleen.) With Nina he could look into the meaning of the original trauma through the eyes of a woman, and so take hold of the ambiguity in the experience—the level on which he was not his hero brother satisfying himself upon the prostitute, but a woman submitting to a rape by the hero. Through Nina he could arrive at a realization, detached from himself, of the presence of the hero in his first sexual partner and in all the subsequent repetitions. Nina says, "They were all the same. Count them all as one, and that one a ghost of nothing." All of them were merely proxies of the hero—and the hero himself, being dead, merely "a ghost of nothing." As

O'Neill wrote Nina's realization of the folly of her promiscuity, he saw the sanatorium in which it took place as a species of inverted brothel, a "house full of men." It was also the sanatorium in Paterson, New Jersey, where his brother had died, so that he really was seeing his hero brother introducing him this time to death, not sex. At any rate, he was clearly obsessed with Jamie's ultimate blindness as he wrote Nina's revelation. He had been haunted by it in *Lazarus Laughed*. One of his first ideas, later cut, was to have Lazarus appear after the resurrection with eyes bandaged to protect them from the hot lights of earth after his sojourn among the stars. The bandaged Lazarus had allowed O'Neill's blind brother to join his father in resurrection. The bandage in Nina's revelation does the opposite. She says, "I seemed to feel Gordon standing against a wall with eyes bandaged and these men were a firing squad whose eyes were also bandaged—and only I could see! No, I was the blindest! I would not see!" Her hero does not triumph over death; he submits to it, as do all the blinded proxies with him. Nina continues that she dreamed "of Gordon diving down out of the sky in flames and he looked at me with such sad burning eyes, and all my poor maimed men, too, seemed staring out of his eyes with a burning pain, and I woke up crying, my own eyes burning." The hero with blinded eyes again flames down to death, and all his proxies go with him. Nina, along with O'Neill, realizes in both cases that the hero, the proxies, and herself are all one—all blind. So the revelation by Nina of the folly of her promiscuity brought O'Neill to an understanding of his own. By seeing the hero in all the sexual partners, he exorcised him from them, and at the same time accepted for his hero and himself and everyone the finality of death.

Of course, O'Neill's woman play had to be pervaded by the shaping woman of his life, his mother, yet he found no place for her among the major characters of his first two acts. So she forced her way in by taking possession of an off-stage maid. By giving her that commonplace name so meaningful to himself, "Mary," O'Neill made his mother's name resound in the first two acts. It sounds in the first line of the play, as Marsden enters saying, "I'll wait in here, Mary." It is repeated, always in answer to the urgent question O'Neill was asking himself as he wrote: "What if there is only the mother—only death?" When Nina abandons the Professor to a house "full of death," she leaves him to Mary. "Mary will look after you," she says, and he echoes, "Mary will do very well, I'm sure." Frightened and alone, he repeats, "Mary will do very well by me." "Mary" resounds again six times at the beginning of act two—where it is repeated obsessively in the stage directions and enters the dialogue not with the old message of eternal life and love, as in *Marco Millions* and *Lazarus Laughed*, but with the assurance of death. "He's dead, Mary says," Nina echoes entering.

O'Neill had to have his mother invisibly present to bring himself to accept death for both life and love. In act two he—and Nina with him—accepts the fact of his father's death and the death of all love with him. Nina says, "Yes, he's dead—my father—whose passion created me—who began me—he is ended. There is only his end living—his death. It lives now to draw nearer me, to draw me nearer, to become my end!"

From the middle of act two on, the off-stage Mary disappears, and O'Neill's mother begins to pervade the action. The plot parallels her major tragedies, cleverly rearranged to fit the story. The great tragedy of his mother's life—and therefore of his father's, his brother's, and his own—had come of a fatal doctor's prescription: the prescription of morphine to which she became addicted. O'Neill made a doctor's prescription the fatal beginning of all the tragedies for the woman of his play and for the three men who love her. It is Dr. Darrell in act two who gives her the fatal prescription. He begins by confidently diagnosing the causes of Nina's sacrificial promiscuity—in what O'Neill made a deliberate echo of Dr. Hamilton's behaviorist talk of how one is "conditioned," seasoned with his Freudian jargon about "normal love objects," and even including one of Dr. Hamilton's favorite circumlocutions in speaking of sex, "spooning." ("Spooning!" Darrell thinks, ". . . rather a mild word for her affairs.") Dr. Darrell prescribes that she marry Sam Evans, "a fine healthy boy," whom she can mother and who will give her children to mother. Sam turns out to be a fatal prescription.

O'Neill had always seen himself as the guilty cause of his mother's addiction, for his birth had given her the pain that began it. He gave Sam Evans just such an innocent guilt, and gave the Evanses a family secret even more disastrous than his own. He deliberately shaped it from the popular scientific theories (surface lies) by which his characters live. In the 1920s, current belief saw heredity alone as the cause of insanity, and placed its hope in eugenic breeding. O'Neill used both beliefs in his plot, to show their fallacies. The secret of the Evans family is the madness that runs in it. O'Neill placed it in Sam's father, and had Sam's birth drive him into it, by making him anxious about its appearance in the boy. So Sam has brought tragedy to his mother—as, in a very different way, O'Neill had brought tragedy to his. O'Neill had Sam repeat his innocent guilt in Nina's case—for he, like O'Neill, has been sent away to boarding school to protect him from learning the secret.

O'Neill used the Evans family secret to give his woman a tragedy like his mother's when she lost her baby, Edmund, and felt herself guilty of killing him. O'Neill knew that his mother had been so shattered in health afterward that she had had to undergo a "series of brought-on abortions." He joined the tragedy of the baby with the later abortions to create for Nina a situation in which she is forced to kill the baby she loves by abortion. Nina's tragedy in act three comes from the revelation by Sam's mother of the family insanity, so that she agrees to abort the baby she loves for its own sake and that of its father. By centering the drama on the revelation of the secret, O'Neill could join his own tragedy, in learning of his mother's secret, to his mother's tragedies, to enter into woman's heritage of suffering in childbearing.

O'Neill took his atmosphere from recollections of late April 1921, when he had gone to Rochester for several weeks of difficult dentistry by his friend Saxe Commins. He had suffered much pain and much lonely longing for Agnes. The countryside, he told her, reminded him of the area around her house at West Point Pleasant, except that it was "more fertile" and had a look of "comfortable prosperity" with its "big orchards." He set the Evans farmhouse among those blossoming upstate orchards and gave the house all the horrible inner empti-ness he had then felt. He had written Agnes that, without her, "I have a poign-ant pain of emptiness inside as if I'd lost the vital spiritual organ without which the rest of the machine is a mere whirring of wheels and a futile noise." He felt the same spiritual emptiness as he was writing this act, having exorcised his old heroes with their assurance of eternal love, and it poured into Nina's intuitions about the Evans house. She says, "I feel it has lost its soul and grown resigned to doing without it. It isn't haunted by anything at all—and ghosts of some sort are the only normal life a house has—like our minds, you know." (At this point he was possessed again by the death of love when his father died in his suffo-cating hospital room, and he had her add, "I lay awake and found it difficult to breathe, as if all the life in the air had long since been exhausted in keeping the dying living a little longer.")

In the midst of O'Neill's Rochester dentistry, Saxe and his family had been suddenly plunged into grief by the death of his brother's child. That "terribly tragic" death of a child joined his mother's to shape this scene of sudden dis-aster and allowed O'Neill to become one with his woman and her unbelieving horror as the family secret is revealed and she is forced to lose her baby. Mem-ories of his mother's addiction also went into his picture of a mad Aunt Bessie hidden upstairs in that house of death. She resembles his later haunted image in the last act of *Long Day's Journey into Night,* of his mother wandering about somewhere upstairs "like a mad ghost" under the drug. O'Neill ended the act by uniting the two tragic mothers—Sam's mother with Nina at her feet—in woman's age-old heritage of pain in childbearing. The older woman accepts the younger as "daughter of my sorrow" and kisses her bowed head.

O'Neill was shaping his life as he shaped his play. Act one had come as a cry from the heart of loneliness. He was in the midst of his despairing act two when he met Carlotta Monterey in Maine on July 15, 1926, and felt magnetically drawn to her warmth and strength. (He had barely noticed her when first introduced at the time she took the role of Mildred for the uptown production of his play *The Hairy Ape* in April 1922.) He saw Carlotta five times more that summer, and that fall he turned to her when Agnes left him alone in New York to supervise rehearsals for a revival of *Beyond the Horizon*. Agnes thought that they could ease the tensions in their marriage by taking vacations from it (on fatal advice from her cynical society friends), and she returned to Bermuda, leaving him without even the support of letters. So he found himself totally abandoned at the point when he had reached the depths of despair with the first three acts of *Strange Interlude*. Carlotta was also lonely. She had been divorced from Ralph Barton in March of that year, and so that fall she joined O'Neill in lunches and dinners and concerts, and even in rehearsals of his play. On November 26, the day before he was to leave for Bermuda, she helped him shop at Macy's in the morning, and after the dress rehearsal of *Beyond the Horizon* he joined her again in her apartment. When he left at 2:30 in the morning he knew he was in love. All the way back to Bermuda he felt himself "shot into the sky" with "only my shadow moving down on the earth where there are houses and people who live in them." For nine years his life had rested on his love for Agnes. Blasted out of it, he felt himself blown about in the clouds "without a destination." He told Carlotta that for the whole trip he had kept to his cabin, taking "many strange journeys into diverse exquisite torture chambers of the soul." At home he confessed all to Agnes. He told Carlotta, "I have been quite frank here. There are some things I couldn't be about—even by silence." (He was living *Strange Interlude*, where speech can only express "imperfectly" or conceal the truth behind.) At this point, O'Neill began his final struggle to preserve what had been his religion, his love for Agnes. Afterward Agnes harked back furiously to that bitter time, urging him to remember how he had told her he wanted a divorce, to remember his hostile silences in the days that followed. Could she forget all that? Never! O'Neill was writing his own agonized attempts to cross the abysses of his shattered marriage into acts four and five of this play with their picture of the collapsing marriage of Nina and Sam after her abortion. As he took up these acts, he told his friend Kenneth Macgowan (who knew of Carlotta), "With all that's inside me now, I ought to be able to explode in that play in a regular blood-letting."

He expressed all his own alienation in the divided thoughts of his play husband and wife, as in Nina's wish that her spouse would "disappear . . . leave me free . . . if he'd die." His uncertainty and his miserable realization that he had failed to make Agnes happy went into Sam's desperate self-urging, "Go on and wake her up! . . . say you're willing to give her a divorce so she can marry some real guy who can give her what she ought to have!" When the divorce came O'Neill told Agnes, "You are still young and beautiful and, with any sort of even break from fate, you should have every chance for a real happiness before you—a happiness that it has become indubitably evident I never did and never can give you." All the appalling silences filled with tormenting thoughts poured into the soliloquies of Sam and Nina in acts four and five. He identified so completely with the anguished Sam, who is likely to be driven mad by losing his wife, that he told Agnes during one of their brief separations (she was in New York to see her sick father), "If I lost your love, I'd go mad with grief!" So in *Strange Interlude* the shaping of his life and the shaping of his play were inextricably intertwined. The pain of his marriage began bleeding into his play at this point and could only go on hemorrhaging into all the scenes to follow.

Of course, in acts four and five he aimed consciously at dramatizing life's push to renew itself through the woman except that he no longer saw her as the Earth Mother, the Cybele-Demeter of his old affirmations of life. Riddled by doubt and disillusion, he saw her in *Strange Interlude* very much in the way of Schopenhauer, as the chief instrument of a great mindless force sweeping individuals—deluded by the belief that they pursue their own happiness—into fulfilling the needs of the species. O'Neill had discovered Schopenhauer at the very time that he himself had been swept into his procreative involvement with Kathleen Jenkins. He would apologize, later, for his gloomy "Schopenhauer musings." Schopenhauer had been with him when he had Kubla Khan say, observing the acquisitive Polos, "My hideous suspicion is that God is only an infinite, insane energy which creates and destroys without other purpose than to pass eternity in avoiding thought." Such an insane energy sweeps Nina and Darrell in act four toward begetting a baby. Their pretense at scientific reasoning on begetting a healthy baby to save Sam's sanity is swept aside by the life drive within them, and their thoughts break into a crescendo of expectations of personal happiness, ending with Darrell's thought "I shall be happy for a while!" and Nina's "I shall be happy! . . . I shall make my husband happy!"

This push of life naturally brought with it the idea that had been obsessing O'Neill through his last plays, the myth of the endlessly reborn hero. It had come to him when he made his first note for *Strange Interlude* in the fall of 1923, for he called it first "Godfather," a pun on a father god, and a proxy father. Even after he abandoned this title, he kept the idea. But the hero came forth quite ambiguously in the actual writing, for he was being exorcised even as he was being summoned. In the play it is Nina who is bemused by the hero—

in the person of her aviator Gordon Shaw. In her biography she treats him "as if he had been a demi-god," and she sees him as the father of her aborted baby. She tells Darrell, "I loved it so it seemed at times that Gordon must be its real father, that Gordon must have come to me in a dream while I was lying asleep beside Sam!" Darrell responds, "Ha! . . . the hero again! . . . comes to her bed! . . . puts horns on poor Sam! . . . becomes the father of his child! . . . I'll be damned if hers isn't the most idiotic obsession I ever. . . . ." Yet Darrell himself has become a proxy for the hero, from the moment he enters and she takes his hands thinking, "Strong hands like Gordon's . . . take hold of you." By the end of the play even Darrell says, "I'm quite sure Gordon isn't my son, if the real deep core of the truth were known! I was only a body to you, your first Gordon used to come back to life."

O'Neill wanted to contrast the push of life in these acts with the pull of death. As Nina moves toward conception of her baby in act four, Marsden worries over his mother's dying, and in act five, Nina is pregnant and Marsden is in mourning. The death of Marsden's mother allowed O'Neill to continue his try-ing-on of the Oedipus complex. He could easily have used his mother's dying to fill out that of Marsden's mother had he really believed that she had been his most powerful attachment; instead, he used for her the loss that had ob-sessed him from the beginning of this play, the death of his father. Up to act four, Marsden's mother (who never appears) is merely a gossipy snob. Dying, she suddenly becomes invested with the attributes to O'Neill's father. In *Long Day's Journey into Night* James O'Neill has "never been really sick a day in his life." Marsden says twice that his mother has "never been sick a day in her life." After the custom of the elderly James O'Neill, who was always "the best walker of the lot," "she walked miles every day, she loved bathing and boating in the summer even after she was sixty." O'Neill gave her the "dull, constant pain" in her stomach that had first revealed his father's cancer of the intestines, and Marsden echoes his own anguish in the spring of 1920, when the doctors first diagnosed it. O'Neill had told Agnes, "I'm all broken up and begin to cry every time the meaning of it all dawns on me." He had responded to the specialist "Doctor Erdmann's verdict" that his father's heart was too weak for an opera-tion by saying, "It seems so damned awful that nothing can be done." After-ward, when his father's suffering had been prolonged by his strong heart, O'Neill had exclaimed, "And that fool in New York was afraid to operate on him months ago because he claimed his heart was *weak!* Isn't it all a ghastly joke? Who could ever trust a doctor's word after this revelation of their criminal ignorance?" In *Strange Interlude* Marsden "breaks down chokingly" at Dar-rell's verdict, "trembling all over" and crying miserably, "Damn it, you're condemning her without—!" The doctors he calls in are able to do "nothing for her—absolutely nothing!" And Marsden ends like O'Neill, exclaiming, "I think you doctors are a pack of God-damned ignorant liars and hypocrites." Once again O'Neill told himself that love—his father—had died.

So he reached darkest despair at the same point his woman reached fulfill-ment. Her mystical oneness with the life force renewing itself through her be-came jangled by the discord of his pain. Of course, technically, he saw *Strange Interlude* as a two-part, two-night play, and so the end of part one had to be spiced with enough unresolved conflict to lure an audience back for a second night. Actually, act five seethes with hatred. Darrell and Nina have overturned their scientific planning by falling in love, but the love is corroded by the cruelty of the triumphing woman and the resentment of the trapped man. Indeed, Darrell takes over O'Neill's feelings of entrapment when he had to marry Kath-leen Jenkins. All his own old wish to behave honorably, conflicting with fear and hatred, went into Darrell, who thinks, "Her body is a trap! . . . I'm caught in it!" Desire itself becomes horrible, with Nina luring Darrell like a prostitute, and Marsden shrinking in horror at the currents of desire he senses beneath the surface, thinking, "There's something in this room! . . . something disgust-ing! . . . like a brutal, hairy hand, raw and red, at my throat! . . . stench of human life!" The image comes out of O'Neill's memory of the time in his flight from Kathleen that he had reached blackest despair in Argentina sorting bloody rawhides in the midst of a stink he shuddered to recall. These memories cor-roded his attempt at a mystical vision of woman's fulfillment in pregnancy. He had Nina think, "I am living a dream within the great dream of the tide . . . breathing in the tide I dream and breathe back my dream into the tide . . . suspended in the movement of the tide, I feel life move in me, suspended in me . . . no whys matter . . . there is no why . . . I am a mother . . . God is a Mother." This sea imagery reflects his plan to write a series of autobiographical plays called "The Sea-Mother's Son" and shows that even at this point the idea was emerging stillborn. O'Neill had been exorcising all his old gods, and with God the Father dead any kind of God the Mother, including a Sea Mother, could only join Him. All Her peace had been overwhelmed in a tumult of negative emotion. Hatred runs through this act and reaches a climax when Darrell runs away from the pregnant Nina—even as O'Neill had once fled the pregnant Kathleen—to leave her murderously frantic. At the same time, in this act the cry of loneliness that had sounded from the beginning of the play reaches a scream of pain, for O'Neill found himself doubly bereft of love. His love for Agnes was hopelessly dead, and he had left Carlotta, telling her, "My soul is a black cell of loneliness and longing, longing for you, my love. . . . God has turned his back and slammed the door and gone away and all the prison is darkness." In act five his loneliness swelled out in Sam's suicidal panic, went into the bereaved Marsden's wail, "No longer any love for me in any room," and ended in the woman's anguished cry, "Oh, afternoons . . . dear wonderful afternoons of love with you, my lover . . . you are lost . . . gone from me forever!" By the end of part one, God the Father had gone from O'Neill's world, and love had gone with him.

SECOND PART

O'Neill meant part two to carry his woman from fulfillment through all the inevitable losses of age. Nina reaches peak possession in act six with her baby, her husband Sam, her proxy father Marsden, and her lover Ned Darrell, who comes back to her, defeated by desire. All her old idealism has been shattered, and she is inspired only by sheer possessiveness. She plots to possess lives while her husband Sam plots to possess money. While he schemes to get Marsden to invest in his advertising agency, knowing "he'd be an easy partner to handle," Nina schemes to hold Marsden's love, thinking triumphantly, "I can always twist him round my finger!" When Ned Darrell returns, totally subjugated by desire, Nina takes possession of him too, for now she will not divorce Sam. She answers Darrell's objection "How can you be so inhuman and calculating?" by retorting, "It was you who taught me the scientific approach, Doctor!" In the end Sam has lured Marsden and Darrell into becoming silent partners in his business, and Nina has lured them into becoming his silent partners in her love.

O'Neill put into this scene all his horror of the loveless life he was leading in the midst of his "success." Even as far back as the summer of 1924 he had confessed to his friend Kenneth Macgowan that he wished he had never gone in for "playwriting, mating and begetting sons, houses and lots." He was, he said, "homesick for homelessness." In the fall of 1926, when he left New York to rejoin Agnes in the huge house they were refurbishing in Bermuda, he wrote back to Carlotta that all the way there he had felt his old dead and drowned Hairy Ape soul—the soul of his anarchism—running under the keel of the ship, asking him mockingly what he had gained with his "money" and "house," his "wife and kids," his "security and ease." When the break came he would tell Agnes that "not until the 'possessive' stuff has died out in each of us" could they meet as friends. "The old destructive habits of thought and feeling have got to be erased from our reactions to one another." All his horror of his possessive marriage—of his success—went into his image in part two of a world without values. Marsden thinks of the acquisitive Sam: "Typical terrible child of the age . . . universal slogan, keep moving . . . moving where? . . . never mind that." He sees it in the newspaper, "in every headline of this daily newer testament . . . going . . . going . . . never mind the gone." And he, Marsden, feels that he is not even going; he has already reached "nowhere." At the heart of the web is the possessing woman—who is life, reproduction, eternal recurrence. She thinks, hysterically triumphant, "My three men! . . . I feel their desires converge in me! . . . to form one complete beautiful male desire which I absorb . . . and am whole . . . they dissolve in me, their life is my life . . . I am pregnant with the three! . . . husband! . . . lover! . . . father! . . . and the fourth man! . . . little man! . . . little Gordon!"

She joins the possessive Agnes to O'Neill's most negative recall of his mother with her three men—his father, his brother, and himself—and the fourth man, the "little man," her beloved dead baby. Nina's husband Sam, at this point, emerges from O'Neill's most negative image of himself joined to that of his father as sheer money-maker. Dr. Darrell—who like Jamie had been the brilliant and promising one—disintegrates as he hangs about, sharing the woman bitterly with her husband Sam, just as Jamie had wasted his promise, hanging about his mother year after year, bitterly sharing her love with his father. Darrell's bondage is that of both Jamie and O'Neill in the "prostitute" mother. Just how intimately Darrell emerged from family memories appears in his full first name as preserved in the list of characters (he is *Ned* in the dialogue), for it is "Edmund," giving him the name of O'Neill's dead baby brother. Through it Edmund Darrell mirrors the destruction of all three—the baby, Jamie, and O'Neill himself—in his bitterest recall of the family past.

The eleven years between acts six and seven complete the destruction. Darrell has tried to escape his trap, as Jamie had, through "drink and women," only "to come back each time more abject," more visibly dissipated. Like Jamie's, his eyes have become "embittered and they hide his inner self-resentment behind a pose of cynical indifference." He echoes Jamie's venomous tongue, speaking "with a nasty laugh—cuttingly" and ever "more mockingly." Into his bitter bondage O'Neill poured all his pain in the possessive woman of his present, Agnes. At the same time, he entered the woman too, as she asks herself, "Why did he give up his career? . . . because I had made him weak?" and as she tells herself, "No woman can make a man happy who has no purpose in life!" Those were O'Neill's thoughts about Agnes. One of the most painful aspects of their marriage had been her disintegration as a writer under the impact of his overwhelming success. Although he kept urging her "not to attempt easy things, or junk for money," she had done little else, and finally had degenerated altogether into apathy and idleness. The waste of Agnes's talent was as much in Darrell as the waste of Jamie's.

Indeed, all O'Neill's unhappiness with Agnes erupted into the unhappiness of Darrell and Nina. They have paid for "afternoons of happiness" with "years of pain." As he and Agnes in their quarrels, they have broken only to come together again. Either Nina has "gotten so lonely again living this lonely lie of my life" and called him back, or he has gotten "lonely" in his "lie" first. After the first joy of reunion, they have quickly reached—as he and Agnes did—the "ugly bitter stage" of reproach and recrimination. Agnes herself later that fall answered O'Neill's pleading for her to join him in New York by writing him furiously that he needed her and loved her at this point only because he was lonely and bored. If they came together, his love would turn into sheer annoyance with her inside of two weeks. So much of his own disintegrating marriage went into the tension between Nina and Darrell that his answer for them had to be his own answer too.

O'Neill also released his anxiety about the children caught up with him in unhappiness. It is little Gordon's eleventh birthday in act seven, and O'Neill used for it his memories of meeting his eleven-year-old son by Kathleen Jenkins for the first time. O'Neill had no money in 1912, and so they had divorced without alimony. Kathleen brought up their boy to believe that her second husband, George Pitt-Smith, was his real father. Only when she read newspaper articles on the success of *The Emperor Jones* did she realize that the ne'er-do-well she had divorced had become a famous playwright. Immediately she opened negotiations through her lawyer James Warren (of the divorce) for support of the boy. O'Neill agreed to pay his son's board and tuition at Horace Mann School in New York City, and in the fall of 1921 he met his son, restored to his real name, Eugene O'Neill, Jr. O'Neill's own sensations gave him Darrell's awkward agony before the boy brought up as another man's son. His own insight into the baffled sensations of the boy gave him the feelings of young Gordon. Gordon also takes from O'Neill's understanding of his other son Shane by Agnes. As the marriage foundered, Shane had become (so O'Neill later told Harold DePolo) "extremely—if secretly—sensitive to the undercurrents and he was worried by them, I know." All O'Neill's compassion for his sons and hurt for himself at the threatening dissolution of his home went into the tensions between Darrell and his son.

In part two the lies are becoming threadbare. Sam is not mad but "healthy as a pig," although "his great-grandfather, his grandmother, his father, were all insane." Darrell sees "the huge joke": "Sam is the only normal one! . . . we lunatics! . . . Nina and I! . . . have made a sane life for him out of our madness!" Darrell's prognostics for human life have turned out so badly that he has taken up the biology of one-celled animals in place of medicine. His old arrogant faith in current theories and surface facts has turned itself inside out and shown itself for what it really is—sheer irrationality. He comes in the end to believe, "Thinking doesn't matter a damn! Life is something in one cell that doesn't need to think!" Nina responds, "I know! God the Mother!" Marsden also sees the lie he has lived by and admits to himself, "I've been a timid Bachelor of Arts, not an artist! . . . my poor pleasant books! . . . all is well! . . . is this well, the three of us?"

With the breakup of the lies, O'Neill showed the beginning of the pull toward death in his characters. Nina longs to "rot away in peace!" Darrell says, "My life work is to rust—nicely and unobtrusively!" Marsden's hope of Nina has moved out of life. "I would be content," he thinks, "if our marriage should be purely the placing of our ashes in the same tomb . . . our urns side by side and touching one another." Nina feels that she is "only a mother," for "the wife and mistress in me has been killed," and yet even her grip on her son has begun to slip. In his "Diagram," O'Neill had broken off his love for his mother sharply at the point when he learned the secret of her addiction. His young Gordon begins to break away from his mother when he sees into her secret, her love for Darrell. O'Neill's own self-understanding gave him Darrell's analysis to Nina that Gordon feels "cheated of your love" so he concentrates "his affections on Sam whose love he knows is secure." So O'Neill had concentrated on his hero father when he lost his faith in his mother.

Act eight, ten years later, brings the woman to menopause. The end of her reproductive cycle ushers in a new cycle, for her son Gordon has reached the age of her lost Gordon and has found a Nina of his own, his fiancée Madeline. Nina struggles to hold onto him, just as her father had struggled to hold onto her, and she loses, just as he did. O'Neill wanted to express the "hazy quality" of the "passage of time" moving "past the leading characters who stand still, growing old," so he put them aboard Sam's anchored yacht, watching "in the soft golden haze of late afternoon sunlight" the race of life—literally a boat race in which the young hero Gordon strokes his way to glory. Nothing shows more clearly how drastically O'Neill had exorcised his own gods and heroes than his ambivalent image of the reborn hero Gordon. Young Gordon is heroic as a swimmer and oarsman, just as O'Neill had become in the image of his father and was encouraging his sons to become. He told Shane, for instance, that he wanted him to grow up big and strong so he could "row on the crew and be on the swimming team when you go to college." He also wanted Shane to be a top student like young Gordon and told him later: "Eugene is studying very hard at Yale now. He is eighth in a class of five hundred. That is awful good, don't you think? I know you will work as hard as he does when you go to college."

Yet his curdled image of Gordon's victory shows how negatively he felt toward the image of his own success, first as swimmer and boater, then as hardworking student (as he had been at Harvard in play-writing, not at Princeton). Gordon's victory parallels O'Neill's first big success, the opening of *Beyond the Horizon* on Broadway, which his father had watched from a box. O'Neill himself said of it, "Yes, it was the greatest satisfaction he knew that I had made good in a way dear to his own heart." Shortly after, his father had been felled by a stroke leading to his final illness and death. Gordon's "father" Sam watches, with apoplectic pride, his son make "good in a way dear to his own heart," and then he too is felled by a stroke. O'Neill shows all his self-loathing for the "fame" he would so gladly have exchanged for some of Alexander Berkman's "infame," by having Gordon triumph in a "bedlam" of noise—in a "perfect pandemonium" of sirens and whistles. The culmination of the noise, for O'Neill, had been the death of love—the death of his father. He had Marsden stand over the prone body of Sam and deliver an epitaph that seems almost a sardonic parody of his own epitaph on his father, who had been, he had told Agnes, "a *good* man, in the best sense of the word—and about the only one I have ever known." Marsden says, "A good man—yes, a good man!"

With Sam gone, O'Neill could resolve the long, unhappy love of Nina and Darrell, and he could not help finding the answer for his own love by finding the answer for theirs. Before the scenario of September 1925, when he was still calling the play "Godfather," he found an answer in his religion of romantic love. His two lovers were to break out of the long lie at last. Nina was to say, "This is our truth. We love." Darrell was to reply, "Truth is a secret. Sometimes by a miracle of grace, two people learn the one secret together—and keep it!" By the time he wrote the scenario, he found that resolution too easy for all those years of pain. He ended with Nina and Darrell left in the garden, "two people alone in a great silence under the sky, huddling each other for warmth and courage." Each confides a dream. Nina's dream is that she has flown to heaven with the hero Gordon—which is really O'Neill's old dream of eternal life and love with the hero—and Darrell's dream is that he has discovered "the secret of life to heal mankind of all fleshly ills"—which is the dream behind *Lazarus Laughed.* They were to end hoping, "Perhaps those dreams will begin to come true."

This was the resolution O'Neill clung to in real life—clung to with all the strength of desperation—long after he had rejected it for his play. Even on

April 16, 1927, he was telling Agnes (who was in New York to care for her sick father) that Spithead, their new Bermuda home, seemed to him their reward. He saw it as symbolic of his love for her and of their nine years' struggle that had at last won through to the peace of this "ultimate island," where they might "live toward" their "dreams." He still clung to that hope late in August when he left for New York. He told Agnes, "Everything seems so right in our relationship now after all the nervous bickerings and misunderstandings of the summer." He felt that they had achieved fresh understanding of their married life and renewed faith to carry them on united.

Yet months earlier he had seen in the deeper vision of his play that the dream was hopeless and the love was dead. His actual finale of *Strange Interlude* had told him exactly what the end would be. In act nine of *Strange Interlude,* the heroes, the "Sons of the Father have all been failures." They "flew away." The reborn hero, Gordon, has literally flown away in an airplane like the first Gordon, still clinging to the lie of his mother's virtue. Darrell asks Nina to marry him because Gordon expects him to, but both know their love is dead. Nina refuses, recalling, "Those were wonderful afternoons long ago! The Nina of those afternoons will always live in me, will always love her lover." When O'Neill relinquished Agnes almost a year after he wrote that ending, he told her, "I want always to have your image in my mind as the Agnes I loved so entirely over so many years." Nina refuses Darrell's proposal with "No. Certainly not. Our ghosts would torture us to death!" When O'Neill broke with Agnes forever he told her there had been "too many torturing scenes that one may forgive but which something in one cannot forget." For his play O'Neill redeemed Darrell so that he could take the break. He works out his salvation assisting a young biologist who is what he might have been "if I'd had more guts and less vanity, if I'd hewn to the line!" He leaves Nina saying, "I'm going back to work." All through the last years of his marriage O'Neill had been urging Agnes to get back to work. When the break came he asked her, "Have you started to work yet? Please do, Agnes! You know as well as I that that is what you deeply need." When she told him she was writing again he said, "Now you are all right and on your own feet in your own life!" If she had had that, he thought, they might have won through to happiness together—but ironically his being around was exactly what had made it impossible for her. If she hewed to the line, he was sure she would come into her own as a writer and thank the day he left her free to do so. So he had seen—and yet not seen—what the end of his love for Agnes had to be when he wrote the finale of *Strange Interlude*.

He had even seen—yet not seen—that he was working out his life in his novel-play. In act eight he had the novelist Marsden finally decide—in a mood of drunken recklessness—to break out of his lies and write the truth of his and Nina's and Darrell's and Sam's entangled lives. He "scrambles to his feet and peers about him with hectic eagerness," saying, "Here I am talking while my last chapters are in the making—right here and now—you'll excuse me, won't you, Nina? I must watch—my duty as an artist!" Indeed, so clearly did O'Neill see—while not seeing—that he was working out his life in his novel-play that as soon as he finished it he got the idea for a play about a man who works out the fate of his marriage—without realizing it—in a novel he is writing. O'Neill even thought he might have his protagonist put himself into the woman of his novel, as he had done in his novel-play. Yet the real meaning of this plan never entered his head, for when the time came for writing it he told his dentist, Dr. Lief, that he could not do it "until all my personal affairs are cleared up and forgotten." He added, "It's a funny coincidence. I had the idea all mapped out before I left Bermuda and before there was any suggestion of a smash in my domestic life! It was quite objective. And yet now it would appear as most subjective and autobiographical because of the turn events have taken. A strange business! Maybe something inside me was doing a brilliant clairvoyant job in future reading!" Something inside him had already done its major job of clairvoyancy in *Strange Interlude,* and the plan for the play about a man who works out the fate of his marriage in a novel (*Days Without End*) only showed a further understanding by that "something inside" of exactly what he was doing while he did it.

What answer did he foresee for himself after the breakup of his love for Agnes? Nina turns to Marsden and proposes by asking him, "Will you let me rot away in peace?" The union of these two figures in mourning is a union in death. Their marriage will be celebrated, Marsden says, in a funereal "gray ivied chapel full of restful shadow," and in it the colors of Cybel's parlor, of Tiberius's brothel-palace, are already of the past. Marsden says, "The crimsons and purples in the window will stain our faces with faded passion." In a darkening garden the two of them sit, hoping to "sleep with peace together—to die in peace!"

At first O'Neill closed with thanks to "Our Mother who art in heaven." Then he cut the words and expressed his acceptance of the long sleep in the final night by showing Nina already asleep and Marsden contentedly watching "the evening shadows closing in around them." This resolution in death—and Darrell's resolution in work—was all that O'Neill could see when he asked Agnes to divorce him just before the Christmas of 1927. He told her, "Something in me is so damn utterly dead that I don't care about anything anymore—except doing my work." He felt so exhausted by the cruel futility of all his "dead dreams" that he could welcome death as an excuse to sleep.

But O'Neill did not die with his dreams and his heroes. He turned to Carlotta and proposed to her, gritting his teeth and repeating, "I need you. I need you." He turned back also, as Darrell, to his work. Nothing could have been more prophetic of the truth he found in this play than its title "Strange Interlude." The interlude is the empty space, the irrelevant diversion between the acts of a play. The play, for O'Neill, was life, was truth. Day-to-day living was the interlude. Nina had observed, "The only living life is in the past and future . . . the present is an interlude . . . strange interlude in which we call on past and future to bear witness we are living!" She had seen "our lives" as "merely strange dark interludes in the electrical display of God the Father." For O'Neill, his father's play had been the primal reality, and he had made the play the purpose of his life. After *Strange Interlude* he turned from two-part, two-night plays to three-part, three-night plays and wrote trilogies for the next six years. Then he thought of a cycle of four plays to be played on four nights in the theater, which grew and grew as he worked on it until it became a cycle of eleven plays to be played on eleven nights in the theater. "It goes on forever," he said. He was trying—it seems—to wipe out the interlude altogether, and actually make the play go on forever.

O'Neill had finished his first draft of *Strange Interlude* and was having it typed up when Lawrence Langner of the Theatre Guild came to Bermuda in March 1927. O'Neill gave him the typed first six acts, and Langner stayed up late on a stormy night reading it. Langner thought it was the "bravest and most far-reaching dramatic experiment" since Ibsen and said that it knocked George Bernard Shaw's *Back to Methuselah* "into a cocked hat." So O'Neill sent the first draft to the Guild as soon as it was all typed, explaining that it needed only "intensive cutting." By May, when he went to New York to talk it over with them, it was "greatly condensed," and after the conference he worked "like a dog" on it again, "thinking over every line" and cutting still more. He had met all the committee's objections except, he said, "Helen Westley's for all intro-spective psychological plays, which I can't do much about!" The Guild finally took it on September 20, 1927.

O'Neill had wanted Katharine Cornell to do Nina, but her husband, Tyrone Guthrie, insisted that no one would "pay for two nights to see one play" and declared that the asides probably could not be done. O'Neill's next choice was Ann Harding, who, he thought, "would look it better than anyone." The Guild then offered it to Alice Brady, "a good scout but rather a rough neck," O'Neill thought. She made "the mistake of her career," she confessed later, by turning it down. So Lynn Fontanne became Nina. O'Neill thought her acceptable, but far from his Nina. The men, he thought—Tom Powers as Marsden, Glenn Anders as Darrell, and Earle Larimore as Sam Evans—would be "splendid." When rehearsals began, O'Neill was "tickled to death" with the whole cast's "fine feeling."

Philip Moeller directed it, and his first suggestion was that instead of doing the play in two nights they do it starting in late afternoon, then having a dinner break, and continuing in the evening, after the manner of the Wagner operas at Bayreuth. O'Neill agreed, and set to work cutting more, although he found it far from "easy" or "grateful work." Moeller's greatest inspiration was his plan for doing the asides. He discarded trick effects like moving the characters to a certain part of the stage or monkeying with the lighting. Instead, he froze all physical action during the asides and directed the actors—so Glenn Anders said—"to think our thoughts and speak our lines." Moeller worked hard for restraint, urging the actors, "Hold back, don't give everything, always seem to have something left." His only conflict with O'Neill came over "laughs." At one point he confided to Langner, "I hope he doesn't realize that line is funny, for if he does, out it'll go." O'Neill, of course, was resisting turning the irony of his play into farce and destroying the emotional build of his scenes. As a matter of fact, that actually happened during the road tours, particularly after police had attacked the play as obscene. Glenn Anders never forgot watching "the mood of the play disintegrating before a volley of titters discharged by an audience bent on finding the suggestive." In Philadelphia, he recalled, Judith Anderson (as Nina) became so angry that "she stamped her foot with rage." They had to play down their lines, he said. "Sometimes we'd murmur the asides so low you couldn't make them out." All that, however, came much later. When the play first opened on January 30, 1928, the balance was right, and O'Neill thought Moeller's the "most imaginative" directing he had ever had.

Although O'Neill assured the Guild that *Strange Interlude* would probably be "the big bacon-bringer"—over *Marco Millions*, which they were also producing—the Guild predicted the reverse. So they put *Strange Interlude* into the small John Golden Theater, thinking it could not last more than "the usual subscription period of only six or seven weeks." To their amazement it became a triumph, with almost universally brilliant reviews—it "cleaves the skyline of tomorrow," said Gilbert Gabriel in the *New York Sun*. They had standees at all performances as late as April. "That trends on fanaticism it seems to me," said O'Neill when he heard about it. "Myself, I wouldn't stand up 4½ hours to see the original production of the Crucifixion!" *Strange Interlude* ran seventeen months in New York, and by 1929 the Theatre Guild had two traveling companies playing to crowded houses on the road.

Of course, the great gods Brown had at it, before and after it left New York. Providence and Boston banned it as a "disgusting spectacle of immorality and advocacy of atheism, of domestic infidelity and the destruction of unborn human life"—and this although the play had won a Pulitzer Prize and had excellent reviews from Catholics who grasped the moral retribution in it. Since Boston had outlawed it, the Guild decided to play just outside the city limits in Quincy, and the Mayor of Quincy allowed it a trial performance before civic leaders. Clergymen present decided that it had been "absolutely misrepresented," and the Mayor of Quincy declared it "a beautiful play, worth a hundred sermons." So the Guild arranged special trains and buses from Boston to Quincy and had another triumph—and as usual the "Banned in Boston" notices brought crowds to the other cities in which it played. Productions in Berlin, Budapest, Stockholm, and Denmark were highly successful, although O'Neill found that the reviews had an "obvious chauvinistic anti-Yank color." He told Langner that he hoped his beloved country appreciated the lickings he was taking in the front lines.

The book of *Strange Interlude* sold like a new novel as soon as it appeared in February 1928. Paramount offered a film contract. At that point, on May 27, 1929, O'Neill, the Guild, and Boni & Liveright found themselves sued for $1,250,000 in damages by a woman calling herself "Georges Lewys" who charged that O'Neill had stolen *Strange Interlude* from her privately printed novel *The Temple of Pallas-Athenae*. O'Neill confided to Saxe Commins, "Of course, her claim is a ridiculous hold-up that would never be permitted in any other country but our land of free blackmail, but still she has already spoiled a movie sale that would have netted me thirty-seven thousand and will cost me nearly fifty by the time the suit is over." Although it was always far cheaper to pay a little blackmail money out of court rather than pay the expense of winning such suits, O'Neill hoped that fighting it would "direct attention to the injustice of such cases" so as to get "the law revised." As soon as his old friend and lawyer Harry Weinberger won it, he joined with Representative Fiorello La Guardia to place an amendment to the Vestal copyright bill before Congress to protect authors from similarly absurd charges of plagiarism.

O'Neill told Stark Young: "I've had about as much of a certain kind of success in *Interlude* as could be hoped for. You might add, as much as my stomach can stand! What a success! This plagiarism suit is the fitting final note of cheapness to wind up the whole affair!" The final "success" came when Metro-Goldwyn-Mayer, starring Norma Shearer and Clark Gable, created of *Strange Interlude* what O'Neill described as "a dreadful hash of attempted condensation and idiotic censorship." Even his unlimited hopes for the technique of asides proved vain. He soon decided that for any but neurotic characters it could only be "superfluous show-shop 'business.'" Later, when he again became entranced by the possibilities of masks, he would describe *Strange Interlude* as an attempt at "the new masked psychological drama" without using masks. It had been, he thought, successful for revealing "surfaces and their immediate subsurfaces, but not where, occasionally, it tries to probe deeper."

He always placed *Strange Interlude* among his representative works, but it never was a favorite. Through it he had exorcised his gods, his heroes, and his most intimate dreams in order to face a terrible truth. No sooner had he finished it than he began a search—in plays—for renewed values, for a tenable faith to live by.

6

Dynamo

Strange Interlude picked up O'Neill's plan for his next play and exploded it out into three. He needed a trilogy to cope with the death of his gods and heroes and thought to call it "God Is Dead! Long Live—What?" The original play had come to him in August 1924, when he wrote Kenneth Macgowan about a "queer and intriguing" idea for a play he would call *Dynamo*. It probably sprang from a scene he was writing in *Marco Millions* in which his American businessman Marco is given up by his Chinese tutors. They think he might make a scientist because he worships "Matter as his gross God," but decide not because he always escapes from "scientific truth into infantile fantasies." Later, in 1926, O'Neill made his first note: "Play of Dynamos—the despairing philosopher-poet who falls in love with balance equilibrium of eternal energy—his personification of it—his final marriage with it—the consummation ending with his destruction." Even before he finished *Strange Interlude*, O'Neill began moving into *Dynamo* and the search for God in theories of the universal force electricity, as its talk of the "electrical display of God the Father" shows. The other two plays came on August 12, 1927. One would seek God in romantic love, the other in money.

He wanted his trilogy to "dig at the roots of the sickness of today as I feel it—the death of an old God and the failure of science and materialism to give any satisfying new one." Each play was to be a "symbolical and factual biography of what is happening in a large section of American (and not only American) soul right now." *Dynamo* is set in the midst of the furious controversy that exploded with the 1926 Scopes trial when the schoolteacher of that name fought and lost his case for the right to teach evolution in the Tennessee schools. All over America, fundamentalists had burst into furious denunciation of evolution, insisting on a literal belief in the words of the Bible. They were answered furiously by pseudoscientists who demanded an equally unquestioning faith in current theories. O'Neill hoped to show the absurdities of that conflict by taking his characters from two battling American families, one of them belonging to the "boomingly overassertive" fundamentalist minister Hutchins Light, and the other to the atheist Ramsay Fife, superintendent of the local hydroelectric plant, a good-natured humorist "except where the religious bigotry of his atheism is concerned." Fife is so full of the Scopes trial that his daughter Ada, finding him scowling over the newspaper, asks, "What's the bad news, Pop? Has another Fundamentalist been denying Darwin?"

The first act begins with the distant flashes of lightning and growls of thunder of an approaching storm, becoming ever more violent until it bursts with the act's finale. What O'Neill wanted, he said, was "thunder with a menacing, brooding quality as if some Electrical God were on the hills, impelling all these people." The thunderbolt of God's vengeance had entered the controversy set off by the Scopes trial, when newspapers had misreported Sinclair Lewis's comment during a Kansas church forum that if there were actually the vengeful God, in which some people believed, He would strike him dead for what he was going to say in the next fifteen minutes. Lewis had taken out his watch later and observed that the time was more than up. The newspapers had Lewis leap into the pulpit of a Christian church, pull out his watch, and give God fifteen minutes to prove Himself by striking him dead. A spate of sermons on this myth swept the country afterward. O'Neill parodied it by having his atheist make just such a challenge, speeded up to five minutes. As the act opens, the Reverend Light petulantly asks his God, "Is not the time ripe to smite this blasphemer who defies Thee publicly to strike him dead?" Upstairs, his son Reuben, shaken by the challenge, answers it for himself as American ministers had: "Of course there's a God . . . He wouldn't pay attention to a fool like Fife, that's all." As a macabre touch, O'Neill had Reuben repeat the challenge at the end of the act, when he loses faith in his father's God. He grabs his father's raincoat and shouts up to the lightning: "If there is his God let Him strike me dead this second! I dare Him!"

What interested O'Neill was not the absurd controversy but the psychological "roots of the sickness" of which it was symptomatic. He had read, fascinated, Jung's tracing of the strange paths of the "religion-creating incest libido." In *Twelve Essays on Sex and Psychoanalysis* O'Neill had read Wilhelm Stekel's revelation that the "emotional attitude" of fierce mockers of God shows "there is something suspicious about their atheism." "Blasphemy," Stekel had declared, "is only one of the forms of strong belief." In the words of Gottfried Keller, "A passionate lover of God and a passionate sceptic are really yoked to the same wagon, from which one cannot escape any more than the other." So are the two fanatics in *Dynamo*. The minister's overassertiveness in his fundamentalism comes from his uncertainty in living up to the example of his minister father, and Fife's fanatical atheism is a perpetual reaction against his Calvinist father, who had threatened, "I'll put the fear of hell in your heart if I have to kill you."

In act one the two warring fanatics in their neighboring houses with a lilac hedge between are shown to be totally absorbed in one another. Indeed, as O'Neill first wrote *Dynamo* he went far beyond Stekel to analyze the need in these two for each other's opposition. He wrote a stage direction in which they enter "pleasantly engrossed in a violent argument, and it is plain at once that each one's disputatious intolerant religious spirit has found an outlet in the other and, on this basis, they are becoming fast friendly enemies." O'Neill cut most of this study in "strange friendship" when he rewrote *Dynamo* after its production, but the idea stayed in his mind and long afterward went into *The Iceman Cometh*.

Stekel had discovered that many of his neurotic patients were obsessed by the belief that they had a "great historic mission." They saw themselves as "Christ, Satan, Judas" or as "prophets, founders of new religions, saviours and saints." Many expected a "great miracle" that would reveal them as "God's deputy" or the "Saviour" but feared it would not come because they were "stained with sin." Both Light and Fife are obsessed in this way. The Reverend Light expects God to smite Fife and tells Him, "If Thou didst, I would proclaim the awful warning of it over all America! . . . I would convert multitudes, as it was once my dream to do!" But he feels unworthy because his love for his wife has been "one long desire of the senses." On the other side of the lilac hedge, Fife sees himself as one with "Lucifer, the God of Electricity." He wants to turn "the sixty thousand volts of my plant" against the minister and his God. His enmity makes him perpetrate a disastrous practical joke on the minister's son Reuben, in which he sees himself as Lucifer. He mocks Reuben's reluctance to come in to him as fear "to enter the presence of Satan" and teases the boy for his fear of lightning, telling him, "A minister's son has reason to worry, maybe, when he's in a den of atheism, holding intimate converse with a damned man! I'm thinking your Jehovah might aim a thunderbolt at me but Lucifer would deflect it on to you—and he's the better electrical expert of the two, being more modern in his methods than your God!"

The ironic comedy of the fathers sets off the tragedy of their children. Reuben becomes set on a far more dangerous "great historic mission" than either of theirs, and it ends by destroying him and the girl Ada. O'Neill saw in his tragedy an opportunity to come to grips with the cataclysm in his own life. It had been shattered when "something" inside him found out in *Strange Interlude* that his love for Agnes was doomed. He had rested his love on his father's faith in a God of eternal life and love. That was why he had written her from his father's deathbed asking her to help "protect our love against ourselves" so that they would have, as his father had, "the faith to go on." When his love for Agnes died, his faith in his father's God died with it. No wonder he needed almost a year to accept the truth he discovered in *Strange Interlude*. When he did, he told Agnes: "It is horrible to face the end of anything one has hugged to one's heart for years—." The horror began as soon as he found himself alone in New York at the end of August 1927 and wrote Agnes, "This homeless situation—which is entirely your choice, please remember, and against my best judgment—is unhealthy and unhappy (for me) and dangerous for our future, if my premonitions don't lie. Are you willing to accept all responsibility for its possible eventualities?" When Carlotta came back to New York from Baden-Baden on September 9, he wrote Agnes desperately that he could not imagine "why you should deliberately put me in this lonely and distracted situation where I long for love and care and tenderness (knowing as you did what the particular temptation as it now exists, would be) unless you are in love with someone down there and don't care what I do or who I love!" The threatening cataclysm in his home fused with the threatening September hurricanes in Bermuda, and his fear of the hurricanes became part of his frantic insistence that Agnes join him. He told her, "It isn't healthy, you're making our children run the risk of the hurricane down there. Supposing it is a really terrible hurricane like the Florida one?" In the end he burst out, "And if anything happens to either of the children I swear I will never forgive you!" But Agnes did not come. She wrote a furious response instead that brought destruction upon their marriage. O'Neill had seen it coming in the hurricane sweeping down upon his home, and he put both into *Dynamo*. A storm menaces as Reuben is betrayed out of faith in love and God. It breaks with "a tremendous crash of thunder" when he breaks all his bonds, and he runs off as "the sound of wind and rain sweeping down on the town from the hills is heard."

O'Neill had always feared betrayal from Agnes, and so his pleading was fraught with suspicion: "You must have a lover down there as I suspected before! If so, I wish you'd be fair enough to be honest about it and let us quit!" After the divorce proceedings began he felt even more betrayed by her, for Agnes delayed, refused to work through his lawyer, Harry Weinberger, demanded higher and higher alimony, and told "foul fairy tales" about him. They had married on the understanding that each would free the other instantly if ever one of them fell in love with someone else, and so he felt that she was betraying "the pledge on which our marriage was made." As he wrote *Dynamo*, all the remaining love of their marriage burned itself out in a cruel exchange of letters. "The whole perfidious Agnes mess," he said, "was hounding me by every mail." She had "double-crossed" him, and he felt "as if I'd been walloped beneath the belt." He told Benjamin De Casseres, "Nobody ever, 'took me for a ride' before in anything but trifling matters. Even among prostitutes and bums whenever I laid myself open to 'the works' and trusted them, I found I got an even break."

Behind this sense of betrayal, and inextricably linked to it, stood his first shock to his faith in love and women: his mother's addiction. He made Reuben's catastrophe a double betrayal in love, by his mother and by his girl. Even the family secret that broke O'Neill's faith went into *Dynamo*, only it is transformed into a macabre practical joke, and Fife, who plays it, caricatures the mocking Mephistopheles of an older brother who revealed a very different real secret to O'Neill. Fife bets his daughter Ada a new dress that he can show up the boy she is falling in love with as "yellow" like the whole "Bible-punching breed." He does it by revealing "the secret of the family"—actually a confession he finds in the newspaper made by a man named "Clark" to his daughter's fiancé, a minister's son, who instantly had run to the police with it. Fife swears Reuben to secrecy on the Bible and then tells as his own story, even to the name "Clark," this lurid tale of an old murder concerning lovers in a wood, a rival, and a skull split by an ax. Reuben's first horrified reaction to the hoax family secret echoes O'Neill's reaction to his real one. He instantly distrusts the woman, thinking, "She's the daughter of an adulteress! . . . and a murderer! . . . how can I ever trust her? . . . she's gone around with lots of fellows . . . how do I know she never—?" He is overcome by a despair very like O'Neill's in his parting letter to Carlotta: "My soul is a black cell of loneliness and longing. . . . God has turned his back and slammed the door and gone away and all the prison is darkness." Reuben thinks, "Fife's damned me with Him! . . . there's no use praying! . . . it's getting black! . . . I'm afraid of God!" and he runs home "like a frightened little boy," crying "Mother! Mother!"

The final scene brings the two betrayals together. Reuben's mother has discovered her son's love for the atheist's daughter Ada and wants Reuben punished. She pushes the minister into the closet when she hears Reuben rushing to her for help, and swears on the Bible that she will not tell his father. Unexpectedly Reuben then pours out not only his love but also Fife's confession. His father emerges and begins to beat him, but breaks off, thinking God has delivered Fife into his hands, and rushes off to the police with the story. Rage at the betrayal destroys Reuben's faith in his mother with his fear of his father. He breaks out of the room in which his father has locked him and rushes after him. Both are stopped by Fife, leaning out of his window to tease them, and then Ada angrily reveals the hoax. The double betrayal turns Reuben against love and against his father's God, and he vanishes into the storm.

O'Neill made his characters as different from himself, his parents, and his wife as he could. The boy with his reddish-blonde coloring, his family's Old Testament fundamentalism, and the high-school flapper Ada were all far removed from O'Neill, his background, and his love for Agnes. Yet the names he chose are echoes out of the time he loved Agnes best. The last name of their Provincetown Playhouse friend Jimmy Light came just right for a young man seeking God in electricity. His father's name, "Hutchins," is that of Hutchins Hapgood, their older philosophical friend of the Peaked Hill Bar days on Cape Cod, whom O'Neill had come to love and could theorize with far into the night. Another close friend of those days, Wilbur Daniel Steele, gave his name to "Steele's" store, in which Ada saw the dress she bets on. Powerful associations clung to the hoax confession name "Clark," for it belonged to Shane's nurse, whom O'Neill feared Agnes was casting off after their separation, and also to O'Neill's much mistaken biographer, Barrett Clark. Less obviously, O'Neill gave both betraying women—Reuben's mother, Amelia, and his girl Ada—names beginning with the A of Agnes.

Although O'Neill could not have made the Reverend Hutchins Light more unlike his own father, he was filled as he wrote *Dynamo* with two biblical remembrances of his father: as Jacob in *Joseph and His Brethren* and as the father of the prodigal son in *The Wanderer*. He called his boy after a son of Jacob—first after Benjamin in the notes and finally after Reuben. Although the white frame New England cottage of the Lights was meant to contrast with the garishly electric-lit stucco bungalow of Fife, it also recalled the first cottage James O'Neill bought in New London, before he built 325 Pequot Avenue. And O'Neill loaded it with his biblical memories in framed prints of "The Return of the Prodigal, Jacob and Isaac, etc." He had Reuben return fifteen months after the storm, swaggering like the returned prodigal of his early play *The Rope* and actually thinking "the prodigal returns!" as he predicts, "And won't the old man be glad to see me! . . . yes! . . . he'll poison the fatted calf!"

O'Neill went back to his grotesque prodigal of *The Rope*, written ten years earlier, because he himself was back in the prodigal years that had inspired it. He was once again in flight from an unhappy marriage, on the way to a second divorce, and memories of his first marriage swarmed into *Dynamo* and even pushed their way into his life. At the same time, his inner state was one of perpetual rage and bitterness at Agnes—and a sense of agonized loss. He resented Agnes's assumption that she did all the suffering. Furiously, he asked her if she did not think that he suffered, especially with horrible guilt toward Oona and Shane, and toward her because he had made her suffer. He told Harold DePolo that he missed his children more than anyone would believe and that he had black hours when the past rose up and filled him with regret for all that might have endured if he and Agnes had not been so blind to each other's need for growth and fresh understanding. He linked this remorse with his old "shame" and "blame" at his first "dance with Folly"—that is, his involvement with Kathleen Jenkins, and so *Dynamo* took on the tone of his early play, *The Rope*, because it came out of the same spirit of guilt and merciless self-hatred.

Events from that time also found their way into *Dynamo*, transformed and recombined. His own proposal to Kathleen appears comically transformed in Mrs. Fife's remembrance of her romance with Ramsay: "As soon as he knew he'd got me into trouble he spoke right up . . . 'Oh, hell, then I guess I've got to marry you' . . . and I said yes, and I was awful happy." O'Neill married Kathleen on October 2, 1909, at Trinity Protestant Episcopal Church in Hoboken, New Jersey, and then threw himself upon his father for help. Two weeks later James O'Neill had his son on ship for Honduras with a gold-prospector, Earle Stevens, and on his twenty-first birthday he was steaming past Mexico, bound, hopefully, for a new start in life.

His marriage had been a disaster for him and his family. As far as Kathleen's mother understood it, James O'Neill objected because Kathleen was Protestant. The religious difference certainly existed—and it probably went into the religiously warring families of *Dynamo*. But Mrs. Jenkins never realized how desperately Eugene himself wanted to "break the shackles of care" and be "free" of Kathleen, as the poem he wrote on the way to Argentina declares, or of how single-mindedly his father was acting to save him from a marriage he did not want. After the baby was born, Mrs. Jenkins tried to force recognition from the O'Neills by announcing the marriage (moved back to July), as well as the birth of Eugene Jr., to a *New York World* reporter on May 7, 1910. She told him that

James O'Neill had requested secrecy because "Mrs. O'Neill had been ill all winter and the announcement of her son's marriage, it was feared, would have grave consequences to her." It was certainly kept from her, for O'Neill's letters to his parents from Honduras speak of "spells of dejection and the blues" but gave no hint that he had them because he was married. In *Dynamo,* Reuben's mother is made frantic by his involvement with the girl, and during his absence she suffers the "grave consequences" feared for O'Neill's mother. She dies. When Reuben comes back his father greets him with the cry "Murderer! You killed her!" As he wrote this scene, O'Neill felt all the guilt from the time his birth had pushed his mother onto morphine—in his father's words, "the poison." Reuben's father tells him, "You killed her as surely as if you'd given her poison, you unnatural accursed son!"

From act two on, both the girl Ada and her mother May recall O'Neill's first marriage and divorce. Once seduced, Ada becomes very much the simple, loving girl of O'Neill's entanglement, with all her blindness to her lover's inner conflict and all her confidence in a romantic happy ending to her story. Her mother May repeats the same mindless expectation of ultimate happiness of Kathleen's mother throughout it all. Mrs. Jenkins had been utterly stunned after her announcement of the marriage to the *World* reporter, when he returned to tell her that Eugene O'Neill was not in Honduras working to earn a living for his family, but back in New York, where he had been seen with his father in the Green Room Club. With tears in her eyes, she said that he could have come to live with them, for he knew "how we all feel toward him." Pathetically, she added, "There would have been no 'mother-in-law' about it, either, and he knew that. I felt toward him as if he were my own son." May Fife echoes Mrs. Jenkins and her affectionate acceptance of her daughter's seducer. She puts her arm around Reuben sentimentally and says, "I'll be your mother—yours and Ada's. I've always wanted a boy."

Eugene O'Neill had left Honduras after a bout of malaria in time to join his father, touring in *The White Sister* when it opened in St. Louis on March 14, 1910, and that was why he was back in New York with his family when Mrs. Jenkins—believing he was still in Honduras—made the announcement in May. Once again James O'Neill acted swiftly and had his son sailing out of Boston harbor on June 6, bound for Argentina and a job with Westinghouse Electric. The spirit of that flight went into Reuben, who tells Ada that he "never stuck" to a job long: "I wanted to keep moving and see everything." O'Neill always described his wandering from job to job in the same words: "My ambition, if you call it that, was to keep moving and do as many things as I could" or "I hadn't any particular idea or ambition, just to keep moving." The boy's "psy-

chological mess" duplicates his own. A year after *Dynamo* he would tell George
Jean Nathan, speaking of his son Eugene Jr., who had been born of his "Folly"
and who was the same age he had been during it, "When I survey his merits
and think of the rotten mess of a life I was at his age, I have no fatherly supe-
riority assumptions, believe me!" That "rotten mess" had come very close to
ending with the marriage, for he had tried to kill himself. The same pull toward
death of those days was sweeping him along again, for *Strange Interlude* had
left him only God the Mother and the yearning to sleep forever. *Dynamo* had
to find him a way out.

It was perfectly designed to do so. A psychological investigation of religion-
creating impulses would let him continue the exorcism of his gods begun in
Strange Interlude, in order to tackle God the Mother and so free himself from
her pull toward death. Yet had he begun *Dynamo* two years earlier he could
easily have turned it to the savior-begetting of *Lazarus Laughed*, as his 1926
note on it shows:

> Dynamo stops—interlude, pipes of Pan—Dynamo begins again—
> Waterfall—Neanderthal man
> > "Mother Dynamo"
> He who sees Pan, dies.

He meant his Mother God to be accompanied by her old consort Pan-Dionysus,
and probably she was to reveal Pan in the ultimate consummation, for "He who
sees Pan, dies." O'Neill would thus have fulfilled his old unconscious formula
and reached the Father by way of the Mother. When he began his first notes,
Pan-Dionysus still lived in him, for his young man is a college classics instructor
in them and so can blend Greek myths with theories of electricity. By March
13, 1928, the day O'Neill began writing, Pan-Dionysus had vanished from his
Pantheon, so his boy had only religious habits and a smattering of astronomy,
physics, chemistry, and evolution from which to create a new religion of the
"Great Mother of Eternal Life, Electricity," whose "Divine Image on earth" is
Dynamo.

O'Neill meant Reuben's "Mother Complex" to be the heart of his religion-
making. Jung had pointed out that "Americans, as a result of the extreme de-
tachment from the father, are characterized by a most enormous mother complex." So the boy's psychology—as O'Neill explained—fit his theme of American life in the play, America being "the land of the mother complex." The boy's
fight against his father's God, as O'Neill saw it, was "humanly a fight to conquer
his father," and he put into it his own struggle. In his "Diagram" he had shown

how his "resentment" at being exiled to boarding school developed into open "hatred and defiance" of his father after his disillusionment with his mother. Even if his father had never raised a hand to him he knew that he had punished Jamie, the leader of his revolt against him, "physically by whipping," so he linked beating with rebellion. In his revolutionary poem of 1916, "The Louse," he asked the workers if they expected God to reward them:

> God is a father.
> Remember the beatings you received from your own.

A beating by his father provokes Reuben's revolt against both his father and God.

O'Neill was working very consciously with his own longings as he traced the "devious ways hidden from himself"—so he explained—by which Reuben elevates his mother "into God the Mother so that he can possess and be possessed by her." Reuben's path starts with a longing to talk with his mother that brings him home and intensifies when he finds her dead. O'Neill had himself longed for a reassuring message of life and love from his mother after she died. He raised two women from the dead—in plays—to deliver it. He was also working closely with thoughts of blocked communications with Kathleen in the past and with Agnes in the present. Never before in O'Neill's writing had memory, play events, and life action slid into and out of one another as in *Dynamo*. O'Neill had broken communications with Kathleen when he fled to Honduras. In the play, Reuben sends his mother taunting postcards with no return address. His father tells him she had written long letters begging him to come back: "She couldn't mail them, she knew you'd never read them, and that broke her heart most of all!" O'Neill had fled Agnes giving her no address but the Guaranty Trust Company in London, through which all his mail to and from was forwarded. By April he was deliberately misleading her into thinking he was in Prague. (Actually he was in Guethary, outside Biarritz.) By May, not long after writing this scene, he could not bear the agony her letters brought him, and he sent them back to her unopened. His torn feelings over her letters emerged in the play father. He confesses that he destroyed all those letters down to the last scrap because he "felt betrayed" by them and because he "was insane with hatred." These lines were put in a year later when O'Neill realized that his brains had been "wooly with hatred," over Agnes, and could see it now that he was sane again.

Ada's mother May becomes the major means by which Reuben finds his dead mother again in the dynamo. May actually looks like a dynamo. Her body has the huge "inert strength" of the torso of a dynamo, and her eyes have the same "blank" look as those on the exciter set on top of one. Her hair is "like copper wire in the sun." She loves the dynamos and says that they are "singing all the time about everything in the world." She herself can imitate perfectly their "whirring purr." Her name "May" and her easy acceptance of life and love make her redolent of spring and renewal. Through her, O'Neill could look into all his old mystical search into the meaning of life that had created the mother gods of his plays.

Into her he put his own comical reevaluation of his old mysticism and his old mother goddesses. Just as Cybel in *The Great God Brown* had mingled the mystical cow mothers with O'Neill's memories of his mother under the drug, so May is redolent of both. Her husband thinks, "Look at her . . . in a dope dream again . . . I might as well be married to a cow." In comical stage directions, she "raises herself to her feet like a cow, quite placidly" or stares at the night with "moony, placid cow eyes." Her loving-kindness, like the Buddha's, embraces all things. She thinks, "I love little birds—it must be nice to be a bird—except for cats—but I love cats too." She also picks up O'Neill's first feeling in his love for Carlotta of being shot into the sky and "blown about like a cloud" without direction, and of finding "this cloud life not all the poets have claimed for it." May puts a blessing on the cloud life: "I'd like to be a cloud . . . it must be nice to float in the wind."

Through May, O'Neill took comical hold of all his own mystical ecstasies. He would always recall a moment of bliss on the sailing ship carrying him to Argentina, when (as he would write of it later in *Long Day's Journey into Night*) he had lain on the deck and become drunk with beauty, so that "for a moment I lost myself—actually lost my life. I was set free! I dissolved into the sea, became white sails and flying spray, became beauty and rhythm, became moonlight and the ship and the high dim-starred sky!" He would add: "And several other times in my life, when I was swimming far out, or lying alone on the beach, I have had the same experience. Became the sun, the hot sand, green seaweed anchored to a rock, swaying in the tide." He would conclude, "It was a great mistake, my being born a man. I would have been much more successful as a sea gull or a fish." He had already gotten all these mystical high points into perspective by way of May Fife. May recalls (in *Dynamo* as produced), "D'you remember when we went for the day down to Palmer's Beach last summer and I floated way off by myself and you had to row out and tell me to come in unless I wanted to see Europe? Well, I felt that day that I was a fish—and then after that, looking up at the sky, I felt I was beginning to dissolve softly into the water, and finally I felt all of May, Mrs. Fife, was gone and I was the sea and it was me—and I was awful happy, Ramsay, and awful sore at you for bringing me back." O'Neill knew perfectly well that "When you begin to smile at the ghosts in yourself, they never materialize again." He was more than smiling at May Fife. He was so clear on her comedy role that he warned the Guild, "If whoever plays it is even conscious of being funny for a moment, or rides her lines for laughs, I will swim back all the way from China with a Kriss between my murderously-gritted teeth and slay that actorine!" Through May, he exorcised his mother gods, and so effectively did he banish them that, when he tried to work on his plan for "Sea Mother's Son" afterward he never could bring it to birth in his mind. Never again would old love images find their way into his mysticism. Working later on the second play of his God trilogy, he sighed, "Oh, for the good old days when I was content to be either simple-minded or foggily mystical—now I aim to be clearly psychological and mystically clear. . . . A tough ambition!"

The rest of the fog in his mysticism went with his demonstration in *Dynamo* of the perils in the religion-creating unconscious. Long before he started writing, O'Neill knew that his play's force would come from the actual image of Dynamo on stage and of her temple, the powerhouse. So in September 1927, he asked Maurice Wertheim, the financial wizard of the Guild, to put him in contact with the great hydroelectric plants, and at first Wertheim suggested he go to Niagara Falls, which would have given him a thunderous setting for his last act. Then, O'Neill told Agnes, Wertheim found him "a big bug in the Bankers Trust" who arranged for him to see the Stevenson plant, which was much closer, on an "isolated spot on the Housatonic—dirt roads for 5 miles nearest to it," north of Danbury, Connecticut. On September 30 he drove there and "was taken all over and shown everything from roof to cellar. Quite an experience." He used the wash of the Housatonic River over its dam to give Reuben the impression of "some one singing me to sleep—my mother—when I was a kid—calling me back to somewhere far off where I'd been once long ago and known peace!" The horizontally mounted generators of the Stevenson plant actually looked like women, and O'Neill took from them Reuben's dynamo, "huge and black, with something of a massive female idol about it, the exciter set on the main structure like a head with blank, oblong eyes above a gross rounded torso." O'Neill also found minor deities in the oil switches with their "spindly steel legs" and "six cupped arms stretching upward" looking "like queer Hindu idols." O'Neill felt in himself the "permeating possessiveness" of the dynamo's whir, which numbs "the brain with a narcotic palpitation." That sound was to dominate the entire final act, and against it O'Neill set "the startling, strained, unnatural effect of the human voice raised to try and dominate the generator's hum."

O'Neill took away from his visit, a vision of power that might easily go berserk—the machine power that was taking over America more and more in the 1920s. With it O'Neill also saw a concrete image of the psychological perils implicit in the pull to regain old images of felicity. He had been fascinated by Jung's analysis of "The Dual Mother Role" and found it "extraordinarily illuminating in the light of my own experience with hidden human motives." Clearly he was aware of his own double mother-image, and so Jung's idea had reality for him. Jung had explained that the longing for the mother in myths and the unconscious is really a wish to return to the womb "in order to be born again." So the mother in myths represents, on the one hand, life, fertility, rebirth. On the other hand, there is danger in a man's wishing to go back, to give in to the "deadly longing for the depths within, for drowning in his own source, for becoming absorbed into the mother." This destructive pull emerges in myths in the form of a monster, what Jung called the "terrible mother" of mythology. O'Neill had experienced both—the life-giving mother and the "terrible mother" with her pull toward death, and he put Jung's dual mother into his play by way of the two play mothers. May is the mother of fertility, life, and love. Reuben's Mother God Dynamo is the "terrible mother," and O'Neill made his boy half aware of her danger. He confides to Ada that there have been moments "when all these switches and busses and wires seemed like the arms of a devil fish—stretching out to suck me in."

O'Neill meant to symbolize in the dynamo both the psychological dangers of the "terrible mother" and the danger of machine dominance in America. His Dynamo therefore participates in the destruction of the final act (at least in the play as produced). O'Neill had learned that the superintendent of the Stevenson plant controlled his generators by ear and could tell by the pitch of their hum if something was wrong. In the final act of *Dynamo*, Reuben's idol, the Number One Dynamo, goes berserk, and Fife, the superintendent, thinks, "She used to remind me of May—you felt she was simple—and good—you'd never call her good now with that sound crying in her and growing stronger—there's pride in that sound—aye, and there's cruel hunger in it too—she'd like to eat you." Reuben's father has an apocalyptic vision of the dangers of the machine. He sees it as "either the Beast or the Dragon prophesied in the Book of Revelation—both manifestations of Satan. Materially it helps us while spiritually it degrades us to the level of swine!" He also sees its threat to his boy and wants to save him from this "loathsome female deity."

Reuben has become obsessed by the deity he has created and by a full-blown "great historic mission." He believes—as did many of Stekel's neurotic patients—that he is meant to be the new Christ, the savior of mankind, and he expects a miracle to identify him. He tells May Fife that the Great Mother Dynamo "wants some one man to love her purely and when she finds him worthy she will love him and give him the secret of truth and he will become the new saviour who will bring happiness and peace to men! And I'm going to be that saviour—that's why I asked you to come—I want you to be a witness! I know the miracle will happen to me tonight because I had a message from my mother last night." But Reuben doubts the coming of the miracle—as did Stekel's patients with a "great historic mission"—because he feels stained by sin.

He feels compelled to repeat his mother's repressive role on the traumatic night. O'Neill had learned from Stekel that the compulsive acts of a neurotic are an attempt to set "the stage for an old scene which he is determined to re-enact." He knew even more powerfully from himself in this crisis period that the past rises to determine the present, and he was to become ever more acutely aware of its pressure for repetition. He certainly knew that he was repeating his father's solution to an unhappy marriage of shipping him off to another country, as soon as his marriage with Agnes failed. If he had not had rehearsals of *Strange Interlude* holding him in New York until January 30, he might have taken ship at once. As it was, he asked Agnes to divorce him at the end of December, and on February 10, 1928, he was writing in his *Work Diary* "Exit—S.S. 'Berengaria'!" as he sailed for Southampton. (It was a bitter blow to Agnes that he went to Europe at once with Carlotta when she had been trying in vain for years to get him to go there.) Even as he was writing *Dynamo*, O'Neill was already thinking of repeating the second stage of flight from Kathleen—the flight to Argentina with the "ultimate goal" of reaching China. Shortly after he finished he sailed October 5 with the S.S. *Andre Lebon* out of Marseilles bound for Hong Kong. O'Neill's father had put him on ship for the second flight from Kathleen just eight months after his first sailing for Honduras. O'Neill followed even the timing, for he took ship for Hong Kong eight months after he had sailed for Southampton. O'Neill used his own compulsion to repeat the past to analyze Reuben's compulsive repetition of his mother's role on the traumatic night of the storm.

He remembers her rage at him for kissing the girl, and a moment after he has learned of her death he suddenly feels blocked from kissing Ada. As O'Neill explained it, the pull of Reuben's dead mother on him from the grave is perfectly plain when he attempts to kiss Ada and finds that he cannot. Reuben also feels blocked from marrying Ada after he has seduced her. He thinks, "Mother said she was no better than a streetwalker . . . she certainly didn't put up a fight

... marry her! ... what does she think I am, a boob?" The compulsion becomes stronger once he has found his mother again in the dynamo. He begins to have visions of her coming to warn him that he is "living in sin," that Dynamo will not find him worthy, until he has "given up the flesh." He has kept himself from Ada a month on the night he expects the miracle, and is at the snapping point. He has even repeated the beating with a belt that his mother brought upon him and thinks, "But suppose the miracle doesn't happen tonight? ... Ada keeps coming in dreams ... her body ... I've beaten myself with my belt ... I can't keep on much longer." He is pulled apart by desire for the girl and need for his mother who prohibits her.

O'Neill himself had been racked by the pull of two women from the time he had left Carlotta in November 1926. He told Kenneth Macgowan he was torn by the desire—"more than desire, need!"—for the two and bewailed his all-or-nothing devotion to one love ideal at a time. So O'Neill had already experienced in himself the all-or-nothing pulls that drive Reuben to destruction, and he had been particularly torn at the Stevenson plant. In his urgent plea to Agnes to join him when Carlotta came back, he said he was desperate to break out of "this obscene and snaily creeping tedium of dull days" into "some madness— of love or lust or drink or anything else!" He had warned her that he had no interest in little sex affairs for their own sake, that for him it was love or nothing. Did she want him to love someone else? She answered fiercely that she saw through his remark about taking to love or drink, and he could just go ahead and "do" it. So when O'Neill went to the Stevenson plant two weeks later he told Agnes everything, except that Carlotta was with him. He put his acutely torn feelings at the time into Reuben and saw in his sacrifice of the girl his own sacrifice of his love for Agnes. He had always equated the destruction of love with the destruction of life, and he said after the divorce that Agnes could no longer hurt him: "She's too dead."

In the play it is the kindly mother May who triggers the murder of her daughter by her mindless expectation of a happy ending—in a way reminiscent of Mrs. Jenkins's attempt to bring about her daughter's happy ending by the newspaper announcement that had boomeranged so disastrously. Reuben asks May if Dynamo is withholding the miracle because of something to do with Ada, and she—thinking he means to marry the girl at last—answers, "Yes, you've got to do the right thing by Ada, Reuben." So she sets off the "unnatural excitement" in which he tries to carry out both pulls at once by bringing Ada into the powerhouse to worship Dynamo with him, only to give way to passion on the platform before his Mother God. O'Neill made Reuben's cry of anguish to the girl after it (in *Dynamo* as produced) the same he might have directed at his mother after her betrayal, and the same that O'Neill himself might have directed at Agnes when she failed his final plea: "You cheated me—when I trusted you—when I needed your help—when I loved you better than—." O'Neill then had Reuben carry out the sacrifice of the "impure maid" that Jung described in the myths of the world "to pacify the anger of the 'terrible mother'" and to assure the attainment of the "mother-bride," or, in O'Neill's words, "the boy's psychological Mother-struggle-ending-in-girl-sacrificed-to-Mother-God."

The form that sacrifice took shows how possessed O'Neill was by the divorce of his first two wives, by the feeling that he was repeating the sacrifice of Kathleen Jenkins in the sacrifice of Agnes. For one thing, sound echoes of "Jenkins" began reverberating in his brain. Fife is gotten away from the powerhouse (in *Dynamo* as produced) by May's announcement that "Jenn"—never mentioned before—is keeping his supper hot. The only other presence in the powerhouse is the floorman "Jennings." (In *Dynamo* as produced, two floormen are there, Jennings and an Italian named "Rocco" who keeps crossing himself at the doings of the boy—like a curious representative of O'Neill's Catholicism looking upon his divorces.) The elaborate ritual of murder carried out by the boy shows the insistence in O'Neill's mind of Agnes's devastating reply to his final plea. She told him that her pistol was locked into a drawer to which she had lost the key, or she would go out at once in their punt and put an end to it all. Reuben does not strike or strangle Ada. He dashes to the switchboard room, where he flings "the startled and terrified Jennings"—O'Neill's first divorce witnessing his second—away from the desk, "tears out a drawer and gets the revolver." With it he motions Jennings through a back door and "turns the key in the lock after him," and then he springs up the stairs to shoot the girl twice (as if she were the two women of the two divorces). Through the figure of his guilt, the boy, he had torn out the locked drawer of Agnes's suicidal letter so the sacrifice could take place, and what was locked away by key was the haunting remorse at the first divorce—the witness Jennings.

The end of his play repeats the end of the entire story of his first marriage to Kathleen: his suicide attempt. Overcome with horror, the boy cries, "I don't want any miracle, Mother! I don't want to know the truth! I only want you to hide me, Mother! Never let me go from you again!" He takes hold of the carbon brushes of the exciter; there is a flash of blue light; his voice is heard in a moan of "loving consummation" that becomes the "crooning of a baby" and finally is lost in the dynamo's hum. So Reuben succumbs to the pull of death in the wish to be reabsorbed into the mother, even as O'Neill had succumbed after supplying the evidence for the divorce from Kathleen.

O'Neill's final image brings the two mothers together over the body of the boy, for they are both aspects of the same longing. May—the loving mother—whose name is just one letter short of O'Neill's own mother's name, "Mary"—kneels by the dead boy and, turning with bewildered resentment to the dynamo, says, "And I thought you was nice and loved us!" She pounds the steel torso of the dynamo with her fists, and as the curtain drops she has hurt herself and "begins to cry softly." So O'Neill committed the suicide he had attempted after the destruction of his first marriage a second time after the destruction of his second—only this time by proxy in a play, and in a way that brought him understanding and salvation from the pull of death. The first play of his God trilogy left him absolutely shorn of old dreams, exorcised of God the Father and God the Mother, asking himself, "Long Live What?"

O'Neill needed a few months after resolving *Dynamo* to resolve all the hatred of self and Agnes that had tormented him while writing it. The crisis came when he reached China with the flu and had what was really a nervous breakdown, although it took the form of a relapse into his old outlet from intolerable tension, alcoholism. In the release of all that pent-up hatred, he almost demolished his new love with the old, for he quarreled with Carlotta when she tried to rescue him from drinking. They came ecstatically together again on the return voyage to France, and at last he felt completely liberated from the festering hatred of old love and free to enjoy the new.

As soon as he and Carlotta were established at Cap D'Ail on the Riviera he reread *Dynamo*. He had sent it off to the Guild unrevised, in first draft, as soon as it was typed (just as he had done with *Strange Interlude*). The Guild (still drunk with *Interlude*'s success) cabled back at once on October 4: "Dynamo accepted with enthusiasm. All wish you bon voyage." Now, four months later, O'Neill saw as he reread it that it needed cutting, and he told Langner that he hoped "Phil" Moeller had done "that fell deed with unction and thoroughness." He also saw that he had been wrong to repeat the spoken-thoughts technique for this play and later warned himself never to use it again indiscriminately—"that was what principally hurt 'Dynamo,' being forced into thought-asides method which was quite alien to essential psychological form of its characters." He added, "Saw this when I re-read it after return from East—too late!"

As he refused to go back to America until he was divorced and remarried to Carlotta, the Guild had gone ahead and was on the brink of rehearsals without him. He had told them all about *Dynamo*'s being the first play of a God trilogy, and they passed on his statement to the newspapers. He did not explain the theme of this particular play, for he thought it "so plain" as to be almost "too

obvious," so the Guild—and the critics after them—missed it entirely and took
the theme of the trilogy as the theme of the play. Langner admitted that they
"greatly missed 'Gene' at rehearsals for clarification," and as for Theresa Helburn, even after it was all over and O'Neill had explained all about the "mother
complex," she confessed, "That was never clear to me." O'Neill did give them
careful directions on staging. The scheme of the two houses with one or two
rooms open, embodied, he thought, "all that is sound theatre in Constructivism
while giving it an obvious natural reason for being." His acts were cut into brief
scenes punctuated by pauses of darkness, and he warned against lengthening
them with lights up in the theater, which would "ruin the continuity and give a
jerky, intermittent effect." He was dismayed to learn afterward that they had
settled on an "orthodox Russian constructivist set" quite "out of key" with his
play and that they had run all the scenes together, obliterating the meaningful
pauses and leaving all the rooms open with superfluous characters on stage
pretending to be "living naturally in their quarters." O'Neill saw these as the
chief mistakes in their production.

He had urged them to get the sound right and not leave it for the last minute
or they would end up with "a generator sounding obviously like a vacuum
cleaner." At the start of rehearsals he cabled a reminder: "Don't forget perfect
sounds, voices against sound as early as possible." But without him there to
modulate and shape, the Guild bumbled. O'Neill himself said that he had never
gotten credit for the changes he made during rehearsals, but no play of his had
failed to gain by his being on the spot.

Dynamo opened on February 11, 1929. The critics pounced upon it fero-
ciously. O'Neill's friend, George Jean Nathan—a panner of the play himself—
said the reviews read "as if it was O'Neill who stuck that woman into the fur-
nace several months ago, who was responsible for the mysterious deaths of
Elwell and Dot King and who was back of the Charlie Ross kidnapping." Particularly vicious were the two failed-playwright critics, Heywood Broun and St.
John Ervine, but as O'Neill already knew, "when those gangrened failures get
to accepting you it's a sure sign you're good and dead." Not one critic saw the
"human psychological struggle" in the play; they saw nothing but the religious
theme. Burns Mantle, typically, said that O'Neill "boldly pits the God of the
fundamentalist religionists against the God of an atheist protagonist, electricity,
and proves to his own satisfaction that one is as ineffective and shadowy as the
other."

How anyone could think that he would write a play pitting a fundamentalist
God against pseudoscience, O'Neill could not imagine. He thought he had

shown that banal conflict as simply laughable in the comic arguments between Fife and the minister.

He decided that he had "blundered horribly" in giving out the talk of a "trilogy" when he had only one play of it—and he determined to keep absolutely secret the "trilogy" nature of the other two plays until all three were written. As for the reviews, he told his publisher, Horace Liveright, "I know the majority of notices were antagonistic but this is what I have always expected—about the same break in the press that I got on 'Brown' and 'Desire.' " The audiences had made a success of those plays, and O'Neill cabled the Guild on March 18: "Why not move Dynamo to smaller theater? Think it would have chance then of keeping on moderately like Brown and Desire." But the Guild had given up and was ready to let the play die with the last of its subscription audiences.

O'Neill was not disturbed by the "bunk" of the critics; he knew they were only getting back at him for the success of *Strange Interlude*. What had, he said, "dismayed me this time was that no criticism either favorable or not—Atkinson, Krutch, Gabriel, Young etc. included—got what I thought my play was about." Perhaps *Dynamo* had become muddled from trying to do too much. He decided to give it "the works" before allowing it to be published, and "the works" were so thorough that the book of *Dynamo* became a quite different play from the one produced. He got busy "cutting and interpolating and condensing" and, more than anything, "simplifying." He put in two new scenes to give a blow-by-blow account of the boy's religion-creating. He cut everything that distracted from the boy's psychology, and so cut out most of the participation of the other characters in the final scenes—and much that had made the play valuable to him in working out the cataclysm in his own life.

Primarily he cut the boy's father and his efforts to save his son from "the Woman." In his own crazed way, the minister had seen that the boy's mother and the dynamo were one and had thought confusedly, "I must save him from her!—(Then catching himself—pitifully agitated) Her—who?—the flesh?—that's mad—she's dead—I meant some Satanic mother of evil—his electricity!" He tries to save his boy from the pull of death. Apparently O'Neill had become clear on the fact that alliance with his father had meant life for him, while his yearning for his mother had meant death. That was why he chose the name "Hutchins"—the name of an older man he had "grown to love" for the boy's father, crazed as he is. In *Dynamo* as produced, Hutchins Light comes to the powerhouse to save his boy from the "terrible mother." Confused by Ada's voice calling Reuben, he cries: "Beware, Reuben! The hour appointed for me to wrestle for your soul has struck. This is the temple of the Beast, and she who calls you is the woman, full of names of blasphemy—the mother of harlots and abominations of the earth, the habitation of devils!" O'Neill had his effort to save the boy go wild, for it triggers the sacrifice of the girl and the boy's suicide. O'Neill knew that his father's own effort to save him had brought on the sacrifice of Kathleen and his own suicide attempt. By working it all out in the play, he came out with an understanding of what his father had actually meant for him. *Dynamo* as produced carried O'Neill from his unconscious images of his father as Pan-Dionysus, the male life principle, to a firm conscious identification and alliance with him. Although O'Neill cut it all from the published play, he kept the alliance itself, and he showed it at once in response to the attacks of the critics. He told Robert Sisk of the "doleful tenderness" with which people broke the reviews to him, and declared, "Me that was born on Times Square and not in Greenwich Village, and that have heard dramatic critics called sons of bitches—and, speaking in general, believed it—ever since I was old enough to recognize the Count of Monte Cristo's voice!"

He was still hacking away at *Dynamo* right through the galleys, and he told Liveright, "Am sorry to say I have again cut and revised hell out of it but now, finally, I really feel 'Dynamo' is cleared of its rubbish, simple and direct—and a damned good play." But all that work to make the critics understand a psychology unfamiliar to them was naturally in vain. When the book appeared on October 5, 1929, no one understood it any better. By this time he himself was doubtful, and he told Joseph Wood Krutch, "I like it better now, but not enough. I wish I'd never written it—really—and yet I feel it has its justified place in my work development. A puzzle." For a while, he talked of writing a third *Dynamo* for the definitive edition of his works. But for him there was no going back. He gave up this "crippled child of the storm and stress period," and only long afterward did he question whether its debacle might have been undeserved. In 1941 he wanted to convince the Guild that his early play *Anna Christie* was a bad choice for revival. It was written, he said, around characters and a "situation." He would not compare it with his best plays, he said, but with one of his flops—*Dynamo.* Maybe it stepped on its own feet dramatically—and he was not sure even of that, for 1929 criticism had been ready to attack any play that mentioned God—but *Dynamo* had been, he thought, "about characters plus life." And life—seen through no glory of gods or heroes—was what he had gone on with in the superlative play that followed *Dynamo.*

7

Mourning Becomes Electra

"Life is growth—or a joke one plays on oneself!" O'Neill decided. *Dynamo* had been a step back. He felt it wronged his love for Carlotta, and he told her that his next play would "make the world see how much you have done for me." He had battled the forces of hatred and death within himself, and he wanted a theme to fit that struggle. When he found and plunged into it, he exulted to Saxe Commins: "It's the sort of thing I needed to come to me—one that will call for everything I can give it—a glorious opportunity to grow and surpass everything I've ever done before!" He did not know whether he had the "stuff" to do it, but he did know "I'd rather fail at the Big Stuff and remain a success in my own spiritual eyes, than go on repeating, or simply equalling, work I've done before." It would be "the biggest and hardest I have ever tackled."

The first idea had come to him in the spring of 1926, when he thought of "a modern psychological drama using one of the old legend plots of Greek tragedy"—the Electra, or the Medea. The Electra story would set him in direct rivalry with the great Greek dramatists, for Aeschylus, Sophocles, and Euripides had all treated it. He would make it a real trilogy, like theirs, with three plays treating the same characters. Through it he could achieve—what he had always striven to arrive at—a sense, like the Greek sense, "of the Force behind" life, whatever one called it, "Fate, God, our biological past creating our present." It was to be "primarily drama of hidden life forces."

On his voyage to China this play of hidden forces took life, and so the sea washes through it from beginning to end. His fated family became shipbuilders and shipowners, and he had them long for liberation by sea, just as he had felt on the *Charles Racine* that he could "at last be free, on the open sea, with the trade wind" in his hair. The sea chanty "Shenandoah" sounds throughout his play, for he thought that it "more than any other holds in it the brooding rhythm of the sea." Although he set the play in the family house, haunted by the family past, he put one act aboard the *Flying Trades* and very deliberately placed it at the "center of whole work" to emphasize "sea background of family and symbolic motive of sea as means of escape and release." In this act the two lovers, Adam and Christine, plot in vain to escape by sea after the chanty "Shenandoah" ("Way—ay, I'm bound away") has reached an ironic crescendo of longing.

The sea and O'Neill's recall of the white sails of the *Charles Racine* determined his choice of time. He wanted to make this play American, and so he needed an American war to match the Trojan War from which the Greek hero Agamemnon had triumphantly returned to be murdered by his wife and her lover. O'Neill thought World War I was too close; his audiences would not see beyond its surface to the real drama of hidden forces, and he was sure that the American Revolution would also blind them with its "romantic grammar-school-history associations." The "only possibility" was the fratricidal Civil War, which fit a "drama of murderous family love and hate" and provided a detached "mask" for the timeless struggle beneath. It allowed him to make the ships of his play Clippers and to use his old thrill at white sails and his old longing to reach China of his voyage out of Boston to Argentina, for the Clippers had all been bound for China by way of Argentina in the tea trade. He made a China voyage the heart of this play, which began to grow in him on the "Arabian Sea en route for China" and on the "China Sea."

He set his investigation of family fate where his own family's fate had worked itself out, in the small New England "seaport, shipbuilding town" of New London. He actually called it "N.L." in his notes. New England, with its "Puritan conviction of man born to sin and punishment," was the "best possible dramatically for Greek plot of crime and retribution," he thought, and he could reexamine his own guilts through all five members of his New England family. He called his Agamemnon "Ezra Mannon," and "Mannon," suggestive of "Man," became the name of his tragic family, whose struggle would reveal the larger struggle of life-and-death forces within the soul of man.

O'Neill hoped the play would have a "strange quality of unreal reality." He wanted to show that the surfaces of life—which are taken for reality—are meaningless and that the great realities, the "hidden life forces" beneath the surface, are so overwhelming when perceived, as to seem unreal. (He who sees Pan, dies.) So he built his penetration through surfaces into the three plays of his trilogy. Each one has the curtain rise to reveal a painted backdrop of the Mannon house as it looks to the townspeople from the street, set in a splendor of orchards and gardens behind a white picket fence. Then this obviously artificial surface lifts to bring the audience directly before the reality of the house and all the embattled forces within the family. O'Neill had seen at once that he could make his house "Greek temple front type that was rage" at the time and that it was "absolutely justifiable, not forced Greek similarity." He remembered the Greek Revival houses of his boyhood New London, but he took care to buy Howard Major's *Domestic Architecture of the Early American Republic: The Greek Revival,* in which he found just the severe tomblike house he wanted for Ezra Mannon's father, Abe, to have built as a "temple of Hate and Death" after expelling his brother David from the family, supposedly in outraged morality but actually in jealous revenge. O'Neill took for it Marshall House at Rodsman's Neck, New York, with its cold stone base, its pagan portico with six tall columns, its central doorway with a "squared transom and sidelights flanked by intermediate columns," and its arrangement of windows—only he changed its eight steps to four in mercy to the actors and added the shutters he needed for his final catastrophe. This house, like the house in *Desire Under the Elms,* was to participate in the drama. The family is torn between pagan joy in life, and Puritan condemnation of pleasure as sin, and their conflict appears in the facade of the house, where the pagan temple portico is stuck on "like an incongruous white mask" over the "sombre gray ugliness" of its stone walls. In the first play "Homecoming," all the windows of this outraged house reflect the sun "in a resentful glare," and as the murder is planned the inside of the house is stained with the crimson of the setting sun. Whether the columns are bathed in sunlight, haunted moonlight, or bloody sunset, they throw their shadows in black bars against the wall, suggesting the imprisonment of the fated family.

Each of the three plays moves from the embattled exterior of the house to its haunted interior, dominated by the family past in the portraits of the dead Puritan Mannons. Most of the indoor scenes take place at night, and in "the flickering candlelight" the eyes of the portraits take on "an intense bitter life." They glare so "accusingly" at the Electra character after all her crimes, that she justifies herself to them as if they were living judges. O'Neill knew that this haunted interior came out of his deepest self, "whom the past always haunts so persistently." As soon as he had written these plays and had returned to America, he went to New London with Carlotta to "revisit Pequot Ave. old time haunts," and right after that visit he got "Idea play—house-with-the-masked-dead and two living intruding strangers," so much had his own family past in the house at 325 Pequot Avenue haunted him when he designed the haunted interior of the Mannon house.

He even dared to give the same penetration through surfaces, the same sense of "unreal reality" to his characters. Each of the plays begins with a group of townspeople, looking upon the Mannons in a prying, gossiping way as the New Londoners of O'Neill's youth had once looked upon the O'Neills. O'Neill gave them purely "exterior characterization," each with a few emphatic mannerisms. He also made the two fiancés of the tragic young Mannons "almost characterless"—embodiments of simplicity, goodness, and health. All these external people set off the entirely "inner" characterization of the fated Mannons. He wanted to avoid for the Mannons, "as far as possible and consistent with living people, the easy superficial characterization of individual mannerisms." Because they speak directly out of the passions engendered in the family past, O'Neill found that any experiments with asides or stylized soliloquies—and he tried both in the course of rewritings—only got "in the way of the play's drive." His characters were already speaking out of the depths, out of the hidden forces within them, and no technique could cut deeper than that. He thought his play "needed great language to lift it beyond itself. I haven't got that." Instead, he created a prose with a "forceful repeating accent and rhythm" that expressed the "compulsion of passions engendered in family past." The rhythm was so intense that the actors found anything but a letter-perfect reading of their lines broke the headlong drive of the play. All O'Neill's poetry went into the living symbolism of color, light, sound, and action, composed for the theater.

He needed a tragic conflict from the previous generation of Mannons to weigh upon his characters and to motivate his Aegisthus to take revenge on the Agamemnon, Ezra Mannon. A modern audience would not accept the legendary revenge of Agamemnon's father on Aegisthus's father for seducing his wife: serving him up his own children's flesh at a banquet. The "general spirit," not the "details of legend," interested O'Neill, so he eliminated the cannibal banquet and used the rivalry in love of the brothers, but it took hold of him only when he thought to make it a rivalry over a nurse in the family, rather than a wife, and conceived of her as Irish among the Puritan Mannons. This fatal nurse girl came out of his memories of the nurse introduced into his own family, Sarah Sandy. She had been English in a family of Irish, and O'Neill suspected that his mother had chosen an Englishwoman because, as he wrote in his family history, "Husband hates English intensely. Always hostile to nurse secretly and she to him. Was M [Mother] actuated by revenge motives on husband in this choice—to get reliable ally in war with husband?" Sarah's introduction into his family, O'Neill knew, had had fatal repercussions for him, and he thought of putting its reverse—an Irish nurse among Puritans—into his fated family.

One of the striking ideas that came to him as he worked with the second draft of *Mourning Becomes Electra* was to make all the women in the play look alike, starting with the nurse. He had Ezra Mannon select a wife who resembles the nurse he adored as a boy, and had the Aegisthus character fall in love with her because she looks like his mother, that same fatal nurse. O'Neill had read the popular book his friend Kenneth Macgowan had written with Dr. G. V. Hamilton, *What Is Wrong with Marriage,* with data from the research in marriage in which O'Neill had participated. They had pointed out that a man's "ideal of feminine beauty" usually "goes straight back to the mother of his boyhood." O'Neill saw that this idea would give him a chain of fatal attractions among his Mannons in line with modern psychological theory, and he used it because he had seen its truth in the power over his own love choices exercised by his second mother, his nurse Sarah Sandy.

He certainly knew that in Carlotta he had selected, for the first time, a wife with his own mother's beautiful dark eyes and his mother's "long and straight" nose (as described in *Long Day's Journey into Night*). He dedicated the first galley proofs of *Mourning Becomes Electra* to Carlotta "with a large kiss on her long nose." Agnes had been very beautiful in a totally different style, with ash-blonde hair and blue-green eyes and prominent cheekbones. The light hair, blue eyes, and high cheekbones all reflected Sarah Sandy. Moreover, with Agnes, O'Neill had brought another Englishwoman into his Irish family. In a loving note of thanks to her for pictures of herself and Shane (when he had left Provincetown to stay with his parents in New York for his first Broadway production, *Beyond the Horizon*), O'Neill gave her a message, supposedly for his infant son, in which she was to "tell him my advice as one Shin Fein to another: Never trust a woman, or depend on her, especially—as Shane the Proud will be sure to whisper out of the subconscious—a woman born in London, surely!" He told her of the pride and joy he and his parents took in the pictures of her and Shane; she looked so beautiful he feared that she could not really be his. His profound love for Agnes had roots in his attachment for his English nurse, and so in a way all the pain, passion, love, and hatred of his marriage had proceeded from her.

Even before Agnes he had been drawn to a woman who recalled his nurse rather than his own mother when he became caught up in Kathleen Jenkins, who was an Episcopalian, rather than Irish Catholic, with light hair, blue-gray eyes, and broad cheekbones. His involvement with Kathleen went into his story of rivalry between Abe and David Mannon over the nurse girl, for David Mannon, expelled from the family by his brother Abe, repeats the main outline of O'Neill's story. He gets the girl with child, marries her, then is filled with shame, takes to drink, and finally commits suicide—as O'Neill had tried to do. This old suicide hangs over all the action—as O'Neill's old suicide had been hanging over him—and it brings with it a chain of further suicides.

At first O'Neill pictured his Clytemnestra—Christine—in the image of his own mother. His Plot Notes give her "beautiful, large and dark" eyes like his mother's, and the "reddish brown" hair that his mother recalls having in *Long Day's Journey into Night.* After he had decided on a fatal Irish nurse girl for all his women to resemble, he made the appearance typically Irish with "hair black as night and great soft eyes as blue as the Caribbean Seas." Then he decided to erase his own intimate Irish-English conflict out of the nurse, and he made her French-Canadian. He was writing in a French château of the Loire Valley, and if a French nurse pushed her way inexorably into his mind she came probably as the ghost of his son Shane's nurse Fifine Clark, born in and married out of France. O'Neill had been pained by her separation from his children—coming as it did at the same time as his own—for he read his own loss in hers. News of her death came to him in a cable on July 13, 1929, just as he was working on the plot for *Mourning Becomes Electra,* and he wrote in his *Work Diary*: "Deeply grieved—real mother to Shane & Oona." So the "real" mother of his children combined with his own nurse-mother and really real mother, and although he kept the eyes blue as the Caribbean Sea, he gave the nurse girl hair that combined his mother's reddish brown with his nurse's blonde to make a color "partly a copper brown, partly a bronze gold." He also made Ezra's wife part French, as was Carlotta. His own mother ended by setting only one clear sign of her presence on the nurse-mother in his play; she gave her the name "Marie," French for her own name "Mary."

O'Neill wanted all the women of his play—Marie Brantôme, Christine Mannon, and her daughter Lavinia—to share an inner "psychic identity" shown by their physical resemblance. Marie, the Canuck nurse girl, and the French-origin Christine have the same pagan freedom. The family servant Seth recalls Marie to Lavinia as "frisky and full of life—with something free and wild about her like an animile." Christine also moves with a "flowing animal grace." Their postures stand in sharp contrast to the wooden military movements of the Puritan Mannons, who fall into the stiff stances of statues of eminent dead men in parks. O'Neill expressed the same conflict between pagan joy and Puritan life-denial in their dress. At first he thought the color for Christine should be the deep purplish crimson of Cybel's parlor and Tiberius's brothel-palace, but at last he chose green—the color of life—and had her appear first in green satin and then in green velvet. Her first defiant gesture is to carry a great bunch of flowers into the tomblike Mannon house. Her green is set against the black of the life-repressing Mannons, and black is the color of death. It is the color that becomes her daughter, as the title "Mourning Becomes Electra" declares. At the beginning of the play, Electra—called "Lavinia" after her other name in the legends, "Laodicea"—identifies with the Puritan Mannons, wears black, and echoes their wooden posture and military manner. She rejects any comparison with her mother, insisting, "I'm not a bit like her! Everybody knows I take after Father!" But Adam Brant sees at once: "Your face is the dead image of hers. And look at your hair." Lavinia has the same contrast between conscious identification with her parent of the opposite sex and real psychic identity with her parent of the same sex that O'Neill gave Eben of *Desire Under the Elms*—he who had insisted that he was "Maw—every drop o' blood!" although his brothers saw that he was "Like his Paw. Dead spit an' image!" O'Neill had seen just such a contrast in himself, with open hostility toward his father and inner identification with him, like the "strange, hidden psychic identity" between all the women of *Mourning Becomes Electra* and between all the men. In his "Diagram" for Dr. Hamilton he placed his "hatred and defiance" of his father as open and outward, while inwardly he lived in a world of "fantasy— father as hero." This self-knowledge went into all his fated Mannons. They really are quite unlike the orthodox Freudian Oedipus complex, in which the love for the father is outward, while the hostility is inner and repressed. No wonder O'Neill rejected the accusation of such critics as Barrett Clark that he was following psychoanalytic theory in this play, and tried to tell them—what was perfectly evident to him—that he could "have written *Mourning Becomes Electra* almost exactly as it is if I had never heard of Freud or Jung or the others." Out of the psychic identities, and out of the fated attraction of Puritan Mannon men for women with conflicting pagan life-strivings, O'Neill's "modern psychological approximation of Greek sense of fate" emerged.

"HOMECOMING"

Electra had fascinated O'Neill, and even in this first play—essentially the tragedy of her father Agamemnon—he made her his protagonist. So she became the most deeply imbued of all his characters with his own struggle against the forces of hatred and death, his own longing for life and love. He gave her his own profound loneliness, and the feeling of being shut out of love that had come with his exile to boarding school, and his resentment—in his case against his father—for sending him there. He found a way to have Lavinia rejected by her mother, so that she has a similar feeling of being shut out of love—and it served him also to motivate Christine's hatred for her husband—for the legendary reasons did not fit his play. In *What Is Wrong with Marriage,* Macgowan and Hamilton had pointed out that a major cause of sexual disability in married women was "a husband's ineptitude as a lover" and that it was "the husband's *initial* ineptitude that counts" rather than his later abilities in the act of love. Ezra Mannon's Puritan shame cripples his lovemaking into crude lust, so that his first relations with his wife change her love for him to "disgust." The disgust is so intense that she hates even the child born of it. She tells Lavinia, "You were always my wedding night to me—and my honeymoon!" Lavinia feels that her mother "stole all love from me when I was born!" She feels in her way what O'Neill himself felt and wrote into *Long Day's Journey into Night,* that he would "always be a stranger who never feels at home" and "who must always be a little in love with death!" Mourning—the color of death—becomes her, fits her destiny, and her tragic struggle for life and love was O'Neill's own.

As dominated by hatred as Lavinia is at the beginning of his play, O'Neill had been in the year preceding the writing of it. Into this story of betrayal went all his own sense of betrayal during the death throes of his marriage to Agnes, and as always, inextricably intertwined with it, came the crucial betrayal of his life, his mother's drug addiction. Both found their way into the plot he developed from the legends. He found a way to allow Lavinia to share in her father's tragedy, betrayed with his betrayal, and he did so by having Christine bring her lover to the house under the guise of courting Lavinia, and so awaken her love for him. Her love puts her in unsuccessful rivalry with her mother as she had been all her life before for the love of her father and brother. Her discovery that Adam Brant has been cuckolding her father brings discovery that Adam has been betraying her as well. Jealousy—more than protection of her father—moves her to divide her mother from Adam. By doing so she provokes the murder of her father that leaves her doubly bereft of love at the end of "Homecoming."

O'Neill easily put himself into her struggle, into that of her father, and even into that of his betrayer, Christine, whose struggle to free herself from a marriage poisoned by hatred echoes his own struggle to liberate himself from Agnes. The only character who did not immediately invite O'Neill's participation in his tragedy was that of his Aegisthus, Adam Brant, son of the nurse girl. When O'Neill read over his first draft, he found the character "hackneyed and thin" and decided "Must find new one." At that point a complete character walked into his play and blended so fully with his fated family that O'Neill himself never saw that his Captain Brant was really George Bernard Shaw's Captain Brassbound stepped intact out of *Captain Brassbound's Conversion.* (O'Neill had read Shaw's play years ago and had even seen it performed while a student at Harvard.) Once Captain Brassbound had walked out of Morocco and out of Shaw's inquiry into the meaning of justice, he became entirely unrecognizable, for in O'Neill's play he immediately fell passionately in love, which he never would have done for Shaw. Still, he brought with him the same motive for revenge that he had against his uncle in Shaw's play, whom he charges "with the death of my mother and the theft of my inheritance." In *Mourning Becomes Electra* he accuses his cousin Ezra Mannon, and does so out of the same feeling of guilt he had in Shaw's play because he had not been "very fond" of his mother or "very good" to her. In Shaw, "She had unfortunately a very violent temper," and Brassbound confesses that his childhood had been "Hell." In O'Neill's play Brant confesses that his mother had been "very strict" with him, like Brassbound's, even beating him—although this confession conflicts with O'Neill's other picture of her as petting and spoiling the boy Ezra. In both plays the Captain Brassbound-Brant hides his own guilt by accusing his uncle-cousin of letting his mother die "of sickness and starvation," for he himself had fled from her. He is very touchy about her honor in both plays. In Shaw he springs at his uncle, crying, "He did not spare my mother—'that woman,' he calls her—because of her sex. I will not spare him because of his age." In O'Neill's play Brant springs up at Lavinia's taunt at her, crying, "Belay, damn you!—or I'll forget you're a woman—no Mannon can insult her while I—." Probably it was Brassbound who made Brant a "captain," and from there O'Neill went on to make him a Clipper captain and gave him the same romantic appearance, "more like a gambler or a poet than a ship captain," of a notorious Clipper captain who appeared, picture and all, in one of the many Clipper books O'Neill had bought for background. So closely did O'Neill associate Captain Robert H. Waterman with his Brant that he had a chantyman in the ship scene shout up at him, "I don't give a damn if ye air a skipper! Ye could be Bully Waterman himself an' I'd not let you insult me!" In dress, Brant was Bully Waterman. Otherwise, he kept his Brassbound origin, and even took from Shaw's character the irony of judging a judge. Before Brassbound took over Brant, Ezra Mannon had been only "town's leading citizen, Mayor before war." He became a former judge as well when Brassbound came into O'Neill's play.

O'Neill had Ezra look down from his portrait in black judge's robes, as his wife and Brant sentence him to death, and the judge judging him looks so much like him, sitting sternly in his chair, that Christine is frightened and asks him to move. Adam says, when he sees the portrait, "It would be damned queer if you fell in love with me because I recalled Ezra Mannon to you!"

The whole plot became invested with O'Neill's mistrust of Agnes in the last year of their marriage. He had Christine cover her meetings with her lover under visits to a genuinely sick father in New York. Agnes's father had fallen ill with tuberculosis, and Agnes's departures from Bermuda to New York to see after him had aroused O'Neill's old distrust and all his uncertainty of her love. She had only to postpone her return to drive him frantic, and when she did so in April he sent her a telegram that even he realized was, he said, "harsh and unreasonable but I had been counting the days." He said that if she failed him Wednesday he would never trust her word again. Later, when his brains had become "wooly with hatred," he confided to Kenneth Macgowan his suspicion of what a private detective would discover about Agnes's infidelities once set to trace her past. His suspicions even found a vent in his first draft for his second God-trilogy play. In it his hero would be tortured when his wife visited her father by "imagining that she had lied to him about the purpose of her visit, that she was being unfaithful to him." In *Mourning Becomes Electra* Lavinia becomes the detective who spies out the infidelity, and she makes her first threatening hint of her discovery in a pointed question about her grandfather, who "seems to have been sick so much this past year."

Ezra's homecoming became fraught with O'Neill's two crucial homecomings, that of 1926, when he began the last struggle to preserve his marriage, and that of October 1927, when he made his final struggle, telling Agnes, "I'm simply eaten up by impatience and actually counting the days! . . . It will be so marvelous to take you in my arms and kiss you again!" Instead of his imagined homecoming, he had seen the death of their love. In *Mourning Becomes Electra,* Ezra Mannon returns from the orgy of hatred and death of the Civil War, bent on a desperate struggle to save his marriage, to regain his wife's love, to break through his own barriers of silence and give voice to the truth of his feeling for her. He has been always "a strange, hidden man," and he confesses to his wife, "Something queer in me keeps me mum about the things I'd like most to say—keeps me hiding the things I'd like to show." The words were O'Neill's. He knew himself to be a quiet man "hiding within a crevice of the mind," with a voice that "begins and ends in silence." O'Neill went so fully into the "inexpressive" Ezra Mannon that he told the cast of this play on opening night, "Like Ezry Mannon I am a bit dumb when it comes to expressing the things I would like most to say." After years of silence Ezra pleads with his wife in front of the moonlit temple of Hate and Death that has been their home to help him save their marriage. His plea is O'Neill's to Agnes. O'Neill wrote Agnes during her April New York visit: "We must get away alone to beaches and places when you return." He thought they should have a private life together as well as a family life. His Ezra tells his wife they might win through "if we'd leave the children and go off" together. Ezra cries to her out of the silence and alienation since their beginning: "I love you. I loved you then, and all the years between, and I love you now." O'Neill had told Agnes, "I love you! For our nine years I have loved you and you alone, loved you with my whole being." All the ironic futility of O'Neill's own struggle and all the horror of his final smash went into Ezra Mannon's homecoming to a wife who plans to murder him.

She does so in a way that shows how intimately O'Neill's distrust of Agnes was linked to the distrust of his mother because of her addiction. Both shape the murder in his play. Of course, O'Neill needed all his ingenuity to let his characters "commit murder without having to dodge detection, arrest, trial scenes," so that retribution would come directly out of the forces that swept them to their crimes. He had Christine murder her husband through a "medicine" that is actually "poison." She lets it be known that he has a heart condition, deliberately provokes a heart attack by taunting him with her infidelity, and then, instead of his medicine, gives him poison she has had Brant send her—and so he appears to have died of angina. The murder takes Agnes's weapon of deliberately provoking jealousy and joins it to O'Neill's mother's betrayal through a "medicine" that was really "poison." (In *Long Day's Journey into Night* he has his mother call the drug "medicine," and his father call it "poison.")

In dying, Ezra makes a commentary on O'Neill's old dream that his mother would rise out of death to reassure him with a message of life and love. For Lavinia, he had the father rise, and his message is the reverse of reassurance. He gasps, "She's guilty—not medicine!" The words bring suspicion of the murder to Lavinia, who enters in time to hear them, yet they apply equally to O'Neill's distrust of a mother who was "guilty"—in very different circumstances—because the drug she administered was "not medicine" but poison. So powerful was that indelible memory that O'Neill meant at first to have Christine commit suicide with the drug that killed her husband, so that the same "medicine" that was really "poison," destroys both, as it had poisoned the life of both his parents.

"THE HUNTED"

The same double betrayal—Agnes and his mother—shaped the second play of *Mourning Becomes Electra,* "The Hunted." In all the legends the son Orestes—whom O'Neill calls "Orin"—knows at once of his mother's guilt. In O'Neill's play it is the revelation, the realization, of his mother's guilt that is his particular tragedy, as it had been in his own case. As a matter of fact, O'Neill and his mother took over Orin and Christine. Christine has had the same "fierce" affection concentrated on her son, as O'Neill's mother, and she treats him exactly as O'Neill's mother treats him in *Long Day's Journey into Night.* Both call their grown son "my baby"; both promise to "nurse" him and both make him "comfortable" with the same gesture—placing a pillow behind his back. Both mothers play father against son by pointing out the father's jealousy. O'Neill's mother says in *Long Day's Journey into Night,* "He's been jealous of you most of all. He knew I loved you most because—." Except that the words are more cruel in *Mourning Becomes Electra,* they are the same. Christine tells Orin his father was "jealous of you. He hated you because he knew I loved you better than anything in the world!" Of course, Christine appears more treacherous because she is deliberately using her son's love in order to escape to her lover. She moves into O'Neill's old vision of the prostitute mother—and into her reincarnation in the Agnes of his distrust, redolent of betrayal. Certainly O'Neill had begun to see clearly the meaning of that old vision, for in less than two years after he finished *Mourning Becomes Electra* he noted in his *Work Diary* that he had "Idea M-harlot play." "M" was his usual abbreviation for "mother," so he had reached the point where he could write a "Mother-harlot" play, with his old vision made perfectly explicit.

"The Hunted" is largely Christine's tragedy, and O'Neill saw her guilt and horror through his remembrance of his mother's, and through his regret at the loss of innocence and trust which came from learning of her loss. Before the goodness of Hazel, Christine almost lets out the truth of her guilt, as she longs for her lost innocence. "If I could only have stayed as I was then! Why can't all of us remain innocent and loving and trusting? But God won't leave us alone. He twists and wrings and tortures our lives with other's lives until—we poison each other to death!" In *Long Day's Journey into Night* his mother's regret for the "poisoning" within her own family comes when she says, "None of us can help the things life has done to us. They're done before you realize it, and once they're done they make you do other things until at last everything comes between you and what you'd like to be, and you've lost your true self forever."

The more acute agony in Christine's words was wrung from O'Neill by the last agony of his love for Agnes, by his regret for his own "poisoned" family life—the word was *his*—and regret for all the torture of their love.

O'Neill endowed Orin with his own nerves, the nerves he would have his father speak of in *Long Day's Journey into Night,* when he calls himself a "healthy hulk," whereas his son has "always been a bundle of nerves like his mother." In *Mourning Becomes Electra,* Ezra tells his wife of Orin's break-down: "Nerves. I wouldn't notice nerves. He's always been restless. He gets that from you." In fact, O'Neill brought Orin home from the war two days after his father's murder with a head wound and had the horror of the revelation of his mother's guilt, and his own guilt over her suicide after he has killed her lover, complete the shattering of his mind—in line with Euripides' interpreta-tion of the legend, in which Orestes goes mad from the matricide.

Through Orin's haunted war-shattered brain, O'Neill was able to fuse the hidden forces of hatred and death within the nation with those within his fated family, so that the battle of life-and-death forces within the souls of the Man-nons shows itself to be a battle within the soul of man. Orin speaks of "mur-dering" two rebels in a fog. "It was like murdering the same man twice. I had a queer feeling that war meant murdering the same man over and over, and that in the end I would discover the man was myself! Their faces keep coming back in dreams—and they change to Father's face—or to mine—." When he returns to his family's whited "sepulchre" and to his father's corpse laid out within it, the horrors of war become one with the realities of his family. He looks down on the austere face of his dead father in his coffin and says, "Death sits so naturally on you! Death becomes the Mannons!" Orin looks just like the dead man he addresses, and both look like the black-robed judge in the por-trait, so his dream becomes palpable. In the end, when he has murdered his mother's lover, he sees his dead father in him. "He looks like me, too! Maybe I've committed suicide!" Actually he has, because Brant's death causes his mother's suicide, and her suicide brings on his own. The family resemblances make the family destiny visible.

The final horror of this second play comes with Christine's realization that her son has killed her lover, and with her last look of mingled fear and hatred at the daughter who has brought him to do it. Inside the temple of Hate and Death, she shoots herself with a "pistol," like the pistol of Agnes's suicidal letter, sending Orin into an agony of remorse: "I drove her to it!" His cry releases all O'Neill's guilt over Agnes joined to all his guilt at bringing on his mother's trouble.

"THE HAUNTED"

At the beginning of the third play, the blood out of the family past shows in a crimson sunset bathing the portico. Seth, the family servant, has bet a townsman that he will be afraid to stay alone in the empty Mannon house from sundown to moonrise. Although Seth intends the bet to make a joke of the town talk that the house is haunted, it actually serves to accentuate the deeper truth of its saturation with the past. Seth himself admits to Hazel and Peter that there is such a thing as "evil spirit," and he himself feels it in the house "like somethin' rottin' in the walls." Even Hazel feels gripped by "something cold" the moment she steps under its portico. So O'Neill set the homecoming of Orin and Lavinia, the last of the Mannons, returned from their China voyage to make a stand for life in the temple of Hate and Death.

Euripides had sent Orestes on a long voyage to the land of the Tauri to recover from the madness brought on by the matricide, and O'Neill had Lavinia take Orin away on one of their own Clippers to China. O'Neill's own China voyage in flight from the hatred and bitterness of his smashed marriage found its way into theirs, even though he disguised the obvious parallel by sending them on from China to one of the South Sea Islands. Yet even this additional voyage came of intimate personal history. With his second draft, he thought to accentuate the sea-longing of the Mannons by giving them all a dream of finding love, innocence, and peace on an island. The island would be for them—so O'Neill told himself—a "mother symbol" charged with their "yearning for prenatal non-competitive freedom from fear." He put it first into Adam Brant, who, having once been shipwrecked on the islands, thinks that they are "as near the Garden of Paradise before sin was discovered as you'll find on this earth!" Indeed, as he is the first male Mannon to enter the play, O'Neill named him Adam after the biblical first man. Adam tells Christine that he wants to take her away on his own Clipper to China and then to the South Pacific Islands: "By God, there's the right place for love and a honeymoon!" Even Ezra Mannon, determined to regain love, thinks he might win through to happiness with his wife if only they could sail to the other side of the world and "find some island." Orin comes back sure that he will find his mother in an island, from having read Melville's book *Typee,* and then hallucinated a mother-island in the first days of his head wound. Orin's most bitter disillusion, as he spies on his mother through the cabin skylight of the *Flying Trades,* is that she is plotting to go with Adam to "my island I told her about—which was she and I—."

Of course, O'Neill was perfectly clear on the Jungian overtones of the island dream. He went out of his way to point out to Barrett Clark that the only book of the psychoanalysts that had really interested him had been Jung's *Psychology of the Unconscious,* but only "in the light of my own experience with hidden human motives." Long before he had read Jung he himself had had a dream-vision of love in which the woman, the mother, merged with the setting of his deepest joy in life, the sea and the sand. He had once written a poem, "On the Dunes," to Beatrice Ashe—to his "Soul Mother of Mine" as he called her. In it her body had been "warm and undulating" like "the sand dunes," and he had found her in the moods of the sea—in the "laughter of spray," in the "exultant wave-crests," and in the "tender smiling" of its calm. So O'Neill put his own old love into Orin's dream of an island where, he tells his mother, "The breaking of the waves was your voice" and "The warm sand was like your skin."

If O'Neill put this old dream into his fated Mannons, he did so because it was also the dream that had permeated his entire love for Agnes. Their first happiness had been spent by the sea, among the dunes of Peaked Hill Bar. They had always longed for an island of perpetual summer and had found it at last—so they thought—on Bermuda. O'Neill told Agnes that it was their "ultimate island where we may rest and live toward our dreams." The very postmarks on their letters declared Bermuda to be "The Isles of Rest." The futility of his Bermuda dream pervaded the island dreams of his doomed Mannons. Even after he finished *Mourning Becomes Electra,* O'Neill still longed for his island. When he returned to America he sought the blessed isles once again on Sea Island Beach, Georgia, where he built "Casa Genotta," the house of Gene and Carlotta.

Even the two images of health, life, love—Peter and Hazel—for whom Lavinia and Orin make their final struggle, came to O'Neill out of his most intimate dreams of love. The names he chose for them were quite transparent— although partly based on the first initials of Pylades and Hermione, the fiancés of the legendary Electra and Orestes. O'Neill first called Lavinia's lover "Peter Oldham," giving his woman the same love ideal as his old mother-identified self, for the "old ham" was, of course, the old actor, his father. His first idea for Hermione was just as transparent. He called her "Hester Sand"—with "Sand" just one letter off the name of his nurse "Sarah Sandy." The next name he found for her—and kept—was even more transparent: "Hazel." O'Neill knew that Carlotta's legal name before she went on stage had been "Hazel Tharsing." Certainly he saw in her the same goodness and purity he put into Hazel, for a letter of his calls her "my pure and unspoiled one." Once O'Neill decided to make Peter and Hazel brother and sister like Orin and Lavinia, he found the same last name for both, "Niles." At this point he and Carlotta were planning a trip down the Nile, where O'Neill expected to feel his spiritual oneness with the ancient Egyptian conviction of the eternal renewal of life as symbolized by the recurrent overflowing of the Nile, bringing fertility and new growth.

He made Lavinia's China voyage culminate in the South Sea Islands as he had originally meant his own to do, and he put all the meaning of his China voyage into hers. On it Lavinia discards the Mannon black for her mother's green, the color of life, and she takes over her mother's struggle for life and love. In the hospital at Shanghai, O'Neill had felt that "all the bitterness got burnt out of me." He had triumphed over the hatred for Agnes, and he had triumphed over the lure of death, the compulsion to repeat his old suicide attempt. China, he knew, had done "a lot for my soul. I live now. I *can* live."

Indeed, it was only after the China voyage that he could consciously identify with his father and so enter with him the world of life-enjoyment and love that had always radiated from him. Only after China did Eugene O'Neill begin openly calling himself "son of the Count of Monte Cristo," because of the "slumbering director in me" (his father had always directed his own company). After China he could scorn the critics of *Dynamo* because he had been born on Times Square, not in Greenwich Village, and had heard dramatic critics "called sons of bitches—and, speaking in general, believed it—ever since I was old enough to recognize the Count of Monte Cristo's voice!"

But en route to China, O'Neill had still been helplessly bedeviled by compulsions out of the past—the whole voyage repeating, as it did, his flight from his first marriage in a flight from his second. And in his rage, his frustration, he became imbued with that other ubiquitous ghost out of the past, his brother Jamie. To Harold DePolo, who had been as much Jamie's friend as his own, and who had been with Jamie during his last self-destructive year of life, O'Neill confessed: "And now comes a sad tale! Prepare to weep! Whether it was sun-wooziness or what, I was introduced by a Frenchman to a swell gambling joint in Saigon and I bucked the wheel—and the game suddenly got me. I must have that Jim strain in me after all." What O'Neill did not tell Harold DePolo was how fully he had taken on Jamie's identity. He had gone on to a "booze bust" in Shanghai as suicidal as Jamie's, and that catastrophe—part alcoholism, part influenza, part nervous breakdown—had come close to bereaving him of love and life together.

Certainly his third trilogy play was haunted by Jamie's despair after their mother died. Orin's guilt, horror, and flashes of perverse malignity took much from Jamie's agony of self-destruction then. Lavinia is torn by watching Orin's pain and by an exasperation like O'Neill's own as he watched his brother destroy himself. He had wanted to be liberated from that lacerating spectacle, and the remembrance went into Lavinia's desperate impulse to push the brother she loves out of life. O'Neill's old feeling of living with his brother's life, of repeating his tragic destiny, had possessed him as he neared China. Sometime during the third draft of *Mourning Becomes Electra* O'Neill grasped the meaning of it all in one vision of how he could make fate—destiny—compulsion out of the past—both visible and palpable to an audience.

He did it by having his characters repeat words and gestures and even scenes out of the family past. Orin and Lavinia in the third play are the image—even to clothing and posture—of their father and mother in the first. Orin repeats his father's furious jealousy at Brant in the first play, and his own repetition of it with his mother in the second. He explodes into suspicions of Lavinia with all of O'Neill's own expectation of betrayal during his marriage to Agnes, which had culminated in all the mad hatred of the divorce delays. Agnes's way of deliberately provoking his jealousy had found its way into Christine's outbreaks of taunting in his earlier plays, and he had Lavinia repeat them by deliberately provoking her brother to believe his own baseless suspicions. Lavinia herself is bewildered by what she has done, saying, "Oh, Orin, something made me say that to you—against my will—something rose up in me—like an evil spirit!" He laughs: "Ghosts! You never seemed so much like Mother as you did just then!"

The weight of the past upon these two is made tangible by the weapon Orin holds over his sister to keep her from marrying Peter. He writes a family history, and in the earlier versions it goes back to the beginning and merges the history of the country with the history of the family, so that Orin says of it, "I've tried to show that the evil fate goes back to the murder of Indians to steal their lands, to witch burning as a pleasure!" In the published play, it starts with their grandfather Abe Mannon, and Orin tells Lavinia, "Most of what I've written is about you! I found you the most interesting criminal of us all!" This blackmailing weapon comes out of what O'Neill saw as Agnes's "legalized blackmail" in the divorce, and particularly out of the last long dispute between them. O'Neill told George Jean Nathan that it was Agnes's "refusal to accept a clause specifying that she should write no articles about me or our married life or thinly-disguised autobiographical fiction exploiting me. Can you beat it?" In *Mourning Becomes Electra* Orin uses his family history to force Lavinia to give up Peter, and then in his agony seeks safety in irreparable guilt that sums up all the family past. His father had caressed Christine's hair awkwardly, telling her, "Only your hair is the same—your strange beautiful hair I always—," and she had shrunk from his touch. Orin himself had repeated the caress and his father's words, causing his mother to shudder. In the last play he turns incestuously to Lavinia, caressing her hair and saying, "There are times now when you don't seem to

be my sister, nor Mother, but some stranger with the same beautiful hair—."
As she pulls away violently, he cries, "Perhaps you're Marie Brantôme, eh? And
you say there are no ghosts in this house?" Her struggle against him repeats
their mother's against their father, and like her mother she sentences him to
death.

O'Neill's most difficult problem from the beginning had been to find a tragic
ending "worthy" of his Electra. Back in 1926, when his "Greek plot idea" first
came, he had been struck by R. W. Livingstone's idea in *Pageant of Greece* that
Sophocles showed "moral insensitiveness" in having the matricide Orestes live
happily, instead of going mad as he does in Aeschylus and Euripides. O'Neill
went him one further and decided that all the Greek plots were flawed because
their Electra "peters out into undramatic married banality." O'Neill also had
been intrigued by Livingstone's praise for the ending Sophocles found for *Oedipus*. "A lesser poet," Livingstone declared, "would have made him either kill
himself, or drag out his life in obscurity," but Sophocles found a climax "more
worthy" of his greatness. His Oedipus blinds himself, thus shutting himself off
"from the world of sense," because his offense has "set him apart from men
and in a sense, above them, in a world of his own." Sophocles had even given
him a desolate world of his own, appropriate to his fate, on "the mountain of
Cithaeron where his parents cast him forth as a child to die."

O'Neill found a "worthy" tragic ending for his Electra. She—like all the
Mannons—is already set apart from men, for their faces in repose look like
"life-like death masks," so that she and all the Mannons bear the stamp of their
ultimate fate even while they struggle for life. When she gives herself over to
retribution she says, "I'm the last Mannon. I've got to punish myself! Living
alone here with the dead is a worse act of justice than death or prison! I'll never
go out or see anyone! I'll have the shutters nailed closed so no sunlight can ever
get in. I'll live alone with the dead, and keep their secrets, and let them hound
me, until the curse is paid out and the last Mannon is let die!" She turns and
enters the house—as the first shutter slams to—to inhabit a desolate world of
her own, set apart from mankind by the grandeur of her suffering.

In this tragedy of the damned the Mannons have been defeated by the forces
of hatred and death out of the family past. But O'Neill had won through to a
"new era" of life with "my inner self freed from the dead, consciously alive in
the new, liberated and reborn!" His triumphant struggle for life and love had
been the heart impulse of *Mourning Becomes Electra*. His characters were
defeated, but their struggle passionately affirmed life and love, and so they
achieved the exaltation of the original Greek tragedies in celebration of Dionysus—of Life. Christine with her flowers and her green dress is struggling for

life and love. Ezra returns from the murder of the war, declaring, "I'm sick of death! I want life!" Adam Brant reaches love out of revenge and achieves his own spiritual victory by sacrificing his beloved ship and the sea for love. He tells Christine, "You've brought love—and the rest is only the price." His very words echo those of O'Neill, who had given up his whole past for love. He had said then: "For everything real one gets in the vale of beefs one pays on the nail! And I have got something real!" His Orin achieves affirmation at the very brink of death, able to say, "I'm glad you found love, Mother! I'll wish you happiness—you and Adam!" And Lavinia's is the most passionate affirmation of all. In her last desperate struggle she cries, "I want to feel love! Love is all beautiful! I never used to know that!" She wants to "have children and love them and teach them to love life so that they can never be possessed by hate and death!" She is tragically defeated by her own past, doomed by her crimes to the "darkness of death in life." But the exaltation of her affirmation came from O'Neill's own. When he dedicated *Mourning Becomes Electra* to Carlotta, he told her that it represented for him "a victory of love-in-life."

O'Neill had plunged into *Mourning Becomes Electra* in May 1929 and did not come out of it until he had done five drafts and sent the fifth to the Theatre Guild on April 7, 1931. It had been "harrowing labor" all the way. By the third draft he exclaimed to Manuel Komroff, "And the wear and tear of it—it's an intense business from start to finish—leaves me sick with writing at the end of each day." When the Guild wired back enthusiastically accepting it, O'Neill and Carlotta sailed at once for the United States. He wanted to watch over this play's production every inch of the way. The Guild suggested Alla Nazimova for Christine, and O'Neill agreed. It had been the sight of Alla Nazimova as Ibsen's Hedda Gabler—seen during an Easter recess in March 1907, when he was a Princeton freshman—that had, he said, "discovered an entire new world of the drama for me. It gave me my first conception of a modern theatre where truth might live." He told the Guild that Nazimova "would be grand in spite of accent if can be directed to act as she did first Ibsen productions and cut out ham mannerisms acquired later." (She became so "grand" as O'Neill's Christine that Gerhart Hauptmann declared her "the greatest actress I have seen since Duse.") Alice Brady became Lavinia. Earle Larimore became Orin, and O'Neill thought he did "the finest work of them all." Philip Moeller again directed for O'Neill, and his old colleague Robert Edmond Jones did the sets.

After the first complete rehearsal, they saw that the headlong tempo would let them do all three plays on one night with a dinner break, as they had with *Strange Interlude*. O'Neill immediately did an entire sixth draft, cutting to the bone. (He was sorry that he published this acting version, for the fifth draft, he thought, made a better reading play.) All through rehearsals he changed and sharpened lines, so that Alice Brady said she would "wonder with horror" at every utterance whether she had the old words or the new ones. O'Neill saw to it that Brady let no pathos weaken the grandeur of Lavinia's tragic destiny. Particularly at the finale, he told her again and again that "no one should feel sorry for her." He participated completely in bringing his play to life in the theater. At the dress rehearsal he could only think, "Farewell (for me) to the Mannons!" *Mourning Becomes Electra* became a glorious success from its opening on October 26, 1931, but O'Neill felt suddenly "worn out—depressed—sad that the Mannons exist no more—for me!"

He thought this had been "a great Guild achievement against great odds" and "a high example of the combined acting, producing, and writing art of the American theatre." Not one critic grasped the battle of life-and-death forces in the play, but all the critics were deeply moved by it. The more intelligent ones, such as Krutch, were content to say that *Mourning Becomes Electra* meant only in the sense that "*Oedipus* and *Hamlet* and *Macbeth* mean—namely that human beings are great and terrible creatures when they are in the grip of great passions." The rest called it "melodrama" but confessed that it had thrilled them inexplicably. O'Neill was glad that a play beginning at 5:30 with a dinner break played to packed houses in the darkest years of the Depression. Indeed, it was so successful that the Guild added a road company by January 4, 1932, with Judith Anderson as Lavinia, and O'Neill thought that she was often better than Brady.

Almost at once, negotiations were under way for production throughout the world. When the British made an offer, O'Neill responded as his father's son. He said that he wanted "a substantial advance" or it was "no go," and he added, "Tell Bright I've sworn off giving plays to the British for nothing. (If James O'Neill of Monte Cristo fame heard that I ever gave the cursed Sassenach the slightest break he'd come back from the grave and bean me with a blackthorn! My, but didn't he love them!)" Almost every capital in Europe did *Mourning Becomes Electra* in the following years. Even ten years later O'Neill was still following new triumphs in Portugal, Switzerland, and Spain. At first he had been all for a film, but after he saw what Hollywood did to his *Hairy Ape* he shrank from the thought. He told Terry Helburn: "I so deeply regret having sold that play, need or no need, to be boy-and-girled by the Amusement Racket." He could not bear to see Hollywood desecrate *Mourning Becomes Electra* as well. He was right too, for when Dudley Nichols produced it quite faithfully, R.K.O. cut it to ribbons after its premiere, to get it down to standard feature length, and sent it out mutilated.

Later O'Neill was sure that it was largely for *Mourning Becomes Electra* that he received the Nobel Prize. He always loved *The Hairy Ape* and *The Great God Brown* best of his early plays, but he had gotten "the most personal satisfaction" from *Mourning Becomes Electra,* he said, adding, "You know that is Carlotta's play." Later still, he declared it the best of all his old plays—but by that time he had written *Long Day's Journey into Night,* and that, he knew, was "the best of all."

8

Ah, Wilderness!

After his farewell to the Mannons, O'Neill turned to his God trilogy, and the second play that seeks God in romantic love. When his love for Agnes had fallen to pieces, his religion of love had crashed with it. He needed a new faith, and he had to seek it in the desolated America of the Great Depression that he had found when he returned from France. He had seen the breadlines stretching through the "skyscraper canyons" of New York, and he had seen even more sharply the smash of old values that they brought with them. "The old Gods, the old life-values are dead," he told himself. "Life has trampelled them into dust and rushed on—rushed on too fast, too far ahead of any new human values, and we are left floundering in a lost interlude of 'all is permitted!' " He wanted to pull himself up out of it and create a world of new values in a new way. He wanted to free himself from his old "formula of tragedy" and try for a direct and ringing affirmation of life. He told Dudley Nichols, "Even the most positive affirmative Nay! of my past work no longer satisfies me. So I am groping after a real, true Yea!" But the struggle was hard, desperately hard, and on August 31, 1932, he put down "Without Endings of Days," as he was calling his second God play then, and wrote despairingly in his *Work Diary:* "Battle with it again—no flow—sunk!"

The next morning, September 1, he awoke with *Ah, Wilderness!* It had come

out of his dreams "fully formed and ready to write," title and all. All that day
he outlined it, and on September 6 he began, for it seemed "crying to be
written." He became so absorbed that he had to start having lunch brought to
his study so he could "work without interruption." By September 27 he was
declaring in his *Work Diary: "Finished First Draft!"*

His dream play had come to him with a Fourth of July morning in his boyhood home at 325 Pequot Avenue, New London, and brought the old family
room with its screen door to the porch, its doorways to the dining room through
the back parlor and to the front parlor. His last two July Fourths had been
saturated with images of the old house. He had gone back to look at it just
before the Fourth in 1931, and thinking of it had brought his idea for a play
about the "house-with-the-masked-dead." During the Fourth of July holiday in
1932 he had played host to the children of his two previous shattered marriages,
with Agnes's son Shane and Kathleen's son Eugene Jr. (who brought his new
bride, Betty, along) visiting him at Sea Island Beach in his newly finished home
with Carlotta. He was "on the hop leading fishing and swimming parties—and
talking parties," very like the Fourth of July festivities of his New London boyhood yet far from "the old solidarity of the family unit" he had felt around him
then.

That "old solidarity" had been the core of his dream. Family love had been
the world of his childhood, and it returned bringing not his specific family—
though the Millers live in his old home—but a total-recall family redolent of
the time. They are, he explained, the kind of people "I really know better than
any other—my whole background of New London childhood, boyhood, young
manhood—the nearest approach to home I ever knew—relatives, friends of
family, etc. all being just this class of people." His boyhood chum Art McGinley
thought, when he saw the Millers, that they were meant to be the McGinleys.
His mother had been just such an easygoing housewife as Essie. His father had
been a newspaperman like Nat Miller. His own name, "Arthur," went into the
older brother, and the names of his brothers—Tom, Lawrence, and Wint—
went into the little boy Tommy Miller, a grown-up brother Lawrence away from
home, and the Yale man Wint, who leads young Richard Miller astray. Many
other people thought the Millers were their family, and lots of New Londoners
saw in Nat Miller the image of Judge Frederic P. Latimer, editor of the *New
London Telegraph*. Latimer had been a friend of James O'Neill, had given Eugene his job on the *Telegraph* in 1912, and had been the first to see genius in
him. Actually the play was redolent of New London names and New London
ways. Young Mildred Culver came up out of the past so urgently that she gave
her name to Richard's sister Mildred with her nickname "Mid" and even

pushed her last name into the play through Mildred's "going to the beach to Anne Culver's." All the play people came up as total recall of a period of the past—and into them flitted some of the most insistent and lovable spirits from O'Neill's "ghost-haunted inner dark."

The dream play came to him first as July 4, 1905—the crucial time of his life, when he had been sixteen going on seventeen. He kept that age for the boy of his play, Richard Miller, although he changed the year to 1906. The entire dream emerged out of his struggle to find a meaning—a faith—for his new love for Carlotta. On May 25, 1932, he had written a prose poem to her, declaring, "You are my lost way refound," and that lost way haunted him in the following months, as he struggled with the "modern, involved, complicated, warped and self-poisoned psyche" of the way he had actually taken. The *Ah, Wilderness!* dream brought him back to the point in time where he lost the way, where he had taken the wrong turning, and it let him take the turning again as he should have taken it, to go on as he should have gone. Later he confessed, *"Ah, Wilderness!* was a nostalgia for a youth I never had," and still later, "That's the way I would have *liked* my boyhood to have been. It was a sort of wishing out loud."

His wrong turning had been precipitated by his disillusion with his mother (over her morphine addiction), and had taken him away from love to a world of drink and prostitutes, to a disastrous involvement with Kathleen Jenkins and a squalid marriage-divorce, so that in 1914, when he came to the first great romantic love of his adult life, Beatrice Ashe, the girl he wanted so desperately to marry, all of his past stood in the way and destroyed his hope of happiness. In the dream, not only did he go back to the turning point in 1905, he went back also to the great romantic love of his youth ten years after it (1914–16) and refound the lost way to that old enchantment.

Beatrice permeates *Ah, Wilderness!* She came on a wave of poetry, bringing all the music of the verses O'Neill had so passionately quoted to her. His letters to her sing with "The Rubáiyát of Omar Khayyám" and with quotations from the poets that delight Richard in the play: Swinburne, Oscar Wilde, Kipling, Dowson. The very title of *Ah, Wilderness!* came out of "The Rubáiyát" and brought back his love for Beatrice with the books of verses that lent their magic to it.

> A Book of Verses underneath the Bough,
> A Jug of Wine, a Loaf of Bread—and Thou
> Beside me singing in the Wilderness—
> Ah, Wilderness were Paradise enow!

Beatrice had actually been a singer, and their love had flowered on the sands beside the sea of a New London summer. At Harvard that winter of 1914–15, he had told her he longed for her to come to him "a-singing." He sent her a dream poem in which he was transported from his dreary Cambridge room with the "flat-wheeled" trolleys clanging by to a "wave-swept beach" with her in his arms. He even used "The Rubáiyát" to tell her:

> "Summer, indeed, is gone with all its rose"?
> Ah, but the soul of Summer haunts me yet.

The *Ah, Wilderness!* dream brought back his youthful romantic love on the wings of the poetry that had transformed Wilderness to Paradise.

O'Neill had begun devouring those poets before he took the turning and lost the way. He confessed to Art McGinley that, although Richard Miller is not a self-portrait, "the boy does spout the poetry I and Hutch Collins once used to." There—with the poets, the great books—his rebellion had begun. He and Hutch had been first set apart, O'Neill knew, because "the things which interested us, which we found beautiful, had no part in the life of that small town." Only they had not stopped with the beautiful. Both he and Hutch had gone on to drink, to prostitutes, to playing "loose and fast with all the girls" (as another New London chum Ed Keefe put it) until they ended by becoming, O'Neill recalled, "linked as twin disreputables in the village gossip." The dream play kept it all poetry and high-thinking. Richard gets into more and more trouble from the great books he reads, but he never really gets far past the poetry, and so he can find the way to the romantic dream love that O'Neill himself had lost long before it began, back when he was sixteen going on seventeen.

Beatrice never appears in her own person in *Ah, Wilderness!* yet she dominates the play and materializes in three separate characters, so that O'Neill is able to tell the actual truth of their love and at the same time make his old dream come true. Beatrice moves first into Richard's sister Mildred, although Mildred is only fifteen and redolent of many other New London girls. The Beatrice in her is revealed by Mildred's "big, gray eyes" and "fetching smile." O'Neill had written a comic love poem to Beatrice, telling Dante that his Florentine Beatrice could not compare with his:

> Her eyes were not so large or grey;
> She had no such heart-teasing smile.

By entering Mildred, Beatrice becomes sister to Richard, the proxy for O'Neill who will take the turning again, and as a sister she is bound to him in family love and innocence, as she had been in a poem O'Neill wrote her, "From a Child to a Child." By shunting Beatrice into Mildred, O'Neill splits off from her romantic dream image, the aspect of Beatrice that foreshadowed her ultimate faithlessness. Beatrice was an incorrigible flirt and immensely attractive to men. In a "Villanelle" that O'Neill wrote to her he signed himself "Knight One Thousand and One" and complained in the very title that "The Cursed Memory of The Thousand Others Doth Poison His Dreams." In it he reiterates the refrain "I am but one among a multitude." In *Ah, Wilderness!* Mildred fetches a similar multitude. When her brother Arthur teases her about one of them she says, "Pooh! What do I care for him? He's not the only pebble on the beach." Her mother reports at one point that Mildred is "out walking with her latest. I've forgot who it is. I can't keep track of them." In Mildred, Beatrice's flirtatiousness becomes harmlessly comic. Mildred tells Richard, "Gee, it must be nice to be in love like you are—all with one person." The Beatrice in Mildred can even admire in her romantic avatar, Richard's Muriel, the spunk, the loyalty, and the possession of her own soul that the real Beatrice never achieved.

The second avatar of Beatrice absorbs all the hopeless pain of O'Neill's love for her, and the truth of their irrevocably broken engagement. Much of the plot of the dream play came out of O'Neill's last desperate letter to Beatrice of July 25, 1916, urging her to marry him, and with it came Lily Miller, Nat's old-maid sister (eternally the pure Lily) who sprang into life from O'Neill's warning to Beatrice not to clutch her virginity to the end. The real Beatrice had chosen the other alternative he warned against, a conventional husband and a domestic cage. Nevertheless, all the pathos of the waste that he had predicted came alive in the dream play Lily, along with all the frustration of their love. Her only resemblance to Beatrice is her "gray" eyes, dimmed by spectacles, but the essence of their unhappiness went into her.

She and her futile suitor Sid Davis could not be more unlike Beatrice and O'Neill on the surface, or more revealing of what actually happened to their engagement beneath it. Sid took outer shape, it seems, from an irrepressibly comic little man, probably alcoholic like the play Sid, whom O'Neill knew when he was Richard Miller's age. Louis Sheaffer found a photograph of O'Neill at about that age with three unidentified New London friends in whom he saw no significance. The one standing next to O'Neill fits, point by point, O'Neill's description of Sid. He is about forty-five, "short and fat, bald-headed, with the Puckish face of a Peck's Bad Boy who has never grown up." He even wears Sid's "shapeless and faded nondescript" of a once flashy suit, and it looks particularly derelict in the photo because he has no collar or tie under the jacket.

The only clue to his identity as the O'Neill who lost Beatrice is his name. After Beatrice broke the engagement, and after O'Neill had his final terrible collapse into alcoholism that winter, he wrote two one-act sea plays in which there is a sentimental alcoholic who has lost his beloved, a singer, because she became disgusted when he relapsed into alcoholism and broke their engagement. This first embodiment of the O'Neill who lost Beatrice went by the name of "Smith" at sea, but his real name was "Sidney Davidson." Association seems to have brought the second embodiment in *Ah, Wilderness!* his name "Sid Davis."

Uncle Sid and Aunt Lily relive the unhappy part of O'Neill's love for Beatrice. When O'Neill went to bed on August 11, 1932, and dreamed the *Ah, Wilderness!* dream, just sixteen years had passed since Beatrice broke their engagement in August 1916. He kept that time span for his play. Lily tells Sid's sister Essie, "It's sixteen years since I broke off our engagement, but what made me break it off is as clear to me today as it was then." Beatrice broke her engagement to O'Neill because he relapsed into drink. From the beginning she had made him "promise" to cut out all drinking. She had been distressed by his disreputable past, so he swore himself to chastity for her sake. Lily's objection to Sid for drinking and "bad women" is really Beatrice's objection to O'Neill, and Sid's promise to stay sober represents one point in O'Neill's long promise to Beatrice. His letters to her from Harvard are full of his determination, for her sake, to stay teetotal and chaste. He told her that he had given up for her all that in the past had "made life bearable to me and given me pleasure." He was determined not to sin against their love. He felt humiliated by the "grimy smears" of his past and wanted to be cleansed for her. Even the "grimy smears" seem to have found their way into the dream proxy of his alcoholic self, Sid. O'Neill at first had a scene in which the smears become concretely visible. While Sid sleeps off his hangover, Tommy inks black circles over his face. When Richard then sets off a "cannon" firecracker just outside, "Sid jumps from his chair with a frightened yell, his mouth open, his eyes popping, his hair on end. With the ink lines around his eyes and mouth he looks indescribably like a hideous clown doing an act. Tommy and Mildred and Richard double up and roar with glee. Sid looks from one to the other with a foolish sickly smile." Although O'Neill cut this scene of visible degradation during rehearsals, it had been powerfully present in the dream.

It was in the second year of O'Neill's engagement to Beatrice, the second year of enforced chastity and sobriety, that O'Neill cracked under the strain of long frustration and collapsed into a bad bout of drinking. He writes of it in that last letter to Beatrice, telling her how he had been afraid to face her. She had forgiven him, and his letter gratefully calls her "Dear Old Big Heart." The story of Sid and Lily perpetuates the whole cycle of promise, relapse, self-loathing (Sid denounces himself as a "dirty, rotten drunk"), and ultimate forgiveness. Lily personifies "Dear Old Big Heart," and she repeats the endlessly recurring cycle in the play with endless forgiveness. Although their engagement has been broken sixteen years back, theirs has not been the complete separation that came for O'Neill and Beatrice. Nevertheless, it has all the melancholy of that separation for O'Neill: *Ah, Wilderness!* was a comedy "with undertones, oh yes, with undertones!" Only the dream detaches the cycle of relapse-forgiveness from the final tragic rupture and continues it revolving enchantedly forever.

So it is that Lily and Sid participate when Richard is brought upon the carpet before the family for his reading, unexpectedly joining him in enthusiasm for "The Rubáiyát." They are, after all, another aspect of the lost love for Beatrice that Richard exemplifies. Richard gives voice to the romantic dream of "a Book of Verses"—and "Thou." Sid jokingly tells of "how beset" O'Neill's path had been "with gin" in the alcoholic sense of the word, and Lily gives the lines that tell the truth of all the loss that the dream play denies:

> The Moving Finger writes, and having writ,
> Moves on; nor all your Piety nor Wit
> Shall lure it back to cancel half a Line,
> Nor all your Tears wash out a Word of it."

The third avatar of Beatrice is Richard's ideal love, Muriel Macomber, although nothing of Beatrice can be seen outwardly in that plump fifteen-year-old girl with her "big naïve wondering dark eyes." (Beatrice's charms went into the other fifteen-year-old, Mildred, who is safely bound with all her flirtatiousness to Richard in the indissoluble bonds of innocent family love.) The dark-eyed child exterior of this proxy Beatrice came from the last perfectly innocent romance of O'Neill's boyhood before he took the wrong turning. When O'Neill chose Ruth Gilbert with her "enormous brown eyes" for the role of Muriel, he told her that "she resembled a childhood sweetheart" of his "on whom he had based the part." Whether or not O'Neill had actually written the passionate lines of Swinburne's "Anactoria" to this childhood sweetheart, as Richard has in the play, he had certainly later used them to Beatrice. His letters to her burned with Swinburne's ecstasy, and he had written her the lines from "Laus Veneris" with which Richard greets Muriel in the beach scene that makes the Beatrice dream come true:

> And lo my love, mine own soul's heart, more dear
> Than mine own soul, more beautiful than God,
> Who hath my being between the hands of her—.

O'Neill had created his religion of love for Beatrice out of these lines. In *Ah, Wilderness!* the poetry, the separation, and the ultimate union of Richard and Muriel are all a dream rewriting of the actual tragic ending of O'Neill's great love for Beatrice.

O'Neill's last letter had urged Beatrice to break with her parents. He wanted to free her "wild, wayward bird-soul" from imprisonment in all domestic cages—her parents' house first of all, or that of a conventional husband. He wanted to save her from the "mean ambitions" of a vapid small town where an artist could only be misunderstood by the people and "stung by their poisonous bites." In the dream play all the small-town mean-mindedness is concentrated in Muriel's father, the owner of the local dry-goods store, who comes in fiercely on the Fourth of July, after discovering Richard's poetry to his daughter, to charge Richard before his father with being "dissolute and blasphemous—with deliberately attempting to corrupt the morals of my young daughter Muriel" and to demand that he be given a "hiding he'd remember to the last day of his life." He has punished Muriel by literally shutting her up in a domestic cage— that is, by not allowing her "out of the house for a month," and he has forced Muriel to write a letter breaking with Richard forever.

So in the first act of *Ah, Wilderness!* Richard is betrayed by his mother and his girl, even as Reuben had been doubly betrayed in the first act of *Dynamo*— but all the cruelty is out of the betrayal. Essie betrays Richard to his father only in her loving naïveté over the books he reads, and she really repeats the anxiety of O'Neill's own mother. In *Long Day's Journey into Night,* Mary tells her son, "It's the books you read! . . . Your father shouldn't allow you to have them." So the dream Richard is accused by a mother full of loving-kindness and emerges triumphantly before the larger understanding of his father. The same understanding brings out Richard's real innocence of the accusation of Muriel's father, and his wish, like O'Neill's for Beatrice, to marry her.

Nat Miller is as much O'Neill looking back humorously at his own youth, and looking on sympathetically at his sons, as he is James O'Neill, yet he represents entirely the life values of the latter. By entering into him, O'Neill consolidated his identification with his father's faith. Afterward O'Neill described his characters as "loyal, kindly, high-minded." He asked Saxe Commins, "And do you like Pa and Ma and all the rest? Fine people, all of them, to me. Lovable!" He had heard his father voice just these values—just these words—as, for instance,

James O'Neill on Edwin Booth: "It is hard to tell you how lovable he was personally, how high minded and lofty was his purpose and how pure his character." So fully was O'Neill back at one with his father's views that he ended the first act of his dream play with a total recall of one of his most joyful ways of carrying them out. While in France, O'Neill had gone in for a few finely crafted automobiles, including a Bugatti racer, and when he returned to the United States he took advantage of Depression prices to buy a secondhand Cadillac. To Brooks Atkinson he confessed that he was an "A-one snob" in cars and boats, and had been since boyhood. "My father, the Count of Monte Cristo, always got me the classiest rowboats to be had, and we sported the first Packard car in our section of Connecticut way back in the duster-goggle era." The first act ends on this recollection, with the elder Millers all equipped for a ride in their automobile in "the elaborate paraphernalia of motoring at that period—linen dusters, veils, goggles, Sid in a snappy cap."

The nostalgia became even more intimate in act two, set in the dining room at 325 Pequot Avenue. To Saxe Commins, O'Neill exclaimed, after writing it, "How I remember the dinners in New London! I feel I've caught them." He had caught the whole flavor of the period, and in this scene Essie bursts into a medley of all the dinner table clichés of thousands of families to their children: "Tommy! Stop spinning your napkin ring! . . . Mildred! Sit up straight in your chair! . . . Richard! Take your elbows off the table!" Yet with all their redolence of a class of Americans, the Millers became powerfully possessed by the O'Neills, and in the dream play the major tragedy of the O'Neills passes off in laughter—although its "undertones" reverberate insistently with the pain that has been transcended. At the dinner table little Tommy becomes not only universal little boy but little Eugene O'Neill at the seafood dinners of his boyhood, seated at the same table with his later self Richard, at the brink of the turning that changed his life. And his mother and father and brother are there with him.

The easygoing Essie becomes possessed by O'Neill's elegant mother and is shown in Mary Ellen O'Neill's typical struggle to train what she would call in *Long Day's Journey into Night* the "stupid, lazy greenhorns" with whom she had to deal because the "really good servants are all with people who have homes and not merely summer places." Just such a "clumsy, heavy-handed, heavy-footed, long-jawed, beamingly good-natured young Irish girl—a 'greenhorn,'" makes the dinner table scene of the Millers hilarious, even though they have a home and not just a summer place. And the Nat Miller and Sid Davis who return from the Sachem Club picnic, the first "benignly ripened," the second "blurry" from drink, take on and become enriched by the ghosts of

James O'Neill at his most glowingly benevolent, and his son Jamie at the point
before his wit and his teasing of his father took on its biting edge. Sid's drunken
high-jinks at the table—particularly comic transported into his fat "Puckish,
naughty-boy" self—bear all the traces of Jamie's style. Mock toasts were one of
Jamie's specialties. He once sent Eugene a note with a newspaper clipping in
his praise, commenting, "Gentlemen, I give you 'The Babe Ruth of the
Drama.' " Sid delivers his toast raising his soup plate and bowing to all sides:
"We'll drink to the dead already, and hurrah for the next who dies. Your good
health, ladies and gents." Sid's mock circus-barking was another of Jamie's
tricks—and one that O'Neill had already picked up and used ironically for the
ending of his play *The Hairy Ape*. So fully did O'Neill relive his brother's charm
that he entered into Sid himself and made a joke on his own setting-aside of
his heavy labor on "Without Endings of Days" to dash off *Ah, Wilderness!* Sid
says he invented lobster. "Fact! One day—when I was building the Pyramids—
took a day off and just dashed off lobster."

Only after his hilarious exit do the undertones break out in Lily's desolate
cry "That's been his downfall—everyone always laughing," and at this point Sid
enlarges to symbolize both Eugene's drunkenness, which lost him Beatrice, and
Jamie's, which lost him everything. Sid's joke "Waterwagon—Waterbury—Wa-
terloo!" turns out to be only too true of the job Nat has got him on the Waterbury newspaper. He has lost it for drunkenness just as Jamie had lost all the
jobs his father got him with other theatrical companies. Nat takes Sid back on
his own paper, just as James O'Neill had always to take Jamie back.

The Puckish Sid thus absorbs and transforms the tragic alcoholism of the
O'Neill brothers into comedy, and the dinner table scene really cancels out the
family secret that drove them to it. Another harmless family secret is substituted for the terrible revelation of his mother's addiction that pushed O'Neill
to take the wrong turning, and it is revealed, as the tragic one was, by Jamie
(embodied in Sid). O'Neill used his father's actual belief—so he said—that "a
certain peculiar oil in bluefish" invariably poisoned him, and his mother's giving
it to him for years as "weakfish." So the tragic "poisoning" of their family life
by his mother's drug, which had taken shape in *Mourning Becomes Electra* as
the murderous poisoning of the father by the mother, becomes in *Ah, Wilderness!* the laughable revelation of Essie's trick. Sid says, "See how guilty she
looks—a ver—veritable Lucretia Georgia! Can it be this woman has been
slowly poisoning you all these years? And how well—you've stood it! What iron
constitution!"

The other of his father's "idiosyncrasies" that O'Neill recalled in Nat Miller
at the dinner table is James O'Neill's habit of repeating over and over again, as

if it were new, the story of how he once saved a chum's life while in swimming as a boy. Of course, swimming was one of the first and best ways that O'Neill took his father as a model, and that identification had been his own lifesaving, so no wonder the old story and Jamie's teasing variations on it came to O'Neill's mind as the second of his father's ways to be lovingly portrayed in this scene of the dream play that negates the seeds of tragedy in his mother's trouble and saves his life in retrospect.

The scene ends with Richard going forth in full rebellion to meet his brother Arthur's friend Wint at the Pleasant Beach House to take one of the "real swift" Janes from New Haven off his hands while he is upstairs with the other. Richard is driven to go by Muriel's seeming betrayal and by his parents' scolding over his comment on Uncle Sid's drunkenness. Richard thinks it is all Aunt Lily's fault. "It's all because he loves her, and she keeps him dangling after her, and eggs him on and ruins his life—like all women love to ruin men's lives!" The words really describe O'Neill's long, futile engagement to Beatrice and recall his ironic statement on the brokenhearted Sidney of his sea plays: "An' she said she threw you over 'cause you was drunk; an' you said you was drunk 'cause she threw you over."

Richard's encounter with sin at the Pleasant Beach House reverses the outcome of O'Neill's, yet the sin itself is enveloped in the same enchanted nostalgia as the rest of the dream play. Looking back at his own early encounter with "sin," O'Neill fondly recalled the romantic idealization with which he had gilded the blotchy back rooms of his youth. The discrepancy between the actuality of those "fly-specked" haunts and his poetic illusion of them create the humor of this scene, and O'Neill had it in mind when he dedicated *Ah, Wilderness!* to his friend George Jean Nathan, "Who also, once upon a time, in peg-top trousers went the pace that kills along the road to ruin." He had it in mind again when he described *Ah, Wilderness!* for the Wilderness Edition of his plays as "A nostalgic comedy of the sentimental days when youth was young, and right was right, and life was a wicked opportunity." Once drunk, Richard envelops the back room of the Pleasant Beach House with the turgid aura of sincerely bitter remorse and equally sincere enjoyment in the verses of Oscar Wilde's "Ballad of Reading Gaol." Richard is able to see the tart, Belle, as "a romantic, evil vampire" and still later can elevate her into an alluring New York chorus girl. One of O'Neill's urgent telegrams to the company after seeing the dress rehearsal of this play read: "Serious criticism I forgot. Please insist Belle look more cheap: tawdry costume, and make-up less natty, modern, pretty; otherwise out of character and Richard's chorus-girl-story contrast lost."

At the same time as it looks back with loving laughter on the "wicked opportunity" conception of sin, the dream play saves O'Neill's proxy Richard from all the genuinely disastrous effects of O'Neill's own debauch into it. O'Neill had taken to drink when he was fifteen years old, and it had become—so he had told Beatrice—a necessity to make life "bearable" to him. Richard, instead, nurses a beer and is pushed into a sloe-gin fizz only by extreme taunts from the tart—and he gets drunk on it only because Belle has conspired with the bartender to put "dynamite" into it. Richard succumbs to the drink, but he preserves himself from the all-out assault of the prostitute simply by giving her the five dollars she is after. So Richard is preserved from O'Neill's wrong turning, and the dream play even absolves O'Neill's older brother Jamie from all the guilt of leading him astray. Richard goes to the Pleasant Beach House only because his older brother Arthur is away when Wint comes seeking him, and the boy is saved altogether by the entrance of a traveling salesman who is outwardly unlike Jamie but seems to be a dream embodiment of him in his role of a salesman that he acted so long in the play *The Traveling Salesman*. This character first appropriates the prostitute, then has the boy expelled from the place as obviously underage, and finally goes after him to see him safely on his trolley on learning that he is Nat Miller's son, for his father's sake. So he reverses on all points the actual role of Jamie, who had egged on O'Neill's rebellion against their father, had started him drinking when he was a very underage fifteen, and had delivered him up to prostitutes a year later.

In the Pleasant Beach House all the tormenting doubts and distrusts of love that O'Neill had been fighting in "Without Endings of Days" became shunted off into the prostitute. It is she who tries to break Richard's real faith in Muriel, telling him, "Bet you she's out with a guy under some bush this minute, giving him all he wants. Don't be a sucker, Kid! Even the little flies do it." The old resentment at Beatrice's choice of another of the multitude after she broke with O'Neill seems to have surfaced through the other prostitute upstairs with Wint, "giving him all he wants," for her name is the same as that of the singer who broke her engagement and the heart of Sidney Davidson in O'Neill's early play about his loss of Beatrice, *In the Zone*. She is called "Edith."

O'Neill brought Richard home drunk to a family sitting up and worrying over him. Before he comes, Arthur sings to take his mother's mind off her anxiety, and the songs "Then You'll Remember Me" and "Dearie"—with the words, "Dearie, My Dearie, nothing's worthwhile but dreams of you"—bring Sid, the figure of O'Neill's failure in love for Beatrice, to burst out in remorse and break into the sobs of a "sick little boy." Lily, the eternal "Dear Old Big Heart," forgives his broken promise, throws her arms around him, kissing "him tenderly and impulsively on his bald head" and soothing him "as if he were a little boy."

Then Richard—O'Neill at the point of the turning—lurches in full of the quotations from Ibsen's *Hedda Gabler* that the real O'Neill had quoted obsessively during the Princeton Easter Recess of 1907 after going back night after night to see Alla Nazimova in that play. Richard goes green, cries out "to his mother appealingly, like a sick little boy," and is taken in charge by his later avatar, Sid, who had himself been sobbing not long before "like a sick little boy." In the dream play both avatars of O'Neill—and the eternal little boy in him—merge, as one takes charge of the other.

But O'Neill's dream-proxy Richard is saved from Sid's fate, although Sid addresses him sardonically in the next act as "my fellow Rum Pot" and adds familiarly, as O'Neill himself or Jamie might have, of Dowson, "as good old Dowie calls us." Richard reacts to his first drunk as O'Neill himself had finally reacted to the years and years of booze busts when he stopped drinking in 1926. O'Neill had said then that he wondered he had ever "sought such a high-priced release" and that now he looked upon a drunken bout as "dull and stupid." His dream-self Richard sees that at once. He says, "It only made me sadder—and sick—so I don't see any sense in it." His first drunk will be his last.

The impetus of the original dream had been to bring O'Neill back to the moonlit summer "Upon Our Beach" of his first great love for Beatrice. Indeed, at Harvard, he wrote her with passionate longing, recalling one particular moonlit summer night out of the many beautiful ones on "our beach." Moonlight had drenched both the sea plays of 1917 about the loss of Beatrice. He called one *The Moon of the Caribbees* and had his sentimental Sidney-self stare, in *In the Zone,* "at the moon," like a man, "half-daft," brooding over his lost singer. By going back to the moonlit beach, O'Neill negates the betrayal of the real engagement. Richard's Muriel has the spunk to overcome her father's prohibition, to break out of her domestic cage and meet him under the new moon of young love.

O'Neill's letters to Beatrice all urged her to find, to possess, to be true to her "own soul." The real Beatrice never did, never could be. In his first bitterness over Muriel's seeming betrayal O'Neill had Richard say: "I suppose you think I ought to be heartbroken about Muriel—a little coward that's afraid to say her soul's her own, and keeps tied to her father's apron strings!" When the dream reverses the actual betrayal into fidelity and Mildred admires Muriel's spunk, Richard is made to exclaim exultantly, "You don't know her! Think I could fall in love with a girl that was afraid to say her soul's her own? I should say not!" In the dream, Beatrice remains true to her soul. O'Neill never has taken the wrong turning to drink and prostitutes. He is liberated from his "grimy smears" to fulfill his dream. O'Neill brought his two young lovers back to their moonlit beach to pledge their love, and in the first draft, which poured out of him in three weeks, he ended his play there, with Richard declaring, "Gosh, I love you—Darling!" and Muriel responding, "I love you too—Sweetheart!" and the two of them sitting rapt "staring at the moon."

Of course, O'Neill awoke from the dream, and awake he knew that his own happiness, his own future, did not lie back with Beatrice on the moonlit New London beach of his youth. Even the dream logic seems to have recognized that, for the romantic face in the dream play was not that of Beatrice—Beatrice's had been shunted off onto Richard's sister Mildred—but that of the dark-eyed child sweetheart from before O'Neill learned of his mother's addiction. She had been the last love in which O'Neill pursued his own mother's dark-eyed beauty. In all his loves thereafter he had pursued the image of his second mother, his nurse Sarah Sandy—that is, up until Carlotta. Carlotta was indeed his "lost way refound." So when O'Neill picked up *Ah, Wilderness!* again to put in three more weeks of work on it, he took up the ending on the moonlit beach and carried it on to forecast his union with Carlotta. Richard bursts into an ecstasy of Kipling to predict his honeymoon with Muriel. They will set out on the "Long Trail—the trail that is always new" of the open sea, take "the road to Mandalay," and "watch the dawn come up like thunder out of China!" even as O'Neill and Carlotta had. O'Neill gave this version to Carlotta, saying, " 'We've watched the dawn come up like thunder out of China!' Sweetheart, all my love! Your Gene. July 22, 1933."

O'Neill did more. He wrote an entirely new final scene to follow the one on the beach, spelling out all that had been left in the dream shorthand of the first draft and reconciling the whole play even further with his love for Carlotta. In it he allows for the real end of his old love for Beatrice. He has Essie say of Richard's love: "Well anyway, he'll always have it to remember—no matter what happens after—and that's something." O'Neill also consolidates in it his late-won companionship with his father. The whole of his youthful rebellion against his father moves into perspective in Nat Miller's remark that his "young anarchist" would love to have "a harsh tyrant to defy." The new last scene wishes away the part of O'Neill's rebellion that had swept him out of his father's world of faith and love. Richard and his father end in perfect agreement on the question of drink, only it is in the rejection of it that O'Neill had come to so late in life, and both are united in essential purity. O'Neill has the embarrassed Nat explain the dangers of girls like Belle, who are the "one outlet for—unless you're a scoundrel and go about ruining decent girls—which you're not, of course." So O'Neill wishes away his later involvement with Kathleen. Richard takes on at once the idealistic purity that O'Neill achieved only in his love for

Beatrice—after a long history of "grimy smears." He tells his father, "I don't see how you could think I could—now—when you know I love Muriel and am going to marry her. I'd die before I'd—!" Also O'Neill wishes away the blow to his father when he was suspended from Princeton—for breaking glass insulators of the trolley line while walking home from a spree in Trenton—and then decided to leave altogether. In the play Richard's "punishment" for his spree will be to go to Yale and "stay there till you graduate." So O'Neill reverses his past and gives himself the university career that he was proud of in his son Eugene Jr., who had done brilliantly at Yale, and that he wanted for his son Shane. Richard ends his conference with his father impulsively kissing him— and thus consolidating, as O'Neill wished he had, his oneness with his father's world of faith and love.

The new final scene recalls all the beauty of that lost world of love. Lily and Sid, whose tragedy had been resolved dream-fashion in the fulfillment of their other avatars, Richard and Muriel, are now given their own resolution on another beach under their own moon. Essie sums them up, saying, "Sid'll never change, and she'll never marry him. But she seems to get some queer satisfaction out of fussing over him like a hen that's hatched a duck—." Arthur is out courting Elsie Rand, and Mildred is out walking with her latest. Nat sums up: "Then, from all reports, we seem to be completely surrounded by love!" The moonlight that spread enchantment over the young love of Richard and Muriel spreads it over his parents, linking the boy's new love with their mature love. At his father's deathbed O'Neill had determined to make his own love follow his father's faith in his mother's love and his love for her, and his belief "that it will go with him wherever he is going." He had thought then of the "setting moon of life," and now he brought that moon, "way down low—almost setting," into his last scene and the ultimate image of his play, in which Richard's mother and father stand in the moonlight, and his father quotes the lines of "The Rubáiyát,"

> Yet ah, that Spring should vanish with the Rose!
> That Youth's sweet-scented manuscript should close!

O'Neill had him add, "Well, Spring isn't everything, is it Essie? There's a lot to be said for Autumn. That's got beauty, too. And Winter—if you're together." (O'Neill gave these words to Carlotta on a photograph of his mature self with the words "I love you," for Carlotta, he believed, was "my Wilderness regained.") Yet he was profoundly aware that the world of *Ah, Wilderness!* was irrevocably gone. He had his play father and mother—redolent of love and faith—kiss and then "move quietly out of the moonlight, back into the darkness of the front parlor" as the curtain falls. So they move back into O'Neill's "ghost-haunted inner dark," back into the past, into the lost world of his youth when he had been "completely surrounded by love."

The laughter in his play was shot through with "poignant melancholy," with regret, with loss. So delicate was the balance of the two in *Ah, Wilderness!* that at first O'Neill thought he might never "subject it to the humiliation of production and publication." He knew that its "whole importance and reality depend on its conveying a mood of memory in exactly the right illuminating blend of wistful grin and lump in the throat—the old tears-and-laughter stuff on exactly the right delicately caressing note." All its validity for O'Neill lay in its "true evocation of a mood of the past, of an American life that is dead." He had depicted with laughter all the restraints of the time on what could be recognized of life and sex, and with them he had depicted all that was held together by those restraints—affection, respect, protective responsibility, "the old solidarity of the family unit." O'Neill was uncertain of whether others would grasp its laughter, for he had not taken "the usual easy route of being superior to the period and spoofing at it without attempting to understand it or see its contrasting virtues." The whole balance of tears and laughter depended on a tension in the audience between this evocation of a lost American life-style and their own consciousness of how far they had been carried away from it by the "corrupting, disintegrating influences" that had "spoiled it since the War." All the truth of his play lay in the perception of "the startling difference between what we Americans felt about life, love, honor, morals, etc. and what we are conscious of feeling today." It depended on conveying what it had meant to O'Neill himself, a "nostalgia for our lost simplicity and contentment and youth."

O'Neill had succeeded in writing "a real, true Yea," a complete affirmation of life, but only for the life of an irrevocably lost world. So he turned back to his exhausting struggle to find an honest Yea for the world of the present and future. Only after that struggle was he ready to think of producing *Ah, Wilderness!* George Jean Nathan had reinforced his own opinion that the play had depths of meaning beyond its surface values. O'Neill thought his own "judgment might be warped by my personal affection for my nostalgia, as it were." Once the Guild accepted both *Ah, Wilderness!* and his second God play, he worried over which would be the "best showmanship" to do first. *Ah, Wilderness!*—he told himself—should come first because even the dullest critics would realize it could not be compared with "Electra," but if his controversial second God play came next the critics were sure to take out their "resentment and bewilderment" on it. He did not want to send *Ah, Wilderness!* out into the hostile world left by the controversy. The question was whether this gentle comedy would be able to charm the critics who would find it a letdown after "Electra." The Guild thought it could and began casting it in mid-August of 1933.

O'Neill was entirely for "fresh personalities, new blood." Yet he was ready to make an exception for the well-known Guy Kibbee for Sid, who, he declared, *"has something."* (Kibbee could not "be got," and so they chose Gene Lockhart.) O'Neill was even ready to make a greater exception and take up Terry Helburn's idea that they get America's beloved song-and-dance man, George M. Cohan, to play Nat Miller. Cohan would bring his huge popular following to the box office, and everyone would be intrigued by the combination of the comedian with the famous tragic playwright. Cohan had been sketching out his own starring vehicles for years and ad-libbing his lines, so he found a written part very hard work. (Even one month after the opening O'Neill wrote Phil Moeller about a radio performance he heard, from which it was clear that Essie and Nat still did not know their lines and made a "disgraceful, slovenly exhibition" of themselves with ad-libbing and mixing up names. Cohan also was addicted to the "significantly charged" pause before a reply that he had learned from the French actor Lucien Guitry. It pulled out the acting time, and O'Neill had to cut and cut. With a star playing Nat the cuts fell mostly among the other roles. O'Neill eliminated his scene of Sid with the inky smears. He cut Essie's instructions to the "greenhorn," including a reprimand for swearing to which Norah had replied cheerfully, "Ah, sure, if you wasn't a Black Protestant you'd know taking the devil's name in vain wasn't swearing at all!" O'Neill felt that the play had been pulled somewhat out of shape. He had meant it as a family play with no star. Even with the cuts, it had been done successfully all over Europe with the boy as the main character.

With all the cuts, the play was running way over time at the tryout in Pittsburgh. Russell Crouse recalled that he was delegated to tackle O'Neill. "I put it to him point blank, and he said nothing. Walked away. But that night . . . he came over and said: 'All right, I've dropped the fifteen minutes out as you wanted. I've eliminated the intermission between the third and fourth acts!' " O'Neill was always ready to cut, he said, where "it could be done without injury to the play's integrity," and he said that he had cut from *Ah, Wilderness!* "even more than I felt was justified." In the end, Langner, Helburn, and Moeller held a "council of war" with Cohan on speeding his delivery, and for the opening in New York on October 2, 1933, he came through on schedule.

O'Neill thought that the cast "really made it live very close to what I imagined it." Audiences were delighted. He told Kenneth Macgowan that old and young were moved by it. Critics praised it—although a few gave all the credit to Cohan. O'Neill found their views—either for or against—"something between them and their trade but, as far as the reality of my plays goes, totally irrelevant." They could see only theater and had lost the "insights of one living in life." Afterward Brooks Atkinson asked him if *Ah, Wilderness!* might not as well "be tragedy as comedy" because "Lily's blighted love" and "Richard's wild rebellion" were "tragic impulses." O'Neill explained that the difference between comedy and tragedy lies in the characters. Tragic characters are driven from within to violent conclusions; comic characters make comic compromises.

Despite a slump in February 1934 because of icy weather and taxi strikes, *Ah, Wilderness!* drew crowded houses for a year in New York with Cohan and for another year with him on the road, playing from Boston to Chicago and out through the Midwest. The Guild also opened a second company in San Francisco with Will Rogers starring in the role of Nat. They even had a road company in the fall of 1935, although Cohan was leaving the cast and the film rights had been sold. The Guild became so delirious over its success that they were already urging O'Neill in 1941 to agree to a revival. That same year, O'Neill told Robert Sisk as "strictly financial news" that a radio serial had offered to buy the rights to the Millers as "the typical backbone-of-America family of all time." So began *Ah, Wilderness!*'s long theatrical history of what became more than a humiliation, really a desecration, by producers, ignorant of the past, who tried to make it live as a lie about the nature of American life in the present.

As for O'Neill, he was so fond of his recollection at first that he told Saxe Commins, "There were innumerable such people in these United States. There still are, except life has carried us out of their orbit, we no longer see or know them, our gaze is concentrated either above or below them. But if America ever pulls out of its present mess back to something approaching its old integrity and uniqueness, I think it will be owing to the fundamental simple homely decency of such folk, no matter how much corrupting, disintegrating influences have spoiled it since the War." But he quickly lost hope for a return to the "old integrity." He turned instead to a great cycle of plays—"A Tale of Possessors Self-Dispossessed"—on what he saw as the fundamental question for his United States: Why, with all its promise, had it ended as the greatest example of the failure described in the Bible: "For what shall it profit a man, if he shall gain the whole world and lose his own soul?"

9

Days Without End

The critics were meant to be completely unaware that *Days Without End*—as O'Neill came to call this play—was actually the second play of his God trilogy. He had declared that he was "off" the trilogy idea, and he meant to reveal the truth only when all three plays were written and he could combine them with the title "Myth Plays for the God-Forsaken." He knew that he must rewrite *Dynamo,* the play that looked for God in scientific theory, but he wanted first to write his play about the search for God in Romantic Love, and then the third about the attempt to make a God of Money.

So clear was he on doing the *second* play of a God trilogy, that he could not look at it from a different viewpoint, as the *third* in a strange trilogy of love plays. Yet every time a great love had come to him he had sought its meaning in a play—and he was now on his third. His first, *Servitude,* had been sent out for copyright after the first rapturous summer of love for Beatrice in 1914. The second, *Welded,* came in 1923 out of his passion for Agnes. When he tackled the third in the spring of 1932, he was striving for a faith to sustain his love for Carlotta. Of course, *Servitude* had long been "safely buried" in typescript in the Library of Congress, and *Welded* was to be banished from a definitive edition of his plays, but those two earlier struggles to find a faith for love were in him, and they would push for repetition as he wrote his third.

In the two, he had felt so powerfully that he was a playwright striving after his life's meaning that he had made his central character a playwright. That feeling gave him the idea for his third love play, for it arrived on August 12, 1927, right after he had worked out the fate of his marriage to Agnes—without realizing it—in his novel-play *Strange Interlude,* and it came to him as a play about a man who works out the fate of his marriage in the plot for a novel. O'Neill had not seen the connection, for later, on March 16, 1929, in the midst of his divorce agonies, he told his dentist, Doctor Lief, that he would have to postpone writing his second God play until all his marital troubles were over and forgotten. "It's a funny coincidence. I had the idea all mapped out before I left Bermuda and before there was any suggestion of a smash in my domestic life. It was quite objective. And yet now it would appear as most subjective and autobiographical because of the turn events have taken. A strange business!" Even if he never saw the connection between *Strange Interlude* and this second God play, he felt *Strange Interlude* fermenting in him as he worked on it, along with his two earlier love plays, for when he finished it he came up with an idea for a play with a "reverse Interlude theme," about one man and three women. He felt so firmly one with his hero that he was tempted to have him write a play rather than a novel, and in his first notes he shifted between the two.

His first love plays had both juggled two women in order to correct an unhappy end of love with a happier one. *Servitude* examined his miserable marriage-divorce with Kathleen Jenkins in order to find an enduring basis for his dreamed-of marriage to Beatrice. Its playwright hero duplicates the marriage to Kathleen by having taken a woman incapable of sharing his intellectual interests and lacking his cultivated family background, and for the same reason as O'Neill, because the girl became pregnant. Instead of flying bodily from the marriage, as O'Neill had, his hero has lived with his wife and children in complete emotional alienation, so that at one point in the play he wakes up to the "horrible thought" that "I do not even know my own children"—as if he were actually O'Neill who had not seen his child by Kathleen since his birth. Into his unhappy home comes a Beatrice-like young lady who has admired his plays and taken up his Nietzschean philosophy of self-realization. Just as the youthful O'Neill had told Beatrice that even if Nietzsche's higher man had not yet made his appearance the "superwoman" certainly had, and her address was 89 West Street—that is, Beatrice's address in New London—so his playwright comes to call his Beatrice-woman "the superwoman." She has fled her loving husband to search for her soul in a dingy hall bedroom and has come to look at the playwright's own marriage to see whether she has the right to cause her husband so much pain.

Revelation of his own love history had come to O'Neill in 1913 when he first discovered Francis Thompson's poem "The Hound of Heaven" while recovering from tuberculosis at Gaylord Farm Sanitarium. In Thompson's flight from love and God, in his search for meaning, in his urgent images of running and hiding, always pursued by what he fled until he came full circle back to faith, O'Neill saw his own flight from his parents' love and from his boyhood religious faith, saw all his years of wandering and intellectual searching, his despair in a hall bedroom of Jimmy the Priest's rooming house after his witnessed bedding with a prostitute for his divorce, his suicide attempt, and his return to his family just before the tuberculosis got him. He quoted "The Hound of Heaven" afterward to Beatrice, and still later, after he lost her, he would recite the whole of it by heart in the back room of Wallace's saloon "The Hell Hole" to an admiring audience of gangsters and truck drivers. In *Servitude* he put himself into the Beatrice-woman and gave her a similar "Hound of Heaven" flight from love to reach despair like his in a hall bedroom, and had her make the full-circle return to love, bringing his other self, the playwright, back to his own fled love. Thompson's poem had so strong a hold on O'Neill's mind that it came out in the dialogue: "Yea, faileth now dream the dreamer and the lute the lutanist."

O'Neill's model of enduring love had been his father's love for his mother, and hers for him. His father had been "a husband to marvel at," faithful through all the agonies of his wife's addiction. O'Neill had seen his father's ideal of service in his loving care for his wife and had read it when he was eight in his father's Christmas story for the 1896 *Dramatic Mirror*. It had been a true story of helping a desperate little girl who had mistaken him for a Catholic priest in which he had pointed up the moral that "life is really worth living" not merely for one's own sake but "through the fortunate circumstances which enable one to come to the assistance of a fellow-being." This became O'Neill's own ideal of love. When he fell in love with Beatrice he wanted to bear all her ills for her; he swore himself to chastity until they could marry; and he remained true to her for two long years of suffering as "a prince of thwarted ecstasy, of unassuaged desire." Adultery, for him, would have been the great sin against their love.

So he revealed love's meaning in *Servitude* by the test of a seeming adultery between the playwright and the Beatrice-woman. Under this stress the selfless behavior of the playwright's loving wife, and of the equally loving husband of the Beatrice-figure, who has pursued her "Hound of Heaven" style, brings her to tell the playwright that he is not a creator of new values, but only "an egotist whose hands are bloody with the human sacrifices he has made—to himself." She has learned from his wife that "happiness" in love "means servitude," and she converts the playwright. They both return to the love they fled, inspired by a Christian-mystical ideal that combines O'Neill's boyhood faith in God's love and in his father's love for his mother: "Servitude in love, love in servitude! Logos in Pan, Pan in Logos! That is the great secret—." Their Nietzschean striving will all go into creating "a superlove worthy of the superman."

These ideas grew in the two years after O'Neill wrote *Servitude*. Beatrice became, first jokingly and then seriously, Dante's Beatrice—the Beatrice of the *Divine Comedy*, she who makes blessed, who leads to the revelation of God. She also became "Mother of mine who gave birth to all that is best in me," so that she fulfilled O'Neill's infant vision of felicity, in which his mother's love brought the greater love of his hero father. He told Beatrice that her love brought him to his "ultimate goal": "I become a part of God and he of me. For are you not—my God?" And he blended this religion with all that he had learned of marriage from Nietzsche as a spiritual opportunity "not only to propagate yourselves onwards but *upwards*." He brought this religion of love to Agnes when he found her in Greenwich Village a year after he lost Beatrice, and Agnes took it up ardently. Their love, she told him, became a beautiful and *"peaceful"* current eternally flowing beneath her consciousness. She needed no other belief, no other "religion." She had it all in him, in "us."

When he wrote the truth of love and marriage into *Welded*, he gave his playwright hero a wife who is an ardent convert to his religion of love. She tells him, "I'd lost faith in everything. Your love saved me," and she sees their marriage as a "true sacrament." She blends the Agnes he married with the Beatrice he never stopped loving. She is an actress who brings life to her husband's plays and has been made great through them, as O'Neill had hoped that Beatrice would be. Beatrice had taken part in what she jokingly called a "Y.M.C.A. orgy," a play called "A Scrap of Paper," and O'Neill congratulated her on taking up his father's profession. They would form a combination, he said, like Laurette Taylor and her husband who had written *Peg O' My Heart* for her. He could already see her name in lights as "Beatrice O'Neill." This dream-Beatrice became endowed with Agnes's fear of losing herself in love, her need to provoke his jealousy, and her jealousy of his far more successful work. The married lovers explode into a quarrel, like those of the O'Neills, and they bodily run from their love, from each other and their home—only to realize, "Hound of Heaven" style, that their love has pursued them, so that they finally return full circle to it and to each other. The great sin against love is again adultery, and once again it reveals love's meaning, for both of them try to kill their love by it and find they cannot do it. The wife runs to an older man who has spent years "waiting and hoping" to win her, in a combination of James O'Neill's example of selfless fidelity and Eugene O'Neill's futile dedication to Beatrice, and in this scene O'Neill-in-his-character once again waits, hopes, and loses her. From his example she learns that her love for her husband is her own, and she completes rather than loses herself by giving herself to love—and knowing that, she returns to her husband. He has tried to kill his love with a prostitute, but he sees that she bears the same "lonely life of one's own which suffers in solitude," as he, and he learns from her lesson of giving in love (to the pimp who beats her) that "You got to loin to like it!" He tells her, "That goes deeper than wisdom. To learn to love life—to accept it and be exalted—that's the one faith left to us." He says that he has joined her "church," and he returns to love and his wife.

Their ultimate sanctification took shape out of O'Neill's haunting remembrance of his boyhood faith. He had been subject, it seems, to a recurrent dream of it. On the day before his thirty-sixth birthday he noted in his *Work Diary* "The chapel dream." This seems to have been a familiar and recurrent dream, and the chapel must have been the one in which he worshiped steadily from his seventh year until he took his First Communion at his boyhood boarding school of Mount St. Vincent-on-the-Hudson. The most striking feature of that chapel had been the great altarpiece—by an Italian named Brumidi—of Christ on the Cross. Far from appearing suspended in death, Brumidi's Christ has already become radiant with resurrection, aglow with light, and appears to be floating upward, ascending. O'Neill's final gesture in *Welded* stages a similar crucifixion-resurrection.

Symbolic of the ascent of the spirit in love, O'Neill placed a staircase to the bedroom in the home of the married lovers. Consummation of love had Nietzsche's meaning of "the great symbolic happiness of a higher happiness and highest hope." O'Neill's highest hope, as he had told Beatrice, was to "become part of God and he of me." In *Welded* the playwright echoes him, declaring that his love for his wife, and hers for him, "has God in it!" Determined to transcend the pain in their marriage, the two lovers come to the foot of the staircase, where the wife stretches out her arms, and as her husband joins her his hands go out to meet hers, so that for one moment they form a cross together. Then their arms go around each other. So their crucifixion on the cross of life and love becomes resurrection, ascension, apotheosis.

All these ideas would push for entry into *Days Without End*. Of course, when O'Neill got his first idea for it, he thought only of his own question as his marriage foundered: if the great love of his life were to die, could he find the faith to go on living? Another idea came to him as he actually watched his marriage smash during his last devastating homecoming to Bermuda. On November 11, 1927, he worked out "Idea *modern Faust play*—the selling of one's life (instead of one's soul)." He was feeling the pull of death then, just as he had felt it at his first failure in love, when he had tried to kill himself. By May 1932, when he really began his second God play about a man who decides his fate in a novel, it had joined with the modern Faust play.

O'Neill knew that it would "mark a startling departure" from everything he had done before, for it was to break away from his old vein of ironic tragedy, which had come of the tension within him between doubt and belief. "I believe everything I doubt and I doubt everything I believe," he had once said. Now he would strive for a genuine "Yea," and he would do so by taking up and transforming the medieval miracle play in which the real hero is the soul of man, its struggle that between faith and denial, and its climax either salvation or damnation. His hero would exemplify man's "Faustian longing" for the infinite, and O'Neill saw his title as a pun on the word "end," which can mean either a goal or a dead stop. He started with "Without Endings of Days" and rang all the possible changes on those words until finally, by accident, he reached the "obviously satisfactory title" of "Days Without End" when describing the play, after its fifth draft, to his new publisher, Bennett Cerf of Random House. So *Days Without End* would contrast modern man's actual living without spiritual goals with his longing for the eternal and unending in his life and love.

He placed his modern Faust in his own America of the Great Depression in the year of his writing, 1932, and he made him the typical middle-class American—a businessman—of the time, whose lack of personal values were part of his country's lack of values now that their "omnipotent Golden Calf" had exploded "into sawdust" before their "adoring eyes right at the height of his deification." His Faust sees no hope among his fellow Americans of a more meaningful God than money-power. He says, "All they want is to start the merry-go-round of blind greed all over again. They no longer know what they want this country to be, what they want it to become. . . . It has lost all meaning for them except as a pig-wallow." There is no supreme power but money worshiped in his world, and he has long since lost his childhood God.

In this character, superficially as unlike himself as he could make him, O'Neill wanted to go on exploring the psychology of religion—that is, of faith in the meaning of life—that he began with his first "Myth Play for the God-Forsaken," *Dynamo*. He wanted to look at his own faith in life that had received such a shattering blow with the death of his love for Agnes, and to understand all that had acted to destroy it, so he could preserve his new love for Carlotta. He was perfectly clear, by this time, that it was the shock of his mother's addiction that had turned him from his childhood faith in a God of Love, and had created his long distrust of women that had tainted his love for Agnes. He had to find a similar shock for his hero, and he wanted one that could reappear to threaten his love for his wife. It came to him out of a double cycle of memories of influenza.

O'Neill had come down with influenza during the Great Epidemic of early 1920, and a frantic exchange of letters between him in New York and Agnes in Provincetown had taken place in her terror that he, like their friend Hutch Collins in the 1919 epidemic, would get up too soon, catch pneumonia, and die. She begged him not to forget Hutch, to take no chances of catching pneumonia for her sake and for little Shane's, for she would not go on living in the world without him. She simply could not. Even before he caught the flu, he had told her that if her love failed him "my only remaining hope is that the 'Flu,' or some other natural cause, will speedily save me the decision which would inevitably have to come at my own instance. If you and I are but another dream that passes, then I desire nothing further from the Great Sickness but release." He associated the influenza with his own and Agnes's suicidal anguish at the thought of losing love, and he also associated it with his own anguish at losing the love of his parents, for his father had been felled by the stroke that ushered in his death during the influenza epidemic, and his mother had died soon after he did.

These associations had been reinforced by memories of his attack of influenza in Shanghai, which had become both an alcoholic relapse and a nervous breakdown, when his hatred of Agnes had overflowed against Carlotta and almost swept away their love. Both gave him his story. His John Faustus has lost his faith at the age of fifteen, when his father and then his mother died of influenza that turned into pneumonia. Before that he had every reason to believe in a "Divinity of Love as the Creator of Life. His home atmosphere was one of love. Life *was* love for him then. And he was happy." (*Faustus* means fortunate or happy, and for O'Neill being happy and loving were one—hence his name for his modern John Faustus, "John Loving.") In a "frenzy of insane grief" over their death, John Loving turned against a God so "deaf and blind and merciless," who answered love with hatred. He found no other faith until he fell in love, married his wife Elsa, and found his "last religion." When the play begins, she is getting over the flu, and the plot of his novel—and his life— depends on whether she will repeat the fate of his parents.

John is thus split between faith and denial, and his "strange religious hatred" (so O'Neill told Philip Moeller) came from "a boy obsessed with a religious hatred complex" who had sought his help in Bermuda—although he made John

Loving forty years old, as he had been at the time of his Shanghai influenza bout, when he had almost lost Carlotta. By giving his hero a seriously "self-poisoned psyche" he could reveal the neurotic's contradictory inner directives and his compulsion to repeat a trauma he desperately fears. He could use all he had learned from Wilhelm Stekel's brilliant analysis of repetition compulsion to show part of his hero—in direct antagonism to his dearest wishes—pushing his wife into repeating the trauma of his boyhood, driving her into going out in the rain with influenza to catch pneumonia and die, in order to justify his distrust of love and release his anger at being vulnerable. At the beginning of the play he has already set the destructive process in motion by revenging himself on his own anxiety over his wife while she was away by a deliberate act of adultery with a friend of hers who was motivated by the same spirit of hatred and revenge at hurt love as he.

O'Neill selected adultery because he had always seen it as the great sin against love, not because he had committed it. He had told Agnes, "You know damn well I'm not interested in little sex affairs for sex's sake alone, that it is love or nothing!" He had been physically faithful until he committed himself to Carlotta, but even his innocent relationship with her had wounded Agnes. When Agnes went to New York in the spring of 1927, he warned her against the malice of some of her so-called friends who would try to hurt her tattling of Carlotta. He felt that it had been rotten of him to leave her open to their cruelty. It had been "stupid and meaningless!" But Agnes and Carlotta jumped places—and Carlotta became the wounded one after his outburst in Shanghai, and Agnes the threat to her. So a strange fusion between the two took place in his play, and both women found their way into the two women of his play. Elsa took in the Agnes cruelly wounded by his association with Carlotta, and the Carlotta stunned and shattered by his unexpected turning upon her during the breakdown in Shanghai. John's partner in adultery, Lucy, took in both the Carlotta who had been a "meaningless" threat to his long love for Agnes, and the Agnes who had vindictively—as he saw it—set out to ruin his happiness with Carlotta by holding up the divorce.

The Agnes in Elsa makes her the same ardent disciple of her husband's last religion—love—as the wife in *Welded* had been, and she echoes her words on having "lost faith" and being "saved" by the "true sacrament" of her marriage. She says, "I've never had any God, you see—until I met John," and she declares that he had had to argue "like a missionary converting a heathen" to convince her that even if every other marriage were a lie theirs could be "a true sacrament—sacrament was the word he used—a sacrament of faith." The idealism was Agnes's, out of her powerful mysticism; otherwise Elsa took her calm beauty from Carlotta. Agnes had been a careless housekeeper, and he made Elsa a devoted one like Carlotta. He remembered a letter from Carlotta to Agnes—when the two women were exchanging understanding after his 1926 homecoming—in which she confessed that she felt blue but was carrying on. "I hear all the music I can and read my eyes out!" In the play, Elsa echoes her, telling Lucy that she follows her usual "peaceful routine—going to a concert now and then, reading a lot, keeping house." Elsa even has had a former painful marriage like Carlotta's to the brilliant cartoonist Ralph Barton. Barton had had a compulsive need to demonstrate his power over women, and, during the weekend-long drinking parties he often held, he had subjected Carlotta to cruel public humiliations until finally she divorced him, after barely three years of marriage, charging adultery. Barton had killed himself, disgusted (so his suicide note declared) with running "from wife to wife, from house to house, and from country to country," and full of regret over his "failure to appreciate my beautiful lost angel, Carlotta." Elsa has had a similarly painful marriage with a man who has—as Lucy puts it—"slapped your face with almost every filthy thing a man can be," filling her with "disgust and hurt" and "wounded pride" until she, like Carlotta, divorced him for adultery.

Carlotta's former marriage to Barton became Lucy's too, but she is right in the midst of it as the play begins. Her leap into adultery, she says, took place at "one of Walter's parties": "Walter was drunk, pawing over his latest female, and she got him to go home with her. Everybody watched to see how I'd take it." Only now, for O'Neill, Carlotta was his "pure and unsoiled one, whom the world has wounded," so he turned from her reaction to that of the angry Agnes of his own divorce and modeled Lucy's reprisal on her. He had John's business partner say of Lucy: "I hear she's going to pieces." "Booze," he explains in answer to John's guilty defense of her virtue, and adds, "There are children, aren't there?" The words echo O'Neill's own in a letter to Agnes warning her of what one of her "friends" just back from Bermuda had told him of "the gossip down there that you had 'gone to pieces,' were drinking, and at least on the verge of becoming a bit promiscuous with your favors, if you hadn't already fallen," and had commented, "Such a shame for my poor dear little children." O'Neill did not believe it, he said, but it had given him a turn. Agnes retorted that he really had believed a vicious liar in a lie so totally without foundation that—if she did not know him—she would think he had made up. Yet only a few letters later she herself tried pathetically to provoke his jealousy. She wrote him a graphic account of an "indiscretion" of hers—in that she found herself pregnant.

"You have piled an indiscretion upon an indiscretion!" he told her. "Don't you know that your letter—you always have had such an unfortunately vague memory for certain things!—gives me proof positive of adultery in your own handwriting?" He told her that he had no intention of using it and that he would be ridiculous to object to her having lovers, but he did object to her effrontery in trying to lay it at his door—when her own dates showed that that was impossible. He thought perhaps she had written about it to "taunt" him, but he was well past the point where she could hurt him that way.

This was the Agnes that gave him Lucy's revengeful adultery with John, and like Agnes she has taunted her husband with it. John exclaims, "You told him? In God's name, why? But I know. You couldn't resist—watching him squirm!" Lucy has changed—as Agnes—to a dangerous instability. O'Neill had told Agnes: "It isn't that I don't trust you to keep your word—when you're yourself, the fine honorable woman you are at bottom. But when you've had even a few drinks you are neither fine nor honorable—." John tells Lucy, "I'm sorry I can't trust you, Lucy. I can when you're yourself. But full of booze—." With booze in her, Lucy takes John in adultery to revenge herself on love, and half in remorse, half in vindictiveness, she tells his wife about it without revealing who he was. She says, "His happiness filled me with rage—the thought that he made others happy. I wanted to take his happiness from him and kill it as mine had been killed!" O'Neill had told Agnes of rumors that she was planning to wait him out, delay the divorce to keep him upset and unable to work, so that he would give up Carlotta, and he declared, "If you did such a thing deliberately to try to ruin what is now so surely my future happiness, I would hate you as bitterly as you would deserve—and who would blame me?"

The fact that both Carlotta and Agnes had gone into both the loving Elsa and the agonized Lucy shows that, in some fundamental way, O'Neill saw that what had happened to the one love could happen to the other. He had told Agnes that neither of them was to blame for the failure of their marriage: "It is what life does to love—unless you watch and care for it. This time I am going to watch and care." He meant to model his watching and caring on his father's example. Life had not been able to kill his father's love for his mother, despite her addiction, for he had had a larger faith to sustain it. O'Neill wanted to strive for a similar faith. He wanted to complete the unity with his father that he had begun in *Dynamo,* and to cancel out his revolt against him. He had tried to replace his father's faith with faith in romantic love for a woman—first Beatrice and then Agnes—and when the love failed him he lost both faith and God. This time he wanted to find God and faith first, so that no matter what life brought he could be what his father had been, a "husband to marvel at."

He found a way—right in the Faust tradition—to bring his father bodily into the play to participate in an ultimate reconciliation. Christopher Marlowe had dramatized Faust's warring inner directives by bringing onstage his Guardian Angel and his Evil Genius to bombard him with contradictory advice at crucial moments. It occurred to O'Neill that he could give his hero an actual "guardian"—an uncle who adopted him when his parents died—who would be a spiritual father to him in the example of his faith. O'Neill made him first a country doctor with a simple belief in a God of Love like that of his own father, but then became tempted to make him really a spiritual father, a priest, and even to make him specifically Catholic, a priest of his own old faith, the Catholic priest for whom his father had so often been taken.

He was even more sharply torn over the identity of the Evil Genius. At first he saw him as the actual leader of his revolt against his father, his brother Jamie. He was to be a "friend," or maybe actually a "brother," of his hero and "a living reminder and participator in all his past—in all his struggles, dissipations, despairs, love affairs, former marriage—a former Catholic like himself—a sneering sceptic now about religion and everything else—a philosophical Nihilist— dissipated, Don Juan and a bachelor. . . ." But Jamie could offer no well- matched fight with his father, and so O'Neill decided to make the Evil Genius a counter-father-figure—literally the father of John's wife, with a name sugges- tive of the actual spiritual father he had found in Nietzsche after revolting against his father's faith. He called him "Friedrich Hardy," joining Friedrich Nietzsche with the poet Thomas Hardy, who sang a universe of blind chance.

Hardy sprang fully into life by becoming a professor of astronomy, out of an idea for an "Astronomer-Astrologer play" that O'Neill had at the same time as the idea for a modern Faust play. All O'Neill's skepticism, all of his despairing doubt, flooded into this lonely old man, afraid of death, isolated in the immen- sities of Sir James Jeans's expanding universe, looking on at a world and all humanity that appears to be rushing madly off in the direction of the distant constellation of Hercules or of Betelgeuse. "On to Hercules" and "On to Be- telguese" kept ringing in O'Neill's head as a possible title for this play—or perhaps for the third God play—and he had Hardy remark ironically: "On to Hercules! An inspiring slogan for the young, eh? There's nothing like having a sure goal. Remember your Nietzsche? 'He only who knoweth wither he saileth, knoweth what wind is good.' "

O'Neill even turned Hardy's remorseless inquiry onto the collapse of his religion of love. At the time, he had told Agnes of his despair at "what the passage of time has done to us." He had "the intolerable feeling that it is per- haps not in the nature of living life itself that fine beautiful things may exist for any great length of time," the intolerable feeling "that human beings are fated to destroy just that in each other which constitutes their mutual happiness. Fits of cosmic Irish melancholia, I guess!" Hardy took over his cosmic despair and gave it voice. He tells John, "There seems to be an idiotic compulsion in life that men must always pick their happiness to bits—like mad monkeys with sawdust dolls! Or perhaps their meaningless fate is the monkey and they are the dolls." He proceeds—and O'Neill with him—to tear apart John's sacramental conception of love that makes adultery a desecration. "Seems to me, John, your hero makes a great to-do about nothing. As meaningless as one fly with another—and of equal importance to life. Not as much, in fact. The flies' inevitably results in more flies—which life apparently regards as important as anything else."

Hardy slashed away at all O'Neill's longings, particularly his temptation to return to his old boyhood belief. "Once a Catholic always a Catholic!" he taunts, and indeed O'Neill made almost a leitmotiv of the taunt in his early notes. Hardy even quotes Zarathustra's warning: "Beware lest in the end a narrow faith capture thee, a hard, rigorous delusion!" O'Neill even attacked— through Hardy—all the dreams with which he had replaced his childhood belief, and foremost among them the dream of a new Savior, like the one he had dreamed in *Lazarus Laughed*. Hardy says, "Saviors are meaningless—even the Nietzschean one you're evoking for us, John. Not one of them has ever really influenced man's life." Even if such a Savior were to arrive, he says, "we'd put him in an insane asylum for teaching that we might have another ambition for our souls than getting all four feet into a trough of swill!" As for the hope that man may "evolve something like a soul," he declares, "Judging from present brainless antics, man will have destroyed himself and become extinct long before he ever really evolves beyond the ape." So thoroughgoing was O'Neill's reexamination of all his values that he even let Hardy loose on the ideal by which he had lived for years, that of the striving human soul that can create its own truth, opt for its own values, impress its own meaning on life. Hardy sees it all as theatrical posturing, with the striving soul merely a puppet that man sets to climbing toy mountains, and its heroism an absurdity in the face of annihilation when "the puppet becomes a ghost, and the walled garden crumbles and the toy mountains dissolve and the glow worms go out—and what is left is a man alone in space who would like to go back whence he came but must go on—whence he came—to meaningless nothingness in either case."

So O'Neill demolished—through Hardy—everything he had grasped and held to in all his mature years of philosophical searching. The rush of this destruction was so impetuous that it swept away every last faith that had held him to life. So urgent did O'Neill become in the person of this remorseless examiner into all values that Hardy ran away with his play. His voice bore down and silenced that of the Guardian Angel, and he even pushed aside the Faust character by the greater intensity of his struggle with despair. With Hardy in the play, no "Yea" had the ghost of a chance. O'Neill could end his first draft only with his hero heartbrokenly hugging the dead body of his wife and shaking his fist at the sky. A second draft only left him "sunk" on the eve of his *Ah, Wilderness!* dream. Yet he struggled on to a third, trying to get beyond what Hardy had left for him—Nothingness.

His very scheme for the split psyche of John trapped him. He had had John tell his alter ego that he plots his novel in order to discover "the truth about you." His inner self flashes back: "Take care! You may find I am only your long-lost soul." O'Neill dove fiercely into the formless memories out of which he had created his religion of love to come up with his own long-lost soul, and found that it was really his infantile sense of oneness with his mother. So he made John's long-lost soul feminine, and as John moves toward truth the appearance of his split self declares itself. O'Neill directed, "The feminine quality of the face has been intensified. It now seems more than ever the face of a John who is a woman. And the sinister satanic suggestion in this face, also, is now terribly accentuated." The satanic quality reflects O'Neill's realization that the wish to return into and become one with the mother was really the lure of death. John's inner self pleads that he wants "to escape, to die, to go back where love lies forever in the grave!" John sees that this alter ego "is in love with Nothingness! He is in love with Death, I think." In the grip of this old pull, O'Neill found himself resolving his play by suicide, a suicide that actually brought him right back to the core of his infantile dream in which union with the mother brings the love of the father. John goes back to the chapel of his boyhood and ends his struggle with his inner self by a suicide that gives him both. His inner self cries, "Oh, Death, dark tender loving Mother!" and John cries, "I believe! Oh God of Love, my Resurrection and my Life! There is only love in thy love forever!" He had landed back in the old answer—death and the mother.

What had made him particularly vulnerable to it was the flood of memory that deluged the scene of John's dying wife. She became invested by his own dying mother—the scene became his mother's deathbed in California—and the feelings the whole tremendous pull of death that had brought him to the dead-baby dream and the tragic finale of his play *Desire Under the Elms*. At the time of her death, his brother had telegraphed him that she was in a coma and had begged him to come at once. He telegraphed back: "Specialist says means complete nervous collapse if undertake trip present condition. Would that help Mother or you?" In the play, O'Neill—in the person of John—is actually there, "on the verge of complete mental and physical collapse," and the play doctor confirms his telegram to Jamie by pushing him (in John) out of the sickroom, telling him, "Can't you see you're no help to her in this condition?" One of the hauntingly horrible memories of that time had been the effect on his mother of Jamie's relapse into alcoholism. O'Neill had read an eyewitness account from a woman present, who had said, "Well, she seemed to get worse every day and Jamie kept drinking harder all the time and the worst of it, I think she knew he was drinking before she died and realized everything and was helpless." From it O'Neill created the appalling image of his distraught hero—half Jamie and half himself—bringing agony to the dying woman.

With his mother in the dying wife, O'Neill became possessed by his old dream that she would rise out of death to reassure him with a message of life and love. Through his early drafts, he struggled to get her to do it. At first she could awake from coma only to long for death and to die. Finally he got her to rise and deliver the message, but that brought him back to his old religion of love, his old infantile dream, with all the lure of death in the woman-mother. So his creative push deserted him in the final chapel scene. He wrote despairingly in his *Work Diary:* "Again reach same old impasse—play always goes dead on me here where it needs to be most alive or I go dead on it—something fundamentally wrong." He told Saxe Commins that it had "run itself into all sorts of blind alleys and exhausted me mentally and physically to the point where I've had bad nervous indigestion—a new one for me!" He had tried "to thrust it aside, forget it for a while, even abandon it entirely, but it won't let go its hold on me—." Then, suddenly, he simply opted out of his impasse. He took a giant step away from the old lure of death by destroying the feminine inner self of John and accepting an entirely new conception of the nature of his split which had been pushing within him for months.

It had been born in August, when he was forced to take time out of his struggle with *Days Without End* to write an article for his friend George Jean Nathan's new magazine *The American Spectator.* From the 17th to the 26th, he set to work expanding some old notes he had made on the use of masks in the theater—"which," he noted fiercely in his *Work Diary,* "I don't want to bother doing, damn it!" Yet in the doing, he hit upon a brilliant modern way to do Goethe's *Faust* with Mephistopheles wearing a satanic mask of Faust. "The whole of Goethe's truth *for our time,*" he declared, is "just that Mephistopheles and Faust are one and the same—*are* Faust." Only a month afterward the idea of doing just this for his own Faust presented itself, and he pushed it away (got it on October 4, and rejected it on the 7th, and reconsidered it once again on February 26, 1933). When he found himself at the old impasse in March, the idea really caught him, and he instantly felt "renewed life in play and enthusiasm in myself at possibilities." So he made John's inner self a devil of hate who was to wear "the death mask of a John who has died with a sneer of scornful mockery on his lips." In this way he banished the woman-identified part of himself forever. And at this point he took his most gigantic step away from despair and his old impasse. He simply opted to banish altogether the powerful force of his own skepticism, which had virtually taken over the play. On March 7 he wrote in his *Work Diary:* "Decide to eliminate the character of 'Hardy'—gives wrong emphasis on theme."

With Hardy banished, the Guardian Angel could rise into full power with nothing to combat but the sneering devil self in John, and he at once took control of the first act and showed the futility of all of John's intellectual searching, paraphrasing "The Hound of Heaven" on his running and hiding until finally he breaks directly into God's words at the finale of Thompson's poem:

> Ah, fondest, blindest, weakest,
> I am He Whom thou seekest!
> Thou dravest love from thee, who dravest Me.

Yet once again when O'Neill came to the suicide of his hero and his final saving revelation, the whole play went dead. He wrote despairingly in his *Work Diary:* "Blind alley again—sick and fed up!"

So he took yet another giant step away from the old pulls, from the old lure of death. He simply opted out of death altogether for both Elsa and John. He gave them life, faith, and love in this world. And so at last—with his sixth draft—he brought his play to a resolution. He told Saxe Commins that Elsa's death and the final suicide had "seemed to me unconvincing, out of character, no solution, not inevitable, simply a dramatic evasive easy way out. In the present end I find some inspiration and a bit of exaltation and mysticism." Death had lost its pull as the way to God the Father. Only the devil of hate, the sneerer and mocker in his hero was to die, bringing him into ultimate unity, whole and able to love before a vision of faith like Brumidi's altarpiece with the crucifixion that is really resurrection. Dawn is breaking through the stained-glass windows of the church as his hero stands before an immense carved Christ on the cross, and in the rising sun it becomes radiantly aglow with "crimson and green and gold" light. The Christ becomes Brumidi's Christ, vibrantly alive and full of transcendent joy. O'Neill took care to tell the Guild that he wanted none of those horrifying "sadistic Spanish Christs" but a "Resurrection Christ," a living exultant human God. Beside him in this chapel he brought the Guardian Angel, and in this way he brought his own father to his side to offer up thanks with him for salvation in faith and love. "The Hound of Heaven" finale "Ah, fondest, blindest, weakest" echoes in his final acceptance as he cries, "O Lord of Love, forgive Thy poor blind fool!" With his spiritual father beside him he affirms, "Life laughs with God's love again! Life laughs with love!"

Yet even at this point, O'Neill found one more step to take to free himself from the old exploded religion of love that had merged him in the woman and pulled him toward death. Shortly after this version was copyrighted, he took it. He had been wavering back and forth as to the identity of the Guardian Angel, wondering whether to make him a country doctor, a Catholic priest, or a vaguely Christian one wearing a habit that suggests both "Catholic priests and Protestant ministers." He had gone from Father Emmet Boyd to "Matthew Boyd, a priest of the Christian Church," to a "Matthew Baird," who would "avoid obvious Irish-Catholic connotations." At last he had decided on the country doctor, because that would avoid "all the Christian or Catholic priest confusion and still preserve all values—without much change too, for most of his dialogue was written in first draft when he was a doctor as now."

Clearly all this uncertainty had nothing whatever to do with dogma, or he would not have been able to transform him so easily by a mere change of name and title. As a matter of fact, the only theology in the play is the assertion that there is a God "of Infinite Love—not a stern, self-righteous Being Who condemned sinners to torment, but a very human, lovable God Who became man for love of men." Theologically speaking, he had not gone much past what he had asserted at the height of his skepticism in *The Great God Brown,* when he had turned the beginning of the Lord's Prayer into an assertion of belief—"Our Father who Art!"—and had declared, "There is only love." Yet the exact name for the spiritual father's faith was desperately important to him. His revolt against his father and God had been a revolt against a believing Catholic and a Catholic God. To make a complete reconciliation, he needed to accept that fact. In his *Ah, Wilderness!* dream play he had moved a great way toward it. He had put just such a tolerant God of Love into its final scene, in which—not satisfied merely with canceling out his wrong turning—he had created a loving reconciliation between father and son. Now he did his last facing up to a total reconciliation and made the Guardian Angel a Catholic priest, so that at the end of *Days Without End* his hero stands side by side in faith with the Catholic Father, the Catholic priest, and he himself stands with him, a comrade in faith beside his father James O'Neill.

The final barrier between them had been broken down. From this point on O'Neill marched by his father's side. In November of that year, 1933, George

Middleton asked O'Neill for two photographs of him, one for himself and one for the Players Club. O'Neill wrote back that he would be "tickled to death" to send him one, but not the Players. He said, "I can never forgive nor cease to resent" the Players Club having ignored his father's death—the only club that sent no word, no flowers, out of all he belonged to—although he had been a friend of Booth's, had acted with him, and was among the club's oldest members. In the new year of 1934 he dedicated part of his profits from *Ah, Wilderness!* to the Catholic Actors Guild, which his father had done so much to organize; their chaplain, the Reverend Edward F. Leonard, wrote thanking him for his "generous contribution" and adding, "I am sure that your beloved father (R.I.P.) would be greatly pleased if he were alive to see this."

O'Neill had completed his identification with his father, but he had not gone back to the Catholic church. Instead he had snapped his last bond with it. The instant he realized that he could just as easily opt to believe what his father had believed as opt for his old Nietzschean ideals, he freed himself from both. All the passion went out of his skepticism, and he saw that both his father's beliefs and his own had been arbitrary and life-preserving. The reality of Catholicism abolished all the dream substitutes for it that he had conjured up in Mother Gods and Father Gods, in proxy saviors and proxy crucifixions. By agreeing that his father's religion could be true and life-giving for whoever chose to believe it, he had—so he told Kenneth Macgowan—been able "to liberate myself from myself," and, he said, "Whatever the fate of *Days Without End* I'm damned glad I did, for I feel immensely freer inside myself." Even more deeply than *Ah, Wilderness!* he said, this play had been "the paying of an old debt on my part—a gesture toward more comprehensive, unembittered understanding and inner freedom—." He knew now "that any life-giving formula is as fit a subject for drama as any other." He had arrived at the great existential vision of his later plays in which he would look compassionately into and through all man's beliefs and all man's dreams to the need that gave them birth.

By one of the curious ironies of life, exactly at this point of psychological liberation Eugene O'Neill became enveloped in a cloud of seeming commitment that would make it appear that the truth he had found for his play hero had been true for him. It all began with the Guild's public relations men, Robert Sisk and Russell Crouse. They set out to get Catholic support for the play. They saw to it that Richard Dana Skinner, critic for *Commonweal* read it in advance, and arranged for him to dine with O'Neill when the playwright came to New York for the production of *Days Without End*. From what Carlotta told him, Skinner got the idea that O'Neill was about to leap back to the fold. Carlotta certainly thought so. O'Neill had followed his play hero in reading his early drafts to his wife, and she saw clearly that O'Neill was struggling to consolidate their marriage in this play. She herself had sentimental memories of her school-days at St. Gertrude's Academy of the Rio Vista convent, and of the admiring nuns. Right after graduation, when she had won a beauty contest sponsored by the *San Francisco Call,* she had cabled back from London, "Be sure to let the sisters at the Rio Vista convent know about this. They will be pleased." If Catholicism consolidated his hero's marriage, Catholicism was, she thought, the answer for him. So when Skinner turned to the Reverend Michael Earls for help in converting O'Neill he told him: "It may interest you to know that his wife is working very hard to bring about his definite return to the Catholic Church as she feels that that is his one salvation." Even after the production, she told Philip Moeller—so Moeller noted—"that she hopes he will return definitely to the faith and that she would be ready to go with him whenever he is ready but he must not be forced."

Meanwhile, O'Neill went his own way. When Russell Crouse told him that he could get the Catholic Writers Guild to endorse the play if he would make the play wife clearly a widow, not a divorcée, O'Neill's answer was "No." He replied emphatically when his publisher Bennett Cerf suggested getting advance endorsements from Catholic dignitaries for the book: "The very last thing I would want done!" He said it would be totally "misleading" because the play was "a psychological study" of religious faith in general. *"It is not Catholic propaganda!* If, after it comes out, the Church wants to set the seal of its approval on it, well, that's up to them. But I don't give a damn whether they do or not—and I certainly will not make the slightest move to win that approval in advance!"

Meanwhile, rehearsals had gotten under way. In this masked play, sets were very important and O'Neill wanted his old collaborator on *The Great God Brown,* Bobby Jones, to do them, but he was tied up and so the Guild suggested Lee Simonson. O'Neill feared at first that Simonson would be out of "sympathy with the mystic undertones of the play," but he knew that Simonson was "a real artist and knows his theatre," and he decided that they could "battle it out in friendship where our ideas differ." Other than for lighting on the split Faust figure, the sets were to be done with "unobtrusive simplicity" to throw emphasis on the soul-struggle—except for the final scene, in which the vision of faith, Christ on the Cross, had to be a "vivid, beautiful, striking thing," for it was really "a character in the drama."

He rejected Langner's suggestion of Jane Cowl for Elsa, for he thought she was a "starry ham" who would try to steal the show. Earle Larimore was to play

John, and O'Neill knew that he would "have to fight every second to get across."
They chose Larimore's wife, Selena Royle, for Elsa. Philip Moeller directed,
and O'Neill worked away at rehearsals "all day every day, no time out for
lunch," making changes up to the last minute, such as intensifying Elsa's flight
out into the rain by having John's Mephisto self remain on stage focusing his
malignity on her, after John's exit.

The opening was set for January 8, 1934. "What a howl of discussion and
misunderstanding and side-taking and reading-the-author-into-his-character's-
end there is going to be on this one! I grow dead with fatigue even to think of
it!" O'Neill predicted. After it, he told Kenneth Macgowan, "The critical lads
fair beshit themselves." They pounced on it as "holy hokum," "fakey preachment," and "reactionary" Catholic propaganda. O'Neill's friend George Jean
Nathan—a passionate skeptic from his mother's Roman Catholicism and his
boyhood convent training—said that it had been ruined by revisions, revisions
that put the Catholic priest in the play. (Ironically, it was he, the passionate
skeptic, not O'Neill, who would return at the end to the Roman Catholic
church.) O'Neill's other critic friend Benjamin De Casseres, an even more passionate skeptic, was so eager to turn upon O'Neill that he printed up his own
satire of it, calling it "Drivel Without End" and having all O'Neill's characters
from earlier plays mock him for selling out. Catholics had at it too. Cardinal
Hayes saw nothing in it but "filth," "profanity," and a divorced woman. Monsignor Lavelle instantly barred it from the Catholic "White List."

O'Neill found the reactions very "adolescent and hysterical." He told Kenneth Macgowan that no one had seen the "profound human implications" of
his study "except a few psychologists." No one at all had seen its "Faustian
undertheme" or understood why he called it "A Modern Miracle Play." No one
realized that it was not a Catholic play, but "a drama of spiritual faith and love
in general" except for a few "Jesuit and Catholic theologians." And the subscription audiences gave the lie to the critics. O'Neill told Macgowan, "Six to
ten curtain calls nightly at the end—Guild audiences three-quarters Jewish!
And yet the critical jack-asses have the nerve to say the technique doesn't come
off!" But in the depths of the Depression they could not carry it "over the
critics' heads."

Luckily, before it closed, Patrick McCartan saw it and sent a copy off to
William Butler Yeats for Dublin's Abbey Theatre. Yeats asked for the rights at
once, and O'Neill told Crouse, "Evidently Yeats sees what the play is all about
and likes it—and Yeats is Yeats. Also he isn't Catholic." The Irish production
was "the event of the year" there and was followed by successful productions
in Holland and Sweden. The book sold wonderfully well. After the dust of the

controversy settled, O'Neill told a fellow former Catholic, Harold McGee, that he had made no great change, "although to judge from the chatter that reached me, you'd think I was on the verge of joining the Trappist monks." To the Argentinian critic Leon Mirlas he gave a clear answer to the American critics' charge of Catholic propaganda. "As for propaganda, I need not tell you that my plays have never been, and never will be, interested in converting anyone to anything except the possibility of the drama as an art." John's choice had been the truth for a "particular ego—not *The* Truth, for I have no *The* Truth to offer." He had said exactly the same thing to the Theatre Guild when he realized most of them did not "see eye to eye" with him on the play's implications.

If he never went on to write the third play of his God trilogy and combine the three under one title, it was not merely because the "Great Depression caught up with its prophecies." He had really finished his study of the psychology of religious faith in the second. He had won the final battle of his psyche and could move on to a larger vision of the human struggle of which his own had been a part. So he set to work on his cycle of eleven plays, *A Tale of Possessors Self-Dispossessed,* to find the heart meaning of America's failure to realize its promise. And although at the very end—with death facing him—he would move back into his deepest personal history for his final plays, he would do so with all the larger vision of human destiny before him, of which his own had been merely the part he knew best.

Abbreviations Used in the Notes

Alexander	Doris Alexander, *The Tempering of Eugene O'Neill* (New York: Harcourt, Brace & World, 1962).
Angoff	*The World of George Jean Nathan,* edited by Charles Angoff (New York: Knopf, 1952).
Angus	Samuel Angus, *The Mystery Religions and Christianity* (New York: Scribner's, 1925).
Berg	Henry W. and Albert A. Berg Collection, New York Public Library, Astor, Lenox, and Tilden Foundations.
Berkman Collection	Alexander Berkman Collection, Internationaal Instituut voor Sociale Geschiedenis, Amsterdam.
Beyond Good and Evil	Friedrich Nietzsche, *Beyond Good and Evil,* translated by Helen Zimmern in *The Philosophy of Nietzsche,* 369–616 (New York: Random House, 1927).
Birth of Tragedy	Friedrich Nietzsche, *The Birth of Tragedy from the Spirit of Music,* translated by Clifton Fadiman in *The Philosophy of Nietzsche,* 947–1088 (New York: Random House, 1927).

Bogard

Travis Bogard, *Contour in Time: The Plays of Eugene O'Neill* (New York: Oxford University Press, 1972).

Boulton

Agnes Boulton, *Part of a Long Story* (New York: Doubleday, 1958).

Bryer

Jackson R. Bryer, *"The Theatre We Worked For": The Letters of Eugene O'Neill to Kenneth Macgowan* (New Haven: Yale University Press, 1982).

Cargill

O'Neill and His Plays: Four Decades of Criticism, edited by Oscar Cargill, N. Bryllion Fagin, and William J. Fisher (New York: New York University Press, 1961).

Clark

Barrett H. Clark, *Eugene O'Neill: The Man and His Plays* (New York: Dover, 1947).

Columbia

Manuel Komroff Papers, Rare Book and Manuscript Library, Columbia University.

Cornell

Department of Rare Books, Olin Library, Cornell University.

Correspondence

The Correspondence of Agnes Boulton O'Neill and Eugene O'Neill, Houghton Library, Harvard University.

Cowley

Malcolm Cowley, "A Weekend with Eugene O'Neill," *Reporter,* September 5, 1957, pp. 33–36.

Crichton

Kyle Crichton, "Mr. O'Neill and the Iceman," *Collier's,* October 26, 1946.

Dartmouth

The Bella Landauer Collection, Special Collections, Dartmouth College Library.

"Diagram"

Eugene O'Neill's diagram of his emotional life (drawn for his psychoanalysis by Dr. Gilbert Van Tassell Hamilton) in Louis Sheaffer, *O'Neill: Son and Playwright* (Boston: Little, Brown, 1968), 506.

Explanation

O'Neill's explanation of "the mystical pattern" in *The Great God Brown,* published as a letter in the *New York Evening Post,* February 13, 1926. Reprinted in Barrett H. Clark, *Eugene O'Neill: The Man and His Plays,* 105–6 (New York: Dover, 1947).

"family history"

Eugene O'Neill's history of his family (written for his psychoanalysis by Dr. Gilbert Van Tassell Hamilton) in Louis Sheaffer, *O'Neill: Son and Artist*, 510–12 (Boston: Little, Brown, 1973).

Floyd

Virginia Floyd, *Eugene O'Neill at Work* (New York: Ungar, 1981).

Gelb

Arthur Gelb and Barbara Gelb, *O'Neill* (New York: Harper, 1962).

George Bellows

Charles H. Morgan, *George Bellows: Painter of America* (New York: Reynal, 1965).

Glover

Terrot R. Glover, *The Conflict of Religions in the Early Roman Empire* (London: Methuen, 1923).

Goldberg

Isaac Goldberg, *The Theatre of George Jean Nathan* (New York: Simon & Schuster, 1926).

Goldman Collection

Emma Goldman Collection, Internationaal Instituut voor Sociale Geschiedenis, Amsterdam.

Harvard

Houghton Library, Harvard University.

Inscriptions

Inscriptions: Eugene O'Neill to Carlotta Monterey O'Neill, edited by Donald Gallup (New Haven: Yale University Library, 1960).

Jung

Carl Jung, *The Psychology of the Unconscious*, translated by Beatrice M. Hinkle, M.D. (New York: Dodd, Mead, 1916).

Karsner

David Karsner, *Sixteen Authors to One* (New York: Copeland, 1928).

Kathleen O'Neill v. Eugene O'Neill

Kathleen O'Neill v. Eugene O'Neill, Supreme Court, Westchester County, June 10, 1912, before the Honorable Joseph Morschauser, Justice.

Lewys v. O'Neill

Georges Lewys v. Eugene O'Neill, Boni & Liveright Inc. and Theatre Guild Inc., Federal Reporter, 49F, 2d ser., no. 2, June 29, 1931, pp. 603–18.

MBE Notes

Eugene O'Neill's notes for *Mourning Becomes Electra*, reproduced in Barrett H. Clark, *European Theories of the Drama*, 530–36 (New York: Crown, 1947).

"Memoranda on Masks"   Eugene O'Neill's notes on using masks for drama, first published in the *American Spectator,* November and December 1932 and January 1933. Reprinted in *O'Neill and His Plays: Four Decades of Criticism,* edited by Oscar Cargill, N. Bryllion Fagin, and William J. Fisher, 116–22 (New York: New York University Press, 1961).

Memorandum   Eugene O'Neill's memorandum to the Theatre Guild on how to produce *Dynamo,* September 9, 1928, published in part in "Scene Designs of Latest Art Used by Guild," *New York Tribune,* December 14, 1929, and in Lee Simonson, *The Stage is Set* (New York: Harcourt, Brace, 1932), 118–19.

Mirlas   Leon Mirlas, *O'Neill y el Teatro Contemporaneo* (Buenos Aires: Editorial Sudamericana, 1961).

Moeller Collection   Philip Moeller Collection, Rare Books and Manuscripts Division, New York Public Library, Astor, Lenox, and Tilden Foundations.

Mollan   Malcolm Mollan, "Making Plays with a Tragic End: An Intimate Interview with Eugene O'Neill, Who Tells Why He Does It," *Philadelphia Public Ledger,* January 22, 1922.

Morehouse   Ward Morehouse, "The Boulevards After Dark: Four Hours from Paris in his French Chateau Eugene O'Neill Is Writing American Drama," *New York Sun,* May 14, 1930.

Nadir Letter   Agnes O'Neill's despairing letter to Eugene O'Neill, late September 1927, O'Neill Correspondence, Houghton Library, Harvard University.

NYU   Fales Library, New York University.

"O'Neill Off Duty"   Brooks Atkinson, "O'Neill Off Duty," *New York Times,* October 8, 1933.

Patterson   Ada Patterson, "James O'Neill: The Actor and the Man," *Theatre,* April 1908.

Poems   Eugene O'Neill, *Poems 1912–1944,* edited by Donald Gallup (New Haven: Ticknor & Fields, 1980).

Post Collection

Books from Eugene O'Neill's private library, C. W. Post College of Long Island University.

Prideaux

Tom Prideaux, "Most Celebrated U.S. Playwright Returns to Theatre," *Life*, October 14, 1946.

Princeton

Manuscripts, Princeton University Library.

Random House

The Plays of Eugene O'Neill, 3 vols. (New York: Random House, 1967).

Robinson

Henry Morton Robinson, *Fantastic Interim* (New York: Harcourt, Brace, 1943).

Sheaffer I

Louis Sheaffer, *O'Neill: Son and Playwright* (Boston: Little, Brown, 1968).

Sheaffer II

Louis Sheaffer, *O'Neill: Son and Artist* (Boston: Little, Brown, 1973).

SL

Selected Letters of Eugene O'Neill, edited by Travis Bogard and Jackson R. Bryer (New Haven: Yale University Press, 1988).

Stekel

Wilhelm Stekel, *Twelve Essays on Sex and Psychoanalysis*, translated by S. A. Tannenbaum (New York: Critic & Guide, 1922).

Texas

The Harry Ransome Humanities Research Center, University of Texas at Austin.

Virginia

Eugene O'Neill Collection, #6448, Clifton Waller Barrett Library, Manuscripts Division, Special Collections Department, University of Virginia Library.

Work Diary

Eugene O'Neill, *Work Diary 1924–1943*, transcribed by Donald Gallup, 2 vols., preliminary edition (New Haven: Yale University Library, 1981).

Yale

Collection of American Literature, Beinecke Rare Book and Manuscript Library, Yale University.

Yule

The Book of Ser Marco Polo, translated and edited by Colonel Sir Henry Yule, 2 vols. (London: Murray, 1903).

Zarathustra

Friedrich Nietzsche, *Thus Spake Zarathustra*, translated by Thomas Common, in *The Philosophy of Nietzsche*, 3–368 (New York: Random House, 1927).

Notes

1. Desire Under the Elms

page 21:

"UNDER THE ELMS." In "Manuscript Notes for Future Plays" (collection of American Literature, Beinecke Rare Book and Manuscript Library, Yale University [hereafter referred to as Yale]). This note has also been transcribed by Virginia Floyd, *Eugene O'Neill at Work* (New York: Ungar, 1981), 53 (hereafter referred to as Floyd). O'Neill's microscopic notes, written to catch the idea rather than to be read again, are difficult to make out, particularly as his tremor causes starts up and down that have nothing to do with the shape of the letters. I worked with these notes before Mrs. O'Neill restricted them from scholars, and I find wholesale discrepancies between Floyd's reading and my own in many of her transcriptions. In this particular note I read the date as 1922, rather than her reading, 1923. Where she reads "locate on farm," I read "laid on farm"; where she reads "father, hard iron type," I read "father, hard miser type" (the first hump of O'Neill's *m* can easily be taken for an *i*); where she reads "his possessive pride in farm—loves earth to be as hard—in old age in a moment of unusual weakness & longing marries young woman," I read "his possessive pride in farm—loves earth it is so hard—in old age in moment of sensual weakness & longing marries young woman."

SILVER CITY SILVER. See "Manuscript Notes for *Desire Under the Elms*" dated "Ridgefield, 1924," Princeton University Library (hereafter referred to as Princeton).

page 22:

"THE TREASURES OF." Letter of December 9, 1920, *Selected Letters of Eugene O'Neill*, ed. Travis Bogard and Jackson R. Bryer (New Haven: Yale University Press, 1988), 143 (hereafter referred to as *SL*)

GOLD . . . IS . . . "JUNK." In *Gold* the treasure is repeatedly called "junk." *The*

Plays of Eugene O'Neill, 3 vols. (New York: Random House, 1967), 1:626, 630, 641, etc.) (hereafter referred to as Random House). In *Where the Cross Is Made* it is merely revealed to be brass.

"APPALLING HUMANNESS." My correction for the text's "humaneness," clearly an editorial error, as the oppressive elms are not appallingly *kind* but appallingly *human.*

"DIAGRAM." O'Neill sketched this chart of his emotional development for his own clarification during the brief analysis with Dr. Gilbert Van Tassell Hamilton in 1926 that helped him give up drinking. It is one of the most valuable documents found by Louis Sheaffer, and it is published on page 506 of Sheaffer's *O'Neill: Son and Playwright* (Boston: Little, Brown & Co., 1968) (hereafter referred to as Sheaffer I). Because O'Neill's handwriting on this document was particularly microscopic, Sheaffer substituted his own labels for the original writing when he reproduced it. Some of these seem to be incorrect, as well as linked together erroneously. Sheaffer reads "Mother love—meaning—Nurse love" (Sheaffer I, 56), which is meaningless, rather than "Nurse Love meaning Mother Love," although both are equally plausible because the writing goes every which way. Sheaffer also errs, I suspect, in his reading of more than one word of the following: "At early childhood father would give child whisky & water to soothe child's nightmares caused by terror of dark. This whisky is connected with protection of mother—drink of hero father." I think that "Thus whiskey" would be a better reading, since O'Neill is obviously drawing a conclusion. The odd English of "At early childhood" also makes me doubt it. See Louis Sheaffer's *O'Neill: Son and Artist* (Boston: Little, Brown & Co., 1973), 190–91 (hereafter referred to as Sheaffer II). I also doubt Sheaffer's reading "discovery of mother's inadequacy" (Sheaffer II, 506). O'Neill would not have used a euphemism like "inadequacy" for drug addiction in a diagram meant only for his own eyes. As a matter of fact, the word "inadequacy" does not appear in any of his plays. I conjecture that he must have written some kind of abbreviation of "morphine addiction," because O'Neill's *m* can easily be mistaken for *in,* and his *o* for *a,* and so on.

page 23:

THE OBVIOUS ENDING. In his screen scenario for *Desire Under the Elms* O'Neill eliminates the baby and kills the old man instead. "Synopsis—for a Screen Treatment of 'Desire Under the Elms' " (as submitted by Richard J. Madden Play Company), 13 pp., in the Henry W. and Albert A. Berg Collection, New York Public Library, Astor, Lenox, and Tilden Foundations (hereafter referred to as Berg).

MALCOLM COWLEY. Cowley wrote up these recollections in "A Weekend with Eugene O'Neill," *Reporter,* September 5, 1957, pp. 33–36 (hereafter referred to as Cowley). Cowley's report is supported by O'Neill's court testimony for the plagiarism suit *Lewys v. O'Neill,* in which O'Neill uses the fact that he was working on the scenario of *Desire Under the Elms* in the fall of 1923 to date the point when he got one of his ideas for *Strange Interlude.*

See *Federal Reporter,* vol. 49. 2d ser., no. 2, June 29, 1931, pp. 603–18, esp. 609 (hereafter referred to as *Lewys v. O'Neill*).

TWELVE ESSAYS ON SEX AND PSYCHOANALYSIS. In his *Reporter* article Cowley (35) says: "Gene picks up a heavy green medical-looking book from the table beside us: it is one of Wilhelm Stekel's treatises on sexual aberrations — perhaps *The Disguises of Love,* which has recently been translated from the German." It certainly was not *The Disguises of Love,* for that is a light, popular work with no shocking case histories. I believe the book was *Twelve Essays* because it was a title Cowley would be likely to forget — as he clearly did — because it had been translated "recently" (by S. A. Tannenbaum, M.D.) and more because it does recount in great detail a case of a seducing mother, really a stepmother (Stekel uses the terms interchangeably, as the boy had been only six when his own mother died). O'Neill may have taken hints from the "dream-like trance" (Wilhelm Stekel, *Twelve Essays on Sex and Psychoanalysis,* trans. S. A. Tannenbaum [New York: Critic & Guide Co., 1922], 245 [hereafter referred to as Stekel]) in which this man carried out his sexual acts for Eben's hypnotic state during the seduction by Abbie. The most decisive reason for selecting Stekel's book as the one O'Neill showed Cowley in 1923 is that he was certainly building on what he had learned from it for his later play *Dynamo,* as we shall see. For the case history Cowley recalled, see Stekel, 241–56.

WOKE UP ON NEW YEAR'S. In Eugene O'Neill's *Work Diary 1924–1943,* transcribed by Donald Gallup, prelim. ed., 2 vols. (New Haven: Yale University Library, 1981), 1:2 (hereafter referred to as *Work Diary*), O'Neill writes for January 1, 1924: "Got idea for 'Desire Under the Elms.'" In a letter to Kenneth Macgowan he said that the year 1924 was beginning auspiciously as he had awakened New Year's morning with the idea for a play (Yale). He also told Walter Huston that he had dreamed the play one night. See Arthur Gelb and Barbara Gelb, *O'Neill* (New York: Harper, 1962), 539 (hereafter referred to as Gelb).

IT ADDED A BABY. O'Neill instinctively compensated for the addition of the baby to the family, which gives it four sons rather than the actual three of his own family by counting Edmund twice. O'Neill had originally thought of calling one of the two older brothers "James" (the actual name of his older brother) and the other "Peter." By changing "James" to "Simeon" he makes the names those of one person: Simeon whom Christ called Peter ("Manuscript Notes," Princeton).

page 24:

EDMUND WAS MORTALLY ILL. The *Denver Times,* March 2, 1885, announces the arrival of James O'Neill and his wife. There are accounts of the telegram, train journey, and the death of the baby on March 4 in both the *Denver Times* and the *Rocky Mountain News* of March 5, 1885. The *News* reported: "Mrs. O'Neill left Denver for New York yesterday morning, before the telegram announcing her boy's death was received." The *New York Mirror* of April 4, 1885, announces James O'Neill's return to New York City from Cin-

cinnati during Holy Week: "Mr. O'Neill comes home to visit his wife, whose health has not been good since . . . the death of her youngest child." The same paper for April 11 says: "The remains of Edmund, the infant son of Mr. and Mrs. James O'Neill, were last Friday removed from a vault in Calvary Cemetery to New London, Conn., for final interment."

SKETCHED "FAMILY HISTORY." The "family history" is the second valuable document prepared by O'Neill for his 1926 analysis with Dr. Hamilton which was found and published by Louis Sheaffer in Sheaffer II, 510–12 (hereafter referred to as "family history").

"MY BABY." In *Long Day's Journey into Night* he has her exclaim to him, "My baby!" (118). She also tells him, "You're still such a baby" (91). In the Notes, the numbers in parentheses after quotations from O'Neill's plays are the page numbers in the published play. In the main text, the page numbers for quotations from the plays are given in the section following these Notes, entitled "Quotations from the Plays."

"THE BIGGEST BABY." As quoted in Sheaffer I, 4.

HIS BROTHER JAMIE. James O'Neill, Jr., died November 8, 1923, in Riverlawn Sanatorium in Paterson, New Jersey. His death certificate reads: "Arteriosclerosis. Cerebral Apoplexy." The cause might more correctly have read "Prohibition Whiskey."

"MOTHER OF THE BEST." Letter to Agnes dated "On the Train" [November 30, 1919] (*SL*, 97). The whole quote reads: "You are wife of all of me but mother of the best of me." A little further in this letter, Bogard and Bryer transcribe: "A leopard isn't such a bum creation, taking bum all in all." I believe the passage should read "taking him all in all."

"MY OWN DEAR BIG." Letter to O'Neill dated "Thursday evening, Five o'clock" [ca. November 1919], in the Correspondence of Agnes and Eugene O'Neill, Houghton Library, Harvard University (hereafter referred to as Correspondence).

"YOU POOR, POOR." Letter to O'Neill dated "Wednesday night" [ca. February 25, 1920] (Correspondence).

MARRIAGE HAD BEEN "UNHAPPY." In a letter Agnes sent to O'Neill (dated July 31, 1920) when he was in New London at his father's deathbed, she speaks of a devastating quarrel they had before he left and tells him she wished he had not said that their marriage was "unhappy." It made her feel that he had forgotten all their beautiful moments and that he was alien to "us" (Correspondence).

page 25:

COAL STOVES . . . "TO BE SHAKEN." See Agnes Boulton, *Part of a Long Story* (New York: Doubleday, 1958), which is Agnes's account of the early years of her marriage to O'Neill, pp. 248, 260–61 (hereafter referred to as Boulton). Kenneth Macgowan told me that Agnes never seemed quite up to caring for the house or for Shane: "She was a very sweet person, but she was not very strong" (Interview, June 26, 1962).

"ABBIE." "AGGIE." Sheaffer reports from his talks with Old Provincetowners

Notes 219

that the librarian of the Provincetown public library during O'Neill's stay there had had the same name he gave his character: "Abbie Putnam." The librarian was hard of hearing and impatient with soft-spoken people like O'Neill. Sheaffer says that O'Neill got "his revenge when he wrote *Desire Under the Elms:* he gave the name of Abbie Putnam to the adulterous farm wife who slays her own child" (Sheaffer I, 356). Actually, O'Neill needed to feel comfortable with the name for a major character who was intimately related to him. Whether there had been an unpleasant librarian of that name or not, I think it seemed right to him because it had the right New England ring and yet recalled Aggie. The last name, I think, came to him because in those days his theater partner Kenneth Macgowan lived just across the Connecticut state line from him in Putnam County, and he was always seeing the "Putnam" road signs as he drove to and from his house.

page 26:

"PRODIGAL BRIDEGROOM." "PRODIGAL HUSBAND." Letter postmarked November 12, 1914, and letter dated "Saturday" [October 10, 1914] (*SL*, 40, 32). All through their engagement O'Neill was already calling Beatrice "wife," and even "Beatrice O'Neill," to make his hope seem real (Berg).

"*THE WANDERER.*" This play by Maurice V. Samuels had been based on William Schmidtbonn's *Der Verlorener Sohn*, which Max Reinhardt had produced in Berlin. *The Wanderer* opened in New York on January 23, 1917. William Elliott and Morris Gest produced it with some help on the spectacular scenes from David Belasco (*Toledo* [Ohio] *Blade*, January 16, 1917). James O'Neill was still playing in it in October when he celebrated the fiftieth anniversary of his first appearance on a stage (*New York Times*, October 12, 1917).

"SOFT-MINDED" CHILD. "MARY." Her nickname was "Ella," but her full name, which appears on such legal documents as the testament of her father Thomas J. Quinlan (Probate Court, County of Cuyahoga, Ohio, Document G.380), has her as "Mary Ellen Quinlan." Her certificate of baptism at St. Patrick's Church in New Haven, Connecticut, has her as "Mary E. Quinlan."

page 27:

"HER HANDS FLUTTER." There are repeated stage directions like this one in *Long Day's Journey into Night* for her hands to flutter, with such modifiers as "distractedly," "with a distracted aimlessness," and "moving restlessly," "aimlessly moving" (15, 20, 40, 42, 46, 65, 73, 89, etc.).

"MOTHER-CHILD." Letter to Beatrice Ashe dated "Sunday" [March 21, 1915] (*SL*, 66).

"UNCONSCIOUS" SUBSTRATUM. Actually, the "unconscious" element in *The Rope* is clearly memory rather than wish. The imagery of this play came right out of the essential facts of the year 1912, when his own prodigal's return to the love of his family took place. The invitation to the son to take his father's gold (love) by way of a harmless suicide (hanging himself with a rope that brings gold, not death) seems to have emerged from his own harmless suicide attempt not long after supplying the evidence on December 27, 1911, for his divorce from Kathleen Jenkins, and his subsequent return to his family's love. If the major events in *Long Day's Journey into Night* are straight fact, and there is every reason to believe they are, that return to love was turned into frustration for himself and the entire family that fall when his mother had a bad relapse into her addiction.

O'NEILL'S FATHER WHEN HE DIED. Like many actors, James O'Neill let his true age become confused. Eugene O'Neill knew his father's age at death was seventy-six, and he says so in a letter to George C. Tyler of December 9, 1920 (*SL*, 143).

JAMES O'NEILL'S INTERVIEWERS. This particular interview is by J.B.C. and entitled "James O'Neill Recalls Boston Memories," *Boston Transcript*, October 20, 1913. James O'Neill was close to seventy years old at the time.

page 28:

LONGING FOR LOVE. Simeon thinks about his golden-haired dead wife "Jenn" as he looks at the golden sunset (204). The name probably came to O'Neill as a sound-echo of Kathleen Jenkins, his divorced first wife, who had long been "dead" for him.

STRINDBERG AS HIS "MASTER." So he declared him to be in his Nobel Prize speech. See *New York Times*, December 11, 1936.

"BEHIND-LIFE" DRAMAS. So he called it in his Playbill essay for *The Spook Sonata*. It appears as "Strindberg and Our Theatre" in *O'Neill and His Plays: Four Decades of Criticism*, ed. Oscar Cargill, N. Bryllion Fagin, and William J. Fisher (New York: New York University Press, 1961), 108–9 (hereafter referred to as Cargill).

"WHAT I THINK." Letter of March 26, 1925 (Department of Rare Books, Olin Library, Cornell University [hereafter referred to as Cornell]). It is reproduced inaccurately in Isaac Goldberg, *The Theatre of George Jean Nathan* (New York: Simon & Schuster, 1926), 158 (hereafter referred to as Goldberg).

"TO WRITE A SYNTHETIC." David Karsner, *Sixteen Authors to One* (New York: Lewis Copeland, 1928), 120 (hereafter referred to as Karsner).

page 29:

"AS BEETHOVEN DID." Louis Kantor, "O'Neill Defends His Play of Negro," *New York Times*, May 11, 1924. It is significant that he made this statement as he was writing *Desire Under the Elms*.

THE GOLDEN BOUGH. O'Neill's first copy of Frazer's great work was the two volumes of *Magic Art and Evolution of Kings*, inscribed by him "Old Peaked Hill Bar, P'town, Mass." (now at Yale). O'Neill told Kenneth Macgowan [March 29, 1921] he was reading it for *The Fountain*. See Jackson R. Bryer, *"The Theatre We Worked For": The Letters of Eugene O'Neill to Kenneth Macgowan* (New Haven: Yale University Press, 1982), 21 (hereafter referred to as Bryer). Later, in a letter to Manuel Komroff dated March 1, 1926

(Manuel Komroff Papers, Rare Book and Manuscript Library, Columbia University [hereafter referred to as Columbia]), O'Neill asked him to send all the volumes of the unabridged edition of *The Golden Bough* that deal with the worship of water.

THE PSYCHOLOGY OF THE UNCONSCIOUS. Later, in response to objections from Barrett Clark that his play *Mourning Becomes Electra* was too "Freudian," O'Neill told Clark that he was no "deep student" of Freud and that, of the psychoanalysts, "Jung is the only one of the lot who interests me. Some of his suggestions I find extraordinarily illuminating in the light of my own experience with hidden human motives." See Barrett H. Clark, *Eugene O'Neill: The Man and His Plays* (New York: Dover, 1947), 136 (hereafter referred to as Clark).

"I NEVER INTENDED." Karsner, 120.

THE FERTILIZATION OF." Carl Jung, *The Psychology of the Unconscious,* trans. Beatrice M. Hinkle (New York: Dodd, Mead, 1916), 173 (hereafter referred to as Jung).

"BIGGER AN' BIGGER." In this and a few other places the Random House text has 'n' rather than the fairly consistent *an'*. I believe this is merely a slip rather than an attempt to distinguish between sounds, so I use *an'* uniformly.

page 30:

"IT'S JUST THAT—." Letter of March 26, 1925 (Goldberg, 158).

" 'DESIRE,' BRIEFLY, IS." Letter to Grace Dupré Hills of March 21, 1925 (*SL*, 194).

page 31:

"A TOMB IN WHICH." The "interred alive" may have come from the persistent feeling he had at this time (as we shall see) that it was he who was dead and they who were alive.

page 32:

"IT'S A JIM-DANDY." This term was certainly keyed in O'Neill's mind to the two important Jims of his life, his father and his brother. He uses it in *Diff'rent* (1920) in a way that reveals the association: "Ask any of 'em you knows if I ain't a jim-dandy to have for a brother" (Random House, 2:499).

"THE GOVERNOR." O'Neill refers to his father as "the Governor" in letters to Tyler who was an old theater friend of his father. James O'Neill was also called so by such fellow actors as Brandon Tynan in interviews like the January 6, 1915, report in the *St. Louis Globe Democrat*.

"I HAVE A PLACE." So James O'Neill said in his court testimony when a demented dressmaker accused him of being her long-lost husband. Asked whether he had ever been a farmhand (like the husband in question), he replied, "Never, except upon my own farm." See "Dantes's Eyes Are Brown," *New York Sun,* November 11, 1889. The title is a joking reference to the fact that the lost husband's eyes were blue and James O'Neill's were clearly brown. "Dantes," of course, was his name in *Monte Cristo*.

HAD RAISED CHICKENS. O'Neill had given a walk-on part in *Desire Under the Elms* to his cousin Alma Platz—who adopted for the moment her mother's more illustrious maiden name "O'Neill"—and she told of the chickens in "O'Neill in Childhood," *Boston Transcript,* December 19, 1925 (a reprint of its first appearance in the *New York Evening Post*). Shane's rooster was observed and mentioned by Louis Kantor in his May 11, 1924, *New York Times* interview. In later years, O'Neill himself went back to cultivating pet roosters.

HIS OTHER SON. In a letter to Eugene Jr. dated January 22, 1924, O'Neill speaks of the final arrangements for the ticket (letter in Edward Laurence Doheny Memorial Library, St. John's Seminary, Camarillo, California).

page 33:

JOSEPH AND HIS BRETHREN. The play by Louis N. Parker opened in New York City on January 11, 1913. James O'Neill played both the role of Jacob and the role of Pharaoh, and Eugene's brother Jamie did Naphtali, Jacob's son, and Ansu, the Chief Magician of Pharaoh's court. The play was published by John Lane Company in New York in 1913 with pictures of the cast in various scenes.

ECHOES OF THE JOSEPH STORY. O'Neill's name for the old man, "Ephraim," comes from one of Joseph's sons who had bad luck with his sons. (I think that O'Neill chose the name "Ephraim" for the father and "Eben" for the son because both names begin with the *E* of "Eugene" and he was deeply present in both.) When Ephraim asks his wife to pray for a son, he actually sees himself as the biblical Jacob and recites: "An' God hearkened unto Rachel!" (235). O'Neill also used the name of another of Jacob's sons, "Reub," for the fiddler to call out in the square dance scene.

"RIDGEFIELD ALWAYS DROVE." O'Neill to Lawrence Langner, December 4, 1929 (*SL*, 359).

"BOOK OF REVELATION." His *Work Diary* (1:2) shows that he finished the first draft of the biblical adaption on January 14 and began *Desire Under the Elms* the next day.

"WORK, *WORK*, WORK." Actually, James O'Neill took these words from a Chicago critic named John McLandburgh, who in the spring of 1873 had written an extremely encouraging article about him, "Some Words About Mr. O'Neill at McVicker's," evaluating his first year there as a young leading man in support of the great traveling stars, such as Maggie Mitchell, Charlotte Cushman, and Edwin Booth. McLandburgh had said: "After the study of a single year he is the equal of some stars, and the superior of many more. But that is nothing. His work is only beginning. The critical period of his profession is that which lies before him. This year will determine whether he is to become an artist or an egotist." The article concluded, "He must work, *work*, WORK!" James O'Neill was so struck by it that he clipped a number of copies for his personal scrapbook (now at Yale). Over the years, the advice became transposed, in the anecdotes he told during his many interviews, to Charlotte Cushman after she had borrowed him from Mc-

Vicker to be her leading man in a special week's engagement at Buffalo, starting December 1, 1873. As James O'Neill told it, she had left him saying, "Let my parting words be: Work! work! work!" See, for instance, James O'Neill, "Among the Stars," *Sunday Magazine,* April 23, 1905.

"HAMMER AND TONGS." Recalling it, James O'Neill had said: "The critics were right that time. I was bad. I knew it. But I got at the play hammer and tongs. I rehearsed all day in my rooms. By the end of the week the play was going well." Ada Patterson, "James O'Neill—The Actor and the Man," *Theatre,* April 1908 (hereafter referred to as Patterson).

page 34:

"CREATORS ARE HARD." From "Old and New Tables." Friedrich Nietzsche, *Thus Spake Zarathustra,* trans. Thomas Common, *The Philosophy of Nietzsche* (New York: Random House, 1927) (hereafter referred to as *Zarathustra*).

"YEARS OF UNDISTURBED." Letter to Eleanor Fitzgerald dated May 13, [1929] (*SL*, 339).

"EASY" WAS HIS. Take, for instance, his comment on Kaiser's *Morn to Midnight:* "It is too easy. It would not have influenced me" (Clark, 83).

"TRUTH, IN THE THEATRE." "Strindberg and Our Theatre" (Cargill, 109).

"REMAIN TRUE TO THE BEST." Letter to George C. Tyler of December 9, 1920. Doris Alexander, *The Tempering of Eugene O'Neill* (New York: Harcourt, Brace & World, 1962), 285 (hereafter referred to as Alexander). Also *SL*, 143.

"IT WOULD BE TOO EASY!" Cowley, 35.

"MY REAL SIGNIFICANT." Letter to George Jean Nathan of June 20, 1920 (Goldberg, 150; *SL*, 130).

page 35:

"INEXPRESSIVENESS." O'Neill used this word for himself after he had used it for his New Englanders in this play. When the final break with Agnes came, he wrote her of the children: "I love them a lot more than you have ever given me credit for. It is only that I am a bit inexpressive about what I feel toward them." Letter to Agnes dated "Friday" [February 3?, 1928] (*SL*, 276).

"BUT WHAT DO YOU." Letter to Agnes dated "Tuesday" [December 20?, 1927] (*SL*, 270).

"MY OWN." These pet names pervade his letters to her during the first few years of their marriage (Correspondence). He had used the same possessive expressions in his letters to Beatrice Ashe (Berg).

"I LOVE SPITHEAD—." Letter to Agnes of April 16, 1927 (*SL*, 239).

"A HUSBAND TO MARVEL AT." Letter to Agnes dated "Thursday p.m." [July 29?, 1920] (*SL*, 131).

"A MAN IN EVERY SENSE." From the report of the funeral in the *New London Day,* August 12, 1920.

page 36:

"I HAVE ALWAYS LOVED." Letter to Kenneth Macgowan dated September 21, 1928 (Yale). The Gelbs, who look at O'Neill through Freudian preconceptions, interpret this as meaning that Ephraim is a "variant of James O'Neill," as if Eugene O'Neill had said that Ephraim was a character *out of his autobiography* rather than *autobiographical* (Gelb, 541).

A FLURRY OF PRODUCTIONS. O'Neill had also had galley proofs to edit for a new collection of his plays, as well as several interviews, and worries over the uproar created by the publication of his play *All God's Chillun Got Wings*.

JUNE 16, 1924. *Work Diary*, 1:8.

"LAID UP." So he said in his *Work Diary*, 1:8.

"THE HOUSE AS CHARACTER." Letter to Kenneth Macgowan dated by him "after August 12, 1926," from O'Neill (Bryer, 132).

page 37:

"IT RUINED MY IDEA." O'Neill wrote this in a "Memorandum" to the Theatre Guild for production of his play *Dynamo*, which took off from the technique of *Desire Under the Elms*. Part of it was published in "Scene Designs of Latest Art Used by Guild," *New York Tribune*, December 14, 1929. Lee Simonson, scene designer for *Dynamo*, also reproduced part of it in his book *The Stage Is Set* (New York: Harcourt, Brace, 1932), 118–19; the complete draft is now at Yale (hereafter referred to as Memorandum).

"EXACTLY WHAT I HAD." From a letter to Lawrence Langner dated June 26, 1941, in which O'Neill tells him that Walter Huston would be "imperative" for the role of Ephraim in a revival of *Desire Under the Elms* they were considering (Yale).

"GRUESOME MORBID." This typical viewpoint was uttered by Fred Niblo, Jr., in "New O'Neill Play Sinks to Depths," *New York Telegraph*, November 12, 1924.

"BUT DON'T THANK ME." Letter of March 28, 1925, in the Fales Collection, New York University Libraries (hereafter referred to as NYU). He later told Kyle Crichton that the attacks brought "the wrong kind of people" to the play. "They came for dirt and found it in everything. It ruined the actors because they never knew how a line was going to be taken." Kyle Crichton, "Mr. O'Neill and the Iceman," *Colliers*, October 26, 1946, p. 40 (hereafter referred to as Crichton).

"ALL'S WELL WHAT." Letter of March 1, 1925. Bryer (86) reads this as "all's well that ends," not seeing the deliberate mistake typical of O'Neill's humor at being so pedantic as to quote Shakespeare. To George Jean Nathan, O'Neill confided on March 26, 1925 (Goldberg, 158) that Banton's attack on *Desire Under the Elms* had "a background of real melodramatic plot—the revenge of Banton's enraged Southern Nordic sensibilities on the author of 'All God's Chillun' (which he tried so hard to stop, and couldn't 'make it')."

"DO YOU HAVE." Letter of February 26, 1925, in the Bella Landauer Collection, Special Collections, Dartmouth College Library (hereafter referred to as Dartmouth).

page 38:

"YES, 'HARLOT' COULD." Letter [ca. September 10, 1925] (Bryer, 98).

"I HEAR THEY HAVE." Letter of February 21, 1926, Manuscript Department, Lilly Library, Indiana University.

"A WAR RAVAGED." Letter to Lawrence Langner dated August 16, 1941 (Yale).

"STIR RAISED IN MOSCOW" and "IT SEEMS THEY HELD" (SL, 238). Letter to Alexander Berkman of April 14, 1927, at the time Berkman was translating *Lazarus Laughed* into Russian. Berkman replied on April 27, explaining that literary trials had originated among revolutionary intellectuals in czarist Russia as a way of circumventing the censorship. Alexander Berkman Collection, Internationaal Instituut voor Sociale Geschiedenis, Amsterdam (hereafter referred to as Berkman Collection).

"THE INNER SPIRIT." From a letter to the Kamerny Theatre group, June 2, 1930. Reproduced in the *New York Herald Tribune,* June 19, 1932, and in Cargill, 123–24. O'Neill was very proud that of the three plays they had selected for this world tour two were his own: *All God's Chillun Got Wings* and *Desire Under the Elms*.

"THE FREUDIAN BRETHREN." Letter to William J. Maloney, M.D., dated February 18, 1925. In the William J.M.A. Maloney Papers, Manuscript Division, New York Public Library, Astor, Lenox, and Tilden Foundations.

"TO ME, FREUD." Letter to Mr. Perlman dated February 5, 1925. Perlman appears to have been a student of Norman Holmes Pearson at Yale, for he had a copy of it which is now in the American Academy of Arts and Letters (SL, 192). O'Neill speaks of Freud's conjectures about the "emotional past" because at this point he had probably read no more of Freud than his *Totem and Taboo* and possibly *Beyond the Pleasure Principle*. These were the two books by Freud that he recalled reading in a letter of October 13, 1929, to Martha Carolyn Sparrow, which she reproduced in her master's dissertation, "The Influence of Psychoanalytical Material on the Plays of Eugene O'Neill" (Northwestern University, 1931), 77. Part of it is reproduced in Arthur A. Nethercot, "The Psychoanalyzing of Eugene O'Neill," *Modern Drama,* Winter 1960, p. 248.

page 39:

DISPUTES AS TO WHETHER. It is not worth looking at all the ideas scholars have had on this play, depending on the theoretical handle by which they have taken hold of it, but a few may make amusing contrasts. Horst Frenz takes Ibsen's *Rosmersholm* as a central influence, Abbie as the central character, and the theme as "a struggle to escape a burden of guilt and to achieve an inner integrity" ("Eugene O'Neill's *Desire Under the Elms* and Henrik Ibsen's *Rosmersholm,*" *Jahrbuch für Amerikastudien,* vol. 9 [1964], 160–65). Murray Hartman takes Strindberg's plays as a central source of plot and characters, Eben as the central character, and the theme as "the tragic possibilities of man's involvement with the mother-image." (*"Desire Under the Elms* in the Light of Strindberg's Influence," *American Literature,* November 1961, pp. 360–69.) Apropos of this viewpoint, O'Neill told Saxe Commins, as an example of George Jean Nathan's limitations as a judge of his work, that Nathan had "considered 'Desire' imitation Strindberg" (Undated note in a 1932 folder, Princeton). The idea that O'Neill plagiarized Sidney Howard's *They Knew What They Wanted* has had recent advocates. Shortly before his death, Kenneth Macgowan suggested to Louis Sheaffer that O'Neill had unconsciously plagiarized the Howard play. Sheaffer agreed with him that "undoubtedly the Howard play helped to inspire *Desire Under the Elms,*" but he also realized that except for the "basic situation" the two plays "are totally different in all respects" (Sheaffer II, 126). Travis Bogard carried the idea a step further. He thought that "the dubious story of the dream [origin], together with O'Neill's uncharacteristic silence about the play as he wrote it, breeds the suspicion that O'Neill was aware that his planet and Howard's were momentarily in uncomfortable close conjunction." (Travis Bogard, *Contour in Time: The Plays of Eugene O'Neill* [New York: Oxford University Press, 1972], 203 [hereafter referred to as Bogard].) Of course, neither Sheaffer nor Bogard had seen the note O'Neill made for his play in 1922. Bogard's suspicions, because there is "scarcely a mention of the play as a work in progress in his letters to Macgowan" (Bogard, 200), can be dispelled by pointing out that O'Neill and Macgowan were seeing each other constantly during the rehearsals of the four O'Neill plays that came between the writing of part one and parts two and three of *Desire Under the Elms,* so that O'Neill was able to tell him anything he wanted to by word of mouth. In a very different viewpoint, Frederic Carpenter sees resemblances of O'Neill's story to such Greek myths as *Oedipus* and *Medea* but believes O'Neill created a "modern myth with new relationships" (106). Carpenter sees Ephraim as the hero but believes that the "final hero is the spirit of Nature," winning out over materialism (Frederic Carpenter, *Eugene O'Neill* [New York: Twayne U.S. Authors Series, 1964], 109).

Among the psychoanalytic critics, Edwin Engel sees Freud's *Totem and Taboo,* and Jung in general, as major sources; Eben as the hero, happily liberated from a "mother complex" by Abbie; and the theme as "the triumph of pagan naturalism over indurated religion, the victory of mother and son over the father." (Edwin Engel, *The Haunted Heroes of Eugene O'Neill* [Cambridge, Mass.: Harvard University Press, 1953], 129 and 126, respectively.) Doris Falk, on the other hand, interpreting O'Neill by means of the theories of Karen Horney, sees Eben as the hero and his salvation in casting "off the prideful father" and integrating with "the submissive, giving spirit of the mother." (Doris Falk, *Eugene O'Neill and The Tragic Tension* [New Brunswick: Rutgers University Press, 1958], 97.) Finally, a genuine psychoanalyst, Philip Weissman, sees Eben as representing "O'Neill (unknown to himself) with his usually unallowable unconscious wishes." He declares: "O'Neill's father and Ephraim Cabot are identical." Eben's tragedy is that he is "unable to grow beyond his sexual feelings for his mother and his death wishes toward his father" (Philip Weissman, *Creativity in the Theater: A Psychoanalytic Study* [New York: Delta, 1965], 140, 142).

"THE MEGAPHONE MEN." Letter to George Jean Nathan of June 20, 1920 (Goldberg, 150; *SL*, 129).

2.   Marco Millions

page 41:

"MAKE GOOD." In his first letter home from Honduras, on November 9, 1909, O'Neill told his parents: "There is every chance in the world for making good" (Alexander, 134; *SL*, 18). The same hope that he would make good had inspired his father to arrange the drafting job for him at Westinghouse Electric in Buenos Aires. (Edward Keefe told me that James O'Neill had found the job for Eugene, and that seems likely, for he would not have arranged his passage there if no job awaited him.)

"I'VE ALWAYS LONGED." So O'Neill told his dentist, Doctor Lief, in a letter of October 2, 1928 (NYU), just before he set out for China once again.

READ UP ON PONCE DE LEÓN. In a *New York Sun* interview, January 12, 1928, O'Neill explained: "The desire to write a play on Marco Polo developed some years ago when I was reading material before writing 'The Fountain.' So much of that material referred to Marco Polo that I got the idea then."

GAVE HIS PONCE A VISION. The vision scene with the three Chinese is in the 1921 version of *The Fountain* preserved in the Library of Congress copyright script. O'Neill rewrote it drastically in the summer of 1922, changing the free verse to prose and cutting the Chinese from Ponce's vision. *The Fountain* seems to have pushed much of its pattern onto *Marco Millions*. Both plays were written in two summers with other plays between, both gave O'Neill an opportunity to write poetry, both were "romantic" and contrasted higher life values with mere worldly ambition. Both plays are freighted with memories of O'Neill's father.

"EUROPE SOMEHOW MEANS" . . . "WIND UP IN." Letter of O'Neill to Kenneth Macgowan, September 23, 1922 (Bryer, 34).

BY SETTING OUT WITH MARCO. Only after O'Neill cut his Chinese trio did the idea for a comedy on Marco Polo come to him. He had no idea for one at the beginning of the summer of 1922, for he told George C. Tyler, in a letter of July 6, 1922 (Princeton), "I would like nothing better than to be represented by a real comedy if I can ever get the time or the idea for one. At present I am 'up to my ears' in going over—and, I hope, improving—'The Fountain.' "

BEST SCHOLARLY EDITIONS. O'Neill's notes with page references for *Marco Millions* at Yale are chiefly from *The Book of Ser Marco Polo*, trans. and ed. Colonel Sir Henry Yule, 2 vols. (London: Murray, 1903), which gave much peripheral information (hereafter referred to as Yule). Manuel Komroff, who was working on a new edition of Marco Polo's travels at the time, told me that on visiting O'Neill at Nantucket that summer of 1925 he was surprised to discover on his shelves all the scholarly editions he had. Komroff based his work largely on Marsden's edition.

page 42:

"A PRACTICAL MAN." "THE AMERICAN IDEAL!" O'Neill copied the quote (Yule, 1:108) and made his exclamation after it. Floyd (61) presents it all as straight O'Neill.

"WOULD ALWAYS MAKE USE." Yule, 1:6.

"MARCO MILLIONS." The First Longhand Draft at Yale has an American ring with the title, "Mr. Mark Million." After that, the title is always referred to as "Marco Millions."

"THE TRUE VALUATION." So O'Neill told Malcolm Mollan in "Making Plays with a Tragic End: An Intimate Interview with Eugene O'Neill, Who Tells Why He Does It," *Philadelphia Public Ledger,* January 22, 1922. Mollan writes "100 per cent" (hereafter referred to as Mollan).

KATE BUSS'S *STUDIES.* O'Neill's inscribed limited edition (Boston, 1922) is at Yale. It has been republished by Jonathan Cape and Harrison Smith (New York, 1930).

"THE CHILD WILL BE." Letter dated "Friday"—probably June or July 1923, for O'Neill also tells Macgowan that late August will be fine for the Macgowans to visit him in Provincetown (Bryer, 37).

page 43:

"BIG NAÏVE WONDERING." So O'Neill describes Muriel McComber in *Ah, Wilderness!* and he said that she had been based on his childhood sweetheart. All that is known about her will appear in the chapter on that play.

THE TRAVELING SALESMAN. James O'Neill, Jr., was in the second, or road, company, while a first company played in New York City until April 10 and then went on to other big cities, starting with Chicago. As the dates ahead in the *New York Dramatic Mirror* for the road company show, they were playing small towns during January, February, and March of 1909 in New York State, Connecticut, Pennsylvania, and Massachusetts to capacity or standing-room-only audiences. When Eugene O'Neill was in Honduras and after his return, Jamie was still touring in *The Traveling Salesman* and so was doubly associated with a journey.

"THE LURE OF EASY POPULARITY." In a letter to his father's old friend George C. Tyler of December 9, 1920, O'Neill said that his father had given in to "the lure of easy popularity and easy money" (Alexander, 58; *SL,* 143).

A TOUCH OF HIS FATHER. For instance, one of his father's typical comments, "I'm hungry as a hunter" (*Long Day's Journey into Night,* 66), went into the elder Polos: "Well, here we are—and hungry as hunters!" (376).

"I ACTUALLY GROW." [April–July 1924], Bryer, 51.

HIS FATHER HAD BURST. O'Neill told Kyle Crichton: "I began with a background of poetry. My father was reciting poetry all the time. Instead of singing in the bathtub, he'd break out into Shakespeare" (Crichton, 18–19).

THEY COULD LEARN MACBETH'S. O'Neill told this story to Hamilton Basso in
"The Tragic Sense," *The New Yorker,* March 13, 1948, p. 37.

page 44:

"WISE GUY." Recalling those days, O'Neill told Tom Prideaux: "While other
boys were shivering themselves into a fit of embarrassment at the mere
thought of a show girl, I really was a wise guy" ("Most Celebrated U.S.
Playwright Returns to Theatre," *Life,* October 14, 1946, p. 104 [hereafter
referred to as Prideaux]). O'Neill's schoolmate at Betts Academy William
Jenkins told me that most of O'Neill's schoolmates realized how far ahead
of them he was in this respect.

"GENE'S ABUNDANCE OF EARLY." From a letter to me by Corwin Dale Willson, July 27, 1955. O'Neill talked more than he usually did at Harvard, for
he was undergoing a stretch of celibacy to keep stainless for Beatrice Ashe.

MARCO OFTEN INCLUDED. Marco Polo declared in his "Prologue": "Some
things indeed there be that he beheld not, but these he heard from men of
credit and veracity" (Yule, 1:1).

"THE WOMEN WEAR." Yule, 1:160. O'Neill copied this quote into his notes for
Marco Millions (Yale).

page 45:

"SMASHING." O'Neill wanted Kublai's court at this point to offer a "smashing
brilliant contrast," he told Lawrence Langner in a letter of April 5, 1927.
The Harry Ransome Humanities Research Center, University of Texas at
Austin (hereafter referred to as Texas).

"HUNDRED ABLE TEACHERS." Yule, 1:19.

"A RECORD IN THE." Yule, 1:21.

FIRST HORRID REVELATIONS. See the account in Henry Morton Robinson, *Fantastic Interim* (New York: Harcourt, Brace, 1943), 63, (hereafter referred to
as Robinson).

page 46:

TWO HISTORICAL RECORDS. Yule 1:30, 77. O'Neill wrote down both in his notes
for *Marco Millions* (Yale).

TARTAR PRINCESS KUKACHIN. O'Neill made her Kublai's grandchild. In Yule,
she is called a "lady" of the Mongol tribe of Bayant (1:23), but in a footnote
(1:38) Yule declared: "Kukachin was the name also of the wife of Chingkim,
Kublai's favorite son." O'Neill saw a possibility that his Kukachin had been
named for her mother and thus was the daughter of the Khan's favorite son.
O'Neill always followed Yule's chief spelling of her "Kokachin." His publishers changed it to "Kukachin."

"A VERY BEAUTIFUL." Yule, 1:32.

"WATCHED OVER AND GUARDED." Yule, 1:36.

"WEPT FOR SORROW." Yule, 1:36.

"YOUR DANCING SNAPSHOT." Letter to Agnes dated "Saturday evening," apparently written in late August 1921 (Correspondence), as O'Neill tells her,

looking forward to her return from New York to Provincetown, "Here's to September!"

LIKE THOSE OF LI PO. O'Neill's inscribed copy of *The Works of Li Po, The Chinese Poet*, trans. Shigeyoshi Obata (New York: Dutton, 1922), is among his books at C. W. Post College of Long Island University (hereafter referred to as the Post Collection).

CANTONESE LOVE SONGS. O'Neill's inscribed copy, translated by Cecil Clemente (Oxford, 1904), is in the Post Collection.

page 47:

THE *SHE-KING*. O'Neill's inscribed *She-King* and *Shu-King* are in *The Classics of Confucius*, trans. Walter Gorn Old (London: Theosophical Publishing Co., 1918), preserved in the Post Collection. Old uses the spelling *"Shi-King."* The patterns of repetition and refrain in some of the Confucian Odes allow for a blend with those in sea chanties.

HER FIERCE READINESS. During the early days of their love, Agnes's jealousy was a joke between them; they allude to it often in their letters (Correspondence). For instance, when O'Neill told Agnes about the leading lady for his play *Beyond the Horizon* on January 28, 1920 (*SL*, 109) he said, "I am getting to be great friends—now don't be jealous!—with Helen McKellar." Agnes wrote him on February 24, 1920, that Susan Glaspell had brought her the newspapers about *Beyond*'s opening and had told her she was going to make her jealous. Susan had then shown Agnes a page with pictures of the two blond beauties, Miss McKellar and Miss Hayes, who looked "ravishing." Instantly, Agnes felt the gnawing of the "demon" with green eyes, she said. She pictured Miss McKellar coming to cheer O'Neill in his sickroom (Correspondence). In his answer, ca. February 26, 1920, O'Neill told her, "Worry not and gnash not your teeth over the 'blond beauties!'" He explained that Helen McKellar had only sent letters of sympathy—he had influenza—and besides was married and very much in love with her husband, so, "I hardly think her kind letters can be regarded jealously—even by one as green-eyed as Agnes O'Neill." (*SL*, 115. *SL*'s dating of "16?" cannot be right, since the letter answers a letter of February 24.)

HE WROTE IT FIRST. O'Neill's First Longhand Draft of *Marco Millions* has a note at the beginning in O'Neill's hand explaining that the script is "a bit confusing because the last scene was written first—the rest of the play half a year or so afterward, with what is now the Prologue written last of all."

page 48:

MYSTIC KNIGHTS OF COLUMBUS. The burial of James O'Neill in the baldric and sword of the Fourth Degree knights was reported in the *New London Day*, August 10, 1920.

ANDREW MELLON. Mellon justified his tax plan by saying, "Any man of energy or initiative in this country can get what he wants out of life. But when that initiative is crippled by a Tax system which denies him the right to receive a reasonable share of his earnings, he will no longer exert himself and the

country will be deprived of the energy on which its continued greatness
depends" (Robinson, 49). O'Neill's Marco and Mellon had the same values,
wanting to get out of "life" only money and lots of it.

MAYOR HYLAN OF NEW YORK. Mayor Hylan had tried to prevent the opening
of *All God's Chillun Got Wings* by delaying permission for the child actors
to go on until shortly before curtain time on opening night, May 15, 1924,
and then refusing. He refused only because the children were too young, he
said, but he had given permission for much younger children who were then
playing in New York. (See such New York newspapers as the *World*, the
Telegram, the *Post*, and the *Tribune* for May 16, 1924.) The Provincetown
Players responded by reading the opening scene, which had the child actors,
and going on with the play.

VIOLATION OF THE SUNDAY LAW. The attempt to close *The Hairy Ape* on
charges of violating the Sunday Law was made by a policewoman, Anna
Green, who purchased a subscription ticket and then brought charges
against the Provincetown Players by "The People of the State of New York."
The case was dismissed because a subscription theater "is not a place of
public amusement" (*Law Journal*, April 12, 1922). Magistrate Simpson of
the City Magistrate's Court, who tried it, declared, "It would be a calamity
if this organization were hampered in any way. It is a private club, doing a
great service to the cause of American drama, a credit to the Community"
(*New York World*, March 23, 1922).

"IMPURE, OBSCENE, AND INDECENT." This charge by Chief City Magistrate
McAdoo was made before he read the play. When he did, he could only
return it "without comment." Owen Davis, chairman of the censorship committee of the Authors League, declared, "No one would condemn 'The
Hairy Ape' excepting a fanatic. If they were to suppress the O'Neill play it
would be a calamity to the theater" (*New York Telegram*, May 19, 1922).

page 49:

"HOUSES OF ILL FAME." First Longhand Draft of *Marco Millions* (Yale).

A FORM OF "ALCHEMY." Yule, 2:423–25.

"THROUGH WHICH MAN LOSES." O'Neill made these particular notes in a
Notebook 1920–1930 at Yale, probably in the interim of the two summers of
writing.

"MANGONELS" . . . "SURRENDER INCONTINENTLY." Yule, 2:158–60.

"HEROICALLY MEANINGLESS AND CONSTANTLY." *Notebook 1920–1930* (Yale).
Originally, O'Neill also sketched a note for Marco to invent Landlordism,
through which "Man loses all creative contact with the fruits of the earth."

"VEIN OF BOMBASTIC." Yule, 1:113.

"THE ULTIMATE PEACE." As quoted in Elizabeth Stevenson, *Babbitts and Bo-
hemians: The American 1920s* (New York: Macmillan, 1967), 30.

page 50:

"ALL WORKERS ON." Eugene O'Neill, *Poems 1912–1944*, ed. Donald Gallup
(New Haven: Ticknor & Fields, 1980), 46 (hereafter referred to as *Poems*).

ANARCHIST WEEKLY *REVOLT*. O'Neill told Beatrice Ashe of his work on *Revolt* in a letter of July 25, 1916 (*SL*, 73). *Revolt* ran from January 1 through February 19, 1916, and Hippolyte Havel is listed as editor. O'Neill helped get the magazine out—no signed work of his is in it. *Revolt* has been preserved in the Internationaal Instituut voor Sociale Geschiedenis, Amsterdam.

"PROFESSIONAL SWINDLERS." So O'Neill described the so-called statesmen arranging the peace of World War II (which he saw as the "same old game" played at the end of World War I) in a letter to Saxe Commins of July 12, 1944 (Princeton).

"AS MARCO TELLS THE KHAN." Ibid. O'Neill used the spelling "Khan" for Kublai; it was his publishers who preferred "Kaan."

page 51:

HIS FATHER'S FAVORITE STORIES. O'Neill parodied his own father's repetitions of this story in the father of his play *Ah, Wilderness!* and told Brooks Atkinson that he had ("O'Neill Off Duty," *New York Times*, October 8, 1933).

"MARK THE EFFECTIVENESS." Review of *The Three Musketeers*, April 1, 1899. James O'Neill had also been praised highly in the March 18, 1899, *New York Clipper* for his "gallantry, reckless bravado, nimbleness of fence."

"EUGENE, I AND OTHERS." So Stephen Philbin recalled to me in a letter of February 17, 1955.

page 52:

GHAZAN KHAN. O'Neill was following the description of Ghazan Khan in Yule (1:24), in which he is said to have been endowed with the "highest qualities."

HE WOULD LIKE TO HIRE. "Doc" Ganey told this story to me and to several others who interviewed him.

page 53:

"INCREDIBLE TORTURES." Letter from O'Neill to Agnes dated "Thursday p.m." [July 29?, 1920] (*SL*, 131).

"CLOTHED IN CRIMSON." Yule 1:5–6. O'Neill made a note of it with page reference in his notes for *Marco Millions* (Yale). The historical Polos kept to crimson because that was the most expensive dye in the Middle Ages. O'Neill made more contrast by varying the colors of the robes.

page 54:

"WRAPPED IN A WINDING." O'Neill probably got the color white for the Khan's mourning robes from the references to mourning in the *She-King*, but the choice of color for the winding sheet appears to have been his own.

"DO YOU REMEMBER." Letter dated "Tuesday" [February 7?, 1928] (*SL*, 276).

GOOD KING OF T'ANG. O'Neill took extensive notes from the *Shu-King*, particularly from the "Lament of the Five Children." He made a list (in his notes for the play) of "Duties and penalties of rulership" as listed by the Prime

Minister of T'ang after the good King died. See *The Classics of Confucius,* 65–67, 85–87.

"THE NOBLE MAN IGNORES." O'Neill's inscribed copy of *The Sacred Books of China: The Texts of Taoism,* trans. James Legge (Oxford: Oxford University Press, 1891), is in the Post Collection. The words are O'Neill's summing up of the principal tenets of Tao.

page 55:

"LÂO-ZSE AND CHUANG." So O'Neill told Frederic I. Carpenter (in a letter of June 24, 1932) in answer to a question Carpenter had put on his Oriental readings. Professor Carpenter kindly allowed me to transcribe it. Now in *SL,* 401.

"REACHING TOWARD THE." Letter dated "Friday" [Summer 1923] (Bryer, 37).

MARCO POLO'S REFERENCES TO A HOLY. Yule, 1:130–39. Yule derives Marco's tree from the trees of the sun and the dry trees in the legends of Alexander.

"BETTER SORT OF LIFE" . . . "MY MOTHER'S LOVE." Letter dated "Thursday p.m." [July 29?, 1920] (*SL,* 132).

page 56:

"VOTIVE OFFERINGS, PIECES OF." Every single one of O'Neill's details came, word for word, straight out of Yule (1:134–35). So it is clear that an error crept into O'Neill's text with its first typing, and he himself never caught it. Yule's list of offerings includes "amulets, rags, and tapers." All the texts of *Marco Millions* read "bangles, armlets, ornaments." Because every detail comes from Yule, and there are no "armlets" in Yule, O'Neill must originally have written "amulets," as in Yule, which could easily appear in his handwriting to be "armlets." Since "armlets" makes sense, the error was never caught.

"CONTRADICTORY MANNER." "DISTORTED IN HUMAN." O'Neill wrote this in his *Notebook 1920–1930* (Yale), originally in describing the Khan's amazement over "the essential identity" of the ideas of Christ and Buddha and the way both are "distorted" in practice. This idea became a major one throughout the play, particularly in Marco's reaction to the Buddhist beliefs identical to his own and in the parallel between Marco and General Bayan, both inspired to war by the "Prince of Peace." The Prologue, coming out of Yule's comparative legends, extends the idea to the distortions of other major religions.

SPRANG FROM "A TWIG." See Yule, 1:135.

ADAM'S STAFF. Yule (1:135) has a more elaborate story, which has the staff move to Enoch and then to the whole "line of Patriarchs," including Joseph until Moses "got his rod from it."

"TREE OF LIFE." Yule, 1:131.

"STAFF OF MAHOMET." Yule, 1:135.

"IN THE THROES OF." Mollan.

page 57:

"FORESTAGE, MUSIC, MANY SCENES." "IT SEEMS TO." Letter to David Belasco of November 22, 1924 (*SL,* 191). O'Neill explained that it was really a comedy satire of American life and ideals, even if ostensibly about Marco Polo. He also declared that the Eastern part of the story had real beauties of philosophy and poetry.

JANUARY 14, 1925. *Work Diary*, 2:473. He had the condensed *Marco Millions* ready for mailing to Belasco on January 23.

IN THE PRISON. See the First Longhand Draft and First Typescript of *Marco Millions* (Yale).

"BELASCO HAS BOUGHT." Letter from O'Neill to George Jean Nathan, March 26, 1925 (Goldberg, 158). The *Work Diary*, 2:479, February 14, 1925, reports a cable from Belasco accepting *Marco Millions:* "very effusive and loving, the old nut."

FORTUNE WAS $200,000. In a letter to Lawrence Langner of April 5, 1927, O'Neill told him this had been Belasco's plan (Texas). In a letter to Agnes dated "Wednesday night," of late September 1925 (Correspondence), O'Neill told her about a long session that he and Robert Edmond Jones had with Belasco. O'Neill concluded: "He certainly admires 'Marco,' bless him!"

"REPUTATION OF HOLDING PLAYS." Letter from O'Neill to David Belasco, April 28, 1926 (*SL*, 202). O'Neill explained that he had not meant to take the play from him but wanted him to show more clearly that he was going ahead with it.

"ONE OF THE REGRETS." Many newspapers reproduced Belasco's opening night telegram, including the review of Percy Hammond, "Marco Millions a Rich and Sardonic Extravaganza," *New York Herald Tribune*, January 15, 1928.

"ROMANTIC, HANDSOME HERO." So O'Neill told Agnes in a letter dated "Friday a.m." (ca. October 1926, Correspondence). He commented: "Dear Actors, what!"

ARTHUR HOPKINS GAVE UP. Clark, 108.

LAWRENCE LANGNER HAPPENED TO. Langner tells about it in *The Magic Curtain* (New York: Dutton, 1951), 231–34. Exactly what took place is revealed in O'Neill's letter to Theresa Helburn of February 28, 1927 (Yale) and to Lawrence Langner of May 1, 1927 (*SL*, 243–45), as well as in copies of Langner's letters to O'Neill of March 29 and April 1, 1927 (Yale).

"PSYCHOLOGICAL MOMENT." Lawrence Langner wrote a circular letter to the Guild Board on April 2, 1927 (copy at Yale), telling them: "I KNOW I AM RIGHT ABOUT THE PSYCHOLOGICAL MOMENT FOR COUPLING UP WITH O'NEILL."

"HEAVY SPECTACULAR." The Guild's objections are reiterated in O'Neill's answering letter to Langner of April 1, 1927 (Yale).

"A SUPER-GRAND SCALE." To Lawrence Langner, April 5, 1927 (Texas).

page 58:

"IRONIC CLIMAX." Lee Simonson, *The Stage Is Set* (New York: Harcourt, Brace, 1932), 116–17.

"SMASHING BRILLIANT CONTRAST." Letter to Lawrence Langner of April 5, 1927 (Texas).

"WRECK THEIR COMPANY." So O'Neill told Agnes in a letter dated "Tuesday" (ca. October 4, 1927, Correspondence).

MARGALO GILLMORE. O'Neill seems to have thought she was a bad choice for the role. Later, when the Guild was casting his play *Dynamo,* he sent them a "Memorandum" on it (Yale), saying that he was "adamant against" Gillmore for the girl in this play because they needed an actress with "some appealing sex to her." Rouben Mamoulian directed, Dudley Digges played Chu Yin.

"SHOULD MAKE A REMARKABLE." "ONE CAN'T HAVE." Letter from O'Neill to Agnes [November 27?, 1927] (*SL,* 266).

"STILL BRINGING HOME." Letter from O'Neill to Theresa Helburn, originally dated "April" but not mailed until June 9, 1928 (Yale).

3.   The Great God Brown

page 59:

"THE INTELLECTUAL, THE OCCUPANT." A letter of Saxe Commins to his aunt Emma Goldman on September 23, 1925, tells us that O'Neill had been planning a "projected sequel" to *The Hairy Ape.* O'Neill had told Commins of it almost as soon as he thought of it. O'Neill's first note for *The Great God Brown* most likely was this sequel. As Commins said, "In it he has the antithesis to Yank, the intellectual, the occupant of the Ivory Tower ask himself the very same perplexing question that flung poor, inarticulate Yank into the embrace of the gorilla: 'Where do I belong?' " (Emma Goldman Collection, Internationaal Instituut voor Sociale Geschiedenis, Amsterdam [hereafter referred to as Goldman Collection]). By "sequel" O'Neill would have meant merely a further inquiry into the same problem, rather than a play with the same characters, just as he meant by his first *trilogy* three plays with totally different characters on three answers to the religious question.

HIS FIRST NOTE IN 1922. Notes for Future Plays. The date is on the note (Floyd, 41).

ED KEEFE AND GEORGE BELLOWS. My information comes from a long interview with Edward Keefe on April 3, 1955, and from a conversation with Mrs. George Bellows, as well as from Charles H. Morgan's *George Bellows: Painter of America* (New York: Reynal, 1965) (hereafter referred to as *George Bellows*).

page 60:

"HIGHEST HOPES." O'Neill took over this phrase from his many readings of Nietzsche's *Thus Spake Zarathustra* and used it frequently after he initially adopted it in "Bread and Butter."

"BREAD AND BUTTER." The typescript sent in for copyright is in the Library of Congress. The play was never published.

"BREAD AND BUTTER" . . . "MUDDY SPIRITS." "Bread and Butter" typescript, Library of Congress.

A SMALL TOWN IN CONNECTICUT. In the play it is Bridgetown, Connecticut, an obvious parody of Bridgeport.

"DEEP-SET AND FAR APART." "Bread and Butter" typescript. The description is very like a picture of young Ed Keefe painted by George Bellows in those days, which I saw in Edward Keefe's home. It can also be compared with the photograph of Edward Keefe among a group of O'Neill's friends in Sheaffer I, 28. Travis Bogard thinks that the hero of "Bread and Butter" reflects "O'Neill's own appearance" (*Contour in Time*, 37), but O'Neill's mouth was large, not small, his eyes were not "deep-set" or "far apart" or "black," but dark brown, and his face was not oval, but long and thin.

ROBERT HENRI. O'Neill used his own first name for this character, "Eugene Grammont," probably because he is the spokesman of O'Neill's own viewpoint.

LABORING ON THE DOCKS. In O'Neill's own case the dock work came after, not before, his marriage as in the play.

MAUDE WILLIAMS. All that is known of her comes from the testimony in *Kathleen O'Neill v. Eugene O'Neill*, Supreme Court, Westchester County, tried June 10, 1912, before the Honorable Joseph Morschauser, Justice. Maude's address was given as 123 West 47th Street, which places it two blocks from the "house" at 140 West 45th Street, where the witnessed adultery was arranged. I assume this address refers to a "house," for this seems to have been a major red light district of the time, just off Times Square. Whether she actually had been with O'Neill or merely allowed her name to be used cannot be judged. In any case, for O'Neill her name was associated with his first debacle in love and his subsequent suicide attempt, and thus fell naturally into this play. In it he used the spelling "Maud." Hereafter referred to as *Kathleen O'Neill v. Eugene O'Neill*.

"STAN KEITH." So he is called throughout the First Draft (in pencil, at Yale) (hereafter referred to as First Draft).

WITH A PENCHANT FOR DRINK. In a letter to Arthur McGinley, April 9, 1927, O'Neill speaks of an alcoholic "bust" with "Eddie Keefe." Arthur McGinley allowed me to transcribe it.

SEE *DESIRE UNDER THE ELMS*. Right after he had seen *Desire Under the Elms*, Bellows wrote Kenneth Macgowan: "The play is magnificent. I felt I was under the spell of one of the world's great dramatists." He added, "I wish I could paint Gene O'Neill sometime" (*George Bellows*, 282).

page 61:

DEAD OF A RUPTURED APPENDIX. When O'Neill received Bellows's letter forwarded with a note on Bellows's death by Eleanor Fitzgerald, he wrote in his *Work Diary* (2:474): "Queer!" It *was* queer that just then, when he was flooded with memories of him, Bellows had tried to reach him and died. Later O'Neill told his son Shane that although he never liked posing he would have been "tickled to death" to have Bellows paint him (January 18, 1940, *SL,* 500).

HUTCH'S SPLENDID "ATHLETIC" FRAME. In a letter of January 29, 1919, to Susan Glaspell right after Hutch's death, O'Neill wrote a glowing tribute to him as an athlete (Sheaffer I, 314).

"THE PASSING OF HUTCH COLLINS." Letter of O'Neill to Beatrice Ashe, July 25, 1916 (*SL,* 73).

"HERO" OF HIS BOYHOOD. In *Long Day's Journey into Night* his father tells Jamie, "He grew up admiring you as a hero!" (34).

page 62:

JAMIE "HAD NEVER FOUND." Letter of O'Neill to Joseph A. McCarthy, February 18, 1931 (*SL,* 378).

"PLAY OF MASKS." Notes for Future Plays. My reading is "Play of masks — remarkable —." Floyd (41) reads it "Play of masks — removable —."

"CURIOUS AND OPPRESSIVE SENSE." *Masks and Demons* (New York: Harcourt, Brace, 1923), 45. Kenneth Macgowan told about how the book came to be written ("M'Gowan's Masks," *New York Times,* April 4, 1943): "It was actually the Dutch scene designer Herman Rosse who made my interest in the mask deep and enduring by turning it backward to first things — to the primitive masks used equally by African witch doctors and Greek herdsmen, by Hopi Indians and by Swiss peasants just across a ridge from Oberammergau. While O'Neill and Jones and I were planning our Provincetown season, I began to work with Rosse on a book called 'Masks and Demons.' We hunted down hundreds of masks in museums from Chicago to Boston, and across into Europe, and collected scores of photographs. Finally we boiled these down to what we thought were eighty masterpieces, and we tried to trace the story of the mask from demonology to the theatrical performances of Greece and Ceylon, Java and Japan." O'Neill was in on this work from its inception and had already begun thinking out original ways to use masks in the modern theater before the book came out.

"NOT THE WORST THINGS." Friedrich Nietzsche, *Beyond Good and Evil,* sec. 40, *The Philosophy of Nietzsche,* trans. Helen Zimmern (New York: Random House, 1927), 369–616.

"EVERY PROFOUND SPIRIT." Ibid.

HE COULD EXPRESS A SPLIT PERSONALITY. O'Neill followed Nietzsche's idea here that the "contrary" would "be the right disguise for the shame of a God to go about in." Ibid.

DRAMATIZE CHANGES IN PSYCHOLOGY. This idea, along with the idea of dramatizing a transfer of personality with masks, was entirely original with O'Neill. As a matter of fact, Kenneth Macgowan, who was in on O'Neill's intentions, declared, "So far as I know, O'Neill's play is the first in which masks have ever been used to dramatize changes and conflicts in character." He added: "O'Neill uses the naked face and the masked face to picture the conflict between inner character and the distortion which outer life thrusts upon it. With this established, he goes on to use the mask as a means of dramatizing a transfer of personality from one man to another." See Macgowan's "The Mask in Drama" from the Greenwich Playbill, no. 4, 1925–26, reprinted in the *Brooklyn Daily Eagle,* January 30, 1926.

page 63:

PAINTED BACKDROPS FOR SCENERY. Robert Edmond Jones told Jerome Littleby, in an interview on March 7, 1924: "The possibilities of a medium of backdrops and flats as scenery" have "never been realized" (Unlabeled clipping in the Provincetown Players' Scrapbook, vol. 2, Theater Collection, New York Public Library).

"SPOOFING" PRODUCTION OF *FASHION.* Kenneth Macgowan told me that their production of Anna Cora Mowatt's comedy was the first in which part of the comic effect came from "spoofing" Victorian theatrical conventions.

JONES HAD MADE. Reviews of *Fashion,* such as one in the February 29, 1924, *American Hebrew,* described this comic effect.

"FAMILY KODAK" CONCEPTION OF REALITY. O'Neill used this phrase to point out the need for "behind-life" drama in his essay "Strindberg and Our Theatre" (Cargill, 108).

"NOTHING TO DO WITH." O'Neill's actual words were that "the facts of life . . . have nothing to do with the truth" and they appear in a "Forword" O'Neill had tried to write for *The Great God Brown.* He finally gave it up, for he always hated expository writing. A clear photocopy of the manuscript appears in Mardi Valgemae's "Eugene O'Neill's Preface to *The Great God Brown,*" *Yale University Library Gazette,* July 1968, pp. 24–29. It reassures me that my reading "nothing to do with the truth" is correct, not Floyd's "to do with truth" (52). Otherwise Floyd transcribes correctly here, and even corrects Valgemae's error of reading "dangling symbol," for the correct "doughy symbol."

TO LIVE IN IMITATION. In *Long Day's Journey into Night* (33) O'Neill had his father tell Jamie: "When he was in prep school, he began dissipating and playing the Broadway sport to imitate you."

REAL GENIUS OF HIS FAMILY HAD BEEN JAMIE. Saxe Commins was one to whom O'Neill confided this conviction, and Commins relayed it to his Aunt Emma Goldman (Goldman Collection).

JAMIE HAD "LOST ALL HOLD." Letter of O'Neill to Joseph A. McCarthy, February 18, 1931 (*SL,* 378).

page 64:

"BANG TAILS." So O'Neill told his agent Richard Madden in a letter of February 26, 1925 (Dartmouth). Boxing Day is, of course, the first weekday after Christmas.

"TOO MISERABLY DISORGANIZED." *Work Diary,* 2:472, January 4, 1925.

JANUARY 28, 1925. *Work Diary,* 2:476. By January 11 he had quit both drinking and smoking, and by the 14th he could begin work condensing *Marco Millions* (2:473). After finishing *Brown,* he relapsed into drinking again (April 3, 2:487) and did not get sober until after the birth of his daughter Oona on

May 14 (2:488). He relapsed again on July 17 (2:489), then sobered up in September, only to have a week-long relapse after visiting New London again in October. With the beginning of "Fountain" rehearsals on November 23 (2:494), he had another relapse and drank all through December, until Kenneth Macgowan made a first appointment for him with Dr. Gilbert Van Tassell Hamilton, so that he could write in his *Work Diary* on New Year's Day 1926: "Welcome to a new dawn, I pray!" (2:495).

"SOILED AND TRUE." These quotes are from O'Neill's poem "Interlude," probably (from its Roman imagery) of Spring 1925, when he was reading for the Roman background of *Lazarus Laughed* (*Poems*, 96).

"THAT DREARY ORDEAL." O'Neill felt this way about productions for a long time, but he did not say so until May 13, 1929, in a letter to Eleanor Fitzgerald (*SL*, 339).

"A GREAT AND SELF-BLIGHTING." So O'Neill told Oliver Saylor in a letter written late in 1921. Saylor reproduced it in " 'The Hairy Ape' a Study in Evolution of a Play," *New York Evening Globe*, May 6, 1922.

"MOST DISGRACEFUL SCENE." From a telegram of O'Neill to C. Hadlai Hull, the attorney for the O'Neill estate, February 17, 1923 (Sheaffer II, 107) asking him to "restrain" Jamie in New London.

"I WOULD FEEL A SUCCESS." Letter to Benjamin De Casseres, August 11 (1927), Dartmouth. He had expressed the same idea in an interview with Flora Merrill in the July 19, 1925, *New York World*, when he was still full of the philosophy of *The Great God Brown*. "The only success is in failure. Any man who has a big enough dream must be a failure and must accept that as one of the conditions of being alive. If he ever thinks for a moment that he is a success, then he is finished. He stops."

page 65:

"THAT THE MORE I SHOULD URGE." Letter to C. Hadlai Hull, December 13, 1922 (Sheaffer II, 105).

"NEW CALEDONIA, CONNECTICUT." First Draft.

"NOLAN'S DUMP." The name came by association with that of the closest crony of Jamie's last months, whose name was Dolan. O'Neill connected Dolan so closely with Jamie's last days that he called his plans for *A Moon for the Misbegotten*, which centers on Jamie's dying, his "Dolan play." See Notes for *A Moon for the Misbegotten*, Floyd, 372.

LOUIS MONTAGUE'S "GAMBLING JOINT." In a letter to Agnes dated "Saturday" [July 31, 1920], O'Neill tells her: "Jim and I go up to Louis' gambling joint" after the hours at the hospital where their father lay dying (Correspondence). Thomas Dorsey, Jr., told me he recalled driving Jamie and Louis Montague up to Provincetown from New London to see Eugene in the summer of 1921.

JAMIE HAD ACTUALLY BEEN ROLLED. Thomas Dorsey, Jr., told me he had been rolled while sleeping off a drunk in a hotel lobby.

page 66:

"CAPERING . . . IN THE NUDE NERVES." First Draft.

"SAINTED" MOTHER. So Jamie spoke of her according to Harold DePolo and /
or his wife Helen (Sheaffer II, 106).

MAMIE BURNS'S BROTHEL. Apparently the real madame of the New London
brothel was named Addie Burns. The names O'Neill chose for her (Madame
May in *The Great God Brown* and Mamie Burns in *Long Day's Journey into
Night*) both echo his mother's name, Mary—Mamie being actually a nickname for Mary, although not one by which his mother was called. There is
also reason to think that the original of the prostitute "Fat Violet" at Mamie
Burns's was actually named "May" and that her name went into Madame
May. At any rate, one of his poems, "Ballad of Old Girls" (1912), asks
"Where's May the queen of the burlesque 'time'? / Not averse to a schooner
of beer, / Tipping the scales at two hundred and nine" (*Poems*, 8). O'Neill's
original name for Cybel in *The Great God Brown*, "Estelle," also recalls his
mother's nickname, "Ella."

page 67:

"FAT" FROM HER CURE. For instance, Mary herself says that she is "too fat"
(14), and her husband calls her "fat and beautiful" (17) and "fat and sassy"
(20).

HER HANDS HAVE BECOME CRIPPLED. Mary says, "I couldn't play with such
crippled fingers" (104).

"WITH AN ETERNAL CUD." I have corrected an error that has persisted in all
printed versions of this play, which read, "with an eternal end." O'Neill
himself finally caught it and told Saxe Commins in a letter dated May 24,
1942 (Princeton): "There is one bad error in the stage directions. It makes
one sentence describing Cybel completely meaningless. It must have always
been there since I find it in the Liveright first edition. Last word of this
sentence should obviously be 'cud' not 'end.' End means nothing." It takes
no master detective to discover how this error came about. The printers set
up their galleys from a copy (now at Yale) typed on a machine whose *c* and
e as well as its *u* and *n* are virtually indistinguishable.

page 68:

"FAR-OFF VOICE." The stage directions for Mary under the drug in *Long Day's
Journey into Night* echo those for Cybel. Mary too speaks with a "blank far-
off quality in her voice" (121). Just as Cybel stares "ahead unmoved as if she
hadn't heard," Mary "Goes on as if nothing had been said" (109) or "As
though he hadn't spoken" (113). Jamie recites bitterly from Swinburne's "A
Leave-Taking": "Yea, though we sang as angels in her ear, / She would not
hear" (173).

HIS MOTHER BECOME EARTH. So conscious was O'Neill of New London as
holding his dead father and mother that he had Dion refer to the town
ironically in the First Draft as "Heaven, Connecticut."

"MEPHISTOPHELEAN." O'Neill's editors used this spelling consistently in *The Great God Brown* instead of the usual "Mephistophelian."

THE SAME ACTOR TO PLAY BOTH. On July 6, 1925, O'Neill sent John Barrymore a copy of *The Great God Brown* as a potential "vehicle," telling him, "Dion in first half and Brown in rest of play should be played by same actor but you alone could do this" (Dartmouth).

"HE HASN'T HAD A DRINK." Letter to Harold DePolo of January 10, 1922 (*SL*, 162).

page 69:

"IF THE SAVAGE IGNORES." P. 163.

"THE LAY OF THE SINGER'S FALL." *Poems*, 38–39.

page 70:

"HE SEEMED SOMEHOW TO MEET." Corwin Willson recalled these talks to me in a letter of July 27, 1955.

page 71:

SUCH A PERIL TO NEW LONDON PARENTS. O'Neill had his mother say to him in *Long Day's Journey into Night:* "Now no respectable parents will let their daughters be seen with you" (44).

"ALSO YE LOVE THE EARTH." Sec. 27, "Immaculate Perception," *Zarathustra*.

HE ENVIES DION'S CREATIVE POWER. O'Neill was thinking of Nietzsche's scorn of the spiritually empty seekers of worldly power: "Wealth they acquire and become poorer thereby. Power they seek for, and above all, the lever of power, much money—these impotent ones!" (sec. 11, "The New Idol," *Zarathustra*). O'Neill was also thinking of Zarathustra's accusation "They steal the works of the inventors and the treasures of the wise. Culture, they call their theft—" (ibid.) when he described Brown's library: "A backdrop of carefully painted, prosperous, bourgeois culture" (294).

"HURRY, BROTHER!" I have omitted one unimportant stage direction after "Our wife is waiting!" (308) to throw emphasis on the significant ones.

LOVE SPREADS ITS GLOW. The romantic Margaret enters singing the popular song from *The Rubáiyát*, "Ah, moon of my delight." The poem was so powerfully associated for O'Neill with his youthful romantic loves that he wove quotes from it throughout his later play about romantic love *Ah, Wilderness!*

THE NAME OF FAUST'S MARGUERITE. O'Neill called her "the modern direct descendent of the Marguerite of Faust" in his explanation of "the mystical pattern" of *The Great God Brown*, first published as a letter in the *New York Evening Post*, February 13, 1926, and reprinted in Clark, 105–6 (hereafter referred to as Explanation). He actually called her "Marguerite" in the First Draft before settling on "Margaret." The *Work Diary*, 2:483–84, shows that O'Neill was reading Goethe's *Faust* in translation from March 5 through March 10, 1925, while working on *The Great God Brown*.

"ETERNAL GIRL-WOMAN." Explanation.

page 72:

"SCOTT'S WHARF." O'Neill sets the Prologue on "the pier of the Casino" (257). When Margaret's voice comes to Dion, it comes from the end "of the wharf" (266). I think that the choice of synonym here came from the context of his memories of loving Maibelle Scott on Scott's wharf. In the Epilogue his woman grown old appears "on the same dock" (324).

"HIS LETTER FROM THE TRAIN." Letter of Agnes to O'Neill dated "Happy House, Tuesday" [November 1919], Correspondence.

"A WHOLE, A TRUTH." The quote from *Welded* (Random House, 2:488) is of weight, for O'Neill was struggling very consciously in that play to resolve the difficulties in his marriage to Agnes.

"THE SACRIFICE OF ALL FREEDOM." *Beyond Good and Evil*, sec. 46.

page 73:

"A HUSBAND TO MARVEL AT." Letter of O'Neill to Agnes dated "Thursday p.m." [July 29?, 1920] (*SL*, 131).

"LIFE IS REALLY WORTH LIVING." With these words James O'Neill summed up the "moral" of an actual occasion when he had been able to come to the aid of a little girl and her dying mother. He had written it up—years later—as a Christmas story for the Christmas edition of the *New York Dramatic Mirror* of 1896.

"THERE HAVE BEEN TOO MANY INSULTS." Letter to Agnes dated "Monday eve" [December 26?, 1927] (*SL*, 271).

page 74:

"THE INTOLERABLE CONDEMNATION." First Draft.

"DOWN-GOING ONES." Sec. 56, "Old and New Tables," part 6, *Zarathustra*.

"TEST." "SELF-JUSTIFICATION." "EACH VISIT." Letter of August 11 [1927] (Dartmouth).

"WHAT WONDER EVEN." Sec. 73, "The Higher Man," part 15, *Zarathustra*.

page 75:

AGNES WAS PREGNANT. O'Neill's daughter Oona was born on May 14, 1925.

"I WANT DION TO LEAVE." I have corrected the obvious error "leave the sky to me" in the Random House edition to read "leave the sky for me."

REREADING *THE BIRTH OF TRAGEDY*. The *Work Diary*, 2:484–86, shows that O'Neill was reading in *The Birth of Tragedy* from March 12 through March 26, 1925. Later O'Neill took Barrett Clark to a rehearsal of *The Great God Brown*, and Clark noticed that, as they left the hotel, O'Neill stuffed "a worn copy of Nietzsche's *Birth of Tragedy* into his coat pocket" (Clark, 5).

"ALL THE CELEBRATED FIGURES." Friedrich Nietzsche, *The Birth of Tragedy from the Spirit of Music*, sec. 10, in *The Philosophy of Nietzsche*, trans. Clifton P. Fadiman (New York: Random House, 1927), 947–1088.

"TRAGIC MYSTERY DRAMA OF LIFE." In a letter to Saxe Commins of May 24, 1942 (Princeton), O'Neill says that *The Great God Brown* "does succeed in conveying a sense of the tragic mystery drama of Life revealed through the lives in the play."

DECIDED TO CALL HIS HERO "DION." The decision came late in his writing, for throughout the Second Draft of the play at Yale, one can see where he has inserted the *i* to change the name "Don," by which he had been calling his character, to "Dion." He also crosses out the former last name "Avery" and substitutes "Anthony." O'Neill pointed out the significance of this final name in his Explanation: "Dion Anthony—Dionysus and St. Anthony—the creative pagan acceptance of life, fighting eternal war with the masochistic, life-denying spirit of Christianity as represented by St. Anthony—the whole struggle resulting in this modern day in mutual exhaustion—creative joy in life for life's sake frustrated, rendered abortive, distorted by morality from Pan into Satan, into a Mephistopheles mocking himself in order to feel alive; Christianity, once heroic in martyrs for its intense faith now pleading weakly for intense belief in anything, even Godhead itself."

"A TRACE OF PAN." This was to happen in act three, scene two, in which Brown is seen changing into Dion's clothes to go to Margaret (Second Draft).

page 76:

"DISSIPATED, BITTER, DIABOLICAL QUALITY." This was to happen in act four, scene one, in which Brown tears up the plan for the capitol building, throws aside his mask of Brown, and escapes in this rejuvenated Pan-mask of Dion (Second Draft).

"THE REMOTE, OBJECTIVE QUALITY." The mask was to become pure God in act four, scene two, in which the "Man" dies out of it, and was to remain so in the Epilogue, where it is seen in tableau with Margaret become the Eternal Mother (Second Draft). A great modern production of this play would try to express this idea in the masks without obliterating the idea that Brown has taken from Dion a poisoned creativity.

"ALWAYS SPRING COMES AGAIN." I omit the stage directions.

page 77:

"ALICE" FOR ALICE CUTHBERT. O'Neill and Agnes had met Miss Cuthbert in Bermuda. In the poem "To Alice" (*Poems*, 95) he sees her as a " 'Sweet spirit' of Innocence." He told his dentist Dr. Lief in a letter of March 28, 1925 (NYU) that he was sending him as a patient "Miss Cuthbert—young and charming—one of the few good friends we have made on the Island."

"THE ETERNALLY CREATIVE PRIMORDIAL MOTHER." Sec. 16, *The Birth of Tragedy*.

SHE STANDS AS THE ETERNALLY PREGNANT MOTHER. When the Argentinian critic and director Leon Mirlas told O'Neill that he thought the Epilogue was superfluous, O'Neill replied (in a letter of May 1, 1935) that he might possibly agree, if ever he could see the play objectively. "But I love that Epilogue! For me, it rounds out the whole piece like an inevitable poetic experience of life. It moves me deeply. And that's that. It is a case of love, you see. So it's no use asking me to act like a critic about it!" This is probably not a letter-perfect transcription, for Mirlas translated the quote into Spanish for his book *O'Neill y el Teatro Contemporaneo* (Buenos Aires: Editorial Sudamericana, 1961), 212, and I have retranslated it back into English (hereafter referred to as Mirlas).

"I MEANT IT ALWAYS TO BE MYSTICALLY WITHIN." Explanation.

"HOT AT WORK ON 'BROWN.' " Letter from O'Neill to his agent Richard Madden of February 6, 1925 (Dartmouth).

O'NEILL FORCED HIMSELF TO TURN HIS BACK. O'Neill told his publisher Horace Liveright in a letter of March 14, 1925, "But what the hell, I got angry about it when they got after 'Ape' and 'God's Chillun' and this time my mind was made up beforehand to preserve the proper philosophical calm, as I'm deep in the second half of 'The Great God Brown' and can't afford to get emotionally sidetracked" (Princeton).

page 78:

HE CONCLUDED IT ON MARCH 25, 1925. In the *Work Diary,* 2:486, he finished all revisions on March 25, and after "Curtain" in the Second Draft, he wrote: "This finished March 25, 1925."

"I'VE JUST FINISHED A DEVASTATING." Letter of March 26, 1925 (Goldberg, 159).

"OLD THING." Letter to Kenneth Macgowan of July 31, 1925 (Bryer, 94).

"WORTH A DOZEN 'FOUNTAINS.' " Letter of September 2, 1925 (Bryer, 96).

"DO THE MASKS IN 'BROWN.' " Monday [after August 12, 1926] (Bryer, 131).

"I QUITE UNDERSTAND." "THEY SUGGESTED ONLY THE BROWNIDIC." Letter of June 22, 1927 (Dartmouth). O'Neill's play on the name of his muddy character Brown has been misread by Sheaffer II (194), Gelb (594), and *SL* (246) as "bromidic." I have capitalized "brownidic" to assist recognition.

"I SHOULD HAVE MADE THEM TWICE AS LARGE." So he told Barrett Clark, who quotes him without date (Clark, 116). Later he used the double-sized masks for *Lazarus Laughed,* but still later in a letter of December 15, 1944, he told Clark that he had thought of a simplified way of doing that play with "no double-sized mask idea for Chorus" (Clark, 149), so perhaps by this time he would have rejected the idea for *The Great God Brown* as well.

"YOU MAY BE RIGHT." Clark, 106. Clark had begun collecting material for his biography of O'Neill at this time, and that is why he was privileged to learn about the play in advance.

AUDIENCE OF CRITICS. In his *Work Diary* (1:21) for January 22, 1929, O'Neill says that the performance for the special audience "went off well, by accounts." On January 23 he lists the regular opening without comment. In the cast were William Harrigan as Brown, Robert Keith as Dion Anthony, Leona Hogarth as Margaret, and Anne Shoemaker as Cybel.

"EVERYONE SEEMS TO THINK NOW." Letter to Horace Liveright of February 17, 1929 (Dartmouth).

"BOTHER TOO MUCH OVER." Clark, 106.

page 79:

" 'BROWN' LOOKS LIKE BIG HIT." *Work Diary*, 1:21, January 27, 1926. O'Neill adds "they tell me," for he did not attend the play after the last rehearsal on January 21.

"PSYCHOLOGICAL, MYSTICAL, AND ABSTRACT." O'Neill said so in his "Memoranda on Masks," a series of notes he made on using masks in the theater which were first published in George Jean Nathan's *American Spectator*, November 1932, with additions in December 1932 and January 1933. It is reproduced in Cargill, 116–22 (hereafter referred to as "Memoranda on Masks").

"THE DEEPLY RESPONSIVE POSSIBILITIES." "Memoranda on Masks," 117.

"ONE OF THE MOST INTERESTING." O'Neill said this in a letter to his editor Saxe Commins on May 24, 1942 (Princeton) apropos of an anthology of plays that Whit Burnett was planning in which he wanted to use *The Moon of the Caribbees*. O'Neill thought that his old sea plays were by this time "stale stuff" and suggested instead that Burnett use act one, scene three, of *The Great God Brown*, in which Dion wakes up in Cybel's cottage.

"FAVORITE." O'Neill called "Brown" his "favorite" play to both David Karsner in 1926 and S. J. Woolf in 1931. See Karsner, "Eugene O'Neill at Close Range in Maine," *New York Herald Tribune*, August 8, 1926, and Woolf, "O'Neill Plots a Course for the Drama," *New York Times*, October 4, 1931.

"IT'S VERY NEAR—AND DEAR." Letter from O'Neill to Frederick C. Packard, Jr., who had been assistant stage manager for the original production; reproduced by Packard without the date in "Eugene O'Neill—Dramatic Innovator," *Chrysalis* 5 (1952): 12.

4. Lazarus Laughed

page 81:

"GERM OF IDEA." *Work Diary*, 1:11. O'Neill noted that he had begun intensive work on *Marco Millions* on July 17, 1924. On August 13 he wrote that he had "started Part Four again—what I've written on it so far is rotten." He was working on this part (with the Princess's story) when the germ came (*Work Diary*, 1:9, 11).

ON SEPTEMBER 1, 1925. *Work Diary*, 2:490.

BIBLE OF HIS YOUTH. O'Neill was never uncertain of his originality and therefore he was always ready to acknowledge joyfully what he had learned from others. When the critic Benjamin De Casseres "found something of 'Zarathustra' " in *Lazarus Laughed*, O'Neill was delighted, for (he told De Casseres) it had influenced him more than any other book he had read. "Although my work may appear like a pitiable contradiction to this statement and my life add an exclamation point" (Letter of June 22, 1927, *SL*, 246). Later, after the play got its Pasadena, California, production, O'Neill told Sophus Keith Winther that Ralph Block's review of it in the June 10, 1928,

New York World was "more significant" than any other. Block had pointed out a parallel between *Lazarus Laughed* and *Thus Spake Zarathustra*. Winther wrote Block on October 21, 1930, asking about it, and then made the parallel his chief tool for treating the play in his *Eugene O'Neill: A Critical Study* (New York: Random House, 1934). Block told me about their correspondence in a letter of November 23, 1964.

"GOOD AND JUST." This is Nietzsche's ironic term. Sec. 21, "Voluntary Death," *Zarathustra*.

page 82:

"A TRANSFIGURED BEING." Sec. 46, "The Vision and the Enigma," part 2, *Zarathustra*.

LAUGHTER IN JOYOUS AFFIRMATION. O'Neill looked into other interpretations of laughter besides this one of Nietzsche's, such as Bergson's and also Freud's in *Wit and the Unconscious*—so he told Manuel Komroff—but in the end he decided to trust Nietzsche for the Greek spirit of laughter. "I agree with him even if he is wrong!" he joked (Letter of March 22, 1926, *SL*, 200). In an earlier letter of March 1, 1926 (Columbia), O'Neill had asked Komroff to send to Bermuda books he needed for background on *Lazarus Laughed* and other plays he was planning. The March 22 letter tells Komroff what he has received and what he wants from Komroff's suggestions.

BIBLICAL WORDS "JESUS WEPT." John 11:35. With the years, O'Neill decided that he no longer liked the title, and he told Barrett Clark so in a letter of February 22, 1944 (Clark, 148).

"PARABLE OF THE HIGHEST THINGS." Sec. 33, "The Grave Song," *Zarathustra*. Nietzsche also sees the dancer as the "epitome" of the "self-enjoying soul" (sec. 54, "The Three Evil Things," part 2).

JEWISH SORCERER WITH A CHARM. O'Neill had read about the fame of the Jews for enchantments in the ancient world in one of the books that Komroff sent him, Samuel Angus's *The Mystery Religions and Christianity* (New York: Scribner's, 1925) (hereafter referred to as Angus). O'Neill's copy is in the Post Collection inscribed "Bellevue Bermuda May '26." O'Neill liked to put in authentic historical touches, and there are many in this play. For instance, he noted the widespread belief in demons as intermediaries between men and gods described in another of the books Komroff sent, Terrot R. Glover's *The Conflict of Religions in the Early Roman Empire* (London: Methuen, 1923) (hereafter referred to as Glover). O'Neill had Tiberius address Lazarus consistently as "Daemon."

WRITTEN OUT THE COSMIC VIEWS. These are in the Notes for *Lazarus Laughed* (Yale).

"ALL THINGS COME FROM DEITY." Of course, O'Neill was able to find lines in the Gospel of John in which the eternal oneness appears—for example, "I am in my Father, and you in me and I in you" (John 14:20–21); and "The glory which thou gavest me I have given to them, that they may be one, as we are one; I in them and thou in me, may they be perfectly one" (John 17:22–23).

"PERVADES ALL, EARTH." O'Neill read this Pythagorean quote from Virgil in Glover, 29. He dated his copy (now at Yale) "April," so he had it for his first draft. O'Neill had planned to use Pythagorean ideas in his play from the beginning, for his March 1 letter to Komroff asks for a volume on the philosophy "of the very early Greeks up to and including Pythagoras."

"FLY UP ALIVE." Glover, 29.

RHYTHMICAL MOVEMENTS AND SCULPTURESQUE POSE. Jones had explained to O'Neill's wife Agnes Boulton that he had ideas "on color, grouping, and rhythmic movement, almost metaphysical in their extent," for her article on their new theater, "An Experimental Theatre: The Provincetown Playhouse," *Theatre Arts Magazine*, March 1924, p. 186. He also explained his ideas in the first Provincetown Playbill for 1923–24: "The director of today thinks in terms of sculpture and arranges his actors in powerfully expressive groups as a sculptor might wish to arrange them."

page 83:

IDEAS JONES HAD FORMED. It is my assumption that Jones took part of his inspiration from his work with Nijinsky. Critics described the dancer's methods as "sculptural" and he himself spoke of making every gesture, every movement express a thought. See, for instance, Romola Nijinsky's *Nijinsky* (Suffolk, N.Y.: Penguin Books, 1960), 266, 269–74, 277.

JONES'S UNUSUAL WAY OF TRAINING. Jimmy Light explained how Jones and he had trained the choruses for the *Ancient Mariner* in an interview with the *New York Evening Sun*, April 23, 1924. He said: "We reached them primarily through an understanding of the meaning of the poem, through an understanding that we wished them to indicate a flow of emotion, not at all to represent action. Unconsciously they developed a sense of form, a sense of rhythm, and because of this, I think, what they do affects the audience much as music does. Unexpectedly they lost all self-consciousness and fell quite naturally into postures and groupings that it would have been impossible to achieve through the regular method of chorus training." Light had already absorbed the feeling for the theater as rising out of the celebration of Dionysus—Life—and the mystery rites that O'Neill conveyed so strongly, and so he described the choruses of the *Ancient Mariner* as "assistants in a ritual, celebrants in a ceremony" and the dramatization itself as "a ritual of sin and repentance." O'Neill had also arranged the "Book of Revelation" for Jones's experiments, but the financial failure of the *Ancient Mariner* discouraged them from ever producing it. Jones himself thought that their production of the *Ancient Mariner* had been a "high-water-mark" of the American theater (so he said in a typed statement now in the Provincetown Players' Scrapbook, Theatre Collection, New York Public Library). O'Neill's *Ancient Mariner* has been published in the *Yale Library Gazette*, October 1960, pp. 61–86.

PYTHAGOREAN ENTHUSIASM FOR NUMBERS. O'Neill was aware of his enthusi-

asm, and in his later play *Days Without End* he sketched the various philos-
ophies he had run through to find "a brief shelter in Pythagoras and numer-
ology" (Random House, 3:503).

"FOR A FUTURE PLAY." "DEAD SELVES." Floyd, 152. O'Neill made these notes
(now at Yale) at Northport, Long Island, in July 1931, according to his own
dating, as part of his preliminary thinking for *Days Without End,* which he
was at that point calling "Without Endings of Days." Each of these "masked
past selves" was to carry its particular "God."

SPEARHEADED EACH CROWD. O'Neill carried out his idea (after the blurry
failure of the masks for *The Great God Brown*) of using double life-sized
masks, but he used them only for the choruses spearheading each crowd so
that audiences could perceive at once from them the essence of the group
personality.

MASKED MASSES WOULD BE THE REAL SCENERY. O'Neill told Kenneth Macgowan this in a letter of January 21, 1927 (Bryer, 145–47).

page 84:

BLEND ALL WORSHIP. Angus treats "syncretism"—the merging of religions and
gods—in the ancient world at length, and O'Neill would have read about
the tendency to absorb all gods into Dionysus on pp. 194 and 195.

DEMETER "SUNK IN ETERNAL SORROW." Sec. 10, *The Birth of Tragedy*.

"A WORLD TORN ASUNDER." Sec. 10, *The Birth of Tragedy*.

page 85:

"A LAMP TO THE PATH." Patterson.

ACHIEVED A COMPOSITE RECOLLECTION. O'Neill had no conscious intention
of turning Lazarus into his father, yet only one detail of Lazarus's appearance is clearly different. His eyes are "black and deep-set" (274), whereas
in *Long Day's Journey into Night* his father has "deep-set light-brown eyes"
(13). Otherwise the figures are similar. Lazarus is "tall and powerful" (274).
The description of James O'Neill in *Long Day's Journey into Night* runs like
this: "About five feet eight, broad-shouldered and deep-chested, he seems
taller and slenderer because of his bearing . . ." (13). Normally James O'Neill
had neither the "mass" of hair nor the "heavy beard" that Lazarus has right
after his resurrection (274), but James O'Neill always had both the hair and
the beard at the moment of his own resurrection from "burial" in the dun-
geons of the Château d'If in his play *Monte Cristo,* which his son had
watched so often as a boy.

"ONE OF THE HANDSOMEST." Amy Leslie, *Some Players: Personal Sketches*
(Chicago: Herbert S. Stone, 1899), 537.

"TILL HE DIES." "James O'Neill's Marvelous Secret of Eternal Youth Laid
Bare," *Chicago Chronicle,* February 28, 1897.

IN THE FALL OF 1907. O'Neill was able to watch all the rehearsals of *Virginius*
before he started work in the New York—Chicago Supply Company.

"I NEVER KNEW HOW MUCH." So said the review in the *Dramatic Mirror,*
October 5, 1907.

"JAMES O'NEILL's MARVELOUS SECRET." *Chicago Chronicle,* February 28, 1897.

"BOYISH EYES, THE EYES." So James O'Neill appeared in 1908 (Patterson).

"YOUNG TO LOOK AT." "Alan Dale Hurls Satire at James O'Neill's 'Monte Cristo,'" *Los Angeles Examiner,* December 15, 1907.

"GIVE SPEECH THE QUALITY OF MUSIC." Letter of O'Neill to Barrett Clark of February 22, 1944 (Clark, 148). O'Neill even told Kenneth Macgowan that he would let Chaliapin do it in Russian, so important did he consider the sheer sound of the voice. He added, laughing, that as for the usual audience's understanding of the play, it would probably be clearer to them in Russian. Letter [December 1926] (Bryer, 140).

"MELODIOUS SPLENDOR." Amy Leslie, *Some Players,* 538.

"UNAFFECTEDLY AND UNFORCEDLY." James O'Donnell Bennett, Review of *Virginius* in *Chicago Record,* February 5, 1908. Bennett's praise of James O'Neill's voice in this article is typical. "The chief charm of his acting is the rare beauty of perfect enunciation and pronunciation of the English language. If the reader can imagine the roll of Milton's verse to the accompaniment of a pipe organ he will get some notion of the richness, power and dignity of this actor's utterance."

page 86:

"AN ARROWHEAD OF CONCENTRATION." Letter to Macgowan of January 21, 1927 (Bryer, 146).

"WITH A SPOTLIGHT." Letter to Macgowan of January 12, 1927 (Bryer, 144).

A STAR HE COULD HOPE TO JOIN. James O'Neill would usually come up from New London, where the family were already established, to get his son Eugene at term's end. For instance, a note in the June 25, 1898, *Dramatic Mirror* says: "James O'Neill spent Thursday in New York, and returned to New London with his youngest son, who has just finished his term at the Mount St. Vincent convent school. Mr. O'Neill is enjoying his vacation, amusing himself with gardening and aquatic pastimes."

page 87:

A SISTER MARY. O'Neill included both the Bible's sisters Mary and Martha in the early scenes, with Martha a simple housewife and Mary a masochistic fanatic (from her gestures in the Bible of prostrating herself and kissing feet). O'Neill used the sisters and Lazarus's parents to dramatize the division into hostile sects through fear and to give Lazarus his first trial of faith in eternal life when his entire family is killed. The episode roughly parallels the trial to O'Neill's faith in the loss of his whole family.

"A FARMER AND NOTHING BUT." "James O'Neill's Marvelous Secret of Eternal Youth Laid Bare," *Chicago Chronicle,* February 28, 1897. The same article gives a typical picture of James O'Neill's family life: "His domestic affairs have been very happy and serene. Almost always his wife, a handsome woman of charming personality, is with him, and one of his two sons also travels with him. The other son, young James, is at college. In the summer-

time you will find the family far from the garish glare and the plaudits of the
theater in a villa near New London, Connecticut."

"A HUSBAND TO MARVEL AT." So O'Neill said of his father in the letter to Agnes
dated "Thursday p.m." [July 29?, 1920] (*SL*, 131).

"FRIGHTFUL" FEELING OF HOPELESSNESS. Letter of Agnes to O'Neill of July
31, 1920 (Correspondence).

"MY MOTHER'S LOVE." Letter to Agnes dated "Thursday p.m." [July 29?, 1920]
(*SL*, 132). "So let us protect" starts a new paragraph in the letter.

page 88:

"AND ALL THROUGH LIFE." Ibid., 131.

"SURPASSING CLEARNESS." This stage direction for Lazarus's final message
(367) takes on particular poignancy set into the reality of the memory that
produced it.

"INCREDIBLE TORTURES." Letter to Agnes dated "Thursday p.m." [July 29?,
1920] (*SL*, 131).

"LAST ILLUSION." Ibid.

"THEN WHY SHOULD HE SUFFER." Ibid.

PRESIDENT SAM OF HAITI. In his introduction to *The Emperor Jones* in the
Wilderness Edition of his plays, O'Neill told how he had heard this story of
the silver bullet about the "flamboyant Sam" from an old circus friend.

A STUDY IN THE PSYCHOLOGY OF FEAR. When O'Neill inscribed a copy of *The
Emperor Jones* to his friend Saxe Commins, who had just completed a psychology book, he wrote: "To Saxe with a million grateful feelings that would
look foolish in words—and in the hope that he'll never write the psychology
of my fear into an 'Emperor Gene.'" Mrs. Saxe Commins kindly allowed
me to transcribe the inscription from the copy in her possession, which
happened to be Eugene O'Neill's *The Emperor Jones, Diff'rent, The Straw*
(New York: Boni & Liveright, 1921).

THE EMPEROR JONES. O'Neill began writing this play only a few weeks after
his father's funeral, for he dated his "T.C.F." (the curtain falls) "Peaked Hill
Bar—P'town Oct. 2, 1920" (see the manuscript at Princeton).

page 89:

AT 4:15. The time of James O'Neill's death is given in his front-page obituary
in the August 10, 1920, *New London Day*.

JULIUS CAESAR. James O'Neill was playing a repertory of *Virginius, Julius
Caesar,* and his usual *Monte Cristo*.

"HAVE YOU EVER SEEN." "Memoranda on Masks," 120.

"AND WHEN WE BEHOLD." " 'But Hither Comes Virginius!': James O'Neill
Tries to Galvanize the Old Play," *New York Telegraph*, September 17, 1907.

"MOB PSYCHOLOGY." "Memoranda on Masks," 120.

"RANDOM COLLECTION." Ibid.

"CROWD MIND." Ibid.

"HARMLESS HUMAN UNITS." O'Neill told Kenneth Macgowan the idea for this play, "The Guilty Are Guilty," in a letter of May 14, 1926 (Bryer, 112). He never found time to write it.

LIKE HIS EMPEROR JONES "BUT *WHITE*." BOTH HIS STUDIES OF FEAR—*THE EMPEROR JONES* AND *LAZARUS LAUGHED*—JOINED IN HIS MIND TO CREATE THIS IDEA. HE COMBINED THE MOB PURSUING THE EMPEROR WITH THE FEAR-RIDDEN MOBS OF *LAZARUS LAUGHED* TO GET THE PLOT FOR IT.

PAGE 90:

"HOWLING MONOTONOUSLY WITH EVERY." Letter to Agnes dated "Thursday p.m." [July 29?, 1920] (*SL*, 132). Bogard and Bryer read "howling monstrously," but O'Neill goes on to compare the howls to the "ticking of the clock of agony," so "monotonously" is certainly correct.

SALTUS'S *IMPERIAL PURPLE*. O'Neill's copy of Saltus, now at Yale, is dated "Peaked Hill, Fall '24." In his letter to Manuel Komroff of March 1, 1926 (Columbia), O'Neill told him that he had both Saltus and Suetonius.

HE HAD READ MANY OTHER BOOKS. O'Neill told Komroff that he had "Ferrero," by which he probably meant Guglielmo Ferrero's five volumes of the *Greatness and Decline of Rome*, for his copy is now in the Post Collection. This book ends before the period of the play, but O'Neill liked to have a solid historical background. Also in the Post Collection are his copies of *The Legacy of Rome* (edited by Cyril Bailey), Grant Showerman's *Eternal Rome*, and M. Rostovzeff's *History of the Ancient World*.

"ILL-SHAPED." "VERY SLENDER." O'Neill's copy of Suetonius's *Lives of the Twelve Caesars* has not survived. I have used the Bohn's Classical Library edition (London, 1909) and these quotations come from p. 285. From the account on the same page of Caligula's hollow eyes and temples and broad knitted brows, O'Neill created Caligula's "bulging, prematurely wrinkled forehead" and "hollow temples" (299). O'Neill also took from Suetonius Caligula's delight "in witnessing the infliction of punishments" (257). His Caligula says, "I like to watch men die" (301). O'Neill adapted details from Saltus in the same way. Saltus quotes Caligula (59) as saying, "Let me be hated, but let me be feared!" O'Neill's Caligula says, "Let them hate—so long as they fear us!" (301).

"MORE OF AN APE." "Zarathustra's Prologue," part 3.

"RATHER GO BACK." "Zarathustra's Prologue," part 3.

"EXCESSIVE CONFIDENCE." *Lives of the Twelve Caesars*, 285.

page 91:

"CHILD OF THE CAMP." Caligula speaks of himself this way in Suetonius, *Lives of the Twelve Caesars*, 256, 266.

CNEIUS CRASSUS. This character is purely imaginary, and O'Neill created his name from those of two members of the first triumvirate, Cneius Pompey and Marcus Licinius Crassus.

TO COWER IN TERROR. Carlotta O'Neill told me that when they visited Mount St. Vincent together, O'Neill pointed out the window of the cottage where he had slept and told her of his terror when the branches of the great tree outside moved against it.

"BEFORE A MIRROR." Suetonius, *Lives of the Twelve Caesars*, 285.

DOMITIAN'S LINING OF HIS ROOM. O'Neill read his self-loathing into all the Roman Emperors. In his poem "Interlude" (Spring 1925) he put himself into Domitian, Caligula, and Nero (*Poems*, 96–98).

HE HAD GOTTEN DRUNK. O'Neill wrote out a schedule of his drinking bouts during 1924 and 1925 on the stationery of Dr. Gilbert Van Tassell Hamilton's "Bureau of Social Hygeine" at 47 East 61st Street, New York City. (Max Wylie copied it when it was in Agnes Boulton's possession, and allowed me to transcribe his copy. It is duplicated in the unbowdlerized copy of his 1925 *Work Diary*, which had been in Agnes's possession.)

DECEMBER 31, 1925. *Work Diary*, 1:495. On this day, for the first time in weeks of solid drinking, he wrote: "On wagon."

"THE VOID LEFT BY THOSE." Letter from O'Neill to Kenneth Macgowan of August 7, 1926 (Bryer, 122).

page 92:

EDGAR SALTUS SAW "IMPERIAL PURPLE." P. 18.

"ABOMINABLE LEWDNESS." *Lives of the Twelve Caesars*, 219.

"RARE-COLORED FLOWERS." See the final longhand script of *The Great God Brown* (Yale).

TIBERIUS'S PALACE IN SCENARIO. *Lazarus Laughed* had been scenarioed "wonderfully," O'Neill told Kenneth Macgowan in a letter of September 28, 1925 (Bryer, 100).

"NUTS COMPLETE." Letter from O'Neill to Saxe Commins of August 7, 1923 (*SL*, 181).

A PERSISTENTLY REPEATED NAME, "LUCIUS." The Third Senator is the only other with a name, "Sulpicius," mentioned once. "Lucius" is pronounced four times.

HAD PLAYED THE ROLE OF "LUCIUS." The review in the September 28, 1907, *Dramatic Mirror* disposes of his performance tersely: "James O'Neill, Jr. was not suited to the role of Lucius." The February 4, 1908, *Chicago Tribune* reported: "James O'Neill, Jr. played Lucius, and ran all the way from Rome to the battlefield without turning a hair in his smoothly plastered locks, parted in the middle—which may and may not have been the style in 450 B.C."

page 93:

"YOUR UNCLE JIM." This comes from a letter to his son Shane (*SL*, 318–19) responding to letters that Shane had dictated to his nurse "Gaga" and one that he wrote himself. It is undated, but in it O'Neill apologizes for not writing before because he was busy finishing *Dynamo*. His *Work Diary* says he finished *Dynamo* on August 18, 1928 (1:57). *SL* dates it [late September 1928].

"*ALMOST BLIND* FROM BAD BOOZE." So O'Neill told Saxe Commins in a letter of August 7, 1923 (*SL*, 181).

"WHAT THE HELL CAN BE." Letter to Saxe Commins of August 7, 1923 (*SL*, 181). Actually there was no problem of what Jamie would do when he got out of this second sanatorium of the year; he died there on November 8, 1923.

page 94:

O'NEILL MADE HIM "79." The scenario with the age of Tiberius is at Yale. In the play he is an "old man of seventy-six" (337).

"IT IS ONLY PAPA'S." O'Neill underlines "marvelously strong heart" because the New York doctor had said months earlier that his heart was too weak for an operation. Letter dated "Friday p.m." [July 30?, 1920] (*SL*, 133).

"IT'S PRACTICALLY A MIRACLE." Letter to Agnes dated "Saturday," of July 31, 1920 (Correspondence).

"ALL THOSE 'IN THE KNOW.' " Letter to Agnes dated "Sunday eve" [August 1?, 1920] (*SL*, 134).

"INTERNAL DECOMPOSITION HAS SET IN." Letter to Agnes dated "Thursday p.m." [July 29?, 1920] (*SL*, 131). In Caligula's speech his reference to the smell comes first, then the reference to Tiberius's thick speech, and then the references to the heart. This happens to be the same order in which they appear in the letter to Agnes.

"THIS SORT OF LIFE—FROTH!" Ibid., *SL* 132. This image found its way into the play through Tiberius's despair, but there it is turned into a negation of his father's hope. He calls it "a bubble of froth blown from the lips of the dying toward the stars!" (353).

"COMPANIES OF GIRLS." Suetonius, 219.

"TRAIN OF LESBIANS." Saltus, 93.

page 95:

FAVORITE MISTRESS POMPEIA. This character is fictitious. O'Neill probably took her name from "Pompeia, sister of Sextus Pompey," who, Suetonius (197) tells us, sent gifts to Tiberius. Of course, as the "mistress" of Tiberius, the negative father image, she fits easily into O'Neill's image of the prostitute mother.

ALTHOUGH LAZARUS SHOULD KNOW THIS. O'Neill had to rationalize this sudden doubt of what Lazarus has been proclaiming out of direct knowledge by having him say: "You have never laughed with my laughter. Will you call back—Yes!—when you know—to tell me you understand and laugh with me at last?" (346).

page 96:

IN IT, SHE SAYS. Agnes allowed Max Wylie to transcribe the fragment when they were helping each other while he wrote *Trouble in the Flesh* and she wrote *Part of a Long Story*. Max Wylie allowed me to photocopy his transcription; he labeled it "Agnes: Thoughts on Her Marriage." It is typical of

Agnes's way of fighting O'Neill that her heroine implies a threat to her husband's demand for "loyalty."

"YOU'VE TORTURED YOUR LAST." Letter from O'Neill to Agnes dated "Tuesday" [December 20?, 1927] (*SL*, 269).

"INCREDIBLE TORTURES." Letter to Agnes dated "Thursday p.m." [July 29?, 1920] (*SL*, 131). In the first longhand script (Yale) a canceled passage of Miriam predicting the second death of Lazarus shows how fully O'Neill identified Lazarus's torture with that of his father. She says, "My fear hears the shrieks of agony of an old man who might be my father."

page 97:

EXPRESSIVE OF THE CREATIVE PUSH. In one of his pencil notes for *Lazarus Laughed* (Yale), O'Neill defined "Laughter" as "the Creative Will of Superabundant Happiness."

"TERRIFIC FLASHES OF LIGHTNING." O'Neill was probably echoing the "flashes of lightning" and "peals of thunder" (Rev. 16:18) that underline events in the "Revelation of John," which he had dramatized for Robert Edmond Jones.

ONE TRULY ALIVE IS THE CORPSE. This feeling that love was in the grave appears explicitly in the message he first gave to the dead Miriam in his first longhand script (Yale). She says, "Yes! Lazarus, come forth! Be not lonely! Come home!" She is echoing the words of Jesus to Lazarus at his resurrection into life, only this time, life, love, and home are to be found in the grave. Even at the time his father was dying, O'Neill had felt this curious inversion. In his letter to Agnes dated "Friday p.m." [July 30?, 1920] (*SL*, 133) he told her: "The town and the people are dead. I despise both."

page 98:

HAVING HER ACT THE ROLE OF POMPEIA. Writing to Kenneth Macgowan, January 21 [1927] (Bryer, 147), O'Neill suggested actresses for Pompeia: "Ann Harding—or Helen Gahagan—or Carlotta might do it."

"I AM YOUR LAUGHTER—." The carbon copy typescript with this inscription is now at Yale. It has been reproduced in *Inscriptions: Eugene O'Neill to Carlotta Monterey O'Neill*, ed. Donald Gallup (New Haven: Yale University Library, 1960) (hereafter referred to as *Inscriptions*). Compare with *Lazarus Laughed*, 324.

ALL THE UNCERTAINTIES. O'Neill shows uncertainty when he moves Lazarus from perfect faith (as his father) to doubt, loneliness, and fear (as himself) in the moment when Miriam dies. The character also is never clearly defined as a contemplative mystic or a man of action in the world (hero), and although his voice can stop armies and he at times uses it to do so like a man of action, he also remains rapt in contemplation when his entire family is being slaughtered beneath him.

page 99:

"LAZARUS—MY HUSBAND—DIED." From the first longhand script (Yale). Of course, O'Neill meant to express the eternal rebirth of Dionysus through the

Earth Mother, Demeter, but he was caught by the idea because it also expressed his wish to *be* his hero father.

MARCH 6, 1926. *Work Diary*, 1:23. He said on that day that he did not like his first scene. On March 9 he declared, "Doping out new scheme for it—not satisfied with old method used so far." On March 10 he wrote, "Mask-chorus conception shapes up wonderfully." On March 12 he decided, "Much reconstruction needed and sloppy writing in 1st draft to be pruned—written in too much of a hurry last fall—mind too distracted."

"PROGRESSION OF HIS IDEAS." Letter from O'Neill to Isaac Goldberg of July 7, 1926 (Harvard).

"FINE STUFF." *Work Diary*, 1:28 (1926).

"THERE CAN BE NO SUCH THING." Karsner, "Eugene O'Neill at Close Range in Maine." O'Neill was also worrying about the fact that *Marco Millions* was still unproduced.

"SWALLOWED UP BY A VASTLY INFERIOR." Letter from O'Neill to Kenneth Macgowan of August 7, 1926 (Bryer, 119).

page 100:

"THE DECISION OF THE CATHOLICS." Bryer, 121.

"IMPRESSED—BUT DIDN'T." So Hopkins told Agnes when she visited New York in April of 1927 and she reported back to O'Neill in an undated letter (Correspondence). Hopkins had already written O'Neill turning it down.

THE THEATRE GUILD, WHICH. O'Neill spoke of the Guild rejection in a letter to Lawrence Langner of May 1, [1927] (*SL*, 243–45). After the great success of the Guild's production of *Strange Interlude*, O'Neill tried again to interest the Guild in *Lazarus Laughed*. He said that done "with a grand gesture" it would be "as startling a sensation as 'Interlude' " (Letter to Robert Sisk of April 10, 1928 [Yale]). Lawrence Langner told O'Neill he had tried to "work up some enthusiasm for a spectacular production by Rouben Mamoulian, with huge crowds on the Reinhardt scale" (Letter of May 10, 1928 [Yale]). Nothing came of it.

"IT WOULD OFFEND THEIR ORTHODOX." O'Neill told Agnes that Schwarz had rejected it in a letter dated "Friday" [September 9?, 1927] (*SL*, 254).

"ONLY TALKING BIG." So O'Neill told Agnes in a letter of September 13, 1927 (Correspondence).

MAX REINHARDT SPOKE. So O'Neill told Eleanor Fitzgerald in a letter of September 11, 1926 (Texas). He told Helen McAfee of the *Yale Review* that he still hoped for a German production by Reinhardt in a letter of January 20, 1928 (Yale).

THE GREAT RUSSIAN DIRECTOR DANTCHENKO. In an April 14, 1927, letter to Alexander Berkman, the Russian translator of *Lazarus Laughed* (*SL*, 238), O'Neill said that he knew only what he had heard from Kenneth Macgowan, Eleanor Fitzgerald, and Bulgakov, the actor from the Moscow Art Theatre working with the Provincetown Players. They all thought that, as soon as his contract with the movies ended, Dantchenko would do *Lazarus Laughed*. On February 2, 1927, Eleanor Fitzgerald wrote Berkman that Dantchenko

might do a film of *Lazarus*. (All the correspondence on Berkman's translation of *Lazarus Laughed*, including carbon copies of Berkman's letters, is in
the Berkman Collection.) Dantchenko's eagerness to get the new O'Neill
play, even before he had read it, is understandable considering O'Neill's
great prestige and popularity in the Soviet Union.

"YOU HAVE BECOME FAMOUS." Letter from Berkman to O'Neill, January 6,
1927 (Berkman Collection). Berkman thought this was " 'wie es sich ge-
ziemt' as my German friends say," or only "right and proper."

"AS FOR MY FAME." Letter to Berkman of January 29, 1927 (*SL*, 233). O'Neill
offered the old anarchist 50 percent of the royalties for his translation, instead of the usual 40 percent. He also reimbursed him for the money he
spent to have the play typed in Russian, and offered an advance on the
contract a little later on. "I say a little later on because just at present I am
cash poor as a church mouse and living on borrowed money, but things are
due to pick up soon" (O'Neill to Berkman, August 11, 1927, Berkman Collection). Berkman replied that both he and the friend with six children who
helped him translate *Lazarus Laughed* could "use money," but "not from
your pocket, dear Gene, not until you know that you yourself will be able to
get something out of Russian performances of the play" (Berkman to
O'Neill, August 27, 1927, Berkman Collection). O'Neill told Berkman afterward: "Bulgakov of the Moscow Art thinks your translation a wonderful one.
He has sent it on to Dantchenko. Why don't you tackle Tairov of the Kamerny with it when he comes to Paris? (O'Neill to Berkman, October 16,
1927 [Berkman Collection]).

WHEN DANTCHENKO LEFT. O'Neill met Dantchenko the day before he left
for Russia, and Dantchenko told him that he was such "a great authority in
Russia" that after his death there would be long arguments as to whether he
was American or Russian, and it would be decided that he was Russian.
From a report on the interview between them, "Eugene O'Neill's 'Lazarus'
to Laugh on Russian Stage," *Pawtucket (Rhode Island) Times*, December
28, 1927.

FOUND "TOO MYSTICAL." Dudley Nichols, who had been present at the interview, looked up Dantchenko on a visit to the Soviet Union in 1936 and asked
him what had happened to the plan for producing *Lazarus Laughed*.
Dantchenko told him that it had been found "too mystical." From an account of his relationship with O'Neill that Dudley Nichols typed up to ac-
company their correspondence when he deposited it at Yale.

"EFFECTIVE, TENSE, TERRIBLE." George C. Warren, review of *Lazarus
Laughed*, *San Francisco Chronicle*, April 10, 1928 (Cargill, 178–80, 179).
Gilmor Brown directed, and Arthur Alexander (former head of the Eastman
Orchestra at Rochester) composed music for it. O'Neill was always eager to
learn all he could about this production and asked Jack Cambell about it at
a Russian performance of *All God's Chillun Got Wings* in Paris. See Cambell, "O'Neill Talks at Paris Interlude," *San Francisco Chronicle*, July 6,
1930.

"OF THE GREEKS AND ELIZABETHANS." "Memoranda on Masks," 121–22.

O'Neill told George Jean Nathan, in a letter of August 11, 1927 (Cornell), that he wanted to write a "brief introduction" to *Lazarus Laughed* to explain "my notions of what an Imaginative Theatre should be." He finally incorporated these notions into his "Memoranda on Masks." Jimmy Light got the idea that O'Neill was "obsessed by the Eleusinian mysteries" in *Lazarus Laughed* and that he would have liked a community production of it like those of the Oberammergau Passion Play. From a carbon copy of Light's essay "The Parade of Masks," Theatre Collection, New York Public Library.

page 101:

"A DIVINE DRAMA." See the notes for *Lazarus Laughed* (Yale).

"LIVE AS LIFE." Benjamin De Casseres had told O'Neill that *Lazarus Laughed* read better than it could be acted. O'Neill answered, "Of course, *Lazarus* reads better than it will ever be acted! It simply can't be done on any stage of today." He added that only in his Imaginative Theatre would it "live as Life and be better than the book" (Letter from O'Neill to De Casseres, ca. March, 1929 [Dartmouth]).

"BEST WRITING I'VE DONE FOR THE THEATRE." O'Neill told Ward Morehouse this in an interview (" The Boulevards After Dark: Four Hours from Paris in His French Chateau Eugene O'Neill Is Writing American Drama," *New York Sun,* May 14, 1930) (hereafter referred to as Morehouse).

"A PRODUCER'S PLAY." He told Theresa Helburn in a letter of April 8, 1928 (*SL,* 290) that *Lazarus Laughed* was "a producer's play" with "unlimited opportunities for imaginative collaboration" by theater artists. Indeed, he told Richard Watts (in "A Visit to Eugene O'Neill, Now of Arcady," *New York Herald Tribune,* June 8, 1930) that "not despite but because of the difficulties of staging, it might have a positive influence on the course of the theater."

"IT'S A GOOD HUNCH." Letter to Agnes of September 11, [1927] (*SL,* 257).

"SPRANG FROM THEIR LAUGHTER." Letter from O'Neill to Barrett Clark, December 15, 1944 (*SL,* 567).

"CONDENSED VERSION WITH MASKS OMITTED." Letter from O'Neill to Barrett Clark, February 22, 1944 (Clark, 148). He summed up that it could be done along the lines of the opera *Boris Gudinoff.* In his World War II letter of December 15, 1944, to Barrett Clark, O'Neill gave his blessing to any university group that wanted to try *Lazarus Laughed.* He said that it was "practically virgin" and just what "their theatre should stand for"; he also pointed out that Hitlerism had the same murder-madness and death drive he had shown in Tiberius and Caligula (*SL,* 567).

5. Strange Interlude

page 103:

"WOMAN PLAY." O'Neill called *Strange Interlude* his "woman play" in a letter to Kenneth Macgowan of September 28, 1925 (Bryer, 100).

APRIL 1923. A very valuable detailed account of the genesis of *Strange Interlude* was submitted in evidence when O'Neill was sued for plagiarism (see
*Georges Lewys v. Eugene O'Neill, Boni & Liveright Inc. and Theatre Guild
Inc., Federal Reporter*, 49F, 2d ser., no. 2, June 29, 1931, pp. 603–18 [here-
after referred to as *Lewys v. O'Neill*]). George Jean Nathan testified that
O'Neill had talked over his idea for the woman play with him right after he
finished *Welded* (ibid., 610), which would place the conversation in April
1923.

ONE WHO HAD LOST. George Jean Nathan testified that O'Neill said the play
was to deal with "a young woman who had lost her idealism and was attempting to recapture it" (*Lewys v. O'Neill*, 609). It is not mere chance that
O'Neill's two earlier "woman" plays, *Diff'rent* and *Anna Christie*, had both
dealt with lost idealism and an attempt to recapture it. Because of his mother's addiction he associated women with disillusionment.

"AN AVIATOR, FORMERLY." *Lewys v. O'Neill*, 609. I suspect that O'Neill heard
the story from Sidney Howard, who had been in the Lafayette Escadrille
and who was in Provincetown in the summer of 1923. It was not the kind of
story that a writer of conventionally well-made plays like Howard could have
ever used himself, so O'Neill was taking nothing from him. If the name of
the "aviator" was suppressed at the trial, it was certainly because the lawyers
were afraid that an author's name might prove a red herring during a plagiarism trial.

"THE THEME FOR A NOVEL." O'Neill wrote the *New York Times* about this plan,
probably to prepare the way for his play *Chris Christopherson*, which was
exactly such an experiment, being primarily a character study of Chris's fatal
fear of life (George Tyler was just putting it into production). O'Neill said
that *Beyond the Horizon* had been projected at first in his mind as such a
hybrid novel-play, as "a series of progressive episodes, illustrating—and, I
hoped, illuminating—the life story of a true Royal Tramp at his sordid but
satisfying, and therefore mysterious, pursuit of a drab rainbow. It was hardly
an idea for a play, but for that very reason I decided that I would make it
one" (reproduced as a "letter" in the April 11, 1920, *New York Times*).
O'Neill gave up the experiment when he rewrote *Chris Christopherson* into
a conventionally well-made play, *Anna Christie*. It appears that his first plan
for the "woman play" harked back to the "series of progressive episodes"
and the character study, for he described it to George Jean Nathan as "a
series of psychological plays depicting the outer and inner life of a woman
from the age of young womanhood until forty-five" (*Lewys v. O'Neill*, 609).

"THE OUTER AND INNER." *Lewys v. O'Neill*, 609.

O'NEILL WROTE THE SCENARIOS. His *Work Diary*, 2:490, shows him working
on the scenario for *Lazarus Laughed* from September 1 through September
10, and on the scenario for *Strange Interlude* from September 11 through
September 15.

BEGAN *STRANGE INTERLUDE*. His *Work Diary*, 1:26–27, shows him from May
16, 1926, "scheming out" *Strange Interlude* in the mornings and going over
Lazarus Laughed in the evenings until he called that play done on June 10.

page 104:

TO BRING A NOVELIST." Bernard Simon, Press Agent for the Theatre Guild, gave an account of the genesis of O'Neill's method in *Strange Interlude,* which he most likely got from O'Neill. O'Neill's first idea, Simon said, had been to have a Greek-chorus–like character "to inform the audience of what had occurred in the interim of years between the acts." Then he decided to have the same character appear in the play and give information "by means of 'aside' comments and soliloquies." In this way O'Neill discovered that the character took on vitality "precisely because" he was "speaking aloud words he would never say to anyone directly" (as quoted in the *Indianapolis Times,* January 26, 1929).

"METHOD: START WITH." Floyd, 74. On O'Neill's having the whole play a thinking-aloud, my reading of the parenthesis is "or this extreme for other play." Floyd's reading is "or this entrance for other play."

"SPECIAL TYPE OF MODERN." So O'Neill described this method for himself in his notes for *Mourning Becomes Electra,* which have been reproduced in Barrett Clark, *European Theories of the Drama* (New York: Crown, 1947), 530–36, esp. 534 (hereafter referred to as *MBE* Notes).

MANNER OF HENRY JAMES. In the notes O'Neill made on his novelist Charlie Marsden (Yale), he wrote: "His style is modeled after James; it is eminently cultivated and detached, full of noiseless humor and irony, but in the present era an anachronism. He has traveled much abroad and lived there on a small income from his mother. On the surface, he is a Europeanized male but this is his superior defense against what he knows is his inferiority as a modern American." Of course, O'Neill meant more than Marsden's style to recall Henry James. Van Wyck Brooks's *Pilgrimage of Henry James* had come out in 1925, and O'Neill had probably read it. His Marsden was to be—as Brooks thought James to have been—a man dominated by fear of life, and so O'Neill used other James traits for him. He had Marsden echo James's habit of using the Italian for "dear," *Cara.* Professor Frederick Carpenter asked O'Neill about Marsden's "Nina, cara Nina," and O'Neill told him in a letter of June 24, 1932 (*SL,* 401) that it came partly from Marsden's ostentation in using a foreign language endearment and partly as a literary play on the name "Anna Karenina." As O'Neill explained to George Jean Nathan, Marsden was meant to be "a sentimental throwback, a kind of Yellow Book period reversion." See *The World of George Jean Nathan,* ed. Charles Angoff (New York: Knopf, 1952), 409 (hereafter referred to as Angoff).

MAKE HIS FORTUNE BY SELLING LIES. O'Neill may have put Sam Evans into advertising in memory of his friend Edward Ireland, who had shared the studio with Keefe, Bellows, and himself and who always had money for the rent as he was already in advertising. Edward Ireland had participated in producing the adultery evidence for O'Neill's divorce from Kathleen. He had testified at the trial that he was "engaged in the advertising illustrating business at No. 20 West 27th Street" as a partner in "the Ireland Rieger Company, of which company I am the president" (*Kathleen O'Neill v. Eugene O'Neill*).

page 105:

MAGNIFICENT ATHLETIC BODY. Beatrice's stupendous figure was recalled to me years later by such of her New London contemporaries as Thomas Dorsey, Jr. Agnes, on the other hand, was slender and delicate, as her photographs testify.

AGNES'S FACE. The crucial features of jaw, mouth, cheekbones, and forehead can be checked in photographs of Agnes. Louis Sheaffer (Sheaffer II, 173–77) thinks that Nina's "extraordinarily large" eyes must have come from the eyes of O'Neill's acquaintance in Bermuda Olga Collinson, who suffered from a thyroid condition. But Nina's eyes are large, not protuberant as in cases of thyroid. Agnes's eyes in photographs were certainly very large and beautiful. Sheaffer thinks the rest of Nina's features must have come from another Bermuda friend, Alice Cuthbert, who did have blonde coloring. I think Agnes is more likely because O'Neill's poem "To Alice" (*Poems*, 95) sees Miss Cuthbert as simple and "whole"—that is, not emotionally torn or complicated, as his Nina was meant to be and as Agnes certainly was.

HER LAST NAME. "LEEDS." O'Neill had had Anna, daughter of the old captain Chris Christopherson, in his play of that name which was later rewritten into *Anna Christie*, grow up in a refined family in Leeds, England. (The typescript of *Chris Christopherson*, sent in for copyrighting, is in the Library of Congress.)

"NINA" RECALLS NINA JONES. In an undated letter to Felton Elkins [June? 1915] (*SL*, 70), O'Neill describes his meeting with Nina Jones on boat day. A reference to Nina Jones as a member of the social elite like Felton Elkins comes in a letter that O'Neill wrote Agnes on January 17, 1920 (*SL*, 104), telling of a meeting with Richard Bennett and his wife, who had heard O'Neill's praises from both Felton Elkins and Nina Jones and so treated him as if he were also of the "400." The editors of the *Selected Letters* (107) are mistaken in identifying the Nina of his January 23, 1920, letter to Agnes as Nina Moise. His calling her a lady of genuine breeding and his speaking of how easy it is to make fun of "them"—that is, the members of the 400—make it clear that he means Nina Jones.

FIANCÉ GORDON SHAW. O'Neill constructed the name of this hero from two of his own literary heroes in youth: George *Gordon*, Lord Byron, and George Bernard *Shaw*. Louis Sheaffer believes that O'Neill modeled Gordon Shaw on Hobart Amory Hare Baker of Princeton, who had been a great college athlete and an aviator in the Lafayette Escadrille killed in France (Sheaffer II, 244). Possibly Baker's figure did merge with the aviator of the story that O'Neill heard in Provincetown, but I think Gordon Shaw became an athlete from O'Neill's conception of him as an avatar of the reborn god, for the athlete is the only authentic American hero of the 1920s who might appear like a Greek god, and Gordon was meant explicitly to resemble one, as, for instance, in the uncut first longhand script (Yale) when Nina thinks, "But the only Gods that didn't make me feel ashamed of their creators were the old Greek ones—beautiful men—as beautiful as Gordon—I believe in Gordon—."

LONG, FUTILE ENGAGEMENT. O'Neill's engagement to Beatrice began in the spring of 1914 and was broken during the summer of 1916.

THE PROFESSOR INVITED HIM. In a letter to Beatrice Ashe dated "Sunday" with an envelope postmarked January 31, 1915 (*SL*, 51), O'Neill described the Friday night visit, which had lasted from 7:30 until after 10 o'clock. O'Neill found the talk more valuable than all the classes put together, and he described to Beatrice everything in the professor's study down to the gold tips of his cigarettes.

page 106:

"INSTINCTIVELY, THAT WE WERE NOT." So O'Neill told Olin Downes in an interview, "Playwright Finds His Inspiration on Lonely Sand Dunes by the Sea," *Boston Post*, August 29, 1920.

"PEEVED." "PINS AND NEEDLES." Letter to Beatrice Ashe dated "Wednesday night" [December 16, 1914] (*SL*, 43). O'Neill wrote her daily and had begun to count the days to Christmas Eve on December 9, when he began to await the money from "the dear old Governor," who by December 13 has become his "stern" parent but (as he points out on December 14) has, up to now, been "exemplary in promptness" (Berg).

"ABOMINABLE HUMOR." So O'Neill predicted to Beatrice in a letter [January 8, 1915] (*SL*, 46) when he learned of the closing of *Joseph and His Brethren* from a member of the company, Malcolm Morley, who had just joined Professor Baker's class.

"CAGE FULL OF WOUNDED." From a letter to Beatrice [January 11, 1915] (*SL*, 48), in which O'Neill tells her that his family is in New York and he can guess "the Pater's mood."

ALL THE FRUSTRATION. For O'Neill, deprivation of love, his parents, and Christmas were all closely connected. It was just before Christmas that O'Neill asked Agnes to divorce him, and Carlotta recalled to me how he told her at the time about how lonely he had always been at Christmas because his father would be acting in some far-off city, and of how he had once been left without the fare to go home. It was easy for this frustration in love at Harvard to melt into the old frustrations he had experienced when exiled to boarding school by his father.

HE HAD BEEN THE "HONORABLE." All the letters to Beatrice show the idealism of his love for her. In a letter dated "Thursday" [October 8, 1914] (*SL*, 30), he tells her of his shame at the "grimy smears" of his past, and in one of January 10, 1915, he tells her that if he did not remain free from stain he would die of shame the first time he looked into her "clear" eyes (Berg).

"THE RACK." Letter to Beatrice Ashe of January 6, 1915 (*SL*, 44).

"SELF-OVERCOMING." Letter to Beatrice Ashe of January 12, 1915 (Berg).

"LONELINESS UNUTTERABLE." Letter to Beatrice Ashe of January 6, 1915 (*SL*, 43).

"SUSAN IS IN BAD SHAPE." Letter to Kenneth Macgowan of August 1924 (Bryer, 56).

page 107:

> SUSAN HAD TRIED TO MASTER. Susan Glaspell's first conception of the book about Jig appears in a letter O'Neill wrote her on June 3, 1924, saying, "I think the idea of the collection of sketches is an excellent one and Agnes and I would be only too happy to try and do something worthwhile for it. We can talk it over when we see you. Provincetown is the place to write it. To me Jig is always in the air there." Eugene O'Neill Collection (#6448), Clifton Waller Barrett Library, Manuscripts Division, Special Collections Department, University of Virginia Library (hereafter referred to as Virginia). Norman Matson, who was Susan's husband after George Cram Cook, told me that O'Neill visited Susan and him several times at Truro when Susan was writing her biography of Jig. Something of the ambivalent attitude of Nina's men toward her idolatry of Gordon Shaw is evident in Matson's feeling for Jig, and perhaps O'Neill noticed it and felt the same himself. At any rate, Matson wrote Susan when she finished *The Road to the Temple* in the spring of 1926 (Berg): "I kept reading it all that day and evening. Couldn't stop. And felt my old feeling of interest, sympathy and profound irritation with Jig. I doubt if we'd been friends. But you've made him live. You've given him continuing life. What a beautiful thing for a woman to have done for a man!"

> HE AND O'NEILL HAD BEEN DRUNK. In an interview of November 15, 1964, Norman Matson told me Susan Glaspell had talked much about Jig's terrible quarrel with O'Neill, and about how resentfully Jig had kept recalling that quarrel right up until his death.

> "ALL JIG'S FAULT." "BEAT IT TO GREECE." Letter to Eleanor Fitzgerald from O'Neill dated "Saturday" [May 27?, 1922] (*SL*, 168).

> "AS FOR JIG—WHEN." Letter to Susan Glaspell from O'Neill, May 26, 1924 (*SL*, 186).

> "HAVE MADE A GRAND." Letter from O'Neill of March 22, 1926 (*SL*, 200).

> FROM A PROFESSOR OF PSYCHOLOGY. The scenario in O'Neill's *Notebook 1920–1930* (at Yale) describes Nina's father as "a gentle, mildly cynical and liberal professor of psychology," who has called in an old friend, "one of the best neurologists," to see his daughter. Later O'Neill realized that if he made his scientist Darrell a neurologist he could put into his play all the explicit psychological analysis he wanted.

page 108:

> "MORAL EXCESS BAGGAGE." Letter to Beatrice Ashe from O'Neill, July 25, 1916 (*SL*, 71).

> "MISTRUST." This was Agnes's word for his doubts of her fidelity, as in an undated letter to O'Neill, ca. late September 1927 (Correspondence).

> DR. GILBERT VAN TASSELL HAMILTON'S. Both Kenneth Macgowan and James Light told Louis Sheaffer that Dr. Hamilton had diagnosed O'Neill as having an Oedipus complex, and Sheaffer reports Agnes as saying that O'Neill "was disappointed in his findings" (Sheaffer II, 190).

> O'NEILL TRIED OUT THE OEDIPUS. O'Neill's ideas on mechanical applications

of Freudian theory are pretty well expressed in Marsden's thoughts (34): "Pah, what an easy cure-all! . . . sex the philosopher's stone . . . 'O Oedipus, O my king! the world is adopting you!'" O'Neill had expressed the same idea before his analysis with Dr. Hamilton in his letter to Mr. Perlman of February 5, 1925 (*SL*, 192), where he spoke of Freud as meaning to him "uncertain conjectures and explanations" and added that he respected Freud but was not an "addict!"

TWO OF O'NEILL'S CRUCIAL MEMORIES. In his first version of Marsden's soliloquy (Yale), O'Neill put many details of his memory of the August heat when his father lay dying, as, for instance, "hot sunlight, sun-scorched grass of the lawn between brick walls and the hot gray asphalt—nurses in hot white, wearily noiseless in hot felt soles, vexed red nurses' faces under white caps perspiring with the vanity and vexation of others' pain—pain—low smouldering moans escaping over open transoms into the cool dark halls. . . ."

"ITS REAL MATURITY BLOCKED." This is O'Neill's own note made in 1926 (Yale) on how Marsden's experience with the dollar tart gave a "terrible shock to his sensibilities resulting in his love for Nina always being a brother love, its real maturity blocked." Marsden's trouble was thus a form of sexual infantilism. Louis Sheaffer believes that O'Neill called this character "Charlie Marsden" in order to combine the names of *Charles* Demuth and *Marsden* Hartley, who (he says) "were homosexual—as is the play's Marsden" (Sheaffer II, 242). Marsden is not even meant to be latently homosexual. O'Neill probably picked up the name "Marsden" from the great Marco Polo scholar of that name whose edition of the *Travels* O'Neill took copious notes (now at Yale) from for *Marco Millions* and whose book Manuel Komroff told me he was surprised to find on O'Neill's shelves.

"I FEEL COLD . . . ALONE! . . ." This is my first quotation of one character's thoughts that is long enough to show the way those thoughts are linked by chains of dots for ellipses in the published versions of the play. This method was adopted after O'Neill looked over the first typescript and discovered (as he told Lawrence Langner when he sent him the typescript) that "the punctuation of the thinking as opposed to the talk is not sufficiently differentiated and causes a bit of confusion" (Letter to Langner of April 4, 1927 [Yale]).

MANILIUS'S *ASTRONOMICA*. The Latin quotation of Manilius from p. 72 of O'Neill's copy of Angus's *Mystery Religions and Christianity* (Post Collection) can be found on a sheet of yellow paper with other star quotes for *Lazarus Laughed* (Yale) and begins with Angus's introduction: "Plotinus argues that the reverent contemplation of the world brings the soul into contact with the God of the cosmos. Manilius discovers man's distinguishing dignity in the fact that he—

Stetit unus in arcem
etc.

O'Neill cut his quote in the play a little before Angus does.

page 109:

TWO UNSUCCESSFUL VERSIONS. O'Neill told Kenneth Macgowan in a letter of August 7, [1926] (*SL*, 209) that he had torn up two versions of his second scene before he got going on the right one. (He was calling his episodes "scenes" at this point, and later changed them to "acts.") The *Work Diary*, 1:31, says on August 22, 1926: "Finished damned 2nd scene (or act) at last!"

AS HE READ ASTRONOMY. Nina's astronomical musings show that O'Neill had been reading astronomy, as does the fact that he wrote in his *Work Diary* for November 10, 1927 (1:48) that he had "Idea for Astronomer-astrologer play." He had at least one of Sir James Jeans's books when he began work on *Days Without End*, for in his notes (Yale), he reminded himself at one point, " 'Converse Equation'—look up equation in Jeans' book."

page 110:

LAZARUS APPEAR . . . WITH EYES BANDAGED. In the first longhand script of *Lazarus Laughed* (Yale), Lazarus "utters a cry of pain and shields his eyes with his hands" when the servants bring lights, and then binds his eyes with a black scarf, causing a frightened silence among his guests, "for Lazarus is a strange, majestic figure seated at the tablehead, the black band cutting his face into a broad and serene forehead above lips whose understanding smile now seems terrible and enigmatic."

MARY RESOUNDS AGAIN. Marsden hears people approaching and thinks, "No, let Mary go." The stage directions read: "Mary is heard shuffling to the front door which is opened. Immediately, as Mary sees Nina, she breaks down and there is the sound of her uncontrolled sobbing and choking. . . ." They follow with "as Mary's grief subsides" Nina is heard saying, "Isn't Mr. Marsden here, Mary?" (26).

page 111:

A DELIBERATE ECHO OF DR. HAMILTON'S. The results of Dr. Hamilton's investigation, *A Research in Marriage*, was first published by Boni (New York, 1929), and has been reissued by Lear (New York, 1948). O'Neill was able to absorb Dr. Hamilton's style as he answered his elaborate questionnaires as one of one hundred men and one hundred women, all married, who took part in the research, before Dr. Hamilton gave him a private analysis. Card 25, page 39, for instance, uses both "spoon" and "spooning." O'Neill testified in *Lewys v. O'Neill*, (609) that he had also later brought up his ideas for *Strange Interlude* and "discussed its psychological aspects with Dr. G. V. Hamilton." O'Neill's earlier participation in answering the questionnaires probably alerted him to some of the matrimonial problems he stressed in his play. For instance, card 1, page 89, asked, "Does your wife ever make you feel uncomfortable because she contributes toward the family support?" O'Neill would have recalled the uneasy period when he lived in Agnes's house in West Point Pleasant, and it perhaps suggested Sam's misery working in the Professor's old study and Nina's resentful thought "I even have to give him a home" (69).

CAUSE OF HIS MOTHER'S ADDICTION. In the "family history" he sketched at the time of Dr. Hamilton's analysis, O'Neill noted that he had been "born with difficulty" and that had led to his mother's "treatment with Doc. which

eventually winds up in start of nervousness, drinking & drug-addiction. No signs of these before" (Sheaffer II, 511).
"SERIES OF BROUGHT-ON ABORTIONS." Sheaffer II, 511.

page 112:
"MORE FERTILE." "COMFORTABLE PROSPERITY." "BIG ORCHARDS." Letter to Agnes dated "Thursday," when O'Neill had moved with Saxe to "the half-farm, half suburban villa establishment of Saxe's brother-in-law" (Correspondence). O'Neill's letters to Agnes at this time have only the day of the week. Agnes's are dated and range from April 23 to May 4, 1921.
"I HAVE A POIGNANT PAIN." Letter to Agnes from O'Neill dated "Friday" (Correspondence).
"TERRIBLY TRAGIC." So O'Neill said it was to Agnes in a letter dated "Wednesday" [April 27?, 1921] (SL, 153).

page 113:
WHEN HE MET CARLOTTA. His meetings with Carlotta and his work schedule are in his Work Diary, 1:29–31, 33–34.
SHE TOOK THE ROLE OF MILDRED. When Carlotta gave the Yale University Library one of the first photographs she had given O'Neill in 1926, she noted on the back of it: "I met Eugene O'Neill in 1922 when Arthur Hopkins sent for me to play in the 'uptown' performance of 'The Hairy Ape'—we were introduced and said a very few words—neither of us very excited about meeting the other!"
LEAVING HIM WITHOUT EVEN. In a letter dated "Sunday eve" written on the boat from Bermuda to New York, apparently on his May 1927 trip (Correspondence), O'Neill told Agnes, "Don't think you have to try the policy of never letting me hear a word from you. Under the circumstances that would be very bad business. I need to hear from you. It was partly your never sending me any word when you went to Bermuda and left me alone in New York that helped me to forget myself."
DIVORCED FROM RALPH BARTON. The interlocutory judgment was filed on March 19, 1926. The case had been tried on March 5, 1926, on grounds of adultery before the Honorable Isidor Wasservogel.
SHE JOINED O'NEILL. Their meetings are listed in his Work Diary, 1:34, including those on November 26.
"SHOT INTO THE SKY." From the first draft of a letter to Carlotta written on December 1, 1926, the day after Beyond the Horizon opened in New York, for it refers to receiving a cable from her on it (Correspondence). O'Neill's references to "houses" and "people who live in them" show his feeling of alienation in the midst of his family.
"I HAVE BEEN QUITE FRANK." This part of the first draft of the December 1, 1926, letter to Carlotta (Correspondence) has been read by Sheaffer II (236) as "There are some things I couldn't lie about—even by silence." The correct reading is "I have been quite frank here. There are some things I couldn't be about—even by silence." O'Neill is not only considering silence

as more truthful than speech, as he shows it to be in *Strange Interlude*, he
is conceiving of silence as the only language of love—and yet even that as
inadequate to express his feeling for Carlotta. In his letter to Agnes of April
16, 1927 (Correspondence), he told her that his feeling for her would sound
"bald and shallow when forced into words," for "here silence, the silence of
a love that knows itself loved in return, is the only eloquent speech."

AFTERWARD AGNES HARKED BACK. This comes from an undated (late September 1927) letter to O'Neill from Agnes (Correspondence), in which she
reaches a nadir of despair over her relationship with O'Neill (hereafter referred to as the Nadir Letter).

TO CROSS THE ABYSSES. One of the most boring of the O'Neills' neighbors at
Bermuda, Montiville Morris Hansford, who was quite oblivious to the marital crisis, wrote up O'Neill's behavior in the midst of his family as if it all
came of odd quirks of genius ("O'Neill as the Stage Never Sees Him," *Boston Transcript*, March 22, 1930). Hansford says: "His mental slumps inspire
one with a great desire to take a walk, get away. He is best left alone at such
times. Yet, in some respects, he is most comical. Coming slowly down the
back stairs to join a group on the porch at Bellevue, I have watched him
stand for two minutes, trying, evidently, to decide upon which chair to sit,
and wondering (certainly by his expression) what sort of human beings were
these gathered together. Often there comes to his face an expression of
astonishment, even on seeing his own family, as if undecided just where this
or that child fitted into the general scheme of things."

"WITH ALL THAT'S INSIDE." Letter to Macgowan of December 7, 1926 (Bryer,
137).

page 114:

"YOU ARE STILL YOUNG." From O'Neill's letter dated "Tuesday" [December
20?, 1927] (*SL*, 269) asking Agnes to divorce him.

"IF I LOST YOUR LOVE." From O'Neill's letter to Agnes of April 16, 1927 (*SL*,
240).

IN THE WAY OF SCHOPENHAUER. I have pointed out all the parallels between
this play and Schopenhauer's philosophy in "*Strange Interlude* and Schopenhauer," *American Literature*, May 1953, pp. 213–28.

"SCHOPENHAUER MUSINGS." O'Neill speaks of them in a letter to Agnes of
January 24, 1920 (Correspondence).

SCHOPENHAUER HAD BEEN WITH HIM. Schopenhauer is certainly evident in
Strange Interlude. Sheaffer II, 240–41, believes that O'Neill "based"
Strange Interlude on George Bernard Shaw's *Man and Superman*. O'Neill
was certainly perfectly familiar with *Man and Superman*, and also with its
sources, mentioned by Shaw in his preface: Nietzsche, Schopenhauer, and
Westermarck. (O'Neill's copy of Westermarck's *History of Human Marriage*,
in three volumes and dated by him "Nantucket Sept. '26" is now at Yale.) In
Man and Superman, Shaw sees Nature as struggling to evolve an ever higher
consciousness by way of the woman who chooses to propagate the rational
philosopher and revolutionary social thinker John Tanner over the romantic

dreamer Octavius. Shaw has the philosopher recognize and accept his role in achieving Nature's great purpose. Nothing could be more unlike O'Neill's view in *Strange Interlude* of woman dominating a meaningless, purposeless universe in which "Life is something in one cell that doesn't need to think!": that is, "God the Mother" (170) or Schopenhauer's blind striving of the "Will to Live."

HE CALLED IT FIRST, "GODFATHER." O'Neill submitted a photostat of his first note with the title "Godfather" for *Lewys v. O'Neill,* 609.

page 115:

"THE BEST WALKER." The following report on James O'Neill during the run of *Joseph and His Brethren* appeared in the *St. Louis Globe Democrat* on January 6, 1915: "Mr. O'Neill is a wonderful man. He is an advocate of the vigorous life. Yesterday, in spite of his age, he started out early with Brandon Tynan, who plays 'Joseph' in the company—a fine young Irish actor—and walked from his downtown hotel out to Forest Park, marched around it, and tramped back to his hotel for dinner. He arrived swinging his cane as jauntily as if he had been 30 years of age instead of double that—and more." When they arrived Tynan had declared, "The 'Governor' is the best walker of the lot. A lot of us are younger, but there isn't one of us who is more virile."

HIS FATHER'S CANCER OF THE INTESTINES. In a letter to Agnes [March 1, 1920] *(SL,* 118), O'Neill reports that his father has had another stroke. Dr. Aspell had told them that James O'Neill had a fatal cancer of the intestines that ought to be removed, but his weak heart would not survive an operation.

"I'M ALL BROKEN UP." Letter to Agnes [March 1, 1920] *(SL,* 118).

"DOCTOR ERDMANN'S VERDICT." "IT SEEMS SO." So O'Neill spoke of it in a letter to his father's old friend George C. Tyler on April 20, 1920 (Princeton).

"AND THAT FOOL IN NEW YORK." Letter to Agnes dated "Friday p.m." [July 30?, 1920] *(SL,* 133).

page 116:

THE END OF PART ONE. In his *MBE* Notes (536), made in August 1931, O'Neill decided that in *Mourning Becomes Electra* he had succeeded in making each of its three plays "complete," but with an ending that demands the next play as its "inevitable sequel." He realized that *Strange Interlude* "never got credit for this technical virtue," which allowed it to succeed in spite of the break between the two parts: "no other two-part play, as far as I know, has accomplished this synthesis of end and beginning."

ACT FIVE SEETHES WITH HATRED. The words "hate" and "hated" run through the thoughts, as, for example, "She's beginning to hate you" (92); "Sometimes I almost hate her!" (96); "Mother hated her" (99); "Oh, I hate him!; I'll make Sam hate him!" (108).

BLACKEST DESPAIR IN ARGENTINA. This job with Swift Meat Packing Company at La Plata was the final and worst job that O'Neill took in Argentina, and he recalled it shudderingly to Hamilton Basso for his February 28, 1948, *New Yorker* interview, "The Tragic Sense."

SEA IMAGERY REFLECTS HIS PLAN. The basic image of Nina's pregnancy musings comes, of course, from the tides of the sea. O'Neill worked on an outline for "The Sea-Mother's Son" on March 8, 1927 (*Work Diary*, 1:39).

"MY SOUL IS A BLACK." From the first draft of a letter to Carlotta, December 1, 1926 (Correspondence).

page 117:

"PLAYWRITING, MATING AND." "HOMESICK FOR HOMELESSNESS." Letter of August 19, 1924 (Bryer, 53).

"MONEY." "HOUSE." "WIFE AND KIDS." From the draft of a letter to Carlotta, December 1, 1926 (Correspondence). O'Neill has crossed out "wife and kids," for he had been led into this confession by his actual Hairy Ape's lament: "Tree square a day, and cauliflowers in de front yard—ekal rights—a woman and kids—a lousy vote—and I'm all fixed for Jesus, huh? Aw, hell! What does dat get yuh?" (Random House, 3:250). Carlotta, having played in *The Hairy Ape*, could be expected to understand the allusion.

"NOT UNTIL THE 'POSSESSIVE' STUFF." Letter to Agnes from O'Neill dated "Tuesday" [February 7?, 1928] (*SL*, 277).

page 118:

"MY THREE MEN!" Nina's sense of herself as eternal reproduction, source and aim of all life urges, takes something not only from Schopenhauer but also from Jung, Frazier's *The Golden Bough*, and the ancient Egyptian myth in which the elemental forces of life are pictured as a Great Mother and her three son-consorts, the first being the father of the other two. O'Neill had read about this myth in his copy (dated by him "Bermuda '25") of Albert Churchward's *Origin and Evolution of Religion* (New York: Dutton, 1924) (Yale). That he was particularly intrigued by the Egyptian view becomes evident in a letter that O'Neill wrote to Manuel Komroff on August 23, 1930 (Columbia), when planning a trip up the Nile. O'Neill told Komroff, "Egypt has always called me. I've a greater intuitive hunch for their feeling about life and death than for that of any other culture—."

SHARING THE WOMAN. O'Neill's biographers have supposed that Darrell's sharing of Nina in *Strange Interlude* with her husband Sam Evans mirrors O'Neill's sharing of Louise Bryant with her husband John Reed. This idea was set in motion by Agnes Boulton's *Part of a Long Story*. Actually, Agnes had never met Louise, and all she knew about O'Neill's relationship with her was what she picked up a year later from Greenwich Village gossip. For her account of O'Neill and Louise, Agnes used bits of Darrell's asides to portray O'Neill's feelings and bits of Nina's for Louise's. Agnes also strained events to give the impression of a long, continuous sharing of one woman by two men comparable to that of the play. Agnes has O'Neill start a love affair with Louise in the summer of 1916 and continue it through fall and winter and the next summer until just before Agnes came into his life in the fall of 1917. All biographers have followed her lead, adding to the story of what took place from what took place in the play. Although Agnes did not know it, O'Neill was still very much in love with Beatrice Ashe in the summer of 1916, as his letter to her from Provincetown of July 25, 1916 (*SL*, 71–72), now reveals, and in this letter he asks Beatrice to come to Provincetown to see his first play production *(Bound East for Cardiff)*. She can stay, he says, with Reed and Louise "as chaperons" or with Mary Heaton Vorse. O'Neill tries also to convince Beatrice to marry him in a union of two struggling artists, with the help of other struggling artists. After the production of the play, he apparently returned to New London to convince her in person. Either her refusal started him drinking, and she then broke completely with him, or she broke completely with him and he then began to drink. Arthur McGinley told me that Eugene's father, James O'Neill, then begged him to get Eugene back to Provincetown from New London. McGinley told me that both O'Neill and he were drunk on the way back and after. A number of letters to Louise from people who had been in Provincetown show that by late September she had undertaken to save O'Neill from drink for his work and was so far successful.

One fact that has weighed heavily with biographers to substantiate a *Strange Interlude* sharing on O'Neill's part of Louise with Reed is that the three of them gave the address "43 Washington Square" in New York for mailing manuscripts that fall. It seems that Reed had rented a group of studios there and allowed several of his friends to use them. He had money from reporting and was always a *practicing* socialist. Reed and Louise used 43 Washington Square for writing and for late nights at the Provincetown Playhouse, where they were both very busy with productions of their own works that fall, but their actual home was their cottage at Croton. O'Neill likewise was actually living at the Prince George Hotel with his family. Louise Bryant wrote a fairly long autobiographical sketch (now in the Syracuse University Library) for Granville Hicks when he was preparing his biography of John Reed, and these facts are revealed in it.

Reed and Louise were legally married on November 9, 1916, and on November 21 they went to a Baltimore hospital, for Reed needed a kidney operation. Almost as soon as she returned to New York, Louise became very ill herself with a female complaint. Reasoning by analogy with *Strange Interlude,* biographers have assumed that she really had an abortion, for, in the play, Nina passes off her abortion to her husband as some kind of woman's trouble. The actual nature of Louise's illness can be checked from her day-by-day account in letters to Reed in Baltimore. (All their correspondence at this time has been preserved in the John Reed Collection at Harvard University Library.) Louise described all her daily symptoms and exactly what Dr. Lorber prescribed, and tells of the nursing care of their friend Becky Edelson, at whose apartment she remained in high fever throughout all of December. From recent medical examinations of this evidence it is clear that Louise was suffering from a tubo-ovarian abscess. As soon as she could be moved and Reed had been released from the hospital in Baltimore, they went to Croton to recuperate together.

Meanwhile, in a letter Jig Cook wrote to his wife, Susan Glaspell, on December 23, 1916, he said that without Louise's help O'Neill had reached "snapping point" (Sheaffer I, 366). He must have relapsed into alcoholism around Christmas 1916. In her autobiographical sketch Louise says that some time in late February, on pleas from O'Neill's mother, she searched for, found, and rescued O'Neill from his long bout of desperate drinking and brought him back to his family at the Prince George Hotel for sobering. As soon as he was well again, O'Neill told her he was going to Provincetown to stay sober and work, and he got there early in March. From Louise's autobiographical account (substantiated by a telegram she sent Reed, now in the Reed Collection), she payed him a surprise visit in Provincetown for one week in May, and that seems to have been the last time she saw O'Neill.

Certainly Louise's feeling for Reed was not Nina's, for Nina has never really loved her husband Sam, whereas Louise was unquestionably very much in love with Reed. But she was trying to live by Reed's belief in an open marriage without possessiveness, in which both parties can give love (physical as well as spiritual) to others. It was a difficult philosophy to put into practical operation, and it seems that early in June 1917 Reed managed to do so in a way that hurt Louise badly. He himself told her on June 11, 1917: "In lots of ways we are very different, and we must both try to realize that—while loving each other. But of course on this last awful business, you were humanly right and I was wrong. I have always loved you my darling ever since I first met you—and I guess I always will. This is more than I've ever felt for anyone, honestly." In another letter, June 25, 1917, he told her that he had confessed to Lincoln Steffens, "I'd been a fool and a cad," and that "he just told me most people were at some time, in some way." Louise had fled to France on a war-reporting assignment as soon as it happened, and she told Reed that if anything happened to her "you will always know that I loved you with all my being. I know you don't think that's as fine as the love that's scattered but, dearest, it's the best thing, the deepest thing in my life" (July 14, 1917). As soon as she returned to New York in August 1917 she and Reed left immediately together on a reporting assignment to Russia.

Louise may very well have given O'Neill physical as well as spiritual support, but she could have done so on only a few occasions, during brief periods, for they were geographically separated for the major part of 1916–17 and were not together after the week in May. There could have been no such sharing of the one woman by two men like the sharing of Nina by Darrell and Evans.

In *Part of a Long Story* (114), Agnes declares that Louise solicited O'Neill's love by giving him a book of poems with the note: "Dark eyes. What do you mean?" This seems to be a fossil remain of the actual event that had set off all the gossip in Greenwich Village about Louise and O'Neill that Agnes picked up when she met and fell in love with him in the fall of

1917. In the *Masses* for July 1917, a poem by Louise Bryant called "Dark Eyes" appeared:

> Dark eyes,
> What shall I do?
> Your mouth smiles
> Persistently,
> But says never
> Anything;
> Do you think then
> That I love you?

The eyes might have been O'Neill's, although with his habitual gravity it is difficult to imagine him smiling "persistently." At any rate, Greenwich Village gossip thought they were O'Neill's and took the poem as a confession of love. Some mixed-up memory of that gossip seems to have gone into Agnes's story of the book of poems and the note. One thing is clear: Agnes herself was very jealous—on her own confession in *Part of a Long Story*—of O'Neill's admiration for Louise and of her power to keep him sober. Agnes (a drinker herself, although never alcoholic) never could. Agnes seems to have filled out the rest of her story of O'Neill and Louise with her more clearly remembered jealousy of Carlotta. She describes satirically how O'Neill wrote a careful draft of a letter to Louise, revising and crossing-out, which would seem when copied a direct outpouring of his heart. Agnes had just such a draft in her possession, but to Carlotta not Louise. (It is the draft of a December 1, 1926, letter that Agnes later sold with the rest of her O'Neill correspondence to Harvard.)

A decisive reason for discounting Agnes's interpretation of the source of Darrell's sharing of Nina with Sam lies in the fact that the play's Nina is shared by three men—Darrell, Evans, and Marsden—along with the fourth man, the baby Gordon, and so makes a closer parallel to O'Neill's recall of his mother with her three men (his father, brother, and himself) along with the fourth man, her beloved dead baby.

I am indebted in my reworking of the story of Louise Bryant, O'Neill, and John Reed to Virginia Gardner (who was then planning a biography of Louise Bryant) for sharing evidence and arguing points with me in a stimulating series of letters.

"NOT TO ATTEMPT EASY." Letter [ca. April 8, 1928] (*SL*, 283), in which he recalls his old encouragement of her to do her best. O'Neill had even helped Agnes with her "junk." He made about 2,000 words of changes to sharpen scenes and dialogue, for instance, in the comedy "Little Hope" that Agnes wrote under the pseudonym "Elinor Rand" (Virginia).

page 119:

THAT HE NEEDED HER. From Agnes's Nadir Letter, late September 1927 (Correspondence).

IMMEDIATELY SHE OPENED NEGOTIATIONS. Negotiations with Kathleen's law-

yer, James C. Warren, were clearly under way by late April 1921, for among
O'Neill's letters to Agnes during the Rochester dentistry is one dated "Saturday p.m." [April 23?, 1921] (*SL*, 153), in which O'Neill tells Agnes that
Shane's nurse, Mrs. Clark, had forwarded to him a letter from the lawyer
and asks for Warren's address.

"EXTREMELY—IF SECRETLY—SENSITIVE." From an undated letter to DePolo
[postmarked May 9, 1928] (*SL*, 299).

page 120:

"HAZY QUALITY." "PASSAGE OF TIME." "PAST THE LEADING." This is a separate
note on "Bellevue" writing paper, so O'Neill must have made it after the
move to Spithead on December 20, 1926, when the "Bellevue" paper became scrap. The sentence here is genuinely garbled, and Floyd (75) does
not make it less so in the part about the passage of time with its events and
people past the leading characters, by inserting a comma after past, so that
it reads "passage of time with the events and people past, the leading characters who stand still. . . ."

"ROW ON THE CREW." Letter to Shane, September 25, [1927] (*SL*, 261).

page 121:

"EUGENE IS STUDYING." Letter to Shane, May 27, 1930 (Virginia).

"YES, IT WAS THE GREATEST." Letter to Nina Moise, August 29, 1920 (Alexander, 277; *SL*, 135).

HIS FATHER HAD BEEN FELLED. *Beyond the Horizon* opened on February 2,
1920. On March 1, 1920, O'Neill wired Agnes: "Excuse not writing. All
upset. Father had stroke. Very serious" (Yale).

WITH APOPLECTIC PRIDE. Sam's death follows the events in James O'Neill's,
but it also takes elements from the death of Jamie, O'Neill's other hero. Sam
appears apoplectic with high blood pressure, and Jamie's death certificate
had read "Cerebral Apoplexy." Also, Sam complains about his eyesight in
act eight, recalling Jamie's loss of vision: he "can't see anything up there!"
(159), and he says that his "eyes are getting old" (171).

"FAME" HE WOULD SO GLADLY. So O'Neill had said in his letter to Alexander
Berkman of January 29, 1927 (*SL*, 233).

"A *GOOD* MAN." Letter to Agnes from O'Neill dated "Thursday p.m." [July
29?, 1920] (*SL*, 132).

"THIS IS OUR TRUTH." O'Neill wrote out this ending on a separate page of
notes for his "last scene," which is labeled at the top "—G—f," so it must
have been written when he was still calling the play "Godfather," before he
took the title "Strange Interlude" in the scenario of September 1925 (Yale).

"TWO PEOPLE ALONE." From the scenario in his *Notebook 1920–1930* (Yale).

page 122:

"ULTIMATE ISLAND." Letter to Agnes from O'Neill of April 16, 1927 (*SL*, 239).

"EVERYTHING SEEMS SO RIGHT." Letter to Agnes from O'Neill dated "Sunday a.m." from the S.S. *Fort St. George* bound for New York from Bermuda [August 28, 1927] (*SL*, 251–52).

"I WANT ALWAYS TO HAVE." From an undated letter to Agnes, [early May 1928] (*SL*, 297).

"TOO MANY TORTURING SCENES." When O'Neill sent his letter dated "Tuesday" [December 20?, 1927] (*SL*, 269–70) to Agnes asking for a divorce, Agnes cabled back, and he at once sent a second letter dated "Monday eve" [December 26?, 1927] (*SL*, 271), this time making it clear that he had found a new love.

ASSISTING A YOUNG BIOLOGIST. Darrell's friendship with the young biologist Preston, who becomes a "compensating substitute" (166) for the son he has given to Sam, probably took something from O'Neill's observation of his father's friendship with Brandon Tynan, the star of *Joseph and His Brethren*, who like Preston had "the rare gift of gratitude" (166), which James O'Neill's sons rarely demonstrated. Tynan would speak of James O'Neill with "a distinct note of reverence" in his voice, as in an interview for the *Chicago News* of September 26, 1914, in which he said, "To talk with Mr. O'Neill is to realize that he is a human, sentient bridge between two generations of playgoers and players. His retrospect goes back beyond the actors I worshiped as a boy to the actors of whom I have heard from the lips of my elders or about whom I have read in biographies or memoirs. Yet here he is, playing night after night, with as much respect for an observation of the modern naturalistic method of acting as if he had made his debut only last season after a course of Ibsen." When Tynan's play *The Melody of Youth* opened, James O'Neill volunteered to do the small role of a blind beggar in it during the first performances. In the *New York Sun* of February 13, 1916, he is quoted as saying: "As one of the older generation of players I want to make a little offering to one of the most promising representatives of the younger generation." When he went on as the blind piper, the *New York Star* of March 1, 1916, reported, "This character is on the stage for perhaps five minutes, and only in one act, and yet so great is the player's artistry that the role stands out as something to be remembered. Mr. O'Neill has long been Mr. Tynan's friend and counsellor." This came five months before the first production of one of Eugene O'Neill's one-act plays at Provincetown that summer.

"HAVE YOU STARTED." Letter to Agnes from O'Neill dated "Monday night," ca. January 1928 (Correspondence).

"NOW YOU ARE ALL RIGHT." From an undated letter to Agnes [ca. April 3, 1928] (*SL*, 283).

HE HAD SEEN—AND YET NOT SEEN. In part, O'Neill's inner knowledge that his love for Agnes was doomed manifested itself through persistent recurring attacks of hives in the spring of 1927. For instance, right after the passionate reaffirmation of his love for Agnes in his letter to her of April 16, 1927 (*SL*, 241) he added a postscript that his "detestable hives" had come back in spite of his diet, and the next morning yet another crop of them had erupted. He bewailed the fact that such a ridiculous malady should make so many splendid days miserable for him (242). The hives seem to have been a psychosomatic reaction to loss of love, for he also broke out in hives when he learned that his father was dying. He was able to tell Agnes—thanking God and Dr. Hiebert's medicine—that they had cleared up as soon as he got to him (*SL*, 133). In part, of course, he was perfectly conscious of the threat to his marriage. He tried to convince Agnes of the dangers in her insistence that they take vacations from one another. He wrote her on August 29, 1927 (Correspondence): "I insisted I had premonitions against this trip as is. I have them worse now." He reminded her that putting him into a homeless situation was entirely her choice and dangerous for their future.

page 123:

PLAY ABOUT A MAN WHO WORKS OUT. This play finally became *Days Without End*. In his early notes for it, while he was calling it "Without Ending of Days" (Yale), his protagonist, then called "Russell," was to have a scene with his wife "in which he reveals that the marriage in his plot is an exact replica of his own." Then, in parentheses, O'Neill speculated: "Or in plot he transforms himself into a wife who is fathered by husband (?)." He was clearly working from inner knowledge of how he had worked out the fate of his marriage in *Strange Interlude*, transforming himself, in much of it, into the woman of his novel-play.

"UNTIL ALL MY PERSONAL AFFAIRS." Letter to Dr. Lief from O'Neill of March 16, 1929 (NYU).

THE COLORS OF CYBELE'S PARLOR. It was important for O'Neill to realize that the "crimsons and purples" of his Mother-Goddess's parlor in *The Great God Brown* and of the brothel-palace in *Lazarus Laughed* were gone for him, for it came of his inner acceptance that his love for Agnes was dead. The lines seemed meaningless to Philip Moeller when he directed *Strange Interlude*, and he urged O'Neill to cut them—in vain. O'Neill dedicated the typescript to him: "To Phil with my humblest felicitations on his putting back my stained-glass-window ecstatic Charlicism" (Moeller Collection, New York Public Library; hereafter referred to as Moeller Collection).

"OUR MOTHER WHO ART." This comes from the "Curtain" of *Strange Interlude* that O'Neill dated "2 / 24 / '27" (Yale), in which Charlie, automatically wincing at Nina's "dear old Charlie," realizes, "No, God bless blessed dear old Charlie—Our Mother who art in heaven!" O'Neill had explicitly equated the evening shadows with the coming of death and the mother by having Nina think: "God the Father is flying away to some other world. Night is the Mother's."

"SOMETHING IN ME IS SO DAMN." *SL*, 269.

page 124:

"I NEED YOU." Brooks Atkinson and Seymour Peck of the *New York Times* made a tape recording of an interview with Carlotta, shortly before the Broadway opening of *Long Day's Journey into Night*, during which she said of O'Neill, describing his courtship, "He didn't say, 'I love you; I think you

are wonderful; I think you are grand.' He kept saying, 'I need you; I need
you; I need you;' and sometimes it was a bit frightening. I had been brought
up in England and nobody had ever gritted their teeth and said they needed
me, and he did need me, I discovered" (from a transcript that Croswell
Bowen kindly allowed me to duplicate).

"IT GOES ON FOREVER." From an interview O'Neill gave to the *Seattle Daily
Times* at the time he was awarded the Nobel Prize (November 12, 1936). Of
course, the long cycles were part of O'Neill's lifelong struggle to capture
more and more of the truth of life in play form.

LANGNER STAYED UP LATE. Lawrence Langner wrote an account of that first
reading of *Strange Interlude* in his book *The Magic Curtain*, 232.

"BRAVEST AND MOST FAR-REACHING." Langner's comments are from a circular
letter he sent to all members of the Theatre Guild Board of Managers on
April 21, 1927 (Yale). On April 4, 1927, O'Neill wrote Langner to say that
he would send the completed typescript of his first draft to the Guild by way
of Elizabeth Sergeant (Yale).

"INTENSIVE CUTTING." Letter to Lawrence Langner from O'Neill of May 1,
1927 (*SL*, 244).

"GREATLY CONDENSED." Cable to Lawrence Langner from O'Neill of May 7,
1927 (Yale). On May 13, 1927, Agnes cabled Langner asking if he still expected Gene to stay with him and saying he would arrive Monday (Yale). A
report in the May 16, 1927, *New York Telegram* says that O'Neill would
arrive from Bermuda that day to confer with the Guild on *Marco Millions*
and *Strange Interlude*. By May 31, 1927, O'Neill was writing Langner from
Bermuda to thank him for the "week at your place" (Yale).

"LIKE A DOG." Letter to Theresa Helburn of August 22, 1927 (Yale).

"HELEN WESTLEY'S FOR ALL." Letter to Theresa Helburn of August 22, 1927
(Yale).

SEPTEMBER 20, 1927. O'Neill cabled the news to Agnes on that day (Yale).

"PAY FOR TWO NIGHTS." Agnes reported Tyrone Guthrie's reaction to O'Neill
in an undated letter from the April 1927 visit to New York, just as Elizabeth
Sergeant had told it to her (Correspondence). Agnes told O'Neill that
Katharine Cornell had read "most of it" and liked it, but Guthrie had given
his reaction merely from glancing through it. Elizabeth Sergeant had carried
a typescript to Katharine Cornell at the same time as she brought one to the
Guild, for O'Neill had promised to let her see it before Langner's interest
was aroused. O'Neill thought Cornell and the Guild might produce it together, if both were interested. Langner says he learned with joy of Cornell's
rejection of it from a conversation with Guthrie, who did not know the Guild
wanted it (*The Magic Curtain*, 233).

"WOULD LOOK IT BETTER." O'Neill had already suggested Ann Harding for
Nina in a letter to Langner of April 4, 1927, "in case Cornell should be out"
(Yale).

"A GOOD SCOUT." Letter to Agnes [November 27?, 1927] (*SL*, 266).

page 125:

"THE MISTAKE OF HER CAREER." Langner says that Alice Brady told him so
"years later" (*The Magic Curtain*, 236).

LYNN FONTANNE BECAME NINA. Letter to Agnes [November 27, 1927] (*SL*, 266). When performances began, O'Neill told Theresa Helburn he hoped that Lynn and the cast were only half as pleased with their work as he was (April 8, 1928, [*SL*, 291]). Two years later he told Ward Morehouse that he had been "remarkably lucky" in actors, and he spoke particularly of Walter Huston in *Desire Under the Elms*, Paul Robeson in *The Emperor Jones*, and Lynn Fontanne in *Strange Interlude*.

"TICKLED TO DEATH." So O'Neill said in a note to Philip Moeller (Moeller Collection) on a day when he was laid up on doctor's orders and could not come to rehearsals.

"EASY." "GRATEFUL WORK." So he told Agnes in the letter of Tuesday [December 20?, 1927], (*SL*, 269).

MOELLER'S GREATEST INSPIRATION. Moeller described his search for the right way to do the asides in "Some Thoughts on the Production of O'Neill's *Strange Interlude*," *Theatre Guild Quarterly*, February 1928, and also in "Silences Out Loud," *New York Times*, February 26, 1928. In the latter he said that the idea of arresting the motion came to him on a train from Baltimore to New York which suddenly stopped. "Unconsciously I may have taken a hint from that," he said. Also, in "Mr. O'Neill and the Audible Theatre," *New York Times*, March 3, 1929, Moeller said that he saw the asides throughout as "a sort of contrapuntal melody."

"TO THINK OUR THOUGHTS." So Glenn Anders declared in an interview (on the film version of *Strange Interlude*) in the *New York Herald Tribune*, September 4, 1932.

"HOLD BACK, DON'T GIVE." So Moeller told Harvey Gaul in an interview, "Meet Philip Moeller, Guild's Ace Director" (Unlabeled clipping, probably from the *Pittsburgh Post Gazette* [Moeller Collection]).

"I HOPE HE DOESN'T." So Langner recalled Moeller as saying (*The Magic Curtain*, 236).

"THE MOOD OF THE PLAY." Interview in the *New York Herald Tribune*, September 4, 1932.

"SHE STAMPED." "SOMETIMES WE'D MURMUR." Interview in the *New York Herald Tribune*, September 4, 1932. This occurred in Philadelphia, after the publicity on the Boston banning had taught audiences to look for indecencies where there were none.

"MOST IMAGINATIVE." So O'Neill said in a letter to Terry Helburn of April 8, 1928 (*SL*, 291).

"THE BIG BACON-BRINGER." In a letter to Robert Sisk of April 10, 1928 (Yale), O'Neill told him: "I hate to say 'I told you so' to the Guild Com. but I always did stoutly assert that 'Interlude' would be the big bacon-bringer of the two, quite outside of its proving the biggest artistic success."

"THE USUAL SUBSCRIPTION PERIOD." So O'Neill said in his note to *Strange Interlude* in the Wilderness Edition of his plays.

"CLEAVES THE SKYLINE." Review of the opening night, January 31, 1928. The critics were almost unanimously enthusiastic about *Strange Interlude*. O'Neill declared that their reaction was "a miraculous exception which won't happen again" (Letter to Richard Madden of February 28, 1929 [Dartmouth]). O'Neill had allowed his friend George Jean Nathan to read it before production, and he had set the tone of enthusiasm in the August 1927 *Mercury.* O'Neill told Theresa Helburn in a letter of August 22, 1927 (Yale), that it was "grand stuff" for arousing interest, and as to its disclosure of the method, "In a way now it's copyrighted."

"THAT TRENDS ON FANATICISM." So O'Neill told Theresa Helburn in a letter of April 8, 1928 (*SL*, 290).

page 126:

THE GREAT GODS BROWN. *Strange Interlude* ran into trouble the spring of its opening in New York. The District Attorney had closed a Shubert Brothers production, *Maya,* and their lawyer declared that if they closed *Maya* they should "on principle," close *Strange Interlude* as well. Reporters went off into wild speculation on what vendetta the Shuberts were carrying out on the Theatre Guild and O'Neill, but in reality their lawyer was working on the realization that the District Attorney would find it very embarrassing to act against *Strange Interlude,* because it had just received the Pulitzer Prize. Helen Arthur, executive director for the producers of *Maya,* declared in a statement in the April 25, 1928, *New York Evening Post,* "It would be a great misfortune to the theatre to close those two fine plays." In fact, the District Attorney ended by clearing both plays, announcing that there was nothing in either to corrupt youth and therefore the Wales Law did not apply to them (see the May 2, 1928, *New York Times* and *New York Herald Tribune*). Lawrence Langner wrote ironically to O'Neill on May 10, 1928 (Yale) that he ought to thank Lee and Jake Shubert for increasing the already enormous publicity on his play.

"DISGUSTING SPECTACLE OF IMMORALITY." These were the words of Mayor Nichols of Boston as recorded in the September 19, 1929, *Boston Daily Record.* In Providence it was Police Captain George W. Cowan who banned it. He had not read it, he said, but had seen excerpts sent to him by Frederick Pool of the Theatre Board of Control of Philadelphia. Cowan said, "These excerpts from the manuscript contained many references to abortion. In fact, the whole play is mostly about abortion. It also has to do with adultery and is blasphemous and atheistic" (quoted in the *Providence Bulletin,* September 17, 1929).

"ABSOLUTELY MISREPRESENTED." The clergyman quoted was the Reverend Edwin F. Noble of the First Universalist Church, who admitted he had gone to the play with a "prejudiced mind." *Quincy (Mass.) Patriot Ledger,* October 1, 1929.

"A BEAUTIFUL PLAY." These were the words of Mayor McGrath of Quincy as quoted in the *Boston Post,* October 1, 1929.

"OBVIOUS CHAUVINISTIC ANTI-YANK." So O'Neill said in a letter to Lawrence Langner, December 4, 1929 (*SL*, 358). O'Neill discovered from the reviews the astonishing liberties European producers took with his plays. He decided to put a clause into his London contract for the play stipulating that they follow the Guild acting script verbatim. He told Terry Helburn, "I've suffered enough from European directors' antics, which I couldn't help; but let it not be said of an O'Neill that he let the English massacre him!" (Undated letter of Summer 1929 [Yale]).

SOLD LIKE A NEW NOVEL. So O'Neill told Terry Helburn in a letter of April 8, 1928 (SL, 290).

"OF COURSE, HER CLAIM." Letter of April 29, 1930 (Princeton).

"DIRECT ATTENTION TO." Letter to Saxe Commins from O'Neill of December 5, 1929 (Princeton). At that point he was thinking of getting Henry Taft, the "famous" corporation lawyer, to do so.

HARRY WEINBERGER WON IT. The case was tried under Federal Judge John Woolsey in March 1931 and won by O'Neill on April 22, 1931. Lewys's lawyer first had to prove "direct evidence of access" by O'Neill to her book. She could prove only that she had sent copies to Courtney Lemon and Lawrence Langner of the Theatre Guild and to Thomas Smith of Boni & Liveright, all three of whom testified that they had neither given the book to O'Neill nor spoken of it to him, so that she was reduced to suggesting that O'Neill could have gotten the books "because charwomen had keys to their respective offices." Judge Woolsey found this "unworthy of consideration." What she put forth as "fingerprints" of theft by O'Neill turned out to be a few grossly generalized similarities from the fact that ideas of eugenic breeding entered into both works, or such meaningless specific similarities as the fact that O'Neill had a Doctor Darrell in his play and she had a Doctor Cramwell in her book and both had been to Munich. Judge Woolsey, summing up, cited a few more examples that reached even "more fantastic heights" and declared in favor of O'Neill, the Guild, and Boni & Liveright, awarding them their costs of $17,500, which, of course, all knew would never be payed as she had no money. See Lewys v. O'Neill.

AN AMENDMENT TO THE VESTAL COPYRIGHT BILL. The amendment asked that plagiarism suers either prove a prima facie case in advance or file security for payment of costs; otherwise the suit was to be dismissed. See "Seek Cash Bond," New York Telegraph, April 26, 1931.

"I'VE HAD ABOUT AS MUCH." Letter of June 20, 1929 (Gelb, 704; SL, 343). O'Neill did confess that the money was welcome, "even though I feel the play earned it under the false pretences of a ballyhooed freak."

page 127:

"A DREADFUL HASH." Letter to Theresa Helburn from O'Neill of May 16, 1944, in Theresa Helburn, A Wayward Quest (Boston: Little, Brown, 1960), 277. Also in SL, 558.

"SUPERFLUOUS SHOW-SHOP 'BUSINESS.'" MBE Notes, 534.

"THE NEW MASKED PSYCHOLOGICAL." "Memoranda on Masks," 119.

6.   Dynamo

page 129:

"GOD IS DEAD!" O'Neill suggested this as a title for his trilogy in a letter to Benjamin De Casseres of September 15, 1928 (SL, 317). The answer from science, he thought, would feed primitive religious instinct no better than a puppy biscuit would feed a lion. The title is, of course, a parody of "The King is dead! Long live the King!" "God is dead" echoes Nietzsche.

"QUEER AND INTRIGUING." Letter of August 19, 1924 (*SL*, 189).

MARCO IS GIVEN UP. O'Neill's *Work Diary*, 1:10–11, shows that he was doing this scene from the original two-night, two-part play in the days before he told Macgowan of his idea. He cut it out when he condensed *Marco Millions* into a one-night play.

"MATTER AS HIS GROSS." Quotations are from the First Longhand Draft of *Marco Millions* (Yale).

"PLAY OF DYNAMOS—." Floyd, 125. Her reading is "—the despairing philosopher—poet who falls in love etc.," instead of "philosopher-poet."

AUGUST 12, 1927. The *Work Diary* (1:45) notes here: "Wrote brief sketch in note book for ideas for the plays 'Without Ending of Days'—'It Cannot Be Mad' and the *new Negro play* I have had in mind."

"DIG AT THE ROOTS." O'Neill gave these explanations of the theme of his trilogy in a letter of August 26, 1928, to George Jean Nathan, and Nathan printed it in the *American Mercury*. It was widely reproduced in newspapers, as, for instance, in the *Boston Transcript*, December 29, 1928 (now in *SL*, 311).

page 130:

THE 1926 SCOPES TRIAL. There is much more of the Scopes trial in *Dynamo* as produced, for the *Dynamo* O'Neill published was drastically cut and reshaped to emphasize the psychology of its main character. The best source of the produced play (which I refer to as *Dynamo I*) is the typescript sent in for copyright (granted October 4, 1928) in the Library of Congress, and I have used that typescript throughout. There is also a typescript in the Berg Collection of the New York Public Library, and the original longhand script at Yale is almost identical to the typescripts. In *Dynamo I* the minister and Fife argue evolution, and Fife answers the minister's question of why he wants to believe he came from a "filthy chattering monkey" very much as O'Neill himself might have: "I'd rather a damn sight! For as the remote descendent of the ape I've come a long distance up and made a man of myself while as the image of God I've come down in the world and I'm the lousiest failure that ever was!"

"THUNDER WITH A MENACING." From the Memorandum O'Neill sent the Theatre Guild on September 9, 1928, with instructions on how to produce *Dynamo*.

SINCLAIR LEWIS'S COMMENT. There is no verbatim transcript of what Lewis said. My account is based on Mark Schorer's reconstruction of what happened in *Sinclair Lewis: An American Life* (New York: McGraw-Hill, 1961), 447.

page 131:

"RELIGION-CREATING INCEST LIBIDO." Jung, 230.

TWELVE ESSAYS ON SEX. Malcolm Cowley's report on O'Neill's volume of

Stekel, and the reasons for identifying it as *Twelve Essays on Sex and Psychoanalysis* are covered in my chapter on *Desire Under the Elms*.

"EMOTIONAL ATTITUDE." "THERE IS SOMETHING." "BLASPHEMY IS ONLY." The chapter in Stekel that had the most influence on *Dynamo* is entitled "The Masked Piety of the Neurotic" (275–84), and my quotations are from pages 215 and 276. Stekel's Gottfried Keller quote comes from his novel *Der Grüne Heinrich*, which can be found in the translation by A. M. Holt, *Green Henry* (London: Calder, 1960), 644.

"I'LL PUT THE FEAR." *Dynamo I.* Fife adds that his father would then "whale the hide off my behind."

"PLEASANTLY ENGROSSED IN." *Dynamo I.*

"STRANGE FRIENDSHIP." George Jean Nathan reported that O'Neill's "dominant intention" in *The Iceman Cometh,* as "he confided it to me," was "a study in the workings of strange friendship" (Angoff, 397). The way Fife and Light get reinforced belief in the reality of their opinions from the fierce opposition of the other is paralleled in *The Iceman Cometh,* where it is one of several ways the denizens of Harry Hope's support each other's pipe dreams.

"GREAT HISTORIC MISSION." "CHRIST, SATAN, JUDAS." "PROPHETS, FOUNDERS OF." Stekel, 233, 277, 283.

"GREAT MIRACLE." "GOD'S DEPUTY." "SAVIOUR." "STAINED WITH SIN." Stekel, 216, 234. Speaking of a particular case Stekel (234) says, "He is awaiting a miracle that will mark him as God's deputy, that will 'identify' him as the Saviour. But he feels himself stained with sin."

"THE SIXTY THOUSAND VOLTS." *Dynamo I.*

"PROTECT OUR LOVE." Letter to Agnes dated "Thursday p.m." [July 29?, 1920] (*SL,* 132).

"IT IS HORRIBLE." Letter to Agnes, "Monday eve." [December 26?, 1927] (*SL,* 272).

"THIS HOMELESS SITUATION." Letter from O'Neill to Agnes of August 29, 1927 (Correspondence).

"WHY YOU SHOULD DELIBERATELY." Letter from O'Neill to Agnes of September 11, 1927 (*SL,* 258).

"IT ISN'T HEALTHY." Ibid.

page 133:

"YOU MUST HAVE A." Ibid.

"FOUL FAIRY TALES." In a letter of May 11 [1929] (*SL,* 338), O'Neill speaks to Harold DePolo of the "foul fairy tales" with which Agnes had "poisoned" the minds of their friends against him. Certainly, in her suffering, Agnes seems to have confused what she had done with what she should have done, and what had taken place with what should have taken place to justify her. For instance, all O'Neill's letters begging her to join him make it clear that she insisted on leaving him alone against his will and his best judgment. Yet when she gave out the news of the divorce she made it appear that he had insisted on the "freedom" and she had kindly gone along with him, only to be injured and deserted. She declared, "This illusion of freedom—so long maintained by the male sex, particularly by the artistic male—is very much an illusion. Now I know that the only way to give a man the freedom he wants is to open the door to captivity." She added that she had "attempted the experiment of giving an artist-husband the freedom he said was necessary for his dramatic success." "Our Love Problem Dramatist Fights to Solve His Own," *New York Journal,* August 11, 1928.

"THE PLEDGE ON WHICH." In a letter to Benjamin De Casseres of April 29, 1928 (Dartmouth), O'Neill told him: "My wife is evidently going to take advantage of the present situation and try to 'Take me for all I've got,' in spite of the pledge on which our marriage was made."

"THE WHOLE PERFIDIOUS AGNES." Letter to Eleanor Fitzgerald of May 13, 1929 (*SL,* 339).

"DOUBLE-CROSSED." O'Neill said so in a letter to Benjamin De Casseres of September 15, 1928 (*SL,* 317).

"AS IF I'D BEEN." Letter of O'Neill to Theresa Helburn of July 13, 1928 (*SL,* 306).

"NOBODY EVER 'TOOK.' " Letter of September 15, 1928 (*SL,* 317).

THIS LURID TALE. The confession murder story has some of the elements— quite rearranged—of the sensational Hall-Mills case of that time.

"MY SOUL IS A BLACK." From the first draft of a December 1, 1926, letter to Carlotta (Correspondence).

page 134:

HUTCHINS HAPGOOD. See O'Neill's letter to Agnes, "Monday evening" [January 5?, 1920] (*SL,* 100). Memories of O'Neill's other friend, "Hutch," Charles Hutchinson Collins, may have mingled in the form of the minister's bullish masculinity. His death by pneumonia may have suggested to O'Neill death by pneumonia for the minister's wife.

MISTAKEN BIOGRAPHER BARRETT CLARK. On April 28, 1926, the *Work Diary* (1:25) shows O'Neill reading proofs on Clark's biography, finding "personal stuff in it mistaken." There were other associations with *Clark*—such as his nurse at Gaylord Farm—but those of Shane's nurse, associated with Agnes's betrayal, and of his erroneous biographer are probably the ones that brought "Clark" to his mind for the false confession in the girl's betrayal.

A OF AGNES. He had also chosen such a name for Abbie, the betraying wife of *Desire Under the Elms.*

BENJAMIN IN THE NOTES. Notes and Outline for *Dynamo* (Yale).

WHITE FRAME NEW ENGLAND. Years later, O'Neill said of his white frame New England cottage at Marblehead in a letter to Saxe Commins of July 26, 1948 (*SL,* 580) that it reminded him of the first house his father had bought in New London very close to the one he later built. O'Neill probably set the play "in a small town of Connecticut" (419) because the power plant he used as a model was there, for he made the surface facts of the play as unlike his own background as he could.

"THE RETURN OF THE." Notes and Outline for *Dynamo* (Yale). Probably he meant to write "Abraham and Isaac, Jacob etc." and it telescoped into "Jacob and Isaac."

page 135:

PERPETUAL RAGE AND. See O'Neill's letter to Eleanor Fitzgerald of May 13, 1929 (*SL*, 339).

FURIOUSLY, HE ASKED. See O'Neill's letter to Agnes [late March 1928] (*SL*, 281).

HE TOLD HAROLD DEPOLO. See letter postmarked May 9, 1928 (*SL*, 299).

"SHAME." "BLAME." "DANCE WITH FOLLY." From O'Neill's poem "Free," written on the deck of the *Charles Racine* bound for Buenos Aires, June 1910 (*Poems*, 1).

page 136:

"SPELLS OF DEJECTION." Letter from O'Neill to his father and mother of November 9, 1909 (*SL*, 18).

"HOW WE ALL FEEL." The *New York World* published this story on May 11, 1910.

ST. LOUIS ON MARCH 14. The March 15, 1910, *St. Louis Star* has an account of the opening with compliments to Viola Allen and James O'Neill as "surpassing in their naturalness."

"MY AMBITION, IF." Interview in the *New York Tribune*, February 22, 1920.

"I HADN'T ANY PARTICULAR." Alta May Coleman, "Personality Portraits: No. 3 Eugene O'Neill," *Theatre*, April 1920, p. 302.

pages 136–37:

"PSYCHOLOGICAL MESS." O'Neill told Lawrence Langner in a letter of March 25, 1929 (*SL*, 331) that his rewriting aimed at clarifying the boy's "psychological mess" over the betrayal by his mother and the conflict with his father.

page 137:

"WHEN I SURVEY." Letter from O'Neill to Nathan of August 31, 1929 (Cornell).

"DYNAMO STOPS—INTERLUDE." Floyd, 125.

BEGAN HIS FIRST NOTES. Notes and Outline for *Dynamo* (Yale).

MARCH 13, 1928. This day, the *Work Diary* (1:54) says, "Began work on 'Dynamo.' " He had moved into the "Villa Marguerite" on March 10.

"AMERICANS, AS A RESULT." Jung, 208.

"THE LAND OF THE MOTHER." Letter from O'Neill to Robert Sisk of March 11, 1929 (*SL*, 326).

"HUMANLY A FIGHT." Letter from O'Neill to Benjamin De Casseres of March 12, 1929 (*SL*, 328).

page 138:

"PHYSICALLY BY WHIPPING." Family history (Sheaffer II, 510).

"THE LOUSE" OF 1916. O'Neill gave this poem to John Reed to place for him.

I found it in the John Reed Collection at Harvard. No copy of it came to Yale, so Donald Gallup overlooked it when he edited *Poems*.

"DEVIOUS WAYS HIDDEN." So O'Neill expressed the theme of *Dynamo* in a letter to Benjamin De Casseres of March 12, 1929 (*SL*, 328).

HE SENT THEM BACK. In a letter to Lawrence Langner, probably late September 1928 (Yale), O'Neill says of Agnes; "And I no longer have the benefit of the lady's confidence, having decided months ago that any friendly basis was no longer possible, and since then sent back all letters unopened." Several of these letters have been preserved (Correspondence). Because they were sent from New Preston, Connecticut, they help to date the cut-off, for an article by John O'Donnell, "Wife Has Silent Part in O'Neill's Drama of Home" in the April 27, 1928, *New York Daily News*, reports that Mrs. Agnes O'Neill had arrived from Bermuda the day before and had gone to her mother's Connecticut farm without talking to reporters, so her letters date from the end of April or the beginning of May. One of them is particularly pathetic, for it gives a vivid account of Oona's attempts to write her father letters and of her eager questions, "Where is he? Is he coming back? Why doesn't he come back, I want him, Mummie," and her tears over his loss.

"WOOLY WITH HATRED." Letter to Eleanor Fitzgerald of May 13, 1929 (*SL*, 340).

page 139:

"LIKE COPPER WIRE." *Dynamo I.*

"RAISES HERSELF TO." "MOONY, PLACID COW." *Dynamo I.* In his review based on a typescript of *Dynamo I*, George Jean Nathan had made particular fun of the stage directions, and although O'Neill refuted Nathan's opinion that the play was "far, far below me," he added: "Not that you're not right about the excessiveness of the stage directions, but then I thought you knew that my scripts get drastically weeded out in that respect when I read proof." Nathan's joshing probably caused him to be particularly drastic in cutting stage directions of *Dynamo*, and much of his "cow" characterization of May went with them. Part of O'Neill's letter is reproduced in Angoff, 35.

"I LOVE LITTLE." *Dynamo I.*

"BLOWN ABOUT LIKE." "THIS CLOUD LIFE." First draft of a letter from O'Neill to Carlotta of December 1, 1926 (Correspondence). May has this thought right before Reuben carries out the imagery in the same letter of being locked in a black prison by an angry God the Father (act one, scene four), and the same scene completes the imagery when Reuben is locked in his room by his father.

"D'YOU REMEMBER WHEN." *Dynamo I.*

page 140:

"WHEN YOU BEGIN TO SMILE." Letter from O'Neill to Agnes, April 16, 1927 (*SL*, 240).

"IF WHOEVER PLAYS IT." Memorandum (September 9, 1928) (see Abbreviations).

"OH, FOR THE GOOD." Letter from O'Neill to Barrett Clark of November 15, 1932 (Sheaffer II, 409).

ACTUAL IMAGE OF DYNAMO. The letters to Agnes (Correspondence) show clearly that the idea for *Dynamo* came long before his visit to the power plant. All O'Neill's biographers have copied an erroneous story that Kenneth Macgowan set in motion (while doing a lecture series designed to coordinate with the Guild's road companies) when he learned from the Guild's public relations that O'Neill had visited a hydroelectric plant near Danbury. Macgowan assumed that O'Neill visited the plant by chance when he was living in nearby Ridgefield, Connecticut, and got his initial idea for the play from it. This error is repeated in Clark, 119–20; Gelb, 675; and Sheaffer II, 306.

GREAT HYDROELECTRIC PLANTS. So O'Neill wrote Agnes in a letter dated "Monday," September 19, 1927 (*SL*, 259), in which he also tells her of Wertheim's suggestion of the Niagara Falls plant.

"A BIG BUG." Letter from O'Neill to Agnes dated "Tuesday," September 27, 1927 (Correspondence).

"ISOLATED SPOT ON THE." O'Neill wrote Agnes of the Friday, September 30, trip to the plant in a letter dated "Tuesday," October 4, 1927 (Correspondence).

"PERMEATING POSSESSIVENESS." *Dynamo I.*

pages 140–41:

"THE STARTLING, STRAINED." Memorandum. O'Neill wanted the Guild to realize that this was an important part of his conception for the final scenes.

page 141:

"THE DUAL MOTHER ROLE." Chapter 7 of Jung's *Psychology of the Unconscious* bears this title.

"EXTRAORDINARILY ILLUMINATING." This is part of a letter that O'Neill wrote to Barrett Clark denying his idea that *Mourning Becomes Electra* follows Freud too precisely. He explained that Jung was the "only one of the lot who interests me" (Clark, 136).

"IN ORDER TO BE BORN." Jung, 251.

"DEADLY LONGING FOR." Jung, 390. In the same passage, Jung explains that this pull of death is "a deep personal longing for quiet and for the profound peace of non-existence."

"TERRIBLE MOTHER." Jung, 423. Jung (405) explains that "the power of the 'terrible mother' is magical and irresistible (working upward from the unconscious)."

SUPERINTENDENT OF THE STEVENSON. O'Neill shows that he understood the superintendent's control by pitch through Fife's reaction to the sound of the dynamo in *Dynamo I.* Later, when Lee Simonson, the scene designer, visited the Stevenson plant at O'Neill's suggestion, taking the cast along, the superintendent told him this, as he had probably told O'Neill, and Simonson marveled: "Here was a technician, like a violinist tuning his instrument, relying on his sense of musical pitch to control a machine where fluctuations had to be mathematically exact" (*The Stage Is Set*, 459).

"SHE USED TO REMIND." *Dynamo I.*

"EITHER THE BEAST." *Dynamo I.* Jung himself had analyzed the "terrible mother" Babylon in the New Testament book of Revelation and even quoted the words the minister uses: "Mother of Harlots and Abominations of the Earth" (Jung, 242–43). O'Neill was himself very familiar with Revelation, having dramatized it for Robert Edmond Jones's experiments with choral movements.

"LOATHSOME FEMALE DEITY." *Dynamo I.*

page 142:

"THE STAGE FOR AN." P. 254. Stekel goes on at this point to describe an exchange of role just like Reuben's compulsion to play his mother's role on the traumatic evening.

"EXIT—S.S. BERENGARIA!" *Work Diary*, 1:53.

IT WAS A BITTER BLOW. Agnes wrote a depressed little letter to O'Neill on February 17, 1928 (Correspondence), when she found out that he had gone to Europe with Carlotta, asking him to think of her when he saw the Europe she had once longed for them to see together.

"ULTIMATE GOAL." So O'Neill said in his letter to Doctor Lief of October 2, 1928, mailed a few days before he sailed for China.

JUST EIGHT MONTHS. The two sailings in flight from Kathleen began a few days before October 16, 1909 (when he was already at sea) and June 6, 1910. The two sailings in flight from Agnes were February 10, 1928, and October 5, 1928. Of course, O'Neill had reason for flight in his fear of being discovered by reporters.

THE PULL OF REUBEN'S. Letter from O'Neill to Benjamin De Casseres of March 12, 1929 (*SL*, 328).

page 143:

"GIVEN UP THE FLESH." O'Neill gives Reuben a psychology in line with Stekel's analysis of fetichism. For instance, in *Twelve Essays*, Stekel says: "*Fetichism is the refuge from women from ascetic motives*. To a fetichist woman is the personification of sin." Stekel's book on fetichism did not appear in English until 1934, long after O'Neill finished *Dynamo*. Yet a comparison of *Dynamo* with this work shows how creatively O'Neill was working with ideas from *Twelve Essays* and his own observations, for his picture of Reuben is very like the more complete picture of fetichism that Stekel arrived at in the later work.

"MORE THAN DESIRE." Letter from O'Neill to Kenneth Macgowan, ca. December 1, 1926 (Gelb, 624; Bryer, 138).

"THIS OBSCENE AND SNAILY." "SOME MADNESS." Letter from O'Neill to Agnes of September 11, 1927 (*SL*, 258).

SHE ANSWERED FIERCELY. "I see through." Agnes's Nadir Letter (Correspondence).

CARLOTTA WAS WITH HIM. *Work Diary*, 1:46, September 30, 1927.

"SHE'S TOO DEAD." So O'Neill said of Agnes in a letter to Kenneth Macgowan of September 21, 1928 (Bryer, 185).

page 144:

"YOU CHEATED ME—." *Dynamo I.*

"IMPURE MAID." Jung, 244.

"TO PACIFY THE ANGER." Jung, 475.

"MOTHER-BRIDE." Jung, 244.

"THE BOY'S PSYCHOLOGICAL." Letter from O'Neill to Eleanor Fitzgerald of May 13, 1929 (*SL*, 339).

"JENN." *Dynamo I.*

JENNINGS AND AN ITALIAN. *Dynamo I.* Although the Italian Rocco is a colorful character and Jennings is perfectly colorless, it was Jennings that O'Neill preserved in the published play. I believe he made the selection on the basis of their inner meaning for him: he needed his first divorce symbolically present, more than his former Catholicism.

THAT HER PISTOL WAS LOCKED. Agnes's Nadir Letter (Correspondence).

page 145:

AS SOON AS IT WAS TYPED. The date of completion, August 18, 1928, is written at the end of the first longhand script of *Dynamo* at Yale and also in his *Work Diary*, 1:57. O'Neill's letters to Saxe Commins (Princeton) show that Commins did the typing of *Dynamo*. He had given up dentistry and was trying to become a writer in Paris. As soon as O'Neill finished *Dynamo*, he set off for Paris on August 23 (*Work Diary*, 1:58).

"DYNAMO ACCEPTED." All the radiograms to and from O'Neill on the Guild's acceptance are at Yale.

"THAT FELL DEED." Letter from O'Neill to Langner of January 8, 1929 (Yale).

"THAT IS WHAT PRINCIPALLY." *MBE* Notes, 534. O'Neill made this note on July 18, 1930.

pages 145–46:

"SO PLAIN." "TOO OBVIOUS." So O'Neill told Robert Sisk in a letter of March 11, 1929 (*SL*, 326).

page 146:

"GREATLY MISSED 'GENE.'" See *The Magic Curtain*, 241.

"MOTHER COMPLEX." Theresa Helburn said that Gene had written her "that the play was about a mother complex, but that was never clear to me" (*A Wayward Quest*, 261).

"ALL THAT IS SOUND." Memorandum.

"RUIN THE CONTINUITY." Memorandum. O'Neill thought that they might make rapid changes by creating the sets "in sections on roller platforms" and could find a way to open or close rooms quickly by a "little ingenuity in a method for clamping on lowered wall sections." The Guild published his directions—but they added four words, "or perhaps even simpler," and so presented their actual complete change from what he asked for as fidelity to his suggestions. See "Some Designs of Latest Art Used by Guild," *New York Tribune*, December 14, 1929.

"ORTHODOX RUSSIAN CONSTRUCTIVIST." So O'Neill told Lawrence Langner in a letter of March 25, 1929 (*SL*, 331).

"LIVING NATURALLY IN." "Some Designs of Latest Art."

CHIEF MISTAKES IN. See letter to Langner, March 25, 1929 (*SL*, 331). The other mistakes O'Neill took upon himself. He told Robert Sisk on August 28, 1930 (*SL*, 267–68), that *Dynamo* had been a series of his mistakes. He had started writing while still too upset over the divorce. He had used the wrong method, sent it out too soon, and had created misunderstanding by talking about the idea for the trilogy when only one play of it was written.

"A GENERATOR SOUNDING." Memorandum.

"DON'T FORGET PERFECT." Cable, February 1, 1929 (Yale).

CHANGES HE MADE. See O'Neill to Benjamin De Casseres, March 12, 1929 (*SL*, 327).

DYNAMO OPENED ON. Langner's estimate of the performance in a letter to O'Neill of February 14, 1929 (Yale) was that Philip Moeller "did a magnificent job with the production"; that Glenn Anders's work as Reuben "was quite astounding"; that Claudette Colbert as Ada "was not as good as we hoped"; that Catherine Doucet as May "couldn't have been better (the suggestion that she burlesqued the part is ridiculous)"; that George Gaul's work as Hutchins Light was "as good as he can do"; that Dudley Digges as Ramsay Fife was "magnificent"; that Helen Westley as Amelia Fife was "very good." He also thought "Lee's sets simply marvelous." He reported that the audiences were all discussing the play and that it "delivers them a staggering emotional blow," but the critics "were all groping in the dark. They seem to think the play ought to solve all the problems of religion and were disappointed that it did not do so."

"AS IF IT WAS O'NEILL." In "Judging the Shows," *Judge*, undated clipping in the Theatre Guild Press Book at Yale.

"WHEN THOSE GANGRENED." Letter from O'Neill to Doctor Lief of March 16, 1929 (NYU). O'Neill told Robert Sisk in a letter of March 11, 1929 (*SL*, 326) that compared to what he had to take on *All God's Chillun Got Wings* the present critical panning was mild. He particularly recalled the viciousness of Heyward Broun, who later admitted that he had neither seen nor read the play. O'Neill also spoke of the imbecility of St. John Ervine to Robert Sisk on March 17, 1929 (*SL*, 330), for he, like Broun, was a disappointed playwright. O'Neill had agreed earlier with Dr. Lief, October 2, 1928 (NYU), "Yes, Ervine is a hidebound, conventional-theatre English-Irish ass." Horst Frenz has collected Ervine's pronouncements on O'Neill, and they certainly show that O'Neill's estimate of him was accurate. ("St. John Ervine on Eugene O'Neill," in *Festschrift für Walther Fischer*, ed. Carl Winter (Heidelberg: Universitätsverlag, 1959.)

"HUMAN PSYCHOLOGICAL STRUGGLE." Letter to Robert Sisk, March 11, 1929 (*SL*, 326).

"BOLDLY PITS THE GOD." Burns Mantle was syndicated. This happens to come from the *Grand Forks (N.D.) Herald*, February 24, 1929.

HOW ANYONE COULD THINK. O'Neill had asked Benjamin De Casseres this in a letter of March 12, 1929 (*SL*, 328).

page 147:

"BLUNDERED HORRIBLY." So O'Neill told Lawrence Langner in a letter of March 25, 1929 (*SL*, 331). He had not meant "trilogy" in the usual sense, and he had not meant to offer a religious answer.

TO KEEP ABSOLUTELY SECRET. When Saxe Commins returned to the United States from Paris, O'Neill gave him some information he wanted disseminated, and part of it concerned the trilogy. In a letter of August 4, 1929 (Princeton), he told Saxe: "Yes, what you gave Atkinson was all right—except that I'm not off the other two plays of the trilogy for good—will certainly write them after a year or two. They're too good to let go. But it's true I am off of having the three combined as a trilogy, as I told you. Probably no one but me would ever see the trilogy relationship, each is so entirely different from the others."

"I KNOW THE MAJORITY." Letter from O'Neill to Liveright of February 17, 1929 (Dartmouth).

"WHY NOT MOVE." Cable from O'Neill to the Guild (Yale). The Guild had put *Dynamo* into the large Martin Beck Theatre to correct their error of putting *Strange Interlude* into the small John Golden Theatre, so that they had not been able to capitalize on its success.

"BUNK" OF THE CRITICS. Letter from O'Neill to Harold DePolo of May 11, 1929 (*SL*, 337).

"DISMAYED ME THIS TIME." Letter from O'Neill to Robert Sisk of March 16, 1929 (Yale).

DYNAMO HAD BECOME MUDDLED. See letter to Robert Sisk, March 11, 1929 (*SL*, 326).

"THE WORKS." "CUTTING AND INTERPOLATING." Undated letter from O'Neill to Doctor Lief, ca. March, 1929 (NYU).

"SIMPLIFYING." O'Neill stressed the simplifying in a letter to Robert Sisk of March 16, 1929 (Yale).

PUT IN TWO NEW SCENES. At first, O'Neill spoke of putting in *three* new scenes, and he told Robert Sisk in the letter of March 16, 1929 (Yale): "They were in my original plan—sketched out—but I was afraid they would make the play too long for one play and not long enough for a double." The letters to Saxe Commins on the typing show also that there were originally to be three new scenes. By the time he had finished, O'Neill had cut them to two. Before Saxe Commins left for the United States, O'Neill told him in a letter of April 6, 1929 (Princeton): "Say that the failure of Dynamo left me cold— that I was not satisfied with it when I read it over on returning from the East and have worked on it for the book, putting in two new scenes I had originally planned for it." The letter to Eleanor Fitzgerald of May 13, 1929 (*SL*, 339) also has two.

"THE WOMAN." "I MUST SAVE." *Dynamo I.*

"BEWARE, REUBEN!" *Dynamo I.* The cry is partly a quote from Revelation.

page 148:

"DOLEFUL TENDERNESS." "ME THAT WAS BORN." Letter from O'Neill to Robert Sisk of March 17, 1929 (*SL*, 330).

"AM SORRY TO SAY." Letter from O'Neill to Liveright of June 14, 1929 (Dartmouth).

"I LIKE IT BETTER." Letter from O'Neill to Krutch of July 27, 1929 (Sheaffer II, 326; *SL*, 350). Krutch too had missed the point of the play entirely, and he has been responsible for a misconception about the origin of *Dynamo* that has persisted (for instance, in Bogard, 319–20; Sheaffer II, 306). In an article in the February 27, 1929, *Nation*, "The Virgin and Dynamo," Krutch had compared O'Neill's play with Henry Adams's chapter "The Dynamo and the Virgin" in *The Education of Henry Adams*. His followers have assumed that O'Neill got the idea for *Dynamo* from Adams. O'Neill had indeed read and admired Adams's book, and his first copy inscribed "Old Peaked Hill Bar, June 1920" is preserved at Yale. But he certainly did not need Adams's description of the 1900 dynamo in the shape of a "huge wheel" as a symbol of "infinite force." By the 1920s the dynamo had become an omnipresent image transforming the country. After he read Krutch's review, O'Neill bought another copy of Adams's book, as he had left the old one with Agnes, to check on Krutch. (His copy, preserved in the C. W. Post Collection, is inscribed "Le Plessis '29," so he must have bought it after he moved there in May.) When he reread it, he must have seen at once how totally different Adams's view was from his own. Adams found it very difficult to reconcile the ancient worship of Woman as a force (as Venus or the Virgin) with the modern image of the dynamo as force. He saw them as "two kingdoms of force which had nothing in common but attraction" (that is, the attraction they had for his mind). O'Neill, by way of more recent physics, had his protagonist amalgamate those two symbols of force, the Woman and the Dynamo, which Adams had felt he could only turn between "as though he were a Branley coherer." From the very beginning O'Neill had been perfectly clear that he was dealing with the failure of "our old Gods and our new sciences, from a psychological and symbolical angle that hasn't been touched before." Letter to Theresa Helburn, July 13, 1928 (*SL*, 306).

HE TALKED OF WRITING. He told Ward Morehouse that " 'Dynamo' had in it the making of a fine play, but I did it too fast." He was also reported as saying in "The Ramblings of Talk with Eugene O'Neill" in the January 3, 1934, *Boston Evening Transcript:* "There is 'Dynamo' to be rewritten, so that matter and form shall more clearly express his design." O'Neill certainly did not want *Dynamo* among his representative work, for a letter from Saxe Commins, then his editor, tells O'Neill on October 7, 1932 (Princeton): "Your condition that GOLD, THE FIRST MAN, WELDED, DYNAMO

and THE FOUNTAIN should be omitted was observed" for a planned Book
of the Month Club collection of his plays.

"CRIPPLED CHILD OF THE." From the dedication of a copy of the first trade
edition of *Dynamo* to Carlotta, October 1929 (he wrote "cripled") (*Inscriptions*).

"ABOUT CHARACTERS PLUS LIFE." Letter to Lawrence Langner, August 24,
1941 (*SL*, 522).

7. Mourning Becomes Electra

page 149:

"LIFE IS GROWTH." O'Neill said so in a letter to Saxe Commins of August 4,
1929 (Princeton).

"MAKE THE WORLD." From a letter to Carlotta of December 4, 1929 (*Inscriptions*).

"IT'S THE SORT OF." Letter of August 4, 1929 (Princeton).

"THE BIGGEST AND HARDEST." Letter from O'Neill to Shane of May 27, 1930
(Virginia).

"A MODERN PSYCHOLOGICAL." *MBE* Notes, 530.

pages 149–50:

"OF THE FORCE." "FATE, GOD." From a letter to Arthur Hobson Quinn, April
3, 1925 (Cargill, 125–26; *SL*, 195), which declares: "Where the theatre is
concerned, one must have a dream, and the Greek dream in tragedy is the
noblest ever!" Among some plays O'Neill thought should be included in a
National Theatre repertory, he listed Aeschylus's *Agamemnon, Choephoroe,*
and *Eumenides;* Sophocles' *Antigone;* and Euripides' *Medea.* "What Shall
We Play?" *Theatre Arts,* February 1941, p. 147.

page 150:

"PRIMARILY DRAMA OF." *MBE* Notes, "April, 1929," 531.

"AT LAST BE FREE." From O'Neill's poem "Free," written on the *Charles Racine* and first published in the *Pleiades Club Year Book* for 1912 (*Poems,* 1).

"CENTER OF WHOLE." "SEA BACKGROUND OF." *MBE* Notes, "March 27,
1930," 533.

"ROMANTIC GRAMMAR-SCHOOL-." *MBE* Notes, "April, 1929," 531.

"ONLY POSSIBILITY." "DRAMA OF MURDEROUS." "MASK." *MBE* Notes, "April,
1929," 531.

"ARABIAN SEA EN." *MBE* Notes, "October, 1928," 530.

"CHINA SEA." *MBE* Notes, "November, 1928," 530.

"SEAPORT, SHIPBUILDING TOWN." *MBE* Notes, "April, 1929," 531.

"N.L." In his Plot Notes (Yale), O'Neill said that his first Clytemnestra, like his
own mother, "has always hated the town of N.L. and felt superior disdain

for its inhabitants" (Floyd, 188, reads "felt a superior disdain"). O'Neill called these notes his "first fruits (very unripe!)."

"PURITAN CONVICTION OF." *MBE* Notes, "April, 1929," 531.

"MANNON," SUGGESTIVE OF "MAN." Sheaffer thinks that O'Neill chose *Mannon* to suggest "Mammon" (Sheaffer II, 338). Because their wealth is largely extraneous to their tragedy, this is not likely. Even in *The Great God Brown* O'Neill had suggested the universal significance of his hero's struggle by having Cybel answer, when the policeman asks his name, "Man" (323).

page 151:

"STRANGE QUALITY OF UNREAL." *MBE* Notes, "August, 1931," 536. The MBE Notes show that O'Neill finished his first draft on February 21, 1930. When he picked it up again on "March 27 (533), he noted that he wanted "more sense of the unreal behind what we call reality which is the real reality!— The unrealistic truth wearing the mask of lying reality, that is the right feeling for this trilogy, if I can only catch it!"

EACH ONE HAS THE CURTAIN. Sean O'Casey was so struck with this idea of penetrating a curtain to a deeper dimension of reality that he borrowed it for his play *Within the Gates*, noting that it came "from Eugene O'Neill's suggestion of a front curtain for his great play, *Mourning Becomes Electra*." See O'Casey's *Collected Plays* (London: Macmillan, 1950), 2:114.

"GREEK TEMPLE FRONT." "ABSOLUTELY JUSTIFIABLE." MBE Notes, "April, 1929," 531.

HOWARD MAJOR'S *DOMESTIC*. O'Neill's copy of Major's book (Philadelphia: Lippincott, 1926) is in the Post Collection; Marshall House appears on plate 23. O'Neill probably lent his copy to Robert Edmond Jones when he designed the settings for *Mourning Becomes Electra*, and Jones followed the plaster walls of the plate, rather than O'Neill's extension of the stone base all the way up the facade.

"WHOM THE PAST." So O'Neill told Harold DePolo in a letter [postmarked May 9, 1928] (*SL*, 299).

page 152:

"REVISIT PEQUOT AVE. OLD." *Work Diary*, 1:104, July 1, 1931.

"IDEA PLAY—HOUSE-." *Work Diary*, 1:105, July 17, 1931.

"EXTERIOR CHARACTERIZATION." *MBE* Notes, "March 27, 1930," 533.

"ALMOST CHARACTERLESS." *MBE* Notes, "March 27, 1930," 533.

"INNER." "AS FAR AS POSSIBLE." *MBE* Notes, "March 27, 1930," 533.

"IN THE WAY OF." *MBE* Notes, "July 18, 1930," 534.

"NEEDED GREAT LANGUAGE." So O'Neill told Arthur Hobson Quinn in a letter of 1932 reprinted in Quinn's *History of American Drama* (New York: Crofts, 1936), 2:165, 206.

"FORCEFUL REPEATING ACCENT." "COMPULSION OF PASSIONS." *MBE* Notes, "July 19, 1930," 534.

THE RHYTHM WAS SO. Alla Nazimova declared that she and the others could not "substitute words or phrases" as they usually did "without throwing the entire passage out of rhythm and spoiling the effect. We have to be letter perfect in our parts, and that's hard work." (Lucius Beebe, "Nazimova Regrets Her Vamping Days," unlabeled clipping in the Theatre Guild Press Book, No. 125 [Yale].)

"GENERAL SPIRIT." "DETAILS OF LEGEND." *MBE* Notes, "April, 1929," 531. O'Neill had a copy of Aeschylus with the Greek on one page and the English translation by Herbert Weir Smyth in the Loeb Classical Library (London: 1926), vol. 2 (Post Collection). He also bought *A Classical Dictionary of Greek and Roman Biography* by Sir William Smith (London: Murray, 1925). His copy inscribed "Villa Les Mimosas '29" is at Yale.

page 153:

"HUSBAND HATES ENGLISH." Sheaffer II, 511–12.

WHAT IS WRONG WITH MARRIAGE (New York: Boni, 1929). Kenneth Macgowan told me in a letter of October 22, 1948: "I believe O'Neill read the joint book and probably some of the articles which appeared in magazines."

"IDEAL OF FEMININE BEAUTY." *What Is Wrong with Marriage,* 124.

"WITH A LARGE KISS." *Inscriptions.* The dedication is dated by O'Neill "Beacon Farm August 1931."

ALL REFLECTED SARAH SANDY. Sheaffer produces a dim photograph of Sarah, squinting in the sun, which has these features, and he declares that she had "reddish-blond" hair and "grayish-blue eyes" (Sheaffer II, 53 and 23, respectively).

"TELL HIM MY ADVICE." Letter to Agnes of January 29, 1920 (*SL*, 111).

KATHLEEN JENKINS. The May 11, 1910, *New York World* printed a large photograph of Kathleen.

page 154:

"HAIR BLACK AS NIGHT." First draft of *Mourning Becomes Electra* (Yale).

SHANE'S NURSE FIFINE CLARK. Part of a letter to Shane from O'Neill in the spring of 1928 (Correspondence) tells him: "You remember how Gaga could speak French? Well, she would be right at home here because that is the language all the people around here speak." A letter to Agnes [April 8, 1928] (*SL*, 284) pleads with her to take Mrs. Clark back, for they had both loved her; their children had loved her; and she had loved and stood by them from the day of Shane's birth.

"PSYCHIC IDENTITY." *MBE* Notes, "March 27, 1930," 533.

page 155:

DEEP PURPLISH CRIMSON. So it is described in the first typescript of *Mourning Becomes Electra* (Yale). In the third play, Lavinia wears a "copy of her mother's dress with the deep crimson color predominating."

"STRANGE, HIDDEN PSYCHIC." *MBE* Notes, "March 27, 1930," 533.

"HAVE WRITTEN *MOURNING*." Apparently Clark read the play before production and made what O'Neill called a "Freudian objection." O'Neill told him, "Authors were psychologists, you know, and profound ones, before psychology was invented" (Clark, 136).

"MODERN PSYCHOLOGICAL APPROXIMATION." His very first note of "Spring—1926" asks if he can get such an approximation (*MBE* Notes, 530).

page 156:

THE LEGENDARY REASONS. For a while, O'Neill thought of including a Cassandra character, but she demanded straight Greek characters, as he noted in his *Work Diary*, 1:75, on September 25, 1929. By September 27 he had become "disgusted" with the idea and abandoned it.

A HUSBAND'S INEPTITUDE. P. 207.

page 157:

"HACKNEYED AND THIN." *MBE* Notes, "March 27, 1930," 532.

CAPTAIN BRASSBOUND'S CONVERSION. In a letter to Beatrice Ashe dated "Wednesday" of May 13, 1915 (Berg), O'Neill tells her that his friend Felton Elkins has invited him to see this play of Shaw's in a box at the Toy Theatre and that he would wear evening clothes. He had been reading Shaw ever since his prep school days.

"WITH THE DEATH OF." *Selected Plays of Bernard Shaw* (New York: Dodd, Mead, 1948), 1:640.

"VERY FOND." "VERY GOOD." "SHE HAD." *Selected Plays of Shaw*, 646–47.

"HE DID NOT SPARE." *Selected Plays of Shaw*, 640. In "Captain Brant and Captain Brassbound: The Origin of an O'Neill Character," *Modern Language Notes*, April 1959, 306–10, I have listed all the similarities between the two.

CLIPPER BOOKS O'NEILL. O'Neill's large, lifelong collection of Clipper books has been preserved in the Post Collection. Among those he probably bought for *Mourning Becomes Electra* are Arthur Clark's *Clipper Ship Era*, Carl Cutler's *Greyhounds of the Sea*, Alfred Lubbock's first two volumes of *Sail: The Romance of the Clipper Ships*, Howe and Matthews's *American Clipper Ships*, and Richard McKay's *Some Famous Sailing Ships and Their Builder Donald McKay*. All O'Neill's Clipper details are authentic, from the black hull of Brant's ship below the waterline to its name, *The Flying Trades*, after such genuine ships as the *Flying Cloud*, the *Flying Dragon*, the *Flying Fish*, the *Flying Scud*, and the *Flying Dutchman*.

CAPTAIN ROBERT H. WATERMAN. I have corrected the erroneous "Watermann" in Random House, 2:105, to the correct "Waterman," which O'Neill certainly used, for he was very exact about all the Clipper lore in *Mourning Becomes Electra*. The picture of Waterman he saw is in Clark's *The Clipper Ship Era* (New York, 1910) opposite page 152, and the Captain's romantic outfit stands in sharp contrast to the sober suits of other skippers. "Bully" Waterman's reputation as a bully reached a climax on his ship the *Challenge*,

New York to San Francisco, when so many of the crew died on the way
(including some mutineers he slew with a belaying pin) that a mob gathered
to lynch him.

"TOWN'S LEADING CITIZEN." *MBE* Notes, "April, 1929," 531.

page 158:

"HARSH AND UNREASONABLE." Letter to Agnes dated "Friday" [April 22,
1927] (*SL*, 242).

CONFIDED TO KENNETH MACGOWAN. The letter, with what he confided suppressed, is in Bryer, 184–86. The nature of the confidence was reported in
Gelb, 679.

"IMAGINING THAT SHE HAD." First longhand draft of *Days Without End* (Yale).

"I'M SIMPLY EATEN UP." Letter dated "Thursday" [September 29?, 1927] (*SL*,
261).

"HIDING WITHIN A." "BEGINS AND ENDS." These words come from an intimate
poem that O'Neill wrote about himself, apparently on August 17, 1942
(*Poems,* 103, 102).

"INEXPRESSIVE." This was a word that O'Neill used to describe himself when
telling Agnes that he loved his children as much as she did, maybe more, in
his "oblique, inexpressive fashion," in a letter [ca. April 8, 1928] (*SL*, 284).

"LIKE EZRY MANNON." From a telegram addressed to "The Mourning Becomes Electra Company," October 26, 1931 (Moeller Collection).

page 159:

"WE MUST GET AWAY." Letter to Agnes of April 16, 1927 (*SL*, 241).

"I LOVE YOU!" Letter to Agnes of April 16, 1927 (*SL*, 240).

"COMMIT MURDER WITHOUT." *MBE* Notes, "July 11, 1929," 532. O'Neill also
managed to make the murder of Adam Brant in his second play appear to
be a ship robbery.

"MEDICINE." "POISON." See, for example, pp. 74, 78, 103, 116, 123, 139.

"O'NEILL MEANT AT FIRST." See the first drafts of *Mourning Becomes Electra*
(Yale).

page 160:

"FIERCE" AFFECTION. In his family history (Sheaffer II, 512) O'Neill's words
are "fierce concentration of affection."

"MY BABY." "NURSE." "COMFORTABLE." Compare *Mourning Becomes Electra,*
76, with *Long Day's Journey into Night,* 118; and *Mourning Becomes Electra,* 80–81, with *Long Day's Journey into Night,* 42–43.

"IDEA M-HARLOT PLAY." The *Work Diary,* 1:159, dates this for April 24, 1933.
It came from a "dream."

page 161:

OWN "POISONED" FAMILY LIFE. O'Neill connected his mother's poison with
the unhappiness of his marriage to Agnes. He talked (for instance, in his
[December 26?, 1927] letter to Agnes) of the "poisonous bitterness and

resentment" in the marriage (*SL*, 271). In his letter to Harold DePolo [post-marked May 9, 1928] (*SL*, 299) he spoke of his "home poisoned" by barely concealed hostility.

page 162:

ONE OF THE SOUTH SEA. In the first typescript (Yale), O'Neill specified the islands that Orin and Lavinia stop at as "the Marquesas" of Melville, but in the later versions, he left the islands vague, partly to enhance their dream-unconscious origins and partly because he realized from his Clipper readings that the Sandwich (Hawaiian) Islands would be the logical stop for a Clipper after a China voyage.

"MOTHER SYMBOL." "YEARNING FOR PRE-NATAL." *MBE* Notes, "March 27, 1930," 533.

page 163:

"IN THE LIGHT OF." Clark, 136.

"ON THE DUNES." This was one of the poems O'Neill left with John Reed in 1916. The Yale copy must have been without title, for it appears in *Poems*, 71, without one.

"SOUL MOTHER OF MINE." From a letter to Beatrice Ashe dated "Friday night," of February 5, 1915 (Berg). He tells her, in the words of Kipling's British soldier yearning for Mandalay, that he would like to wake up in a "cleaner, greener," land with her beside him.

"ULTIMATE ISLAND." Letter of April 16, 1927 (*SL*, 239).

"THE ISLES OF REST." The envelopes in the letters sent from Bermuda in Correspondence are stamped "Come to Bermuda / The Isles of Rest."

"PETER OLDHAM." Plot Notes (Yale). O'Neill's father, in *Long Day's Journey into Night*, calls himself the "poor old ham" (128). "Peter," I suspect, came by association with O'Neill's idea that Electra "peters out into undramatic married banality" in the legends (*MBE* Notes, "November, 1928," 530). Who better to peter out with than Peter?

"HESTER SAND." Plot Notes (Yale).

"MY PURE AND UNSPOILED." Letter to Carlotta of May 25, 1932 (*Inscriptions; SL*, 399).

page 164:

DOWN THE NILE. O'Neill talks of this prospective trip in a letter to Manuel Komroff of August 23, 1930 (Columbia). He tells Komroff that he has "a greater intuitive hunch for their feeling about life and death than for any other culture."

"ALL THE BITTERNESS." Undated letter from O'Neill to Shane and Oona [ca. January 31, 1929] (*SL*, 323).

"A LOT FOR MY." Letter to Eleanor Fitzgerald, May 13, 1929 (*SL*, 339).

"SON OF THE COUNT." Letter to Barrett Clark, June 21, [1929] (*SL*, 344).

"CALLED SONS OF BITCHES." Letter to Robert Sisk, March 17, 1929 (*SL*, 330).

"AND NOW COMES." Letter of May 11, 1929 (*SL*, 336–37).

page 165:

HIS CHARACTERS REPEAT. O'Neill made a note to aim for such repetition on September 21, 1930, in *MBE* Notes, 535.

O'NEILL'S OWN EXPECTATION. Orin suspects Lavinia with the first mate of the ship on which they voyage to China. During rehearsals O'Neill shortened his name to Wilkins, but until then he had been called "Wilkinson." Wilkinson was the name of Agnes's obstetrician for the birth of Oona (O'Neill speaks of him in a letter to Dr. William Maloney of February 18, 1925, Maloney Papers, Manuscript Division, New York Public Library). The name was associated with Agnes, even if O'Neill's distrust of Agnes was not actually directed at Dr. Wilkinson. Of course, O'Neill had other associations with the name, such as Keefe and Wilkinson's store in New London, mentioned in a letter to Beatrice Ashe of "Monday evening," January 14, 1915 (Berg).

"GHOSTS!" O'Neill was thoroughly familiar with Ibsen's play *Ghosts,* and knew the moments when the past suddenly repeats itself in that play. He probably realized that he was taking up Ibsen's idea and giving it a new application.

"I'VE TRIED TO SHOW." First typescript of *Mourning Becomes Electra* (Yale).

"LEGALIZED BLACKMAIL." One of several places in which O'Neill speaks of Agnes's divorce demands as legalized blackmail is his letter to Harold DePolo, postmarked May 9, 1928 (*SL*, 300).

"REFUSAL TO ACCEPT." Letter of February 14, 1929 (Cornell). O'Neill told Nathan that he thought the clause was necessary because "even before we separated I knew she was dickering with an agent about an article of that nature."

page 166:

PAGEANT OF GREECE. Manuel Komroff had sent O'Neill some books, and O'Neill told him in a letter of March 22, 1926 (*SL*, 200) that Livingstone's book looked like just what he wanted.

"MORAL INSENSITIVENESS." *Pageant of Greece* (Oxford: Clarendon Press, 1924), 118.

"PETERS OUT INTO." *MBE* Notes, "November, 1928," 530.

"A LESSER POET." "MORE WORTHY." "FROM THE WORLD." *Pageant of Greece,* 119–20.

"WORTHY" TRAGIC ENDING. It is probably significant that O'Neill, so sensitive to words, repeats Livingstone's "worthy," in his note telling himself he must "give modern Electra figure in play tragic ending worthy of character" (*MBE* Notes, "November, 1928," 530).

"LIFE-LIKE DEATH MASKS." *MBE* Notes, "September 21, 1930," 535.

"NEW ERA." "MY INNER SELF." So O'Neill told Bio De Casseres in a letter of May 10, [1929] (*SL*, 335).

page 167:

"FOR EVERYTHING REAL." Letter from O'Neill to Harold DePolo [postmarked May 9, 1928], (*SL*, 299).

"A VICTORY OF LOVE-." O'Neill dedicated *Mourning Becomes Electra* to Carlotta on April 23, 1931, *Inscriptions.*

SENT THE FIFTH. In a letter to Terry Helburn of April 7, 1931, O'Neill says; "I am sending the script of *Mourning Becomes Electra* by this same mail—two scripts—so that the committee can get quick action on it" (*A Wayward Quest,* 262).

"AND THE WEAR AND." Letter of August 23, 1930 (Columbia).

ALLA NAZIMOVA AS IBSEN'S. *Hedda Gabler* had thirty-two performances, opening March 11, 1907, at the Bijou Theatre in New York with Alla Nazimova in the title role. See *Best Plays of 1899–1909: And The Yearbook of the Drama in America,* ed. Burns Mantle and Garrison P. Sherwood (New York: Dodd, Mead, 1944), 439.

"DISCOVERED AN ENTIRE." Letter from O'Neill to Mr. Olav of May 13, 1938, paying "tribute to Ibsen's memory" (published in *Nordisk Tidende,* "America's Leading Norwegian Newspaper," June 2, 1938 [*SL,* 477]).

"WOULD BE GRAND." The Guild had suggested Nazimova in their cable of acceptance, and O'Neill cabled this message back from Paris, April 28, 1931 (*SL,* 382).

"THE GREATEST ACTRESS." "Dr. Hauptmann Hails U.S. Idea of 'Be Yourself,' " *New York Herald Tribune,* March 17, 1932. Hauptmann said the "two high spots" of his visit to the United States "were my meeting with Eugene O'Neill and attendance of 'Mourning Becomes Electra' last evening."

ALICE BRADY. O'Neill's friend George Jean Nathan had interested him in Lillian Gish, and he gave her the play first, but when she read it for O'Neill and the Guild they all found her too fragile. O'Neill reported to Terry Helburn on August 20, 1931 (*SL,* 392) that he had told Lillian the truth and she took it like a good sport; but he had hated having to do it. They also thought of Ann Harding, but she was tied up with cinema contracts.

"THE FINEST WORK OF." Letter from O'Neill to Dudley Nichols of May 29, 1932 (*SL,* 400).

page 168:

HE WAS SORRY. O'Neill told Barrett Clark in a letter of December 15, 1944: "I made too many cuts in *Mourning Becomes Electra* and let too many of them (but not all) stay in the book. It was a fuller, better play in its final written version, I think" (Clark, 149; *SL,* 567). The book was published on November 2, 1931.

"WONDER WITH HORROR." "NO ONE SHOULD." Morton Eustis, "Backstage with Alice Brady, the Guild's Modern Electra," *New York Evening Post,* October 31, 1931.

"FAREWELL (FOR ME)." *Work Diary,* 1:111, October 25, 1931.

"WORN OUT—DEPRESSED." *Work Diary,* 1:111, October 28, 1931. He started work on his other Greek plot idea, Medea, at once, but for December 30 his *Work Diary,* 1:116, says that he read a description of Lenormand's "Medea" in a *Paris Herald* clipping and that it had "great similarity to way I'd worked it out in my tentative outline—so guess I must abandon idea—too bad!"

"A GREAT GUILD." Letter from O'Neill to Terry Helburn of May 16, 1944 (*A Wayward Quest,* 278–79; *SL,* 558). O'Neill always resented the fact that the Guild left *Mourning Becomes Electra* off the list of achievements at the bottom of their letter paper, particularly as some of the plays on the list were "merely things to hang on a hook in a backwoods privy!"

"*OEDIPUS* AND *HAMLET.*" "Our Electra," *The Nation,* November 18, 1931.

PLAYED TO PACKED. See letter to Terry Helburn, May 16, 1944 (*SL,* 558).

SHE WAS OFTEN BETTER. Letter to Dudley Nichols, May 29, 1932 (*SL,* 400).

"A SUBSTANTIAL ADVANCE." "NO GO." "TELL BRIGHT." Letter to Richard Madden of September 24, 1932 (Dartmouth).

NEW TRIUMPHS IN PORTUGAL. O'Neill speaks of these productions in his letter to Terry Helburn of May 16, 1944 (*SL,* 558).

ALL FOR A FILM. In a letter to Terry Helburn of July 29, 1941 (*SL,* 520) O'Neill tells her he is very much for her idea of a film with Katharine Hepburn and Bette Davis with Pascal as director.

"I SO DEEPLY REGRET." From the May 16, 1944 letter to Terry Helburn (*SL,* 558).

DUDLEY NICHOLS PRODUCED IT. Katina Paxinou was Christine and Rosalind Russell was Lavinia. O'Neill saw the stills and telegraphed Nichols on June 12, 1947 (Yale) that Rosalind Russell "continues to grow and grow" and that Michael Redgrave was an "ideal Orin."

page 169:

R.K.O. CUT IT. O'Neill told Dudley Nichols in a letter of December 4, 1948 (*SL,* 582) that he had no intention of ever seeing the mutilated *Mourning Becomes Electra.* It was just one more sign that culture had been banished from the world in favor of mob negative destiny.

LARGELY FOR *MOURNING.* O'Neill said so in his letter to Terry Helburn of May 16, 1944 (*SL,* 558).

"THE MOST PERSONAL." "Eugene O'Neill Undramatic Over Honor of Nobel Prize," *Seattle Daily Times,* November 12, 1936.

"THE BEST OF ALL." Letter from O'Neill to Professor Frederic Ives Carpenter of March 24, 1945 (in Carpenter's *Eugene O'Neill* [New York: Twayne, 1964], 75).

8.   Ah, Wilderness!

page 171:

"SKYSCRAPER CANYONS." O'Neill's notes for "Without Endings of Days" (December 2, 1931) sets one scene in a canyon-street with a breadline (O'Neill's spelling is *cañons*). Floyd, 152, reads "dead line" for "bread line."

"THE OLD GODS." First longhand script of *Days Without End* (Yale).

"FORMULA OF TRAGEDY." So O'Neill is quoted as saying in "O'Neill Off Duty."
"EVEN THE MOST POSITIVE." Letter of May 29, 1932 (*SL*, 400).
"BATTLE WITH IT AGAIN." *Work Diary*, 1:138.

page 172:

"FULLY FORMED AND READY." So O'Neill wrote in the *Work Diary* (1:138) on
September 1.

TITLE AND ALL. In a letter to Saxe Commins of January 3, 1933 (Princeton),
O'Neill sends him *Ah, Wilderness!* for typing, explaining, "I woke up one
morning with this play fully in mind—never had had even a hint of an idea
about it before—title and all. Immediately laid aside "Without Endings of
Days," on which I was laboring. Wrote the whole damned thing in the month
of September. Evidently my unconscious had been rebelling for a long time
against creation in the medium of the modern, involved, complicated,
warped and self-poisoned psyche and demanded a counter-statement of
simplicity and the peace that tragedy troubles but does not poison." Later,
in a report of an interview with O'Neill ("O'Neill Turns to Simple Folk,"
New York Post, October 11, 1933), a reporter wrote that O'Neill told him,
"Only one play idea has come to him as quickly as that of 'Ah, Wilderness!'
It was 'Desire Under the Elms,' and it arrived in much the same way."

SEPTEMBER 6 HE BEGAN. O'Neill wrote the date September 6, 1932, at the
start of the first longhand script of *Ah, Wilderness!* (Museum of the City of
New York), and wrote "September 27, 1932" at its final curtain.

"CRYING TO BE WRITTEN." So O'Neill wrote in his *Work Diary*, 1:138, on
September 2, 1932.

"WORK WITHOUT INTERRUPTION." *Work Diary*, 1:139, September 11, 1932.

THE FOURTH IN 1931. O'Neill was in New London on July 1, his *Work Diary*
(1:104) says, and he told Lawrence Langner on July 6, 1931 (Yale) that he
had just returned from a trip to Shelter Island and New London and had
been in bed with a cold caught on it.

"HOUSE-WITH-THE-MASKED." *Work Diary*, 1:105, July 17, 1931.

"ON THE HOP." O'Neill wrote Robert Sisk on July 4, 1932 (*SL*, 402) telling him
this, and also that visiting him were Eugene Jr. and his wife and Shane—."
The *Work Diary*, 1:132–33, notes their arrival on July 1 and their departure
on July 15.

"THE OLD SOLIDARITY." O'Neill told Kenneth Macgowan [October 16, 1933]
(Bryer, 204; *SL*, 423) that we hanker after that "old solidarity," and he attributes the popularity of *Ah, Wilderness!* to this hankering. Shane and Eugene Jr. were reminders of the shattering of that unity. Earlier that year
there had been Cynthia Chapman, Carlotta's daughter by a former marriage, and O'Neill thought of his own daughter Oona, who had been too
small to come with Shane.

TOTAL-RECALL FAMILY. O'Neill said that the Millers were "general types true
for any large small-town," in a letter to Arthur McGinley of December 5,
1933. All the letters to McGinley were in his possession when I transcribed
them.

"I REALLY KNOW." So O'Neill told Saxe Commins in a letter of January 3, 1933
(Princeton).

ART McGINLEY THOUGHT. Arthur McGinley told me so.

JUDGE FREDERIC P. LATIMER. See, for instance, Sheaffer I, 228.

REDOLENT OF NEW LONDON. In a letter to Philip Moeller of August 19, 1933
(*SL*, 421) O'Neill told him he must not think of *Ah, Wilderness!* as a New
England play. Connecticut had never been really New England, and the play
might have been laid in the Midwest or the Far West without changing more
than a word or two. He had naturally had his own home town, New London,
in mind, but even in his youth it had been more like New York than New
England.

page 173:

"GHOST-HAUNTED INNER DARK." So O'Neill described his mind in a prose
poem to Carlotta of May 25, 1932 (*Inscriptions; SL*, 399).

"JULY 4TH, 1905." In the first longhand script of *Ah, Wilderness!* (Museum of
the City of New York), O'Neill started with 1905, then changed to 1907, and
finally settled on 1906.

PROSE POEM. I call it a prose poem in that O'Neill said of it to Carlotta, "Well,
you wanted a poem and the above has the right feeling of one, although in
prose . . ." (*Inscriptions; SL*, 399).

"MODERN, INVOLVED, COMPLICATED." From O'Neill's letter to Saxe Commins
of January 3, 1933 (Princeton).

"*AH, WILDERNESS!* WAS A." So O'Neill told Croswell Bowen in "The Black
Irishman," *PM*, November 3, 1946.

"THAT'S THE WAY I." So O'Neill told Hamilton Basso, "The Tragic Sense," *The
New Yorker*, March 6, 1948, p. 48.

HIS LETTERS TO HER SING. There are many literary quotations and allusions
in the letters to Beatrice Ashe (Berg), including quotations from Swinburne's "Laus Veneris" on January 14, 1915, of Oscar Wilde's "The House
of Judgment" (*Poems in Prose*) on February 28, 1915, of Kipling's "Mandalay" on February 5, 1915, and allusions to Ibsen's *The Master Builder* and *A
Doll's House* on December 9, 1914, and to *Hedda Gabler* on February 9,
1915.

"AH, WILDERNESS WERE PARADISE." Some editions of *The Rubáiyát* begin
this line "Oh, Wilderness," and some "Ah, Wilderness." In the Playbill for
Ah, Wilderness! O'Neill explained that because "Oh" carries "an exultant
quality" he chose "Ah," for his title as more expressive of "nostalgia."

page 174:

"A-SINGING." Letter to Beatrice with envelope postmarked October 21, 1914
(Berg).

"FLAT-WHEELED." "WAVE-SWEPT BEACH." The poem, "Just a Little Love, A
Little Kiss," was dated January 9, 1915 (*Poems*, 55–56).

"THE BOY DOES SPOUT." Letter from O'Neill to Arthur McGinley of December
15, 1933.

"THE THINGS WHICH INTERESTED." Letter from O'Neill to Susan Glaspell, January 29, 1919 (Sheaffer I, 314).

"LOOSE AND FAST." So Edward Keefe told me.

"LINKED AS TWIN." Letter from O'Neill to Susan Glaspell, January 29, 1919 (Sheaffer I, 314).

"HER EYES WERE NOT." "Speaking, To The Shade of Dante, Of Beatrices," first published in "The Conning Tower," *New York Tribune*, July 5, 1915.

page 175:

"FROM A CHILD." On January 12, 1915 (Berg), O'Neill sends Beatrice "Just Me N' You (From a Child to a Child)," *Poems*, 57–58.

"VILLANELLE." The full title is "Villanelle To His Ladye In Which Ye Poore Scribe Complaineth Sorely Because The Cursed Memory Of The Thousand Others Doth Poison His Dreams Of His Beatrice" (*Poems*, 73).

SHEAFFER FOUND A PHOTOGRAPH. Sheaffer I, 287.

page 176:

"SIDNEY DAVIDSON." His real name is revealed only in *In the Zone* where his shipmates get into his letters because they suspect him of being a spy—a mishap that had befallen O'Neill shortly after he got to Provincetown from wandering about thinking of his lost singer, even as did Sidney in his play. O'Neill had also included a "Davis" in the crew of this play and *Moon of the Caribbees* from his earlier sea-play *Bound East for Cardiff*. Sid Davis of *Ah, Wilderness!* probably came of mixed memories of the two.

BEATRICE BROKE THEIR ENGAGEMENT. The break with Beatrice seems to have come in August, after his last letter to her, July 25, 1916, and after the productions on July 28 and 29 of *Bound East for Cardiff*, for which he wanted her to come to Provincetown. He then returned to New London to try personally to convince her to marry him, and she seems to have broken decisively with him then, as his collapse into drunkenness at that point indicates.

"PROMISE" TO CUT OUT ALL DRINKING. O'Neill speaks of not violating his "promise" to Beatrice in his letter to her dated "Wednesday-noon" [January 6, 1915] (*SL*, 44).

"MADE LIFE BEARABLE." Letter from O'Neill to Beatrice of ca. March 19, 1915 (Berg).

"GRIMY SMEARS." Letter to Beatrice dated "Thursday" [October 8, 1914] (*SL*, 30).

"SID JUMPS FROM HIS." This scene is act four, scene one, in the first longhand script of *Ah, Wilderness!* (Museum of the City of New York). The scene is also in the typescript submitted for copyright (granted August 8, 1933) now in the Library of Congress.

"DEAR OLD BIG HEART." Letter to Beatrice of July 25, 1916 (*SL*, 73).

page 177:

"WITH UNDERTONES, OH YES." So O'Neill said in his letter to Saxe Commins of January 3, 1933 (Princeton).

"ENORMOUS BROWN EYES." Ruth Gilbert's eyes are described in Mary Brag-
giotti, "Little Girl with a Big Ideal," *New York Post,* December 20, 1946.

"SHE RESEMBLED A CHILDHOOD." "Ruth Gilbert Grows Up from One O'Neill
Play to Another," *Brooklyn Eagle,* November 24, 1946.

LINES FROM "LAUS VENERIS." O'Neill runs the lines together like prose in his
letter to Beatrice of January 14, 1915 (Berg), as does Richard in a second,
rearranged quote: "You are my love, mine own soul's heart, more dear than
mine own soul, more beautiful than God!' " (287).

page 178:

"WILD, WAYWARD BIRD-SOUL." "MEAN AMBITIONS." "STUNG BY THEIR." Letter
of July 25, 1916 (*SL,* 72, 71).

"LOYAL, KINDLY, HIGH-MINDED." So O'Neill is quoted as saying in "O'Neill
Off Duty."

"AND DO YOU LIKE." Letter from O'Neill of January 12, 1933 (Princeton).

page 179:

"IT IS HARD TO TELL." So James O'Neill was quoted as saying in an interview
in the *New York Sun,* April 1, 1917.

"A-ONE SNOB." Letter from O'Neill to Brooks Atkinson of August 16, 1931
(Sheaffer II, 378; *SL,* 392).

"HOW I REMEMBER." Letter from O'Neill of January 12, 1933 (Princeton).

SEATED AT THE SAME TABLE. The idea of bringing together several of his
"dead selves" at crucial ages had been one of his first (dated July, 1931) for
his second God trilogy play, as the Notes for *Days Without End* show (Floyd,
152).

page 180:

"GENTLEMEN, I GIVE YOU." Pencil note from Jamie to Eugene O'Neill (Prince
George Hotel) of May 21, 1920 (Yale).

MOCK CIRCUS-BARKING. Without going into detail, one can note that Yank's
turning to the gorilla is redolent of Jamie. O'Neill's Yank-self addresses the
gorilla as "Brother" (Random House, 3:254) and dying in the gorilla's cage,
says, in *"the strident tones of a circus barker)* Ladies and gents, step forward
and take a slant at de one and only—." Sid in *Ah, Wilderness!* announces
"(in the tones of a side-show barker) In this cage you see the lobster" (231).

"A CERTAIN PECULIAR OIL." O'Neill explained that Nat's two idiosyncrasies at
the dinner table came from his father to Brooks Atkinson ("O'Neill Off
Duty") and to Arthur McGinley in a letter of December 15, 1933.

"IDIOSYNCRASIES." Ibid. For the chum saved in his father's tale, O'Neill borrowed—probably as an in-joke between them—the last name of Robert Sisk
of the Theatre Guild.

page 181:

"WHO ALSO, ONCE UPON." O'Neill dedicated *Ah, Wilderness!* to George Jean
Nathan because his enthusiastic response to it as one of the first readers

encouraged O'Neill to produce it. O'Neill told Saxe Commins, in an undated letter of July 1933 (Princeton) that Nathan thought it "one of the best things" he had done, and he told Lawrence Langner of Nathan's response in a letter of August 8, 1933 (*SL*, 420). O'Neill joked about the dedication to Nathan in a letter of May 13, 1939 (*SL*, 486), recalling the days when they had both been little boys in a convent and were paddled on the behind to the chime of the Angelus by the nuns.

THE TART, BELLE. The name of the tart is perhaps useful for discarding one of the candidates for the original Muriel. Maibelle Scott, whom O'Neill dated in 1912, thought she was the original of Muriel because her parents disapproved of O'Neill and because he had tried to interest her in reading great books. Although Muriel is redolent—as all the characters were—of many persons of that period, Maibelle has no special claim to be her. She certainly wasn't the dark-eyed child sweetheart, as her eyes were blue, and both the parental disapproval and the advanced reading were true of Beatrice and indeed of most of the middle-class girls O'Neill knew. If Maibelle were functioning as an image of romance for him, he would not have used part of her name—sensitive as he was to words—for the tart Belle, who, Richard says, "made everything seem rotten and dirty" (294).

"SERIOUS CRITICISM I FORGOT." Telegram to Philip Moeller of September 30, 1933 (Moeller Collection). I have put in punctuation.

page 183:

BOTH AVATARS OF O'NEILL. O'Neill is so firmly in Sid in this scene that it seems he slides out of the time span in the play and into his own. At the point where Arthur sings "Waiting at the Church" and Sid joins in, O'Neill has Sid recall hearing Vesta Victoria sing this song at Hammerstein's Victoria sixteen years earlier, as O'Neill himself might well have recalled in 1932. But the play time is 1906. It seems that "Waiting at the Church" came out in 1906, so Sid, speaking in 1906, could not have heard it sixteen years before. Later, when O'Neill had his own player piano, he made a list of the songs in its various rolls with their dates, and he has "Waiting at the Church (1906)" listed for roll 3 (now in a folder of miscellaneous O'Neill notes at Yale).

"AS GOOD OLD DOWIE." This familiarity with Dowson is not characteristic of Sid, insofar as he is the fat drunkard of O'Neill's youth—with neither O'Neill himself or Jamie entering into him—for O'Neill had him think in act one that the books Richard might be reading would be "Nick Carter or Old Cap Collier" (193), and he is obviously meeting Swinburne for the first time in Richard's quotes to Muriel.

"SOUGHT SUCH A HIGH-PRICED." "DULL AND STUPID." Letter to Kenneth Macgowan of August 7, 1926 (Sheaffer II, 216; Bryer, 122; *SL*, 210).

"UPON OUR BEACH." This is the title of one of the poems that O'Neill wrote celebrating his love for Beatrice and that he sent to her [September 21, 1914] (*SL*, 27). See *Poems*, 48–53.

PARTICULAR MOONLIT SUMMER NIGHT. The letter of intense longing for this
moonlit night is that of October 21, 1914 (Berg).

"OUR BEACH." O'Neill recalls "our beach" and a picnic there and longs for
their summer days and nights there in a letter [November 1, 1914] (*SL*, 33–
35).

"OWN SOUL." He particularly urges her to find her "own soul" in the July 25,
1916, letter, but earlier ones, such as that of February 18, 1915, are equally
insistent (*SL*, 38).

page 184:

HE ENDED HIS PLAY. See the first longhand script of *Ah, Wilderness!* (Museum
of the City of New York).

THREE MORE WEEKS OF WORK. In the Playbill, O'Neill gave the total writing
time as six weeks, and the first draft took three weeks as the dates on the
first longhand script (Museum of the City of New York) show. O'Neill sent
Saxe Commins the revised *Ah, Wilderness!* on June 15, 1933 (Princeton).
He was also reported as saying that he wrote the play in six weeks (Richard
Watts, Jr., "O'Neill Is Eager to See Cohan in 'Ah, Wilderness!'" *New York
Herald Tribune*, September 9, 1933).

"WE'VE WATCHED THE DAWN." I have added periods after *China* and *Gene*.
O'Neill wrote this on a carbon copy of the first draft typescript with longhand revisions, and it is reproduced in *Inscriptions*.

page 185:

BREAKING GLASS INSULATORS. In an autobiographical note (Yale), O'Neill said
that he was suspended for a year. The decision to drop out altogether was
his own.

"THAT IT WILL GO." Letter to Agnes "Thursday p.m." [July 29?, 1920] (*SL*,
132).

"I LOVE YOU." The words were written February 10, 1933, on a photograph of
O'Neill by Edward Steichen (*Inscriptions*).

"MY WILDERNESS REGAINED." O'Neill dedicated a photograph of him by Carl
Van Vechten to Carlotta "who is my Wilderness regained" on September 5,
1933 (*Inscriptions*). She would not have missed the reference to Milton's
Paradise Regained because, with her, "Wilderness were Paradise enow!"

page 186:

"POIGNANT MELANCHOLY." O'Neill told Saxe Commins in his letter to him of
January 3, 1933 (Princeton) of his affectionate feelings for *Ah, Wilderness!*
"For me it has the sweet charm of a dream of lost youth, a wistfulness of
regret, a poignant melancholy memory of dead things and people—but a
smiling memory as of those who live still, being not sadly dead."

"SUBJECT IT TO THE HUMILIATION." From the letter to Saxe Commins of January 3, 1933 (Princeton).

"WHOLE IMPORTANCE AND REALITY." Letter from O'Neill to Saxe Commins
of January 12, 1933 (Princeton).

"TRUE EVOCATION OF A MOOD." Letter from O'Neill to Philip Moeller of August 19, 1933 (*SL*, 420).

"THE USUAL EASY ROUTE." Letter from O'Neill to Saxe Commins of January 20, 1933 (Princeton).

"CORRUPTING, DISINTEGRATING." "SPOILED IT SINCE." From O'Neill's letter to Saxe Commins of January 12, 1933 (Princeton).

"THE STARTLING DIFFERENCE." From O'Neill's letter to Saxe Commins of January 3, 1933 (Princeton).

"NOSTALGIA FOR OUR OLD." Letter to Saxe Commins of January 3, 1933 (Princeton). O'Neill also told Saxe Commins that this was the "spirit" he expressed in his original subtitle for *Ah, Wilderness!*: "A Comedy of Recollection."

NATHAN HAD REINFORCED. Letter from O'Neill to Lawrence Langner of August 8, 1933 (*SL*, 420).

"JUDGMENT MIGHT BE WARPED." Letter from O'Neill to Robert Sisk of October 15, 1933 (Yale).

"BEST SHOWMANSHIP." "RESENTMENT AND BEWILDERMENT." Letter from O'Neill to Lawrence Langner of August 7, 1933 (*SL*, 419).

page 187:

ABLE TO CHARM. Letter from O'Neill to Lawrence Langner of August 8, 1933 (*SL*, 420). In this letter O'Neill asked Langner to make the decision, and on August 14, Langner wrote back that both he and Terry Helburn agreed with O'Neill that the comedy should come first (carbon copy at Yale).

FRESH PERSONALITIES, NEW." "HAS SOMETHING." Letter from O'Neill to Philip Moeller of August 19, 1933 (*SL*, 420). In this letter O'Neill rejects Helen Westley as the mother because Guild audiences were too familiar with her (Marjorie Marquis played Essie). O'Neill also declared firmly that for Richard anyone who was not thoroughly male boy would be disastrous (they chose Elisha Cook, Jr.).

EVERYONE WOULD BE INTRIGUED. Cohan himself played up the piquancy of the combination in jokes to interviewers. For instance, in "The Theatre" (*Time*, October 9, 1933) he said: "Well, if this play doesn't make a hit, I'll take the kid into vaudeville with me. But I come first. It's got to be Cohan and O'Neill. That's *my* game."

"DISGRACEFUL, SLOVENLY." Letter to Philip Moeller of October 30, 1933 (*SL*, 425). O'Neill urged more rehearsals to get the right lines set.

"SIGNIFICANTLY CHARGED." George Middleton tells of Cohan's admiration for Guitry's pauses in *These Things Are Mine: The Autobiography of a Journeyman Playwright* (New York: Macmillan, 1947), 161, 250. Cohan himself told Paul A. Shenkman of his role in *Ah, Wilderness!*: "It's a real play and it's a great part they've given me. But there are two actors, at least, whom I would much rather see in the part than myself. Unfortunately they are both dead. But what actors!—our own Nat Goodwin and that great Frenchman, Lucien Guitry" (" 'I'm Still a One-Night Trouper,' Says George M. Cohan as Broadway Awaits His Opening in New O'Neill Play" [Unlabeled clipping in the Theatre Guild Press Book 137, Yale]).

"AH, SURE, IF YOU." First longhand script of *Ah, Wilderness!* (Museum of the City of New York). O'Neill made the Millers Protestant as more typical than his own Catholic family, but this was the only reference to it.

HE HAD MEANT. Letter from O'Neill to Barrett Clark of December 15, 1944 (Clark, 149; *SL*, 567).

"I PUT IT TO." From an interview with Crouse by Louis Sobol, "New York Cavalcade," *New York Journal American*, October 22, 1941.

"IT COULD BE DONE." "EVEN MORE THAN." O'Neill said so in an undated letter to Warren Munsell, who had asked him for further cuts when Will Rogers played Nat Miller for the San Francisco company with a tempo even slower than Cohan's (Moeller Collection).

"COUNCIL OF WAR." See Ward Morehouse, *George M. Cohan: Prince of the American Theater* (Philadelphia: Lippincott, 1943), 189–90.

"REALLY MADE IT LIVE." Letter from O'Neill to Kenneth Macgowan [October 16, 1933] (Bryer, 204).

page 188:

"SOMETHING BETWEEN THEM." "INSIGHTS OF ONE." Letter from O'Neill to Robert Sisk of October 15, 1933 (Yale).

"BE TRAGEDY AS COMEDY." "LILY'S BLIGHTED LOVE." "RICHARD'S WILD RE-BELLION." "TRAGIC IMPULSES." See "O'Neill Off Duty."

ICY WEATHER AND. To this O'Neill attributed the drop of attendance in a letter to Warren Munsell of February 18, 1934 (*SL*, 430), but he was sure—and rightly so—that it would pick up.

DELIRIOUS OVER ITS SUCCESS. Langner thought of doing a series of O'Neill revivals starting with *Ah, Wilderness!* and proposed Harry Carey or Walter Huston as the play father. O'Neill told Langner in a letter of June 26, 1941 (Yale) that "revivals need a fresh, intriguing big name casting angle to overcome the public's idiotic attitude toward them." Neither Huston nor Carey would do it, O'Neill knew, and he suggested that they get Lionel Barrymore. He had been the film father and since had been severely crippled, and O'Neill thought he might do it "as a wheel chair father." He told Langner: "Cohan is still fresh in people's minds—or they like to believe so, anyway—and Cohan, even as a memory, sure has color." Langner asked why not Cohan himself? O'Neill replied [ca. July 10, 1941] (*SL*, 519) that, at this point, Cohan would never remember the lines; it would be a straight ad lib performance, but then so would be Barrymore's, if they got him. Langner went ahead with Harry Carey and reported to O'Neill in a letter of November 6, 1941 (copy at Yale): "Wonderful notices—no business."

"STRICTLY FINANCIAL NEWS." "THE TYPICAL BACKBONE-." Letter of January 26, 1941 (Yale).

"THERE WERE INNUMERABLE." Letter of January 12, 1933 (Princeton). O'Neill wrote "U.S."

WITH ALL ITS PROMISE. So O'Neill said in a mass interview at the time of the

New York production of *The Iceman Cometh,* as reported in *PM,* September 3, 1946.

9. Days Without End

page 189:

HE WAS "OFF." O'Neill had Saxe Commins spread this story when he returned to the United States. In a letter of August 4, 1929 (Princeton) he said that he did mean to write all three plays, "But it's true I am off of having the three combined as a trilogy, as I told you." In this way he hoped to avoid the mistake he had made with *Dynamo* when all the critics had taken the theme of the trilogy for the theme of the play.

"MYTH PLAYS FOR." On July 19, 1932, O'Neill wrote out in his *Work Diary* (1:134) this new title for the three plays combined and reiterated that *Dynamo* must be rewritten.

HIS FIRST, *SERVITUDE*. The typescript of *Servitude* with the copyright date of September 23, 1914, is in the Library of Congress. In those days O'Neill sent his plays in for copyright as soon as he finished them.

THE SECOND, *WELDED*. A number of people connected with the production of *Welded* remembered Agnes and O'Neill together at rehearsals, clearly looking upon it as their story.

WHEN HE TACKLED. O'Neill dedicated *Days Without End* to Carlotta. In January 1934 he gave her the uncorrected proofs, quoting the play on making marriage "a true sacrament" and adding, "And ours has, hasn't it, Darling One!" (*Inscriptions*).

"SAFELY BURIED." O'Neill used these words in a letter to Robert Sisk of March 6, 1933 (Yale) telling him that a movie company had bought his early play *Recklessness,* which he thought was "safely buried" in his first volume of plays—self-published—*Thirst,* "dead there—and unmourned." *Servitude* must have seemed even more "safely buried" at this point, as it had never been published at all.

WAS TO BE BANISHED. From the time of his May 1930 interview with Ward Morehouse in France, O'Neill consistently listed *Welded* as one of the plays he wanted to omit from his collected works.

page 190:

AUGUST 12, 1927. *Work Diary,* 1:45.

"IT'S A FUNNY." NYU.

"REVERSE INTERLUDE THEME." *Work Diary,* 1:161, May 23, 1933.

WRITE A PLAY. Of course, the idea came from a novel-play, and that is why he made it a novel, but in the notes he was tempted to make it even closer to his real form, a play. For instance, in a note of November 29, 1931 (Yale), he had his hero say, "You must think me an idiot to turn to playwriting."

THE "SUPERWOMAN" CERTAINLY HAD. So O'Neill told Beatrice in a letter ca.

October 31, 1914 (Berg). O'Neill made the Beatrice-figure physically different from his Beatrice but gave her similar intellectual qualities. As a matter
of fact, he made her a grown-up version of his dark-eyed child sweetheart.

page 191:

HE QUOTED "THE HOUND." O'Neill quotes it to Beatrice in a continuation
dated "Thursday" of his letter October 11, 1914 (Berg), paraphrasing
Thompson's "I shook the pillaring hours / And pulled my life upon me. . . ."

HE WOULD RECITE. Recollections of O'Neill reciting "The Hound of Heaven"
in the "Golden Swan," popularly called "The Hell Hole," on the corner of
Fourth Street and Sixth Avenue in New York's Greenwich Village, can be
found in Mary Heaton Vorse, "Eugene O'Neill's Pet Saloon Is Gone," *New
York World,* May 4, 1930, and in Dorothy Day, *The Long Loneliness: The
Autobiography of Dorothy Day* (New York: n.p., 1952), 84.

"YEA, FAILETH NOW." Thompson's actual lines read: "Yea, faileth now even
dream / The dreamer, and the lute the lutanist."

"A HUSBAND TO MARVEL." So O'Neill described his father at his deathbed in
the letter to Agnes dated "Thursday p.m." [July 29?, 1920] (*SL,* 131).

HE WANTED TO BEAR. See his letter to Beatrice postmarked January 8, 1915,
in which he worries over her illness and wishes he could bear it for her.

"A PRINCE OF THWARTED." O'Neill tells Beatrice so in the letter postmarked
October 11, 1914, in the section written on "Friday." There is no comma in
the original (Berg).

page 192:

DANTE'S BEATRICE. The joking comparison came in his poem "Speaking, To
the Shade of Dante, Of Beatrices" (*Poems,* 65).

"MOTHER OF MINE." O'Neill called Beatrice this in the letter postmarked October 21, 1914 (Berg).

"ULTIMATE GOAL." "I BECOME A PART." From O'Neill's letter to Beatrice of
March 17, 1915 (Berg).

"NOT ONLY TO PROPAGATE." "Old and New Tables," no. 24, *Zarathustra.*

"BEAUTIFUL AND "PEACEFUL." From Agnes's letter to O'Neill of February 9,
1920 (Correspondence).

"Y.M.C.A. ORGY." "A SCRAP OF." "BEATRICE O'NEILL." Letter to Beatrice
[February 13, 1915] (*SL,* 53). Laurette Taylor was married to the playwright
Hartley Manners.

page 193:

"THE CHAPEL DREAM." *Work Diary,* 1:13, October 15, 1924. I assume both
that it was recurrent, because he gave it a name, and that the chapel must
have been the one he saw daily throughout his boyhood. His interest in the
Resurrection-Crucifixion substantiates this assumption.

"THE GREAT SYMBOLIC." "Three Evil Things," no. 2, *Zarathustra.*

"HAS GOD IN IT." This passage was in the first editions of *Welded,* in which the
husband had said: "That may do very well with the common loves of the

world—but ours has God in it! And when the worshipers nod, the God deserts their shrine." It went in the drastic cuts O'Neill made for the 1924 two-volume edition of *The Complete Works of Eugene O'Neill* published by Boni & Liveright. The page proofs with O'Neill's cuts are at Yale.

page 194:

"IDEA *MODERN FAUST PLAY*." The *Work Diary* (1:48) says that he sketched it "tentatively" in his notebook.

"MARK A STARTLING." So O'Neill told Lawrence Langner in a letter of May 8, 1932 (Yale).

VEIN OF IRONIC. O'Neill told Brooks Atkinson he wanted to free himself from "a formula of tragedy that had begun to imprison him" ("O'Neill Off Duty").

"I BELIEVE EVERYTHING." From O'Neill's letter to Grace Dupré Hills of March 21, 1925 (*SL*, 194–95).

A GENUINE "YEA." In a letter to Dudley Nichols of May 29, 1932 (*SL*, 400), O'Neill declared that he was striving for a "real, true Yea!" in this play.

MEDIEVAL MIRACLE PLAY. In a letter to Leon Mirlas of December 19, 1934, O'Neill told him, " 'Days Without End' is an attempt to transform some of the values of the old miracle play, and the old Faustian damned-soul legend, into a psychological mask drama of modern life." Reproduced in Mirlas, *O'Neill y el Teatro Contemporaneo* (Editorial Sudamericana: Buenos Aires, 1961), 204 (hereafter referred to as Mirlas). See also *SL*, 441.

"FAUSTIAN LONGING." In his earliest notes for the play in July 1931 (Yale), O'Neill saw New York's skyscrapers as a symbol of "man's Faustian longing" for "projection of his dreams toward the sky."

PUN ON THE WORD. In the First Longhand Script of *Days Without End* (Yale) O'Neill had his Faust character's inner self explain the double meaning of *end* in "Without Endings of Days," which was to be the title of the novel he is writing in the play as well as the title for O'Neill's play.

RANG ALL THE POSSIBLE. The titles run as follows: "Without Endings of Days" (July 1931); "Endings of Days" (November 26, 1931); "Without Endings of Days" and "Without Ending of Days" (November 29, 1931); "On to Hercules" or "Without Endings of Days" (May 1932); "Ending of Days" (November 30, 1932); "Without End of Days" and "An End of Days" (March 31, 1933); "Days Without End" (July 20, 1933—copyright date). See the notes and manuscripts at Yale and the copyright typescript at the Library of Congress.

"OBVIOUSLY SATISFACTORY TITLE." O'Neill said so in his *Work Diary*, 1:161, May 30, 1933.

SHOCK OF HIS MOTHER'S. O'Neill's notes for May 1932 (Yale), for instance, had John refuse to give in to his "Catholicism-longing" because of "his old resentment against mother, against Elsa as mother substitute (infidelity)." He changed his conception as the play developed, making John resent God, who allowed her to die, rather than his mother, to get further away from his personal religious history. Of course, in *Dynamo* he had really gotten to the heart of his connection of Agnes with his mother.

page 195:

NOT TO FORGET HUTCH. Letter from Agnes to O'Neill of February 11, 1920 (Correspondence). She warned him that the greatest danger in flu came during convalescence.

"MY ONLY REMAINING HOPE." Letter from O'Neill to Agnes dated "Sunday," probably January 25, 1920 (Correspondence). *SL* (108) reads that he wants to die of flu "or some other material cause." I read "natural cause" (in comparison with the unnatural cause of death, suicide).

FELLED BY THE STROKE. O'Neill's telegram to Agnes telling of his father's stroke is dated March 1, 1920 (Yale).

"STRANGE RELIGIOUS HATRED." "A BOY OBSESSED." Philip Moeller took notes on a talk he had with O'Neill and Carlotta, dated January 1, 1934 (Moeller Collection).

page 196:

"SELF-POISONED PSYCHE." O'Neill had described *Ah, Wilderness!* to Saxe Commins in a letter of January 3, 1933 (Princeton) as a rebellion "against creation in the medium of the modern, involved, complicated, warped and self-poisoned psyche. . . ."

"YOU KNOW DAMN WELL." Letter from O'Neill to Agnes of September 11, 1927 (*SL*, 258).

"STUPID AND MEANINGLESS." See the letter to Agnes of April 16, 1927 (*SL*, 240).

page 197:

"I HEAR ALL THE." Letter from Carlotta to Agnes ca. Christmas 1926 (Sheaffer II, 236–37). Carlotta had also told Agnes, "I hope to be as *splendid* as you are—and that's saying a lot."

WEEKEND-LONG DRINKING PARTIES. Nickolas Muray, the photographer, gave me his recollections of Barton's parties.

SHE DIVORCED HIM. The interlocutory judgment filed on March 19, 1926, gives the grounds as "adultery."

"FROM WIFE TO WIFE." After the divorce from Carlotta, Barton had remarried. His suicide note was published in most of the New York newspapers for May 21, 1931. O'Neill and Carlotta had just returned from France, and O'Neill had an interview with reporters scheduled for May 21 at the Guild. The *Work Diary* (1:102) comments: "Not pleasant under circumstances but had to go through with it."

"PURE AND UNSOILED ONE." From the prose poem of O'Neill to Carlotta, May 25, 1932 (*Inscriptions; SL*, 399).

"THE GOSSIP DOWN THERE." Undated letter [late March 1928] (*SL*, 280).

HAD BELIEVED A VICIOUS LIAR. Agnes's reply is also undated (Correspondence).

"YOU HAVE PILED." O'Neill sent this undated letter to Agnes through his lawyer Harry Weinberger [ca. April 8, 1928] (*SL*, 285). O'Neill began it by recollecting their early love in Provincetown and the day Shane was born. They had come a long way from "Happy House" there.

page 198:

"IT ISN'T THAT I." Letter to Agnes dated "Tuesday" [probably February 7, 1928] (*SL*, 276).

"IF YOU DID SUCH." A letter dated "Friday" [February 3, 1928] was O'Neill's response to the first report he had from one of Agnes's catty friends that she was going to delay the divorce to upset his new life and his work so that he would have to give up and come back to her.

"IT IS WHAT LIFE." From O'Neill's letter dated "Tuesday" [February 7?, 1928] (*SL*, 277).

page 199:

"FRIENDS." "BROTHER." "A LIVING REMINDER." From a note O'Neill made on November 26, 1931 (Yale). Of course, he eliminated the hero's former marriage as well as this friend who closely resembles Jamie, except for his "philosophical Nihilism" and a sentimentality for torch songs.

"FRIEDRICH HARDY." In later drafts this character became "David Hardy" to wipe out the obvious recall of Nietzsche. All the drafts of this play are at Yale.

"ASTRONOMER-ASTROLOGER PLAY." He made a note for this play (*Work Diary*, 1:48) on November 10, 1927, the day before he made the note for a modern Faust play. Originally O'Neill meant to work out a contrast between the astronomer father's cosmic viewpoint and his daughter's earth-centered view. He had even called her "Erda," for Earth, at first. O'Neill also wanted to interweave themes from the other two God plays into this one, showing the failure of science and money-power to replace satisfactorily the old God. All that is left of the professor father in the final play is a reference to the wife's trip to Boston (529) during which John committed adultery. Originally she had gone to visit her astronomer father at Cambridge—obviously at Harvard—just outside Boston.

SIR JAMES JEANS'S. O'Neill certainly had at least one of Sir James Jeans's books on hand, for in one of his notes (Yale) he jotted down a reminder to himself: " 'Converse Equation'—look up equation in Jeans' book."

"ON TO BETELGUESE." The third God play, which had started out as "It Cannot Be Mad," became "On to Betelguese" in 1928 and 1929 and then changed to "The Life of Bessie Bowen" (*Work Diary*, 1:141, September 30, 1932).

"ON TO HERCULES!" All the Hardy quotations are from the longhand drafts of the play at Yale.

"WHAT THE PASSAGE." "INTOLERABLE FEELING." Letter "Monday eve" [December 26?, 1927] (*SL*, 271).

page 200:

"MEANINGLESS AS ONE FLY." The comparison of love to the copulation of flies was so painful to O'Neill that he negated it in *Ah, Wilderness!* simply by

attributing it to the sleazy prostitute Belle: "Don't be a sucker, Kid! Even
the little flies do it!" (243).

"SAVIORS ARE MEANINGLESS." In the final play this speech is given to John's
devil self. He says (543), ". . . I'll grant you the pseudo-Nietzschean savior I
just evoked out of my past is an equally futile ghost. Even if he came, we'd
only send him to the insane asylum for teaching that we should have a nobler
aim for our lives than getting all four feet in a trough of swill!"

page 201:

"THE TRUTH ABOUT YOU." This conception of John's inner self appears for the
first time in the second longhand script at Yale and all the quotations from
his speeches are from that version.

"SPECIALIST SAYS MEANS." Pencil script for the telegram (Berg). SL (165)
reads "Would not help Mother or you?" I read "Would that help Mother or
you?"

page 202:

"WELL, SHE SEEMED." This is an undated letter from Mrs. Libbie Drummer
(who had known Mrs. O'Neill for years and was present at her deathbed) to
a friend of the family, Mrs. Phillips, who had written her of the funeral after
Mrs. O'Neill's body arrived in New York (Sheaffer II, 84–85).

"AGAIN REACH SAME OLD." Work Diary, 1:154, March 2, 1933.

"RUN ITSELF INTO." Letter of January 3, 1933 (Princeton). This "nervous indigestion" might actually have been the first symptom of the toxic condition
that finally caused his serious illness in December 1936.

"TO THRUST IT ASIDE." From O'Neill's letter to Robert Sisk of March 6, 1933
(Yale).

TO WRITE AN ARTICLE. This was "Memoranda on Masks," first published in
the November 1932 American Spectator, with additional parts in December
and January.

GOT IT ON OCTOBER 4. Work Diary, 1:141, 142, 154.

page 203:

"RENEWED LIFE IN PLAY." Work Diary, 1:155, March 4, 1933.

"BLIND ALLEY AGAIN." Work Diary, 1:157, March 27, 1933.

OPTED OUT OF DEATH. He decided to do so on June 20, 1933, by rewriting his
entire final act, as his Work Diary (1:163) shows. Long after he had achieved
what he wanted for his own psyche by this ending, he thought of going back
to the suicide for his hero—so George Jean Nathan reported him as having
said in 1946. (The World of George Jean Nathan, 410). By this time Nathan
had confused what O'Neill had first told him about Days Without End with
what he told him of "The Life of Bessie Bowen," for he thought that as
"originally conceived" it had been laid back in 1857 "or thereabout."

"SEEMED TO ME UNCONVINCING." So O'Neill told Commins (Princeton) when
he sent him the sixth draft for retyping (Work Diary, 1:165, July 5, 1933).
Typing it, Saxe Commins got the idea that O'Neill had meant that Elsa was

saved by the prayers of the uncle, and he objected to O'Neill that it did not ring true. Carlotta answered him late in July (Princeton): "Gene and I nearly had a fit when we saw you had taken the end of the play quite from the wrong angle. It has nothing to do with *Christianity* or *prayer* that brings Elsa back—it is her great and all-consuming *love* for her husband." Saxe Commins had been distressed by the whole play. His Aunt Emma Goldman wrote him on February 15, 1935, to ask him about this "pitiful collapse" on the part of O'Neill, commenting, "It is, of course, not the first time that men who have escaped the hold of the church have crawled back." Commins answered on February 18, 1935: "I prefer not to dwell upon Gene's last play, nor even to discuss it as an indication of his affirmation of faith. The memory of all that it meant is too recent to stir up again. I hold, however, that it is his right as an artist to take up the cross or the hammer and sickle, treat it however he chooses and let it stand or fall by its merit. But by merit alone this play could do nought else but fall" (Goldman Collection).

"SADISTIC SPANISH CHRISTS." From O'Neill's letter to Lawrence Langner of October 29, 1933 (*SL,* 424).

page 204:

"CATHOLIC PRIESTS AND." "MATTHEW BOYD, A." So he is described in the fifth draft (Yale), which O'Neill sent off to be typed—as he noted in his *Work Diary* (1:158)—on April 12, 1933.

"MATTHEW BAIRD." "AVOID OBVIOUS." "ALL THE CHRISTIAN." O'Neill's decision for the country doctor came in the sixth draft, finished on July 5, 1933 (*Work Diary,* 1:165) and sent off to Saxe Commins for retyping with this letter of instructions (Princeton), in which he asks him to change "Boyd" to "Baird" throughout and to change the direction "Servant of God" to "an old fashioned country doctor of the old general practitioner type."

HIS LAST FACING UP. The *Work Diary* (1:167) changes the Guardian Angel to a Catholic priest on August 5 and 6, 1933. In a letter to Lawrence Langner of August 7, 1933 (*SL,* 419), O'Neill declared that with the priest-uncle and Catholicism the play was certainly more alive.

page 205:

"TICKLED TO DEATH." "I CAN NEVER FORGIVE." Photostat of the letter November 12, 1933, in the Isaac Goldberg Collection, Harvard; *SL,* 428.

"GENEROUS CONTRIBUTION." "I AM SURE." From a copy of Leonard's letter to O'Neill of February 7, 1934 (Yale).

"TO LIBERATE MYSELF." "WHATEVER THE FATE." From O'Neill's letter to Macgowan of October 16, 1933, written, significantly, on O'Neill's birthday (Bryer, 204; *SL,* 423).

"THE PAYING OF AN." "THAT ANY LIFE-GIVING." Letter from O'Neill to Lawrence Langner of October 29, 1933 (*SL,* 424).

"FOR HIM TO DINE." The *Work Diary,* 1:175, November 23 and 25, 1933, notes engagements with Skinner.

page 206:

O'NEILL HAD FOLLOWED. When he finished his first draft of *Days Without End* on May 12, 1932, O'Neill noted in his *Work Diary* (1:127) "read to C[arlotta]."

SHE SAW CLEARLY. Carlotta knew she was Elsa. When she gave O'Neill her photo-portrait by Steichen that year, she dedicated it with an echo of the play: "To you—darling—who gave me fulfillment and completion—yours to the end and after—" (Yale).

"BE SURE TO LET." The telegram was sent from London with her real name, "Hazel Tharsing," and dated May 4, 1907. The *San Francisco Call* published it on May 5 with an interview, "Story of the Native Daughter Whose Beauty Now Makes Her Famous."

"IT MAY INTEREST YOU." Letter from Richard Dana Skinner to the Reverend Michael Earls, then of St. Mary's Rectory, Boston, of January 11, 1934 (Library of the College of the Holy Cross, Worcester). Skinner was so sure O'Neill would return to the church that he began his critical biography *Eugene O'Neill: A Poet's Quest* (New York: Longmans Green, 1935), interpreting all his plays as a struggle to reach the final answer to life, Catholicism, in *Days Without End*.

"THAT SHE HOPES HE." From the notes Moeller made of a talk with Carlotta and O'Neill, January 1, 1934 (Moeller Collection).

O'NEILL'S ANSWER WAS "NO." So Russell Crouse reported (Sheaffer II, 426).

"THE VERY LAST THING." Letter from O'Neill to Cerf of November 6, 1933 (Sheaffer II, 426–27).

"SYMPATHY WITH THE MYSTIC." Letter from O'Neill to Lawrence Langner of October 29, 1933 (*SL*, 424).

"A REAL ARTIST." "BATTLE IT OUT." From a copy of a letter from O'Neill to Warren Munsell of October 30, 1933, which Munsell had sent to Philip Moeller (Moeller Collection).

"UNOBTRUSIVE SIMPLICITY." "VIVID, BEAUTIFUL, STRIKING." From O'Neill's letter to Lawrence Langner of October 29, 1933 (*SL*, 424).

pages 206–7:

"STARRY HAM." "HAVE TO FIGHT." Letter from O'Neill to Lawrence Langner of November 8, 1933 (*SL*, 426). In a letter to Langner of November 14, 1933, which Langner passed on to Philip Moeller, Carlotta said that she and O'Neill were thinking of Nazimova for the role of Elsa: "Nazimova knows what *to love* and *to suffer* means—even if her hair did become disarranged in the process" (Moeller Collection). Ilka Chase, who played Lucy, told me in a letter of October 22, 1964: "I got a shot at it because Carlotta O'Neill, I think, was fond of me and always kind to me. I read for it and apparently O'Neill and the Guild liked me enough to give me the job." Stanley Ridges played the devil self and Robert Loraine did Father Baird. Philip Moeller, who directed, saw the play as a "metaphysical debate" composed with musical brilliance, "truly contrapuntal" (Elizabeth Borton, "Philip Moeller Discusses Bridge and the Staging of Plays," unlabeled clipping in the Moeller Collection).

page 207:
"ALL DAY EVERY DAY." Letter from O'Neill to Arthur McGinley of December 15, 1933. O'Neill was distressed because they were allowed only four weeks for rehearsals and therefore would have to have an out-of-town tryout week in Boston. He told Lawrence Langner in his letter of November 8, 1933 (*SL*, 426) that he could not react with an audience in the theater.

INTENSIFYING ELSA'S FLIGHT. After the Boston first night, O'Neill sent a note to Moeller asking for a special Sunday rehearsal: "Have grand new ending for Elsa's going out scene" (Moeller Collection).

"WHAT A HOWL." Letter from O'Neill to Robert Sisk of October 15, 1933 (Yale).

"THE CRITICAL LADS FAIR." Letter from O'Neill to Macgowan of February 14, 1934 (Bryer, 207).

"HOLY HOKUM." So Garland declared it in the *New York World-Telegram,* January 10, 1934.

"FAKEY PREACHMENT." So John Mason Brown declared it in the *New York Post,* January 9, 1934.

"REACTIONARY." So Isaac Goldberg declared it in *Panorama,* February 1934.

"FILTH." "PROFANITY." Cardinal Hayes was reported as saying so in the *Boston Sunday Enquirer,* January 21, 1934.

MONSIGNOR LAVELLE INSTANTLY. In a letter to the Reverend Michael Earls of January 28, 1934 (Holy Cross), Richard Dana Skinner remarked on the rejection for the White List, saying, "That in its turn makes it impossible to have various Catholic groups take the play for benefit performances. What strange complexities there are in the Catholic world!"

"ADOLESCENT AND HYSTERICAL." So O'Neill told Leon Mirlas in a letter of December 19, 1934 (Mirlas, 204–5; *SL*, 442).

"PROFOUND HUMAN IMPLICATIONS." "EXCEPT A FEW." "FAUSTIAN UNDER-THEME." From O'Neill's letter to Macgowan of February 14, 1934 (Yale). Bryer, 207–8, omits "human" from "profound human implications."

"OVER THE CRITICS' HEADS." O'Neill hoped that they would in a telegram to the cast on January 9, 1934 (*SL*, 429).

"EVIDENTLY YEATS SEES." Letter from O'Neill of February 27, 1934 (Yale).

"THE EVENT OF THE." From a dispatch to the *New York Times,* April 23, 1934. In it F. J. McCormick was applauded for the "humanity" and "intellectual insight" of his John, and Arthur Shields for making the devil self "a vehement occult presence somewhat eerie in its conception."

page 208:
"ALTHOUGH TO JUDGE FROM." From O'Neill's letter of March 2, 1934 (Sheaffer II, 433).

"AS FOR PROPAGANDA." Letter from O'Neill to Leon Mirlas of December 19, 1934 (Mirlas, 204–5; *SL*, 442).

"SEE EYE TO EYE." Letter from O'Neill to Warren Munsell of February 18, 1934 (*SL*, 430).

THE THIRD PLAY OF. This play about the worship of Gold would have taken off from the story of Eliza or Betsy Bowen, an Irish girl who had set out to get money, first by tricking the wealthy wine merchant Stephen Jumel into marrying her, and then by scheming to get all his money into her own hands. Later she had married and almost immediately divorced the elderly Aaron Burr—the divorce on grounds of his extravagance with her money. She had become increasingly violent in temper and finally altogether mad. O'Neill had intended to bring the story up-to-date, treat the character fictionally, and use a technique in which she alone of all the characters spoke her thoughts. He had first called it "It Cannot Be Mad," then "On to Betelguese," and then "The Career of Bessie Bowen" or "The Life of Bessie Bowen." He spoke of his plans for it in an interview in the September 9, 1933, *New York Herald Tribune.* The manuscript notes for it at Yale are filed under the title "Career of Bessie Bolan," also called "The Life of Bessie Bowen" and "Career of Bessie Bolen." Howard Barnes spoke of its basis in the life of Betsy Bowen in "O'Neill Builds Drama Around Madame Jumel," *Oakland Tribune,* May 27, 1934. When the *New York Times* asked him when "Bessie Bowen" would be ready, he wired back on June 3, 1934: "No plans. Am determinedly resting. Don't even know now if Bessie Bowen will be next one I write when I do start work again."

"GREAT DEPRESSION CAUGHT." Letter from O'Neill to Frederick Carpenter of March 24, 1945 (Carpenter, *Eugene O'Neill,* 135).

Quotations from the Plays

1. DESIRE UNDER THE ELMS

Quotations from *Desire Under the Elms*
(DUE) and *The Rope* (R) are from volume 1 of *The Plays of Eugene O'Neill*, 3
vols. (New York: Random House, 1967),
and quotations from *The Great God
Brown* (GGB) are from volume 3 (these
three volumes are hereafter referred to
as Random House 1, 2, and 3). Quotations from *Long Day's Journey into
Night* (LDJ) are from the Yale University Press edition (New Haven, 1956). I
correct obvious textual errors automatically and less obvious ones with explan-
atory notes.

page 22:
"Two enormous elms," DUE, 202.
"sickly grayish," DUE, 202.

page 23:
"Ye're walkin' like," DUE, 250.
"That's what I," DUE, 260.

page 25:
"come back all," DUE, 209.

page 26:
"For this my," R, 595.

"soft-minded," R, 583.
"She played mother," GGB, 282.
"quickly snatches up," R, 578.
"hugs him with," LDJ, 48.

page 27:
"Her hands flutter," LDJ, 47.
"settles back in," LDJ, 106–7.
"staring fixedly," R, 578.
"Soft-headed," DUE, 246.
"a bundle of nerves," LDJ, 33.
"an' blow his," DUE, 233.

page 28:
"tomb," DUE, 241.
"droppin' off the," DUE, 253.
"fur the gold," DUE, 223.
"looking up raptly," DUE, 269.
"Maw—every drop," DUE, 207.
"Like his Paw," DUE, 211.

page 29:
"Here—it's stones," DUE, 204.
"stone atop o'," DUE, 208–9.
"God's in the," DUE, 237.
"like two friendly," DUE, 206.
"The halter's broke," DUE, 221.
"all slicked up," DUE, 228.
"t' beller like," DUE, 214.
"smells like a," DUE, 211.

"squirms desirously," DUE, 229.
"Hain't the sun," DUE, 229.
"Sometimes ye air," DUE, 236.

page 30:
"Ay-eh! I'm bossin'," DUE, 246.
"Women need homes," LDJ, 88.
"Hum!" DUE, 221.
"A woman's got," DUE, 222.

page 31:
"I left the," DUE, 261.
"prison 'r death," DUE, 267.
"a tomb in," DUE, 241.

page 32:
"Jim," DUE, 268–69.
"It's a jim-dandy," DUE, 269.

page 33:
"it was all," DUE, 232.
"When ye kin," DUE, 236.

page 34:
"When I come," DUE, 236.
"I could o'," DUE, 237.
"God's hard, not," DUE, 237.
"allus lonesome," DUE, 237.
"without knowin' what," DUE,
    238.

page 35:
"fur understandin'," DUE, 238.
"Ye'd ought t'," DUE, 265.
"Purty good—fur," DUE, 269.

page 36:
"Waal—what d'ye," DUE, 268.
"pale and washed," DUE, 203.

2.   MARCO MILLIONS

Quotations from *Marco Millions* (MM)
and *Ah, Wilderness!* (AW) are from
Random House 2.

page 43:
"sentimental singing voices," MM,
    357–58.
"big naïve wondering," AW, 277.
"black pearls," MM, 360.
"bitterly" . . . "contemptuous
    pity," MM, 374.

page 44:
"It was a terrible," LDJ, 136.
"Handsome," MM, 367.
"a gift," MM, 368.
"do it for nothing," AW, 241.
"handsome kid," AW, 240.
"You see I promised," MM, 368.
"an oath I'd be," AW, 243.
"Going! Going! Gone!" MM, 375.
"The women wear," MM, 365.

page 45:
"Died and became," MM, 271.
"A Second Class travels," MM,
    381.
"square," MM, 381.
"You'd think I," MM, 381.

page 46:
"Queen of Beauty," MM, 385.
"Her little feet," MM, 437.
"dancing makes me remember,"
    MM, 423.

page 47:
"pitifully to arouse," MM, 414.

page 48:
"Cock of Paradise," MM, 388.
"Mystic Knights of Confucius,"
    MM, 388.
"child-actor," MM, 389.
"movie star at a," MM, 390.
"sweated out," MM, 391.
"I simply reversed," MM, 392.
"And I got," MM, 392.
"In beggars?" MM, 392.

page 49:
"a poet who had," MM, 386.
"immortal soul," MM, 395.
"Well, you can't," MM, 395.
"of Our Lord," MM, 394.
"heroes who waged," MM, 394.
"workable way" . . . "to conquer everybody," MM, 394.
"You conquer the world," MM, 396.

page 50:
"Buddha, the Prince," MM, 422.
"unscrupulous Japanese trade-pirates," MM, 422.
"has not even," MM, 387.
"He has looked," MM, 387.
"his soul may be," MM, 388.
"I hate idleness," MM, 398.
"If you look before," MM, 406.

page 51:
"a strange, mysterious" . . . "acting the hero," MM, 388.
"brave sword," MM, 411.
"by my bedside like," MM, 412.

page 52:
"whiskey is the healthiest," LDJ, 111.
"My mother's recipes," MM, 412.
"When love is not," MM, 409.
"asleep in green water," MM, 412.
"go to sleep" . . . "I obey! I," MM, 415.
"I never believed," MM, 415.
"You weren't in," LDJ, 147.
"One million!" MM, 415.
"Queen of Love," . . . "Persia shall be," MM, 418.

page 53:
"Here! Guzzle! Grunt!" MM, 419.
"There shall not be," MM, 425.
"glittering multicolored," MM, 429.

"Millions! . . . millions!" MM, 432.
"The Word became," MM, 432.

page 54:
"wrapped in a winding," MM, 434.
"white and clear," MM, 434.
"incense ascending in," MM, 434.
"Greatest of the Great," MM, 435.
"You are a little," MM, 437.
"I—I am dead," MM, 438.
"example has done much," MM, 397.
"The noble man," MM, 401.

page 55:
"Death is," MM, 434.

page 56:
"votive offerings, pieces," MM, 347.
"a twig" . . . "to cleanse his," MM, 349.
"was handed down," MM, 349.
"duped by childish" . . . "Tree of Life," MM, 349.
"staff of Mahomet," MM, 350.
"Say this, I loved," MM, 352.
"of an intoxicating," MM, 352.

3. THE GREAT GOD BROWN

Quotations from *A Moon for the Misbegotten* (MFM) are from the 1952 Random House edition. Quotations from *Servitude* (S) are from *Ten "Lost" Plays* (New York: Random House, 1964). Quotations from *All God's Chillun Got Wings* (AGC) are from Random House 2, and quotations from *The Hairy Ape* (HA) are from Random House 3.

page 61:
"*architects* and builders," GGB, 258.

"athletic," GGB, 257.
"lean and wiry," GGB, 260.

page 63:
　"stereotyped paintings," GGB,
　269.

page 65:
　"You're brothers," GGB, 287.
　"the Big Brother," GGB, 298.
　"You'd think you," LDJ, 21.
　"And my mother?" GGB, 282.

page 66:
　"Never forget the first," LDJ, 163.
　"Fat Violet" . . . "boiled," LDJ,
　159.

page 67:
　"Pah! Imagine me," LDJ, 160–61.
　"a blonde pig," MFM, 149.
　"a come-on smile," MFM, 149.
　"parlor house written," MFM,
　149.
　"stranger" . . . "cold and indiffer-
　ent," MFM, 147.
　"the rouged and eye-blackened,"
　GGB, 279.
　"a blurred impression," GGB, 278.
　"crimson and purple," GGB, 284.
　"nickel-in-the-slot," GGB, 278.
　"a sentimental medley," GGB,
　278.
　"full-breasted and wide-hipped,"
　GGB, 278.
　"chews gum like," GGB, 278.
　"old Sacred Cow," GGB, 285.
　"Mother Earth," GGB, 287.
　"like an idol," GGB, 286, 287,
　288, etc.

page 68:
　"far-off voice," GGB, 288.
　"ahead unmoved," GGB, 289.
　"to be buried," GGB, 282.
　"The earth is warm," GGB, 322.

"reckless, defiant, gayly," GGB,
260.
"habitual expression" . . . "Mephistophelian cast," LDJ, 19.
"All its Pan quality," GGB, 285.
"spiritual, poetic" . . . "childlike,
religious," GGB, 260.

page 69:
　"tongue like an adder," LDJ, 154.
　"I've been the brains!" GGB, 297.
　"And because I," LDJ, 164.
　"When I die," GGB, 295.
　"gnawing of a doubt," GGB, 296.
　"thrive and breed," GGB, 297.

page 70:
　"like a dope fiend," GGB, 307.
　"out one hand," GGB, 319.

page 71:
　"No! That is merely," GGB, 298.
　"Hurry, Brother!" GGB, 308.

page 72:
　"Now I am born—," GGB, 266.
　"O God, now I," GGB, 266.
　"Who are you!" GGB, 266.
　"Watch the monkey," GGB, 268.
　"more selfless and," GGB, 269.
　"more spiritual, more," GGB, 290.

page 73:
　"Servitude in love," S, 294.
　"on his knees" . . . "shining" . . .
　"transfigured," AGC, 342.
　"himself on his knees," DUE, 266.
　"Behold your man—," GGB, 292.
　"radiant with a great," GGB, 292.
　"O woman—my love—," GGB,
　292.
　"kneels and kisses," GGB, 292.
　"Paradise by proxy!" GGB, 305.
　"devastating contempt," GGB,
　311.

page 74:
"What you been," HA, 251.
"Enuf to gimme," HA, 251.
"same courtroom effect," GGB, 269.
"like a cruel," GGB, 297.
"Man!" GGB, 323.
"Spring bearing the intolerable," GGB, 322.

page 75:
"Dion is the moon," GGB, 264.
"And I'll be Mrs.," GGB, 264.
"You are sleeping," GGB, 325.

page 76:
"quick prancing movement," GGB, 318.
"his head thrown back," GGB, 318.
"There is only love," GGB, 322.
"Our Father Who Art!" GGB, 322.
"Always spring comes again," GGB, 322–23.
"My lover! My," GGB, 323.
"You will live," GGB, 323.

page 77:
"It's only our lives," GGB, 325.
"the rouged and eye-blackened," GGB, 279.
"fat-bellied finality," GGB, 313.
"Only to me will," GGB, 313.
"few goatish capers," GGB, 313.
"Long live Chief," GGB, 313.

4.   LAZARUS LAUGHED

Quotations from *Lazarus Laughed* (LL), *Bound East for Cardiff* (BEFC), and *Strange Interlude* (SI) are from Random House 1. Quotations from *The Emperor Jones* (EJ) and *Anna Christie* (AC) are from Random House 3.

page 81:
"To feel one's life," GGB, 286.

page 82:
"love the stars," LL, 309.
"new stars are born," LL, 348–49.
"See! a new star," LL, 289.

page 83:
"a throbbing star-like," LL, 281.
"bestial parody of the dance," LL, 288.
"knives and swords flash," LL, 291.
"in every tense attitude," LL, 291.
"like figures in a frieze," LL, 289.
"out in every direction," LL, 295.
"Sorrowful, Resigned," LL, 274.
"Proud, Self-Reliant," LL, 298.
"a statue of a divinity," LL, 274.

page 84:
"positive masculine Dionysus," LL, 307.
"the old followers," LL, 298.
"the mystic rod," LL, 307.
"sad, resigned mother," LL, 327.
"a group of inquisitive," LL, 279.
"the sheepish shame," LL, 306.
"smiling—as if he," LL, 340.

page 85:
"gently patting his head," LL, 359.
"affectionately as at a child," LL, 359.

page 86:
"a raised platform," LL, 274.
"forward in their seats," LL, 318.
"in a big semicircle," LL, 344.
"deep black," LL, 274.
"pure pallor of marble," LL, 274.
"sun-burned and earth-colored," LL, 274–75.
"dream down on the child," LL, 274.

page 87:
"Say what you like," LL, 346.
"our tomb near our home," LL, 346.
"herds of women," LL, 341.

page 88:
"surpassing clearness," LL, 367.
"a tiny gale," EJ, 190.

page 89:
"queer excitement," . . . "jerky steps," . . . "clenched fists," . . . "threatening talons," LL, 287.
"Shameless! Wanton!" LL, 288.

page 90:
"squatting on their hams," LL, 344.
"concentrated death wish," LL, 347.
"jeering howls," LL, 286.
"almost malformed," LL, 299.
"short, skinny, hairy," LL, 299.
"cuts a hopping caper," LL, 308.
"where he squats," LL, 308.
"a trained ape," LL, 360.

page 91:
"squat, broad-shouldered," . . . "muscular," AC, 5.
"battered features," BEFC, 478.
"a squat, muscular," . . . "a heavy battered," LL, 299.
"Men still need," LL, 328.
"crazy intensity," . . . "with his spear," LL, 370.
"Tragic is the plight," LL, 309.
"half-drunk," LL, 313.
"slave with an amphora," LL, 313.

page 92:
"deep purple, fringed," LL, 337.
"crimson-purple," LL, 335.
"blotched heliotrope," LL, 336.

"crimson and purple flowers," GGB, 284.
"I heard you wish," LL, 317.

page 93:
"lesson," . . . "example for other lions," LL, 328.
"gently pushes the lion's," LL, 329.
"Poor brother!" . . . "Forgive me," LL, 329.
"a stream of reddish," . . . "under the crucified," LL, 331.
"rotten bad influence," LDJ, 165.
"I'll be waiting," LDJ, 166.
"Know you absolve," LDJ, 167.
"raises his hand," LL, 333.
"Judge yourself!" LL, 334.
"Death is dead!" LL, 334–35.

page 94:
"I kept listening," LL, 357.
"His words are a thick," LL, 357.
"He is gone!" LL, 357.
"short, boyish," . . . "harsh, strident," LL, 336.
"women's robes," . . . "anklets and," . . . "affected, lisping," LL, 336.
"Love passed into," LDJ, 159.

page 95:
"perverted passion," . . . "gentle, girlish," . . . "set in an expression," LL, 336–37.
"tender," LL, 274.
"self-contempt," LDJ, 95.
"that's the way," LDJ, 78.
"Up to take more," LDJ, 123.
"laughing with grief," LL, 349.
"the white mask," LL, 350.
"like a young son," LL, 350.
"Now I am love," MM , 352.
"Call back to me!" LL, 347.
"I am lonely!" LL, 347.
"unearthly sweetness," . . . "There is only," LL, 348.

"terrible, unbearable power," LL, 349.

"grief and remorse," . . . "horror and," . . . "the agony and," LL, 349.

page 96:

"Did you think," LL, 361.

"sick of cruelty," LL, 358.

"youth again because," LL, 354.

the "whore" Julia, LL, 356.

"play again about," LL, 355.

"Take a look," LDJ, 63.

page 97:

"My Brother," . . . "to laugh softly," LL, 277.

"smiles back at," LL, 333.

"They charged upon us," LL, 321.

"terrific flashes of," LL, 318.

"a responsive accompaniment," LL, 318.

page 98:

"Is there hope," LL, 365.

"fresh, clear quality," LL, 365.

"I hear him crying," LL, 366.

"I must go," LL, 366.

"flaming toward the stars," LL, 367.

"surpassing clearness," LL, 367.

page 99:

"Sons are always," SI, 199.

"rises and is lost," LL, 371.

"on tip-toes, his arms," LL, 371.

page 101:

"a great bird song," LL, 279–80.

"like a lark from," LL, 345.

5. STRANGE INTERLUDE

page 104:

"a hush-hush whisperer," SI, 176.

"fugitive from reality," SI, 3.

"complacent, superior manner," SI, 6.

"Did you ever know," SI, 41.

"Say lie—(*She says it,*" SI, 40.

page 105:

"striking, handsome rather," SI, 12.

"dreams like sparks," SI, 27.

page 106:

"honorable code-bound," SI, 19.

"No, you mustn't," SI, 19.

"in his arms until," SI, 19.

"Gordon's silly virgin," SI, 19.

page 107:

"very ill" . . . "perilously so," SI, 16.

"And it's true," SI, 11.

page 108:

"flaming toward the stars," LL, 367.

"brought down in flames," SI, 5.

"ashes dissolving into mud," SI, 16.

"I feel cold," SI, 22.

"aloud sonorously like," SI, 23.

page 109:

"I tried hard," SI, 41.

"We should have imagined," SI, 42–43.

"kept on, from one," SI, 45.

"They were all the same," SI, 45.

page 110:

"house full of men," SI, 25.

"I seemed to feel," SI, 45.

"of Gordon diving down," SI, 45.

"I'll wait in here," SI, 4.

"Mary will look," SI, 21.

"Mary will do," SI, 21.

"Mary will do," SI, 22.

"He's dead, Mary," SI, 26.

page 111:
"Yes, he's dead," SI, 39.
"conditioned," SI, 35.
"normal love objects," SI, 37.
"Spooning! . . . rather a," SI, 36.
"a fine healthy boy," SI, 38.

page 112:
"I feel it has," SI, 49.
"I lay awake," SI, 49.
"like a mad ghost," LDJ, 123.
"daughter of my sorrow," SI, 65.

page 113:
"disappear . . . leave me," SI, 69.

page 114:
"Go on and wake," SI, 92.
"My hideous suspicion," MM, 426.
"I shall be happy," SI, 89.

page 115:
"as if he had been," SI, 75.
"I loved it so," SI, 83.
"Strong hands like," SI, 79.
"I'm quite sure Gordon," SI, 174.
"never been really," LDJ, 13.
"never been sick," SI, 77, 100.
"she walked miles," SI, 100.
"dull, constant pain," SI, 77.
"breaks down chokingly," SI, 77.

page 116:
"nothing for her," SI, 100.
"I think you doctors," SI, 101.
"Her body is a," SI, 105.
"There's something in this," SI,
    99.
"I am living a dream," SI, 91–92.

page 117:
"No longer any love," SI, 100.
"Oh, afternoons," SI, 110.
"he'd be an easy," SI, 118.
"I can always twist," SI, 118.
"How can you be," SI, 132.

page 118:
"Typical terrible child," SI, 122–
    23.
"nowhere," SI, 123.
"My three men!" SI, 135.
"drink and women," SI, 143.
"to come back each," SI, 139.
"embittered and they," SI, 138.
"with a nasty laugh," SI, 141.
"Why did he give," SI, 139.

page 119:
"afternoons of happiness," SI, 165.
"gotten so lonely," SI, 143.
"ugly bitter stage," SI, 144.
"healthy as a pig," SI, 149.
"the huge joke" . . . "Sam is the,"
    SI, 139.

page 120:
"Thinking doesn't matter," SI,
    170.
"I've been a timid," SI, 148.
"rot away in," SI, 140.
"My life work," SI, 140.
"I would be content," SI, 148.
"only a mother," SI, 149.
"cheated of your," SI, 144.
"in the soft golden," SI, 158.

page 121:
"bedlam," SI, 181.
"perfect pandemonium," SI, 176.
"A good man," SI, 183.

page 122:
"Sons of the Father," SI, 199.
"Those were wonderful," SI, 196.
"No. Certainly not," SI, 196.
"if I'd had more," SI, 166.
"I'm going back," SI, 196.

page 123:
"scrambles to his feet," SI, 177.
"Will you let me," SI, 197.
"gray ivied chapel," SI, 197.

"The crimsons and purples," SI,
  197–98.
"sleep with peace," SI, 200.
"the evening shadows," SI, 200.

page 124:
  "The only living life," SI, 165.
  "our lives" . . . "merely strange
    dark," SI, 199.

6. DYNAMO

Quotations from *Dynamo* (D) are from
Random House 3.

page 129:
  "electrical display of," SI, 199.

page 130:
  "boomingly overassertive," D,
    422.
  "except where the religious," D,
    428.
  "What's the bad news," D, 431.
  "Is not the time," D, 423.
  "Of course there's," D, 424.
  "If there is his," D, 453.

page 131:
  "If Thou didst," D, 423.
  "Lucifer, the God," D, 437.
  "to enter the presence," D, 436.
  "A minister's son has," D, 437.

page 132:
  "a tremendous crash," D, 452.
  "the sound of wind," D, 453.

page 133:
  "yellow," D, 432.
  "Bible-punching breed," D, 431.
  "the secret of the family," D, 439.
  "She's the daughter," D, 441.
  "Fife's damned me," D, 444.
  "Mother! Mother!" D, 445.

page 134:
  "Steele's," D, 432.

page 135:
  "the prodigal returns!" D, 457.
  "As soon as he knew," D, 430.

page 136:
  "Murderer! You killed," D, 463.
  "You killed her," D, 465.
  "I'll be your mother," D, 477.
  "never stuck" . . . "I wanted to,"
    D, 461.

page 137:
  "Great Mother of Eternal," D,
    477.

page 138:
  "She couldn't mail," D, 465.
  "felt betrayed" . . . "was insane,"
    D, 465.

page 139:
  "inert strength" . . . "blank," D,
    428.
  "singing all the time," D, 458.
  "whirring purr," D, 458.
  "Look at her," D, 429.
  "I'd like to be," D, 441.
  "for a moment," LDJ, 153.
  "And several other," LDJ, 153.
  "It was a great," LDJ, 153.

page 140:
  "some one singing," D, 476.
  "huge and black," D, 473.
  "spindly steel legs," D, 483.
  "six cupped arms," D, 483.

page 141:
  "when all these switches," D, 484.

page 142:
  "wants some one man," D, 477.
  "Mother said she was," D, 471.

page 143:
    "living in sin," D, 478.
    "given up the flesh," D, 478.
    "But suppose the miracle," D,
        478.
    "Yes, you've got," D, 480.
    "unnatural excitement," D, 480.

page 144:
    "the startled and terrified," D,
        487.
    "I don't want any," D, 488.
    "loving consummation," D, 488.

page 145:
    "And I thought," D, 489.
    "begins to cry," D, 489.

7. MOURNING BECOMES ELECTRA

Quotations from *Mourning Becomes Electra* (MBE) are from Random House 2.

page 150:
    "more than any other," MBE, 5–
        6.
    "Way—ay, I'm," MBE, 103.

page 151:
    "temple of Hate," MBE, 171.
    "squared transom and," MBE, 2.
    "like an incongruous" . . . "sombre
        gray ugliness," MBE, 5.
    "in a resentful," MBE, 5.
    "the flickering candlelight," MBE,
        139.
    "an intense bitter," MBE, 157.
    "accusingly," MBE, 168.

page 153:
    "long and straight," LDJ, 12.

page 154:
    "reddish brown," LDJ, 28.

"partly a copper," MBE, 9.
"frisky and full," MBE, 44.
"flowing animal grace," MBE, 9.

page 155:
    "I'm not a bit," MBE, 22.
    "Your face is," MBE, 22.
    "Maw—every drop," DUE, 207.
    "Like his Paw," DUE, 211.

page 156:
    "disgust," MBE, 31.
    "You were always," MBE, 31.
    "stole all love," MBE, 57.
    "always be a stranger," LDJ, 153.
    "who must always be," LDJ, 154.

page 157:
    "very strict," MBE, 26.
    "of sickness and starvation," MBE,
        26.
    "Belay, damn you!" MBE, 24.
    "more like a gambler," MBE, 15.
    "I don't give," MBE, 105.

page 158:
    "It would be damned," MBE, 36.
    "seems to have," MBE, 17.
    "a strange, hidden," MBE, 40.
    "Something queer in me," MBE,
        55.

page 159:
    "if we'd leave," MBE, 55.
    "I love you," MBE, 55.
    "She's guilty—not," MBE, 63.

page 160:
    "He's been jealous," LDJ, 119.
    "jealous of you," MBE, 86.
    "If I could," MBE, 73.
    "None of us can," LDJ, 61.

page 161:
    "healthy hulk," LDJ, 33.
    "always been a bundle," LDJ, 33.

"Nerves. I wouldn't," MBE, 48.
"It was like murdering," MBE, 95.
"sepulchre," MBE, 17.
"Death sits so," MBE, 94.
"He looks like me," MBE, 115.
"pistol," MBE, 124.
"I drove her," MBE, 124.

page 162:
"evil spirit" . . . "like somethin'
rottin'," MBE, 135.
"something cold," MBE, 137.
"as near the Garden," MBE, 24.
"By God, there's," MBE, 39.
"find some island," MBE, 56.
"my island I told," MBE, 113.

page 163:
"The breaking of the," MBE, 90.

page 165:
"Oh, Orin, something," MBE,
155.
"Ghosts! You never," MBE, 155.
"Most of what I've," MBE, 153.
"Only your hair," MBE, 52.
"There are times now," MBE,
165.

page 166:
"I'm the last," MBE, 178.

page 167:
"I'm sick of," MBE, 56.
"You've brought love," MBE, 111.
"I'm glad you found," MBE, 166.
"I want to feel," MBE, 147.
"darkness of death," MBE, 150.

8. AH, WILDERNESS!

Quotations from *The Moon of the Car-*
ibbees (MOTC) and *In the Zone* (ITZ)
are from Random House 1.

page 173:
"going to the beach," AW, 191.
"A Book of Verses," AW, 199.

page 174:
"big, gray eyes" . . . "fetching
smile," AW, 186.

page 175:
"Pooh! What do," AW, 191.
"out walking with," AW, 292.
"Gee, it must be," AW, 273.
"gray," AW, 187.
"short and fat" . . . "shapeless and
faded," AW, 188.

page 176:
"It's sixteen years," AW, 213.
"bad women," AW, 213.

page 177:
"dirty, rotten drunk," AW, 258.
"a Book of Verses," AW, 199.
"how beset" . . . "with gin," AW,
198.
"The Moving Finger," AW, 199.
"big naïve wondering," AW, 277.

page 178:
"And lo my," AW, 277.
"dissolute and blasphemous," AW,
201.
"hiding he'd remember," AW, 203.
"out of the house," AW, 203.
"It's the books," LDJ, 90.

page 179:
"the elaborate paraphernalia," AW,
208.
"Tommy! Stop spinning," AW, 222.
"stupid, lazy greenhorns" . . . "really good servants," LDJ, 61.
"clumsy, heavy-handed," AW, 210.
"benignly ripened," AW, 221.
"blurry," AW, 223.

page 180:
    "Puckish, naughty-boy," AW, 223.
    "We'll drink to," AW, 224.
    "Fact! One day," AW, 231.
    "That's been his," AW, 233.
    "Waterwagon—Waterbury," AW,
      188.
    "A certain peculiar," AW, 227.
    "See how guilty," AW, 227.

page 181:
    "real swift," AW, 219.
    "It's all because," AW, 235.
    "An' she said," MOTC, 467.
    "fly-specked," AW, 236.
    "Who also, once upon," AW, 181.
    "a romantic, evil," AW, 241.

page 182:
    "dynamite," AW, 248.
    "Bet you she's out," AW, 243.
    "sick little boy," AW, 258.
    "him tenderly and" . . . "as if he
      were," AW, 258.

page 183:
    "to his mother," AW, 261–62.
    "my fellow Rum" . . . "as good
      old," AW, 271.
    "It only made me," AW, 270.
    "at the moon" . . . "half-daft,"
      ITZ, 518.
    "I suppose you," AW, 216.
    "You don't know," AW, 273.

page 184:
    "Gosh, I love," AW, 287.
    "Long Trail—the," AW, 288.
    "Well, anyway, he'll," AW, 291.
    "young anarchist," AW, 204.
    "a harsh tyrant," AW, 205.
    "one outlet for—," AW, 295.

page 185:
    "I don't see how," AW, 295–96.

"punishment" . . . "stay there till,"
    AW, 296.
"Sid'll never change," AW, 291.
"Then, from all," AW, 292.
"way down low—," AW, 296.
"Yet ah, that Spring," AW, 298.
"Well Spring isn't," AW, 298.

page 186:
    "move quietly out," AW, 298.

9. DAYS WITHOUT END

Quotations from *Days Without End*
(DWE) are from Random House 3.
Quotations from *Welded* (W) are from
Random House 2.

page 190:
    "horrible thought" . . . "I do not,"
      S, 294.
    "the superwoman," S, 281.

page 191:
    "Yea, faileth now," S, 279.
    "an egotist whose," S, 281.
    "happiness" . . . "means servi-
      tude," S, 270.

page 192:
    "Servitude in love," S, 294.
    "a superlove worthy," S, 295.
    "I'd lost faith," W, 447.
    "true sacrament," W, 448.
    "waiting and hoping," W, 467.

page 193:
    "lonely life of one's," W, 477.
    "You got to loin," W, 478.
    "That goes deeper," W, 478.

page 194:
    "omnipotent Golden Calf," DWE,
      501.
    "All they want," DWE, 542.

page 195:
  "Divinity of Love," DWE, 510.
  "frenzy of insane" . . . "deaf and
    blind," DWE, 511.
  "last religion," DWE, 504.

page 196:
  "I've never had," DWE, 551.
  "like a missionary," DWE, 523.

page 197:
  "peaceful routine—going," DWE,
    516.
  "slapped your face," DWE, 518.
  "disgust and hurt," DWE, 523.
  "wounded pride," DWE, 521.
  "one of Walter's," DWE, 521.
  "I hear she's," DWE, 498.

page 198:
  "You told him?" DWE, 526.

"I'm sorry I," DWE, 527.
"His happiness filled," DWE, 521.

page 202:
  "on the verge of," DWE, 553.
  "Can't you see," DWE, 556.

page 203:
  "the death mask of," DWE, 493–
    94.
  "Ah, fondest, blindest," DWE,
    508.
  "crimson and green," DWE, 566.

page 204:
  "O Lord of Love," DWE, 567.
  "of Infinite Love," DWE, 510.
  "Our Father Who," GGB, 322.
  "There is only," GGB, 322.

Index